COLLECTING

— T H E —

NATURAL

WORLD

Legal Requirements & Personal Liability for Collecting Plants, Animals, Rocks, Minerals & Fossils

Donald Wolberg & Patsy Reinard

ii

Published by Geoscience Press, Inc.
P.O. Box 42948, Tucson, AZ 85733-2948

Cover design by Anne Green.
Book design by Paulette Livers Lambert
Manufactured in the United States of America
10 9 8 7 6 5 4 3 2 I

Publisher's Cataloging in Publication (Prepared by Quality Books Inc.)
        Wolberg, Donald L.
            Collecting the natural world: legal requirements and personal
        liability for collecting plants, animals, rocks, minerals, fossils &
        artifacts / Donald Wlberg, Patsy Reinard.

            p. cm.

            Includes bibliographical references.
            ISBN 0-945005-20-2

            I. Collectors and collecting—Legal status, laws, etc.—United States—Popular works.
        2. Plants—collection and preservation—Law and legislation—United States.
        3. Animals—Collection and preservation—Law and legislation—United States.
        4. Rocks— Collection and preservation—Law and legislation—United States.
        5. Minerals—Collection and preservation—Law and legislation—United States.
        6. Fossils—Collection and preservation—Law and legislation—United States.
        7. Antiquities—Collection and preservation—Law and legislation—United States.
        I. Title.

        KF390.C6W65 1995   340.09'0909
                                       QBI95-20098

Distributed by Mountain Press Publishing Company
P.O. Box 2399, Missoula, MT 59806
I-800-234-5308

CONTENTS

PREFACE

This is the first book of its kind. It surveys all of the state and federal laws that affect those who explore and collect specimens on public land, either as a hobby, profession, or business. This book covers three major categories of collecting: (1) terrestrial and underwater archeology, including ship salvage, (2) fossils and minerals, including gold-panning, other recreational mining, and cave exploration, and (3) wildlife and plant specimens. Each category is divided into two chapters which treat federal and state law separately. The subjects of collecting in other countries and international treaties and customs regulations constitute another large body of law and will have to await another book.

There is no other book available today that treats these issues of collecting as one comprehensive work. It is a necessary companion to technical literature dealing with particular collecting methodologies for antiquities, fossils, gems, mineralogic specimens, or botanical and wildlife specimens. The purpose of this book is to give practical guidelines to the maze of regulations and possible liabilities which confront the collector, particularly on state and federal public land. As such, this book should be of interest to anyone who explores the natural world, including photographers, spelunkers, mineralogists, gold-panners, scuba divers, falconers, herpetologists, ornithologists, entomologists, archeologists, paleontologists, salvagers, and those who harvest plants or wildlife pharmacology, landscaping, reseeding, taxidermy, aquaculture, and propagation. Legislators and government agencies will be interested in this book as the first comparison of collecting laws and policy in the various states and the federal government. This book does not address more general issues of hunting, mining, forestry, agriculture, cruelty to animals, or general criminal conduct on public lands.

Although we have tried to minimize legal jargon, we have kept the exact wording of statutes and legal causes of action where such words have a "fixed and known meaning" in the law. Since this is the language of law enforcement, courts, and legislatures, the reader will be better equipped to comply with and analyze statutes if he or she is familiar with the language. Watch for subtle nouns such as "public land," action verbs such as "excavate" or "destroy," adverbs such as "willfully," and adjectives such as "qualified," because they have a specific meaning in the law that is applied in all cases. For example, whether a crime has been committed or not often depends on if the act required "intent" (done "knowingly" *and* "willfully"). A statute may also be unconstitutional "on its face" or "as applied" to you, because it fails to give proper notice of what constitutes a crime, as required by the Fifth and Fourteenth Amendments to the U.S. Constitution. Hence, we have gone beyond articles that merely recite that "such and such is prohibited or precluded," giving the reader his or her own set of analytical tools.

One will no doubt conclude from this bulky compendium that we are not only a nation of laws, but a nation of many laws. A few states are reversing the trend toward creeping bureaucracy, and we show other states how they may also. For example, South Dakota has taken a small, but significant, step to protect casual collecting from cumbersome mining reclamation laws: "Any person engaged in recreational, hobby, amateur or field activities independently or sponsored by educational institutions, including, but not limited to geology, mineralogy, paleontology, treasure hunting, gold panning, archaeology and noncommercial agate and gem hunting and using hand held tools and equipment is exempt from the provisions of this chapter" (SDCL 45-6B-80). Many states now treat treasure hunting as a joint venture, thereby guaranteeing that significant archeological finds are kept by the state, at no expense to the taxpayers.

The research for this book was based upon the state of the law as it existed in 1995 and 1996. However, archeological, paleontological, mineralogical, and endangered species laws are changing every year as states adopt new laws or update old laws to keep up with the federal government or other states. The Archeological Resources Protection Act is probably here to stay, but federal law regarding fossils will change dramatically when Congress decides on the bills now before it. The federal Endangered Species Act is probably here to stay, but the list of protected species is updated every few years. The law may be modified so that all subspecies need not be protected, nor populations at the margin of their natural range. Most states which have adopted their own Endangered Species Act will review their lists of protected species every two years. Hence, the reader is cautioned to rely on the laws cited in this book only as an overview of the issues and to *always* check with appropriate authorities on the current state of the law.

We appreciate the special contributions of employees of state agencies who have assisted us in capturing some of the regulatory trends in their states, as well as persons who are close to the Black Hills controversy, and the ALAA and other persons behind the various paleontological bills before Congress.

CHAPTER 1

FEDERAL LAWS AND AGENCIES AFFECTING ARCHEOLOGICAL COLLECTING

When Are You Doing Archeological Collecting?

Archeology (or archaeology) is the study of human cultures through time. Archeology is concerned with understanding the evolution, development, and interactions of cultures through their material remains. In America, archeology is a social science based largely in anthropology, while in the Old World it may just as easily be based on the classics. Originally archeology implied the study of ancient cultures of some antiquity and in general this is still a valid association.

However, there is an increased interest in comparatively recent events in the field of historical archeology. State or federal historical preservation laws prohibit activities such as scanning a Civil War battlefield with your metal detector, purchasing a worn-looking Indian pot for your mantel, or taking a timber from a ship which sank in the early 1900s. Thus, there is no bright line between the ancient and modern world, even in an archeological sense. In a similar way, archeology can overlap with art, and as such has long been of interest to collectors, investors, and art historians. Archeology encompasses a society's past and also assumes a political dimension, reflective in national or cultural pride and possessiveness.

Because of these varied interests, archeology has associated with it a rather massive set of laws, regulations, and policies. In the United States there are federal and state laws, as well as the laws of Native American governing authorities. There is little or no opportunity for legal, commercial archeological collecting on public or Native American lands. With increasing frequency government agencies are monitoring the sale of archeological and ethnographic materials, so documentation is a necessity.

Antiquities Act of 1906

The Antiquities Act of 1906 prohibits the appropriation, taking, excavating, injuring, or destroying of any "historic or prehistoric ruin or monument, or any object of antiquity, situated on lands owned or controlled by the government of the United States," without permission from the appropriate federal land manager. Permits are issued by the secretary of the agency responsible for managing the lands involved.

The earliest collecting permit for paleontological work that we have found was issued to paleontologist Charles Gilmore in 1929. This extremely interesting document reads in part:

2

> Pursuant to the provisions of the Act of June 8, 1906 (34 Stat., 225), and the interdepartmental regulations of December 28, 1906, prescribed thereunder, permission is hereby granted to Mr. Gilmore to conduct the proposed archaeological work within the entire eastern half of the Navajo reservation between the San Juan River on the north and the Chaco River on the south; this work to be performed during the field season of 1929. It is understood that all specimens collected will be placed in the National Museum. This permit is issued upon the further condition that all excavated lands will be restored or leveled, in case this is considered necessary by the Superintendent of the Reservation for the protection of stock of the Indians.

The following aspects of this letter are of some importance:

> 1. The U.S. was issuing permits for collecting on Navajo lands, as the area covered is limited to the Navajo Reservation.

> 2. Gilmore was doing paleontology. The permit was issued under the 1906 Antiquities Act and the obvious archeological intent of the permit is acknowledged in the first sentence.

> 3. All specimens collected were to be deposited in the U.S. National Museum and were considered U.S. property, even when found on Navajo lands.

> 4. Lands excavated were to be restored if deemed necessary by the superintendent of the reservation.

The Antiquities Act of 1906 has not fared well in the courts. In 1974, the Ninth Circuit Court of Appeals held that the Antiquities Act was overly vague in its definition of antiquity. The case involved, *United States v. Diaz*, concerned Apache face masks removed in 1969 or 1970 from a cave on the San Carlos Indian Reservation in Arizona. In contrast, in 1979 the Tenth Circuit Court of Appeals in *United States v. Smyer* upheld application of the 1906 Antiquities Act to the theft of 900-year-old archeological artifacts from national forest lands in New Mexico. The only known prosecution under the act for collecting fossils was *United States v. Jenkins*, a 1975 federal district court case in Montana. Farish Jenkins, a well-known paleontologist from Harvard University, was charged with the illegal collection of fossils from Bureau of Land Management lands that he mistakenly entered. The case was dismissed upon the legal argument that the word "antiquities" is overbroad as applied to fossils, and in an archeological context, refers specifically to products of human activity.

Archaeological Resources Protection Act (ARPA)

The Archeological Resources Protection Act of 1979 (ARPA) protects archeological localities and their contents on federal and Native American lands. ARPA is concerned with site or locality context and excavation. It establishes a permit system and civil and criminal penalties for unauthorized archeological activities.

ARPA excludes the release of archeological locality information from the Freedom of Information Act. The collection of arrowheads from the surface is excluded from penalties. Fossils are excluded from ARPA except where they occur in an archeological context, such as animal bones found at a campsite. The fact that ARPA applies to Native American lands is important to archeology and paleontology. ARPA controls who can conduct field studies, and the collection and disposition of materials collected, including fossils.

Although a boon to contract archeologists, ARPA is the bane of the average citizen or local government agency that needs to build roads, drill wells, lay pipelines, or otherwise disturb the surface of the earth on public lands. As an example, ranchers advise us that they cannot drill a new well, two feet from their old well, without paying for an archeological survey to see if any artifacts will be disturbed. In the vast majority of cases, the survey will be negative. Home-builders and road-builders run into the same problem with ARPA, or state versions of the

4

act, when laying pipe, utilities, or roads across the public domain, whether it be a bar ditch or a field. ARPA-based laws could be made more taxpayer-friendly by simply requiring notice to appropriate authorities when artifacts are discovered in the process of construction, or requiring that surveys be done only in areas already shown to be archeologically sensitive. Without legislative change, however, millions more will be spent, and undue delays caused, by the useless digging of holes. Legislators should be forewarned that agencies and archeologists who benefit from the present state of the law should not be called as experts when your legislature studies this issue. If we enact a federal law similar to ARPA for fossils, these same people will have to hire both an archeologist and a paleontologist!

A complete copy of ARPA is found in Appendix H.

National Environmental Policy Act (NEPA)

The National Environmental Policy Act (NEPA) was enacted in 1969 to preserve important historical, cultural, and natural aspects of our national heritage. NEPA requires federal agencies to prepare an environmental impact statement (EIS) for any major federal action that significantly impacts the quality of the human environment. Major federal action can include a change in a land management agency's regulations. Thus, private citizens who have been denied access to public lands for recreation and other purposes may employ NEPA in federal court action to restrain federal agencies from acting outside their statutory powers. NEPA has already proven a fertile ground for suits by environmentalists and ranchers.

Importantly, the human environment is broadly interpreted to include the "natural and physical environment." These impacts include possible effects on the "unique characteristics of the geographic area such as proximity to historic or cultural resources." Although NEPA does not mandate action directly related to the management of fossil resources, the strong historical component in NEPA results in an almost mandatory discussion of impacts to archeology and fossils. The environment is considered to be significantly affected if the proposed actions are likely to "cause loss or destruction of significant scientific, cultural, or historical resources."

An environmental impact statement must discuss the following:

1. Environmental impact of the proposed action.

2. Any adverse impact that cannot be avoided should the proposal be implemented.

3. Alternatives to the proposed actions.

4. The relationship between the local short-term use of man's environment and the maintenance and enhancement of long-term productivity.

5

5. Any reversible and irretrievable commitments of resources that would occur if the proposed action went forward.

Historic Sites Act of 1935 and the National Historic Preservation Act of 1966

These acts provide for the preservation of historical sites, buildings, and objects of national significance for the inspiration and benefit of the people of the United States. The Historic Sites Act authorizes the Secretary of the Department of the Interior to survey, study, acquire, and preserve historical and archeological sites of national significance. The National Historic Preservation Act expanded protection of historical and archeological sites and created the National Register of Historic Places.

The National Natural Landmarks (NNL) program of the National Park Service (NPS) is intended to "identify and encourage the preservation of nationally significant examples of the full range of heritage." A National Natural Landmark is defined as "an area of national significance that contains an outstanding representative example of the nation's natural heritage, including . . . geological features . . . or fossil evidence of the development of life on earth." Thus, paleontology is impacted as well as archeology.

Discovering National Natural Landmarks is the responsibility of the National Park Service. Lands and resources anywhere, including Native American and private lands, can receive the NNL designation. Landowners or land managers are encouraged to enter into voluntary agreements with the National Park Service to manage the designated resources. Thus, collectors should inquire whether Native American and even private lands are NNL designated, even if they have permission from the owners.

The Reservoir Salvage Act of 1960

The Reservoir Salvage Act of 1960 provides protection for archeological and historical sites potentially impacted by federal dam construction carried out by federal authorities or contractors under federal license. It was amended by the Archeological and Historic Preservation Act of 1974, which extended coverage to all projects with federal involvement. The amendment also includes detailed procedures for the study and salvage of "scientific, pre-historical, historical, or archeological data." Paleontology would fall within the "scientific data" section of coverage.

Surface Mining Control and Reclamation Act (SMCRA) of 1977
The Surface Mining Control and Reclamation Act of 1977 (SMRCA) was the first comprehensive federal statute to regulate the surface impacts of coal mining on a national scale. The details of this legislation and how it affects archeology are discussed in Chapter 3.

Native American Grave Protection and Repatriation Act (NAGPRA)
The Native American Grave Protection and Repatriation Act applies to federal lands and includes within its scope human remains and artifacts. The ownership and/or control of these materials is given to the lineal descendants if this fact can be determined, or the Native American group on whose land the material was discovered. NAGPRA also determines who can excavate, where such excavation can occur, and for what purposes any material can be utilized. NAGPRA also requires that materials in collections be turned over to Native American tribal entities.

Federal Land Policy Management Act (FLPMA) of 1976
The Federal Land Policy Management Act of 1976 is the superintending act for the Bureau of Land Management. The BLM is the largest federal land management agency, controlling about forty one percent of the nation's federal lands. In addition to ARPA, that is effective on BLM lands, BLM regulations specifically prohibit archeological collecting. It is, therefore, illegal to "willfully deface, disturb, remove or destroy any personal property or structures or any scientific, cultural, archaeological or historic resource, natural object or area" (43 CFR Sec. 8365.1-5). Anyone who knowingly or willfully violates any BLM regulation under FLPMA is subject to a fine of up to $1,000 or 12 months in jail, or both (43 USC Sec. 1733(a)).

Forest Management Service Act
U.S. Forest Service (USFS) regulations address archeology as well. 36 CFR Section 261.9(g) specifically prohibits "digging in, excavating,

disturbing, injuring, destroying, or in any way damaging any prehistoric, historic, or archaeological resources, structure, site, artifact, or property" or "removing any prehistoric, historic, or archaeological resource, structure, site, artifact, or property" in our national forests. An archeological resource is defined as "any material remains of prehistoric or historic human life or activities which are of archaeological interest and are at least fifty years of age, and the physical site, location, or context in which they are found" (43 CFR Sec. 261.2). Violations are subject to fines of up to $500 or six months in jail, or both.

7

National Park Service
The National Park Service Organic Act of 1916 states that national parks and monuments must be managed "to conserve the scenery and the natural and historic objects." NPS regulations outlaw archeological exploration or digging in the national park system except by authorized personnel.

Bureau of Reclamation
With the passage of ARPA, regulation of archeology is the same in all federal land management areas.

The Federal Aid Highway Act of 1956
This act protects archeological and paleontological resources uncovered during construction of highways, as amended by the Department of Transportation Act of 1966. In many states, the state archeologist or the state historic preservation officer of the State Historic Preservation Office or State Historical Society contracts with the State Highway Department to perform the necessary archeological work, with federal funds.

National Park Service
Under the U.S. Department of Agriculture, the National Park Service manages eighty-three million acres, or eleven percent of public lands. About sixty percent of these lands are national parks, and the rest are nationa preserves.

Bureau of Indian Affairs
The BIA, under the Secretary of the Department of the Interior, acts as trustee of Indian-owned lands that total fifty-five million acres, or seven percent of the total territory under federal stewardship. The 300

reservations, home to more than 500 tribes, are governed by elected leaders who determine activities on their land, including camping, hunting, fishing, and collecting archeological, botanical, geological, and paleontological samples. However, as we saw in the case of Sue, the dinosaur, BIA approval may be required prior to collecting where the landowner's title is not complete because of the trust relationship with the BIA.

Department of Defense
Military reservations and bases total twenty-seven million acres, chiefly in the West and South. The Department of Defense regulates access to these lands. There are more than 220 endangered or threatened species and 100,000 archeological sites on military reservations.

Department of Commerce
The National Oceanic and Atmospheric Administration regulates the national estuarine research reserves and national marine sanctuaries. Estuarine research reserves are located on state-owned lands and are co-regulated by the department and the state involved. There are twelve national marine santuaries for those interested in coral reefs, kelp, and other saltwater habitats.

Department of Energy
The DOE manages 50 sites, totalling 2.7 million acres, including the WIPP underground nuclear waste site in Carlsbad, New Mexico. There is some public access to these sites, should you want to collect.

REFERENCES
Federal Lands in the Fifty States, produced by the cartographic division of National Geographic Society, Washington, D.C., October, 1996.

CHAPTER 2

STATE LAWS AFFECTING ARCHEOLOGICAL
COLLECTING, INCLUDING SHIP SALVAGE

Most states have adopted a version of the federal Archeological Resource Protection Act (ARPA) and require permits for archeological collecting on state lands. Permits are uniformly issued only to persons who are qualified to undertake archeological investigations, and artifacts almost always remain the property of the state. It seems to us that if you own a legitimate private or nonprofit cultural center or museum, and you are qualified, or contract with a qualified person, such regulations would have difficulty withstanding charges of irrational discrimination in the event you are refused a permit. Some states have actually improved on the federal version by offering a share of the recovery as an incentive for collectors to undertake the arduous task of terrestrial or underwater recovery. The state saves its taxpayers the expense of hiring archeologists, and still has its choice of artifacts to keep!

It is not unusual for governments to encourage recovery of underwater antiquities, yet actively discourage excavation of terrestrial antiquities. Perhaps states wish to maintain terrestrial archeological sites in place as tourist attractions, whereas the average tourist is unlikely to visit underwater sites. But from a scientific point of view, the distinction appears to be arbitrary.

Most state laws suffer from the same vagueness as in the *Diaz* case. "Material remains of past life and processes" could equally apply to prehistoric pottery and to Coca Cola bottles, and an "object of scientific or historic interest" is purely in the eye of the beholder.

In a development that preserves sites on private land, many states have created a new form of land ownership, called a "conservation easement." Such easements give a third party, such as the government or a conservation group, the right to enforce limitations on land use against successive owners of said land, far into the future.

Where states have combined archeology and paleontology under the same statute, the reader will find parts of the paleontology and archeology sections in those states redundant.

9

10

ALABAMA

Alabama reserves both the exclusive title and right to explore, excavate, or survey archeological resources (Alabama State Antiquties Act, Title 41, Chapter 3, Sec. 1-6). The act applies to "all aboriginal and other antiquities, mounds, earthworks, ancient or historic forts, and burial sites," on public or private land, "subject to the rights of the owner of the land upon which such antiquities are situated" (Sec. 41-3-1). This means that you cannot obtain permission to excavate from a private landowner, because the landowner cannot sell or give the right to excavate to anyone other than the state of Alabama. However, the state may not explore or excavate private land without the owner's consent (Sec. 41-3-3).

Alabama will seize any antiquities that are "sold or disposed of out of the state," and "the objects so gathered shall be retained in state custody" (Sec. 41-3-5). Furthermore, "person[s] not a resident of the state of Alabama" are specifically prohibited from exploring, excavating, or "carrying away" antiquities (Sec. 41-3-2). While the act does not adequately spell out the consequences to those who excavate antiquities and do not remove them from the state, they would surely be prosecuted under the general crime of trespass and larceny for taking property belonging to the state.

Requests to collect antiquities should be directed to the Department of Conservation and Natural Resources, or the Department of Archives and History. Our guess is that one would have to demonstrate professional qualifications and an "educational purpose," as has occurred in other states.

Fortunately, the word "antiquities" is defined by Alabama law as applying only to archeological finds (human artifacts and structures). The Alabama legislature should be commended for recognizing the difference between archeology and paleontology.

Under Alabama law, the Alabama Historical Commission may contract with private persons for the "recovery or salvage of archeological treasure" defined as "sunken or abandoned ships and wrecks of the sea, or parts thereof or their contents" (Code of Alabama, Sec. 41-9-249.1). Such salvage may take place on state lands or, subject to written consent of the owner, on private lands. The state retains custody of the resulting treasure, but pays a "fair compensation" to the salvager, as determined by the Alabama Historical Commission.

Contacts: State Lands Division, Alabama Department of Conservation and Natural Resources, 64 North Union Street,

Montgomery, AL 36130; Alabama Department of Archives and History, 624 Washington Avenue, Montgomery, AL 36130.

ALASKA
As with many states, Alaska now allows landowners to encumber their land with conservation easements (Alaska State Code, Sec. 34.17.060).

Alaska's Historic Preservation Act protects its "historic, prehistoric, and archaeological" resources, including "fossils or other objects of antiquity which provide information pertaining to the historical or prehistorical cultures of people in the state as well as to the natural history of the state" (Sec. 41.35.230[4]). The Division of Parks, through the Office of History and Archaeology, administers the act. The director of the Division of Parks and Outdoor Recreation issues permits for the "investigation, excavation, gathering or removal from the natural state" to "qualified" persons, but only if the results will be made available to the general public through institutions and museums.

Contacts: Office of History and Archeology, Division of Parks, P.O. Box 107001, Anchorage, AK 99510.

ARIZONA
Arizona requires permits for excavation or collection of "any historic or prehistoric ruin, burial ground, archaeological or vertebrate paleontological site, or site including fossilized footprints, inscriptions made by human agency, or any other archaeological, paleontological or historical feature, situated on lands owned or controlled by the state of Arizona, or any agency thereof" (Arizona Revised Statutes Annotated, Title 41, Chap. 4.1, Art. 4). Permits are issued by the director of the Arizona State Museum, University of Arizona, Tucson, Arizona 85721. Rules governing the permit process clearly include both vertebrate and invertebrate fossils, so don't read the parent statute too freely. Only institutions organized for scientific, research, or land use planning may be awarded one-year permits, and any specimens and records discovered must be placed in a public repository. Anyone who explores, excavates, or unnecessarily defaces or alters any site or object is guilty of a Class 2 misdemeanor (Sec. 41-846) and forfeits all articles to the state museum.

The Arizona trespass statute is so broad that it would outlaw even harmless activities such as rockhounds collecting agates or shark's teeth, casual prospectors panning for a few grains of gold, or a child picking up a pretty stone. It is a Class 2 misdemeanor for one who "knowingly extracts or removes oil, gas, coal, mineral, earth, rock, fertilizer or fossils of any kind or description therefrom" (Sec. 37-501). Surely the legislature did not intend such consequences, but when the crime is on the books, it is subject to abuse.

Contacts: Director, Arizona State Museum, University of Arizona, Tucson, AZ, 85721.

12

ARKANSAS

Arkansas's Department of Libraries, Archives and Cultural Resources houses an Archeological Survey, (Title 13, Chap. 6, Subchap. 2). Its primary purpose appears to be the salvage of archeological and paleontological materials being destroyed or damaged by the construction of highways and dams (Sec. 13-6-210).

The Arkansas Archeological Survey reserves the right to oversee all field archeology on state lands (Sec. 13-6-301).

Contacts: Arkansas State Parks, One Capitol Mall, Little Rock, AR, 72201; Arkansas Geological Commission, 3815 West Roosevelt, Fayetteville, AR 72704; Arkansas Archeological Survey, P.O. Box 1249, Fayetteville, AR 72702.

CALIFORNIA

Although California law on collecting from public land clearly addresses each subject, it is perhaps too broad. The Department of Parks and Monuments regulates terrestrial archeological, paleontological, and historical sites. It is a misdemeanor for any person to "knowingly and willfully excavate upon, or remove, destroy, injure, or deface, any historic or prehistoric ruins, burial grounds, archaeological or vertebrate paleontological site, including fossilized footprints, inscriptions made by human agency, rock art, or any other archaeological, paleontological or historical feature, situated on public lands, except with the express permission of the public agency having jurisdiction over the lands" (Division 5, Parks and Monuments, Chapter 1.7, Archaeological, Paleontological, and Historical Sites, Section 5097.5[a]).

Subsection (b) of the same law defines public lands as "owned by, or under the jurisdiction of a city, county, or district, or fire trails under the jurisdiction of the Division of Forestry in the Department of Conservation" (Chap. 1.7, Archaeological, Paleontological and Historical Sites, Sec. 5097).

Underwater archeology is regulated by the Department of Public Lands. Any person who "removes, without authorization from the commission, or any person who destroys or damages an archaeological site or any historic resource, which is located on or in the submerged lands of, and which is the property of, the state" is guilty of a misdemeanor and is punishable by imprisonment in the county jail not to exceed six months or a fine not to exceed five thousand dollars, or both" (Div. 6, Chap. 4, Sec. 6314[a]). In addition, the commission, or the attorney general or district attorney for that district may seek civil damages for the "damage, loss, or destruction of abandoned shipwrecks, their gear or cargo, or any archaeological site or historic resource located on or in submerged lands of the state", including forfeiture of your vessel (Sec. 6314[b]). Any artifact that has been removed from a "state submerged archaeological site" specified in Subdivision (a) not covered by a "permit as required by Section 6309 or Section 6313" may be confiscated and held up to thirty days. If no agency decides to prosecute, the artifact will be returned to you.

13

Contacts: Division of Forestry, California Department of Conservation; State Lands Commission, California Department of Public Lands, 1807 13th Street, Sacramento, CA 95814.

COLORADO
The state of Colorado reserves title to all "historical, prehistorical, and archaeological resources" including "fossils and other remains of animals, plants, insects, and other objects of natural history" in all lands, rivers, lakes, reservoirs, and other areas owned by the state or any . . . other political subdivision of the state" (Colorado Revised Statutes Annotated of 1973, Sec. 24-80-401). The statute suffers from two vague references, the word "resources," and the phrase "remains of." However, if there is any question that the state owns the site or specimen in question, the collector should request a permit from the Colorado State Historical Society, through the state archaeologist "for the investigation, excavation, gathering, or removal from the natural state of any historical, prehistorical, and archaeological resources within the state" (CRSA Sec. 24-80-406[a]-[e]).

Beware that permits are designed to be difficult to obtain by commercial and casual collectors by a system of onerous stipulations imposed by Sec. 24-80-406[e] on permittees. However, since commercial collectors sell most of their specimens to respected public museums and educational institutions, they should qualify for a permit if they can show a contract with the institution for the exploration or excavation of

14

a particular site or specimen, or both. The stipulations are as follows: (1) investigations, excavations, gatherings, and removals will be undertaken only for the benefit of reputable museums, universities, colleges, or other recognized scientific or educational institutions "with a view to increasing the knowledge of such resources," for "permanent preservation open to the public"; (2) permit holders will provide the state archeologist with a preliminary report of progress within the first year of exploration; (3) an inventory of all materials recovered shall also be supplied; and (4) the state archeologist may require that a "representative collection" be delivered to the state of Colorado. When a permit is revoked, the statute provides that "all recovered materials, catalogues, maps, field notes, and other records necessary to identify the same shall be surrendered immediately to the society" (CRSA Sec. 24-80-406[e]). We suggest that you consult your legal counsel when complying with the last request, as it raises personal property and due process issues. Collectors who have cooperated freely with rogue government agencies without legal counsel have regretted it later.

If you do not have a valid permit, you could be guilty of a misdemeanor as one who "knowingly appropriates, excavates, injures, or destroys any historical, prehistorical, or archaeological resource" and may be fined up to $500 or imprisoned for up to thirty days, or both (CRSA Sec. 24-80-409). An additional problem is that the Colorado Division of Parks and Outdoor Recreation, Office of the State Archaeologist, Board of Land Commissioners, Colorado Department of Highways, and the Colorado Division of Wildlife formerly regulated paleontological collecting in their respective jurisdictions and may mistakenly fail to honor an historical society permit even though its statewide effect is clear under Section 24-80-406.

Contacts: Office of the State Archeologist, 1300 Broadway, Denver, CO 80203; Colorado Division of Parks and Outdoor Recreation, 1313 Sherman Street, Room 618, Denver, CO 80203; Colorado Division of Wildlife, 6060 Broadway, Denver, CO 80216; Colorado Department of Highways, 4201 East Arkansas Avenue, Denver, CO 80222.

CONNECTICUT

Archeological sites in Connecticut, including Native American burial grounds, must be more than fifty years old to be regulated by the State Historical Commission, that issues permits for archeological investigation on state lands.

Contacts: Parks and Recreation Unit, Department of Environmental Protection, State Office Building, Room 267, Hartford, CT 06106; Office of State Archeology, Connecticut State Museum of Natural History, U-23, University of Connecticut, Storrs, CT 06269; Dinosaur State Park, West Street, Rocky Hill, CT 06067.

DELAWARE

Delaware law specifically regulates any attempt to "excavate, collect, deface, injure or destroy" any archeological resource or artifact, or "otherwise disturb or alter an archaeological resource or artifact or its surrounding location or context" on lands owned or controlled by the state. A permit is required from the director of the Division of Historical and Cultural Affairs (Delaware Code, Title 7, Chap. 53, Sec. 5302). Archeological resources and artifacts are defined as any remains of past human life or activity that are at least fifty years old (Sec. 5301).

As in Colorado, permits must be for work done "for the benefit of reputable museums, universities, colleges, or other recognized scientific institutions, with the view to increased knowledge of such objects" (Sec. 5302). Further, the director determines who is "qualified to conduct such an excavation" (Sec. 5302). "Objects of historical or archaeological value or interest" and related records must be deposited in either the Archeological Museum of the University of Delaware or the Division of Historical and Cultural Affairs, except where they go to another institution described under Section 5302 (Sec. 5304).

Penalties for violating the statute have increased from $100 or thirty days imprisonment to a maximum of $10,000 or thirty days, or both (Sec. 5308). Merely to "possess, use or employ" tools or devices "designed, modified or commonly used for the excavation or removal of archaeological resources or artifacts," while on state lands, is a violation of the statute (Sec. 5307). It is also illegal to "sell, transfer, exchange, transport, purchase, receive or offer to sell, etc., any archaeological resource or artifact" defined in Section 5301 and not obtained with a permit (Sec. 5306). Thus, if you merely acquire an artifact that was excavated without a permit, even before it became illegal, you could be prosecuted.

Contacts: Public Lands Commission, Department of Natural Resources and Environmental Control, Richardson Robbins Building, 89 Kings Highway, P.O. Box 1401, Dover, DE 19903; Division of Parks and Recreation, Delaware Department of Natural Resources and Environmental Control, Richardson Robbins Building, 89 Kings

Highway, P.O. Box 1401, Dover, DE 19903; Delaware Division of Historical and Cultural Affairs, Hall of Records, Dover, DE 19903; Delaware Bureau of Archeology and Historic Preservation, 15 The Green, P.O. Box 1401, Dover, DE 19901.

DISTRICT OF COLUMBIA

16

The district has no regulation governing the collection of geological, paleontological, or archeological materials. Parks within the district are controlled by the National Park Service and federal regulation (see Chapter 1).

FLORIDA

Chapter 267 of the Florida Statutes Annotated regulates "historical resources," boasting 10,000 years of human presence in the state (Sec. 267.061[1][a]). It is Florida's public policy that "all treasure trove, artifacts, and such objects having intrinsic or historical and archaeological value which have been abandoned on state-owned lands or state-owned sovereignty submerged lands shall belong to the state with the title thereto vested in the Division of Historical Resources of the Department of State for the purposes of administration and protection" (Sec. 267.061[1][b]). It is also the state's policy to protect and preserve objects of antiquity "which have scientific or historical value or are of interest to the public," including fossil deposits and Native American habitations.

The Division of Historical Resources, through the state archaeologist, only issues permits for surface reconnaissance and excavation on state lands to "accredited institutions" (Sec. 267.13). The division may even designate "state archaeological landmarks" on private land, with the written permission of the landowner. The state archaeologist is also in charge of unmarked human burial sites over seventy-five years old (Sec. 872.05).

Chapter 267 sets forth two grades of crime against historical resources, depending on the means of excavation employed: (1) one who "by means other than excavation either conducts archaeological field investigations on, or removes or attempts to remove, or defaces, destroys, or otherwise alters any archaeological site or specimen located upon, any land owned or controlled by the state or within the boundaries of a designated state archaeological landmark or landmark zone, except in the course of activities pursued under the authority of a permit or under procedures relating to accredited institutions granted by the division, commits a misdemeanor" and forfeits all specimens, objects, and materials collected, along with records (Sec. 267.13[a]), and (2) one who does any of the above "by means of excavation" commits a felony of the third degree, and could forfeit not only all specimens, objects, materials, and records, but also vehicles "involved in" the violation (Sec. 267.13[b]). A collector is required to know when the various laws were enacted because a felony of the third degree could be committed if he or she "offers for sale or exchange any object with knowledge that it has previously been collected or excavated in violation of any of the terms of Sec. 267.11-267.14." The provision is also aimed at any dealer who "procures, counsels, solicits, or employs any other person to violate any prohibition contained in" said sections.

17

Those who explore for, salvage, or excavate treasure troves, artifacts, or sunken ships on state-controlled lands, including submerged lands over which the state has sovereignty, may be fined $500 per day.

Contacts: Florida Department of Natural Resources, Division of Recreation and Parks, 3900 Commonwealth Boulevard, Tallahassee, FL 32399; Florida Department of Natural Resources, Bureau of State Lands, 3900 Commonwealth Boulevard, Tallahassee, FL 32399; Florida Department of State, Division of Historical Resources, R.A. Gray Building, Room 305, 500 South Bronough Street, Tallahassee, FL 32399; Florida Museum of Natural History, University of Florida, Gainesville, FL 32611.

GEORGIA

The state of Georgia, through its Department of Parks, Historic Areas, Memorials, and Recreation, asserts exclusive title and right to "investigate, survey, and recover" all "prehistoric and historic sites, ruins, artifacts, treasure, and treasure-trove" on state-owned or state-controlled lands (Sec. 12-3-52). Thus, Georgia may attempt to apply "prehistoric sites" to paleontogical sites, as well as archeological sites, subject to the statute being declared void for vagueness.

Georgia also owns "submerged cultural resources," meaning "shipwrecks or vessels and their cargo or tackle which have remained on the bottom for more than fifty years, and similar sites and objects found in the Atlantic Ocean within the three-mile territorial limit of the state or within its navigable waters" (Sec. 12-3-80).

The Georgia Department of Natural Resources is authorized to grant permits or enter into contracts with "recognized scientific institutions" or "qualified individuals" to conduct field archeological research or salvage archeology on state properties, including Native American burial sites (Sec. 12-3-52[c]). However, all "findings" must be reported to the department within two days, excluding Saturdays, Sundays, and legal holidays (Sec. 12-3-52[b]) All information and "archaeologically significant objects" derived from archeological research conducted on state land remain the property of the state (Sec. 12-3-52[c]).

Furthermore, the state of Georgia "urges" that all archeological research conducted on private land within the state also be undertaken by recognized scientific institutions or qualified individuals. Thus, there is some opportunity for qualified amateurs and professionals to obtain title to objects from state lands that are not determined to be "archaeologically significant" and that do not belong to a Native American tribe. Of course, there is no permit requirement to operate on private lands. There is also an appeal process for permits that are denied or revoked, in which case the regulations of the department should be scrutinized to see if they comport with due process and the authorizing statute (Sec. 12-3-52[e]).

It is unlawful to "dig, probe, break, crack, carve upon, write upon, burn, or otherwise mark upon, remove, or in any manner destroy disturb, deface, mar or harm the structures, features, surfaces, or contents of archaeological, aboriginal, prehistoric, or historic sites" (Sec. 12-3-621[1]), without a permit from the state or federal government, or the permission of the private landowner. It is also illegal to break or tamper with a lock or gate preventing access to a protected site, or to enter such a site posted against trespassing (Sec. 12-3-621[3][4]). Thus, it appears that a permittee can protect his collection site from vandals and trespassers. However, the statute exempts "artifacts exposed on the surface" from protection, thus recognizing the historical right of hobbyists to collect shark's teeth, pot shards, or other objects that have eroded out and are subject to further damage from the elements if not collected (Sec. 12-3-621[1]).

Contacts: Georgia Department of Natural Resources, State Archeologist, 270 Washington Street Southwest, Atlanta, GA 30334.

HAWAII

Hawaii's Department of Land and Natural Resources regulates all public lands, waters, and mineral resources, including parks, historical sites, forests, forest reserves, aquatic life, aquaculture programs, aquatic life sanctuaries, public fishing areas, wildlife, game, public hunting areas, and natural area reserves through its Board of Land and Natural Resources (Hawaii Revised Statutes, Sec. 171-3).

The Historic Preservation Division of the Department of Land and Natural Resources is charged with protecting historic and cultural properties and regulating all archeological activity within the state (HRS, Sec. 6E-3). The division is managed by the state historic preservation officer who is appointed by the governor (HRS Sec. 6E-5). The Historic Places Review Board, also within the Department of Land and Natural Resources, is charged with maintaining a register of historic places, including those listed on the national register (HRS Sec. 6E-5.5). Alteration of an historic site on private property must be approved by the department as well (HRS Sec. 6E-10).

It is unlawful to "take, appropriate, excavate, injure, destroy, or alter any historic property" without permission from the private landowner or from the Historic Preservation Division if on public land (HRS Sec. 6E-11). "Historic property" is defined as any "building, structure, object, district, area, or site including heiau and underwater site, which is over fifty years old" (HRS Sec. 6E-2). It is also unlawful to offer an historical object for sale (HRS Sec. 6E-12). Violators of either section may be fined up to $10,000 and may also pay restitution damages.

Contacts: State Historic Preservation Officer, Hawaii Department of Land and Natural Resources, 33 South King Street, Honolulu, HI 96813.

IDAHO

The Idaho State Historical Society regulates "archaeological" and "vertebrate paleontological" sites and resources on public lands (Sec. 67-4121). Permits are required for any excavation of any site on public lands, and are granted only to those "qualified by experience or professional training to conduct such excavations in an approved scientific manner" (Sec. 67-4120). No person shall remove from the state of Idaho any artifacts or other objects collected from protectd sites without permission from the Idaho State Historical Society (Sec. 67-4121). Any person violating these provisons is guilty of a misdemeanor (Sec. 67-4122). Collecting geological and paleontological materials within state parks must be approved by the park manager in charge of a specific area.

Contacts: Idaho Bureau of Minerals, Department of Lands, Statehouse, Room 121, Boise, ID 83702; Idaho Historical Society, 610 North Julia Davis Drive, Boise, ID 83702; Idaho Department of Parks and Recreation, 2177 Warm Springs Avenue, Boise, ID 83702.

20

ILLINOIS

The Illinois Historic Preservation Agency regulates archeological and paleontological collecting on public lands under the Archaeological and Paleontological Resources Protection Act (20 ICS 3435).

The agency's chief archeologist issues permits for archeology; the Illinois State Museum issues permits for paleontology. The agency is drafting new regulations that will specify terms and conditions under which permits will be issued, including required qualifications for permit holders (20 ICS 3435/6). However, it is clear that all "materials" and "associated records" derived from exploration or excavation remain the property the state of Illinois. It is doubtful that Illinois will attract academic, museum, or commercial professionals who wish to contribute their time and money to the state.

State law makes it unlawful to "explore, excavate or collect" or "knowingly disturb" or "offer for sale or exchange with the knowledge that it has been previously collected or excavated in violation of this Act," any "archaeological or paleontological resources protected by this Act" without a permit (20 ICS 3435/3). The agency has the power to seek criminal prosecution or sue for injunctive relief or civil damages (20 ICS 3435/3.1). Criminal penalties for violations not involving the disturbance of human remains are Class A misdemeanors, subject to imprisonment and fines up to $5,000. Subsequent violations, or the first-time disturbance of human remains, escalate to Class 4 felonies. Civil damages may also be assessed, including forfeiture of vehicles and equipment.

The act clearly applies to archeological resources on public lands that are "significant material remains or localities of past human life or activities." These may include, but are not limited to, "artifacts, historic and prehistoric human skeletal remains, mounds, earthworks, shipwrecks, forts, village sites or mines." However, statutory language such as "significant" and "material" is unclear and too subjective to give fair notice to the public of the offending activity and should be amended.

Contacts: Illinois Historic Preservation Agency, Preservation Services Division, Old State Capitol, Springfield, IL 62701; Field Museum of Natural History, Roosevelt Road at Lake Shore Drive,

Chicago, IL 60605-2496; Illinois State Museum, State Museum Building, Springfield, IL 62704.

INDIANA

The Indiana Department of Natural Resources issues permits for archeology on all state property through its Historic Preservation and Archaeology Division. Although there are some exceptions, a person who "knowingly, without a permit, conducts a field investigation or alters historic property within the boundaries of property owned or leased by the state" or "disturbs the ground for the purpose of discovering artifacts or burial objects" without a plan approved by the department, commits a misdemeanor (Indiana Statutes, Secs. 14-3-3.4-7 and .4-15). A person who disturbs the ground for the purpose of discovering or removing "artifacts, burial objects, grave markers, or human remains," and thereby disturbs human remains or grave markers, without a plan approved by the department, or in violation of said plan, commits a Class D felony (IS 14-3-3.4-17). To avoid confusion with paleontology and Native American products of later vintage, an artifact is defined as "an object made or shaped by human workmanship before December 11, 1816" (IS 14-3-3.4-1). This definition should be a model for federal and other state legislation.

Contacts: Indiana State Geological Survey, University of Indiana, Bloomington, IN 46204; Indiana State Museum, 202 North Alabama, Indianapolis, IN 46204; Indiana Division of Historic Preservation and Archaeology, Department of Natural Resources, Government Center, 402 West Washington Street, Indianapolis, IN 46204.

IOWA

Iowa has a state archaeologist who oversees both archeological and paleontological finds "in and for the state of Iowa" (Iowa Code Annotated, Sec. 263B.1). This person must be a faculty member of the Department of Anthropology of the State University of Iowa. The statutes are unclear as to whether the state archaeologist controls excavations and finds on private lands, and what consitutes illegal collecting activity.

We suggest requesting a permit from the state archaeologist before proceeding on state-controlled lands. There is likely no formal permit process for private lands, and so you should follow prudent business law and obtain written permission from the landowner to explore, excavate, and own the product of your discovery, subject to mutually agreeable consideration paid the landowner, if necessary. Another Iowa legal convention is to protect landowners from liability for injuries to the public who go on their land for recreation purposes, including "historical, archaeological, scenic, or scientific sites" (ICA Sec. 461C.2).

22

Contacts: Iowa Department of Natural Resources, Wallace State Office Building, Des Moines, IA 50319-0034; Iowa State Geologist and Bureau Chief, Geological Survey, University of Iowa, 109 Trowbridge Hall, Iowa City, IA 52242-1319; State Archeologist, Eastlawn Building, University of Iowa, Iowa City, IA 52242.

KANSAS

The Kansas Antiquities Commission regulates "historic or prehistoric ruins and other archaeological sites" (Kansas Statutes Annotated, Sec. 74-5401). It is illegal to excavate in, remove material from, vandalize, or deface any site so defined on lands belonging to or controlled by the state, local government, or "lands in which a qualified agency is conducting scientific archaeological investigations," without specific authorization (KSA Sec. 74-5403). This could possibly include private lands where a university or other agency has made its claim.

Permits for excavation or investigation may be granted by the commisson to "educational or research institutions, public museums or nonprofit corporations organized for scientific and research purposes" (KSA Sec. 74-5404). However, the commission must be satisfied that the materials recovered will have a "home," and that the permittee has the professional staff and laboratory, storage, or museum space to make the material available to the public. Permit applications must specify the purposes of the investigation, its location, the sponsoring agency, and the professional personnel in charge (KSA Sec. 74-5404). Permit applications are made to the state archaeologist (presently Dr. John Reynolds). Informal regulations exist, but formal regulations are forthcoming.

The Kansas permit process is a model of common sense and is better than ARPA. The Kansas legislature apparently recognized that the state could not afford to own or store all artifacts recovered. Thus, permits are granted to various professional archeologists to accomplish what government contractors do under ARPA—ensure that artifacts are recovered and remain available for research.

Kansas law treats unmarked burial sites separately under the Unmarked Burial Site Preservation Act, and punishes violations with very stiff fines up to $10,000, $20,000, and $100,000, respectively, for subsequent offenses (KSA Sec. 75-2748[b]). Violations consist of "willfully disturbing an unmarked burial site", "knowingly posessing human skeletal remains known to have been from an unmarked burial site, or goods interred with such remains," displaying the same material, selling, trading, or giving away said material, or discarding said material (KSA Sec. 75-2748[a]). The Unmarked Burial Site Preservation Board regulates all public and private lands. Exploration or excavation of unmarked burial sites is strictly the sole domain of the board, acting through the state archaeologist.

Contacts: State Archeologist, Kansas State Historical Society, 6425 Southwest Sixth Street, Topeka, KS 66615.

KENTUCKY
It is the declared policy of Kentucky to preserve "archaeological sites and objects of antiquity for the public benefit" and to limit exploration, excavation and collection of such matters to qualified persons and educational institutions "possessing the requisite skills and purpose to add to the general store of knowledge concerning history, archaeology and anthropology" (KRS Sec. 164.705).

The permitting process is delegated to the state archeologist, presently Dr. Burle Clay. Permits are "regularly" granted, but only "for the benefit of reputable museums, universities, colleges or other recognized scientific or educational institutions with a view to promoting the knowledge of archaeology or anthropology." Again, private or commercial professionals may qualify if the material will be loaned or sold to a reputable institution.

Contacts: Kentucky State Archeologist, 439 Pennsylvania Avenue, Lexington, KY 40506, (606) 257-5735.

LOUISIANA
Louisiana has officially adopted a "public ownership" policy rather than a "state ownership" policy regarding many resources, contrary to the trend in state and federal law to deny public access to what was originally the public domain:

> Public things and common things are subject to public use in accordance with applicable laws and regulations. Everyone has the right to fish in the rivers, ports, roadsteads, and harbors, and the right to land on the seashore, to fish, to shelter himself, to moor

ships, to dry nets, and the like, provided that he does not cause injury to the property of adjoining owners (LCC Art. 452).

24

Louisiana recognizes that, in a representative democracy, the people own the resources, not their representatives. Louisiana's law would also encourage us to reenact the exhilarating experience of unobstructed travel, no longer possible in most parts of this country.

The state, however, asserts ownership of all surface and underwater archaeological sites, including pre-twentieth century shipwrecks and treasure, located "in, on, or under the surface of lands belonging to the state of Louisiana, including its tidelands, submerged lands and beds of its rivers, and the sea within the jurisdiction of this state" (Louisiana Revised Statutes Sec. 41:1605). Thus one cannot conduct archeological exploration or collect "archeological materials, treasure, sunken or abandoned ships, or parts thereof" from state-owned lands without a permit or contract from the state archaeologist (LRS Sec. 41:1606). Permits *shall* be issued for "purely scientific and educational projects," and all recovered materials remain the property of the state with no compensation paid to the permittee. The state may also contract with private individuals to salvage material and pay them compensation based on the value of the recovered remains (LRS Sec. 41:1605).

Permits are requested through the state archeologist, presently Dr. Thomas Eubanks. The state archaeologist is employed by the Division of Archaeology, Office of Cultural Development, within the Department of Culture, Recreation, and Tourism (LRS Sec. 36:209).

It is unclear whether Section 1606 *requires* a state permit for archeological excavation of private land. The words, "may issue a permit . . . on private land if the written consent of the owner thereof is first obtained" could be interpreted as the state offering its expertise to private landowners who cannot afford their own professionals. However, since a violation of any of the archeological laws is a misdemeanor, punishable by fines up to $500 and imprisonment up to thirty days (LRS Sec. 41:1614), this ambiguity should be clarified with the state archaeologist before you take action!

The Division of Archeology also supervises all recovery and study of archeological remains, maintains site files, and acts as legal custodian for all artifacts and objects of antiquity recovered from state lands or donated from private lands, except those donated to the Louisiana State Museum or the Office of State Parks. The Division is instructed to "take into consideration the public nature and research value of these objects and insure that they are accessible to maximum public exhibit consistent with their preservation" (LRS Sec.41:1604).

Regarding the issue of private treasure, Louisiana has enacted some old personal property law definitions:

> One who finds a treasure in a thing that belongs to him or to no one acquires ownership of the treasure. If the treasure is found in a thing belonging to another, half of the treasure belongs to the finder, and half belongs to the owner of the thing in which it was found. A treasure is a movable, hidden in another thing, movable or immovable, for such a long time that its owner cannot be determined (LCC, Art. 3420). One who takes possession of an abandoned thing with the intent to own it, acquires ownership by occupancy. A thing is abandoned when its owner relinquishes possession with the intent to give up ownership (LCC, Art. 3418).

Treasure capable of being acquired, then, may be found on the lands of another, so long as it was previously undiscovered. Then, it must be shared 50-50 with the landowner.

Contacts: State Archeologist, Division of Archeology, Department of Culture, Recreation, and Tourism, 1015 North Third Street, Room 405, P.O. Box 44247, Baton Route, LA 70804.

MAINE

The state of Maine reserves title to all archeological artifacts found on state-controlled land, and the State Museum Bureau is the legal custodian of such specimens (Maine Revised Statutes Annotated, Title 27, Sec. 371). The definition of artifact clearly excludes fossils (27 MRSA Sec. 373A[1]).

It is also the policy of the state that all archeological sites, both public and private, should be "systematically excavated, analyzed and interpreted by a qualified principal investigator" (27 MRSA Sec. 374). The principal investigator must possess minimum qualifications of a graduate degree in anthropology, archeology, or a related field, accompanied by "institutional facilities to ensure proper conservation and curation of the artifacts."

Permits to excavate private land must be obtained from the director of the Maine Historic Preservation Commission, as well as the director of the State Museum Bureau. In addition, a permit to excavate state land must be co-signed by the appropriate state agency. An authorized representative of the state may want to witness and document the removal of artifacts from state-controlled land.

Metal detectors may not be used in state parks or historical sites. This is a common prohibition in most state and national parks.

Contacts: Maine Historic Preservation Commission, 55 Capitol Street, Station 65, Augusta, ME 04333, (207) 287-2132.

MARYLAND

Maryland regulates archeology through its Division of Historical and Cultural Programs Office, and specifically through the Maryland Historical Trust (Maryland Code 1957, Art. 83B, Title 5, Subtitle 6). The trust's archeology office employs a chief archeologist, a state terrestrial archeologist, and a state underwater archeologist (MC Sec. 5-622). State law provides that no one may "excavate, appropriate, injure, or destroy" any terrestrial archeological site on land the state "owns or controls" without a permit from the State Archaeology Office (MC Sec. 5-626). Permittees need not be museums or universities, but investigations must be performed by people who are "qualified" and "for the benefit of reputable museums, institutions of higher education, or other recognized scientific or historical institutions or organizations, so as to increase knowledge and appreciation of archaeological objects and materials." Consequently, any antiquities recovered must be deposited for "permanent preservation" in or with the type of institution described above. Subtitle 6 may also apply to privately owned lands where the owners have petitioned the Maryland Historical Trust for protection (MC Sec. 5-621). Underwater archeological finds may not necessarily be deposited for "permanent preservation," and the trust should be consulted for the exceptions.

Archeology and paleontology in caves receives special attention in Section 5-628. Only a person "trained in archaeology" may apply for a permit from the Maryland Historical Trust to "excavate or remove archaeological, prehistoric, and historic features" from a cave, whether private or public. This statute should offend paleontologists and mineralogists who have serious science to do in a cave but do not qualify as archeologists, as the word "prehistoric" may be interpreted to apply to fossils.

State parks, of course, always have stringent regulations on removing plants, rocks, or animals, and using metal detectors for relic hunting.

Contacts: Maryland Historical Trust, Division of Historical and Cultural Programs, Department of Housing and Community Development, 45 Calvert Street, Annapolis, MD 21401.

MASSACHUSETTS

Archeology in Massachusetts is regulated by a State Historical Commission, a state archaeologist, and a Board of Underwater Archaeological Resources. Massachusetts law addresses underwater archeology specifically, but not terrestrial archeology.

Title to all underwater archeological resources located within the inland and coastal waters of the commonwealth is declared to be in the commonwealth (MGLA 6 Sec. 180). These resources must have "historical value" and constitute "abandoned properties, artifacts, treasure trove or sunken ships, which have remained unclaimed for one hundred years or more or which are valued at five thousand dollars or more," including objects 100 years old or more which are found "inside, upon or around" the above resources. Disagreements regarding an object's historical value may be resolved by a hearing with the board. The Commissioner of Waterways, a member of the Board of Underwater Archaeological Resources, has jurisdiction over wrecked vessels or other shipwrecked property on the shores or waters of the Charles River Basin (MGLA 92 Sec. 72).

No person or entity may "remove, displace, damage or destroy underwater archaeological resources" without a permit from the director of the board (MGLA 91 Sec. 63). However, any "qualified person, organization or corporation" may obtain a permit from the director to conduct "exploration, recovery or salvage operations" if the operations are "in the public interest." Permit applications must be kept confidential by the director's office. The director must grant or deny the permit within thirty days, and his decision may be appealed to the board.

Successful permittees retain seventy-five percent of the value of underwater archeological resources recovered, with the remainder paid to the commonwealth. More states and the federal government should adopt this win-win arrangement whereby adequate reward is guaranteed the private collector with adequate consideration guaranteed the government, at no cost to the taxpayer.

Contacts: State Archeologist, Massachusetts Historical Commission, Boston, MA 02108.

27

28

MICHIGAN

The Michigan Department of Natural Resources may create a bottomlands preserve by regulation whenever a bottomlands area includes a single watercraft of significant historical value, includes two or more abandoned watercraft, or contains other features of archeological, historical, recreational, geological, or environmental significance (MCLA 299.54e). The Lands Division of the Department of Natural Resources provides applications for archeological permits to recover abandoned artifacts in a bottomlands preserve or "aboriginal" records and antiquities on public land. The state archeologist, through the Bureau of History, under the Secretary of State, approves the permits. Permits are issued only for "historical or scientific purposes." Archeological excavators must also obtain a local health department permit for disinterment and potential reinterment of human remains, regardless of whether the site is on public or private property.

Contacts: Michigan State Archaeologist, Bureau of History, Department of State, 208 North Capital Avenue, Lansing, MI 48918.

MINNESOTA

Minnesota reserves the exclusive right and privilege to conduct field archeology on state sites and discourages field archeology on private lands (MSA Sec. 138.32). It is therefore illegal to collect on state lands without a license issued by the Director of the Minnesota State Historical Society (MSA Sec. 138.33). A license *may* be issued to a *qualified* person approved by the state archeologist for field archeology on a specific state site, or simply to engage in purely preliminary or exploratory activity (MSA Sec. 138.36). The state reserves title to all objects found and data gathered in field archeology. If the license names a custodian other than the state archeologist, the title still belongs to the state, and custody can revert to the state for good cause. There are exceptions to state title if the director agrees that a *nonresident school or scientific institution* is the licensee and some other disposition is agreed upon, or that an object may be *bartered for* objects from another state or person (MSA Sec. 138.37).

A "state archaeological site" is defined as a "land or water area, owned or leased by or subject to the paramount right of the state, county, township, or municipality where there are objects or other evidence of archaeological interest." The term specifically includes "all aboriginal mounds and earthworks, ancient burial grounds, prehistoric ruins, historical remains, and other archaeological features on state land or on land subject to the paramount rights of the state."

"Field archeology" means "the study of traces of human culture at any land or water site by means of surveying, digging, sampling, excavating, or removing objects, or going on a site with that intent."

"Scientific institutions" mean "museums, historical societies, foundations for archaeological study, state agencies, and scholarly groups with professional standing and physical facilities for the display, study, and preservation of objects of archaeological interest" (MSA Sec. 138.31). Many private organizations should qualify as scientific institutions when compared with the quality of staff and research at public institutions. There is no definition of "qualified" in the statute.

Contacts: Minnesota Historical Society, Field Services, Historic Sites and Archeology Division, Fort Snelling History Center, Fort Snelling, MN 55111.

MISSISSIPPI

It is the public policy of Mississippi's "Antiquities Law" to "locate, protect, and preserve . . . sites, objects, buildings, shipwrecks, and locations of historical, archaeological, or architectural significance," including aboriginal campsites and dwellings, buried treasure, sunken or abandoned ships and wrecks of the sea, and their contents, and implements of culture (Mississippi Code of 1972, Chap. 7, Sec. 39-7-1 through 39-7-39). All sites or objects of "archeological significance . . . located in, on or under" land belonging to the state or its subdivisions are declared to be Mississippi landmarks and the property of the state (Sec. 39-7-11). Such sites may not be "taken, altered, destroyed, salvaged or excavated" without a permit from the Board of Trustees of the Mississippi Department of Archives and History.

Only the landowner's permission is necessary to excavate most archeological sites on private land. However, if the site is a prehistoric or historic Native American grave, a permit must be obtained from the board (Sec. 39-7-31). We assume that this seeming infringement of private property rights is based on the legal concept that dead bodies are personal property belonging to tribes or families rather than part of the real estate. It is also illegal to "intentionally and knowingly" deface early Native American paintings, hieroglyphics, or other marks or carvings on private or public lands (Sec. 39-7-29).

All shipwrecks and buried treasure on state land are Mississippi landmarks and the sole property of the state (Sec. 39-7-9). However, "qualified private institutions, corporations, or individuals" may contract with the board to salvage sites in exchange for "fair compensation" as a percentage of the cash value of the objects recovered, or a "fair share" of the objects recovered (Sec. 39-7-17). Salvage contracts of this type are the most economical way for the state to acquire antiquities. However, we recommend that no contractor enter into an open-ended agreement in which the percentage is negotiated after the job is completed. Hence, contractors should specify in advance the general nature of articles they intend to keep, and that their selection of items is limited only by the negotiated percentage of the items by weight or value.

Contacts: Department of Archives and History, P.O. Box 571, Jackson, MS 39205.

MISSOURI

Under Missouri's State Historic Preservation Act, the Department of Natural Resources houses the state historic preservation office, and the director of the DNR is the state historic preservation officer (MS 253.408). Because the statutory framework is unclear as to the DNR's jurisdiction, both the DNR and the appropriate state agency with jurisdiction should be consulted regarding restrictions on general archeological collecting. It is, of course, illegal to collect "objects of archeological or historical value" on state park lands (MS 577.073).

Shipwrecks. It is illegal to salvage "submerged or embedded abandoned shipwrecks" that meet the "national register of historic places criteria" without obtaining a permit from the DNR (MS 253.420). Any permit applicant must be a professional archeologist or hire one, and must submit a detailed plan of the salvage operation. "In the event there is a sale," at least fifty percent of each class of artifacts recovered are required to be donated or offered for sale to public or private museums or to other public institutions in the state.

Unmarked Graves. The state historic preservation officer must be notified immediately upon discovery of any unmarked human burial sites, whether discovered in private or public lands or waters (MS 194.400 et. seq.). If the site is encountered as the result of construction or agricultural earth disturbing activities, the DNR decides whether removal of the human skeletal remains is necessary and appropriate for the purpose of scientific analysis (MS 194.407).

The Department of Natural History is also charged with creating and maintaining a future museum in western Missouri that shall be a "conservational" and "historical" museum (MS 184.010).

Contacts: Missouri Department of Natural Resources, State Historic Preservation Program, P.O. Box 176, Jefferson City, MO 65102.

MONTANA

Paleontology and archeology are both covered by the Montana State Antiquities Act (Montana Codes Annotated, Title 22, Chap. 3, Part 4), a practice not recommended because of the profound differences between the two fields. Permits to excavate either "heritage property" or "paleon-tological remains" on state lands are called "antiquities permits," even though fossils are not antiquities (Sec. 22-3-432). Antiquities permits are granted by the Montana Historical Society's historic preservation officer, who must consult with the appropriate state agency. Apparently, the historic preservation officer can be either an archeologist or paleontologist.

Permits are only issued for "work to be undertaken by reputable museums, universities, colleges, or other historical, scientific, or educational institutions, societies, or persons with a view toward dissemination of knowledge about cultural properties." This standard is less stringent than those of other states, such as Maryland's, perhaps because preserving fossils in Montana is like preserving coal in Newcastle.

The law provides that all heritage property and paleontological remains collected under a permit are the permanent property of the state, and must be deposited in museums or other institutions within the state, or loaned to qualified institutions outside the state, unless "otherwise provided for in the permit." In practice, the historic preservation officer may want to keep rare fossils in Montana.

Any person who unearths or discovers a human burial site in mining, construction, or other disturbance of the surface, must immediately notify the county coroner (Sec. 22-3-805).

Contacts: Montana Department of State Lands, 1625 11th Avenue, Capitol Station, Helena, MT 59620; Montana Bureau of Mines and Geology, Montana Department of Highways, 2701 Prospect Avenue, Helena, MT 59620; Montana Department of Natural Resources and Conservation, Energy Division, 32 South Ewing, Helena, MT 59620; State Historic Preservation Officer, Montana Historical Society, 225 North Roberts Street, Helena, MT 59620.

NEBRASKA

The Nebraska legislature funded a Task Force on Historical Preservation that completed its work in 1995. We anticipate that Nebraska will enact an historical preservation law in the future. At present, Nebraska has no statutory framework regulating archeology or paleontology on public or pivate lands except for unmarked burial sites and federally-aided highway projects.

The Nebraska Unmarked Human Burial Sites and Skeletal Remains Protection Act makes it a Class I misdemeanor to "remove, abandon, or conceal" human skeletal remains or burial "goods" or to "receive, conceal, purchase, sell, or transport, trade or dispose of such remains or goods" (Sec. 28-1301).

Contacts: Archeology Division, Nebraska State Historical Society, P.O. Box 82554, 1500 "R" Street, Lincoln, NE 68501-2554, (402) 471-3270, 3314.

NEVADA

Nevada has a pragmatic "multiple use" philosophy regarding its public lands: "The public lands of Nevada must be administered in such a manner as to conserve and preserve natural resources, wildlife habitat, wilderness areas, historical sites and artifacts, prehistoric sites and artifacts, paleontological resources and to permit the development of compatible public uses for recreation, agriculture, ranching, mining and timber production and transmission of energy" (Nevada Revised Statutes, Sec. 321.5977). For example, Nevada's Historic Preservation Act that regulates archeological and paleontological resources (NRS Secs. 381.195-381.227), exempts casual collection of "minerals, rocks, gems, arrowheads, or Indian artifacts," as long as they are not part of a "prehistoric site." Photographing objects of interest is generally allowed without permit (NRS Sec. 381.219).

Permits from the director of the Nevada State Museum are required for archeological and paleontological work on any protected "historic or prehistoric site on federal or state lands" (NRS Sec. 381.197). "Historic" is defined as after the middle of the 18th century, and protected historic sites are described as a site, landmark or monument of historical significance pertaining to the white man's history of Nevada, or Indian campgrounds, shelters, petroglyphs, pictographs and burials. "Prehistoric" is defined as before the middle of the 18th century, and protected prehistoric sites are defined as "any archaeological or paleontological site, ruin, deposit, fossilized footprints and other impressions, petroglyphs and pictographs, habitation caves, rock shelters, natural caves or burial ground" (NRS Sec. 381.195). One should naturally consult with the director of the Nevada State Museum to determine if a particular site is protected or unprotected.

The permittee must also show a valid permit from the proper federal authorities for exploration on land owned or held by the United States (NRS Sec. 381.199). The director may designate agents from other state agencies to issue permits and adopt regulations, so you may be referred elsewhere (NRS Sec. 381.201). The permittee must show a "benefit to a reputable museum, university, college or other recognized scientific or educational institution, with a view of increasing knowledge" and must have sufficient knowledge and scientific training (NRS Sec. 381.203). Upon issuing a permit, the director will immediately notify the Office of Historic Preservation, the sheriff of the county in which the permit is exercised, and the highway patrol, (NRS Sec. 381.205). The permittee must give fifty percent of all articles, implements and materials discovered to the Nevada State Museum, that may accept less than fifty percent by law (NRS Sec. 381.207). Nevada's laws should provide a blueprint for successful cooperation between free enterprise and governmental interests.

It is unlawful for any person to vandalize historic or prehistoric sites, natural monuments, speleological sites and objects of antiquity, or to write or paint or carve initials or words, or deface any of those objects, Native American paintings, or historic buildings (NRS Sec. 381.225). Any object of antiquity taken or collected on historic or prehistoric sites covered by NRS 381.195 to 381.227 without a permit will be seized by state authorities and forfeited to the state (NRS Sec. 381.223). The criminal offense of working without a permit is a misdemeanor (NRS Sec. 381.227). The act is enforced by the Division of State Parks, county sheriffs, and law enforcement officers (Sec. 381.221).

Contacts: Nevada State Museum, Capitol Complex, Carson City, NV 89701; Nevada Historic Preservation and Archeology Office, 100 Stewart Street, Carson City, NV 89710; Nevada Division of State Parks, 1923 North Carson Street, Capitol Complex, Carson City, NV 89710.

NEW HAMPSHIRE

Archeology on state lands generally is regulated by the New Hampshire Historic Preservation Act (New Hampshire Revised Statutes Annotated,

33

Secs. 227-C:1-C:17), through the rulemaking of the Department of Cultural Affairs, and its Division of Historical Resources (also known as the State Historic Preservation Office). We can see no reference to paleontology in the act except for fossils found in the context of archeological sites.

New Hampshire owns all historic resources, except for human remains, on lands owned or controlled by the state or its political sub-divisions, including the bottoms of navigable waters, great ponds, and territorial tidal waters (NHRS Sec. 227-C:6). Historic resources can include buildings or sites that are "significant in the history, architecture, archeology, or culture of this state, its communities, or the nation" (NHRS Sec. 227-C:1[VI]). The commissioner of the Department of Cultural Affairs is in charge of rulemaking (NHRS Sec. 227-C:5). The department also reserves the exclusive right to conduct field investigations of historical resources that involve "the alteration of the surface or subsurface of the resource and removal of any surface or subsurface objects." It may also issue permits to others pursuant to its rules (NHRS Sec. 227-C:7).

The commissioner *may* conduct hearings for those contesting the denial of a permit (NHRS Sec. 227-C:7[V]). The commissioner is the technical custodian of all state historical resources, but must "fairly and equitably allocate and distribute historic resources recovered from a permitted field investigation," provided that:

(a) Custody of isolated finds from the surface of state land, or the bottom of state waters, is granted to the discoverer when these are brought to the division for identification and evaluation;

(b) Assurances are made that the original discoverer of a previously unrecorded historic resource receive custody of twenty-five percent of the recovered material from subsequent field investigations in that resource in which he actively participates;

(c)The formula for the division of the recovered materials shall be based on the percentage of private and public capital invested in a permitted field investigation, with the respective state and priate shares being determined by the ratio of public to private investment, provided that no less than twenty-five percent be retained by the state ad no more than seventy-five percent be released for private custody (NHRS Secs. 227-C:8[III]).

New Hampshire's law on unmarked human burial sites is one of the most onerous we have encountered. For example, if unmarked graves or remains are encountered as a result of construction or agricultural activities, "disturbance of the remains shall cease immediately and shall not resume without authorization from either the county medical examiner or the state archaeologist" (NHRS Sec. 227-C:8a). One can imagine how long it takes to obtain the necessary authorization, and the resulting delays. Then, the county medical examiner must determine if the remains are subject to the Historic Preservation Act. If they are, the state archeologist takes charge of the excavation of the remains, consults with Native American groups, and tries to find a proper home for the remains (NHRS Sec. 227-C:8d,e,f).

The owner or lessee of the land on which unmarked human burials or human remains are found pays for the excavation if the discovery is the result of a "privately-financed commercial land-altering activity," but not if the discovery is the result of "vandalism, erosion, or non-commercial land-altering activity" (NHRS Sec. 227-C:8h). We wonder why anyone would report unmarked burials, except that penalties for non-compliance can be a fine up to $1,000 or imprisonment up to six months, or both (NHRS Sec. 227-C:17). We suggest that a carrot might work better than a stick, especially in the case of a citizen with constitutional property rights under the Fifth and Fourteenth Amendments.

New Hampshire's Act also contains some laudable portions. For example, a program for amateur archeologists provides a means for training nonprofessional persons in technical archeological skills and allows them to take part in field investigations (NHRS Sec. 227-C:10). Also, treasure hunting by use of metal detectors and dowsing rods is exempted from the restrictions of the act on certain state lands such as beaches, athletic fields, school grounds, perimeters of cemeteries, unpaved roads, dumps, and within twenty-five feet of picnic tables and park pavilions (NHRS Sec. 227-C:12).

Contacts: Department of Cultural Affairs, State Historic Preservation Office, P.O. Box 2043, Concord, NH 03301.

NEW JERSEY

New Jersey's State Museum in Trenton falls under the authority of the State Department of Education (NJS 18A:73-1). If New Jersey enacts any laws concerning archeological collecting on public lands, the authority will likely reside with the director of the State Museum.

36

Meanwhile, the Division of Parks and Forestry regulates all collecting on state park and forest lands. No person may "mutilate, destroy, alter or move state park or forest property" including "relics, objects or artifacts of an historical, prehistorical, geological, archaeological or anthropological nature" without the department's permission (NJS 13:1L-10).

Contacts: New Jersey State Museum, 205 West State Street, CN 530, Trenton, NJ 08625; New Jersey Division of Parks and Forestry, P.O. Box 1420, Trenton, NJ 08625.

NEW MEXICO

New Mexico's Cultural Properties Act is administered by the state historic preservation officer and the Cultural Properties Review Committee within the Office of Cultural Affairs (NMSA 1978, Sec. 18-6-8). The Museum Division of the Office of Cultural Affairs maintains all registered cultural properties in its ownership or custody and is the depository for all collections made under the Cultural Properties Act (NMSA 1978, Sec. 18-6-6). A cultural property is defined as a "structure, place, site, or object having historic, archaeological, scientific, architectural, or other cultural significance."

One can be convicted of a fourth degree felony if one "knowingly excavates, injures, or destroys cultural property located on state land without a permit" and if the property is valued at more than $1,000 (NMSA 1978, Sec. 18-6-9). The natural tendency is to overvalue cultural properties or fossils for purposes of prosecution. Likewise, one can be convicted of a fourth degree felony if one knowingly "appropriates" cultural property located on state land without a permit (NMSA 1978, Sec. 18-6-9.1). Here, the threshold for a fourth degree felony is only $200, a subtle trap for the unsuspecting tourist who may not realize that a nondescript pottery shard or broken arrowhead may constitute a valuable cultural property. In addition, violators may suffer civil penalties and forfeit instruments, vehicles, and tools.

Private owners of cultural properties are encouraged to register their properties with the committee. Where the committee deems the property worthy of preservation and inclusion on the official register, the committee may recommend technical assistance to the owner or even purchase of the property for the state or exercise imminent domain (NMSA 1978, Sec. 18-6-10). It is unlawful to excavate an archelogical site on private land with mechanical earthmoving equipment without a permit (NMSA 1978, Sec. 18-6-11A). However, the act later specifies that it does not "limit or prohibit the use of the land on which the archaeological site is located by the owner of the land or require the owner to obtain a permit for personal excavation on his own land, provided that no transfer of ownership is made with the intent of excavating archaeological sites as prohibited in this section." (Sec. 18-6-11D). In exempting the landowner from the permit requirement of Subsection A, Subsection D has been held to exempt employees or agents of the landowner. (*Turley v. State*, 96 N.M. 592, 633 P.2d 687 [1981]). However, permits for excavation on private land may be issued by the Cultural Properties Committee upon approval of the state archeologist and the state historic preservation officer.

Unmarked graves and human remains may not be "excavated, removed, disturbed, or destroyed" by anyone without a permit, regardless of their location (NMSA 1978, Sec. 18-6-11.2). Violation of this section is punishable as a fourth degree felony and a $5,000 fine and/or imprisonment of up to eighteen months, regardless of value. Any person who discovers an unmarked burial shall cease any activity that may disturb the burial or any object associated with the burial and notify the local law enforcement agencies, who shall notify the state medical examiner and the state historic preservation officer.

Contacts: Historic Preservation Office, New Mexico Cultural Affairs Office, 228 East Palace, Santa Fe, NM 87501, (505) 827-6320; Office of Archaeological Studies for Highway Department, La Villa Rivera Building, 228 East Palace, Santa Fe, NM 87501, (505) 827-6343; New Mexico State Natural History Museum, 1801 Mountain Road Northwest, Oldtown, Albuquerque, NM.

NEW YORK

The commissioner of education regulates archeological and paleontological collecting on "lands owned by the state of New York" because most of these are "school trust lands" (McKinney's Education Law, Chap. 16, Sec. 233). It is a misdemeanor to "appropriate, excavate, injure or destroy any object of archaeological and paleontological interest, situationed on or under lands owned by the state of New York, without written permission of the commissioner of education" (Sec. 233[4]).

Permits are issued by the commissioner, through the director of the state museum. Various departments and agencies may also issue permits for lands under their jurisdiction, to persons authorized by the commissioner of education "for the purposes of the state museum or state science service, with a view to the preservation of any such objects worthy of permanent preservation" (Section 233[5]).

The state science service is located at the university and includes the state geologist, the state paleontologist, the state botanist, and the state entomologist (Sec. 235). State-owned objects are generally placed in the New York State Museum (Sec. 233[1]).

Contacts: New York State Museum, Empire State Plaza, CEC 3140, Albany, NY 12230; Office of Parks, Recreation and Historic Preservation, Empire State Plaza, Agency Building 1, Albany, NY 12238.

NORTH CAROLINA

North Carolina has enacted an extensive Archaeological Resources Protection Act (NCS Chap. 70). The act is enforced by the Department of Administration, in consultation with the Department of Cultural Resources. Violators who "excavate, remove, damage or otherwise alter or deface any archaeological resource" located on state lands without a permit can be assessed civil penalties up to $5,000. The act carefully and correctly excludes coverage of paleontological specimens (NCS Sec. 70-12). Private landowners are also urged to refrain from destruction of Native American relics, artifacts, mounds, and burial grounds without turning over excavation to the director of the State Museum and the secretary of the Department of Cultural Resources (NCS Sec. 70-1). The Department of Cultural Resources is charged with issuing permits for archeological investigations on state lands (NCS Sec. 70-13). However, permittees must be qualified and the materials collected remain the property of the state.

The state also asserts title to "all bottoms of navigable waters within one marine league seaward from the Atlantic seashore measured from the extreme low watermark." Title includes "all shipwrecks, vessels, cargoes, tackle, and underwater archaeological artifacts which have remained unclaimed for more than ten years lying on the said bottoms or on the bottoms of any other navigable waters of the State" (NCS Sec.

121-22). The Department of Cultural Resources has authority to issue permits or licenses to conduct salvage operations (NCS Sec. 121-25). A portion of relics or artifacts recovered must be delivered into the custody of the department, but the particular portion is apparently negotiable.

Contacts: North Carolina Division of Archives and History, Department of Cultural Resources, 109 East Jones Street, Raleigh, NC 27611; North Carolina Division of Parks and Recreation, Department of Natural Resources and Community Development, P.O. Box 27687, Raleigh, NC 27611; North Carolina Office of State Property, Department of Administration, 116 West Jones Street, Raleigh, NC 27601.

NORTH DAKOTA

The superintendent of the North Dakota State Historical Board regulates archeological collecting on state lands, or lands owned by counties or municipalities (NDS 55-02-07). The superintendent may issue permits, but only if *all* archeological or historical materials are delivered to the State Historical Society (NDS 55-03-02). Apparently, North Dakota asserts control over private land as well, because a permit on private land requires "human remains and burial goods" be delivered to the superintendent. One must ask whether there is any incentive for nonprofit museums and commercial collectors who sell to them to collect in North Dakota if they may not retain any "sweat equity."

Contacts: State Historic Preservation Officer, State Historical Society of North Dakota, North Dakota Heritage Center, Bismarck, ND 58505.

OHIO

The director of the Ohio Archaeological and Historical Society maintains a state registry of archeological and historic landmarks but must obtain the owner's permission to list the property (OS 149.55). The director also regulates permits for archeological survey and salvage work on public lands (OS 149.51-54) and "Lake Erie Submerged Lands and Abandoned Property" (OS 1506.30-37). The definition of such property is not limited in time to prehistoric or historic Native Americans, but could include any submerged aircraft or watercraft or its contents which has "historical value." Certain areas may be designated as "submerged lands preserves" for recreational and scenic purposes, among others.

The Ohio Department of Natural Resources regulates nonhistorical properties, including state parks, through the Division of

Parks and Recreation (OS Sec. 5401.01). The Department of Transportation regulates roadside parks and roadsides.

Contact: Ohio Archaeological and Historical Society, 1985 Velma Ave., Columbus, OH 43211; Ohio Department of Natural Resources, Division of Parks and Recreation, Fountain Square Building F-I, Columbus, OH 43224.

40

OKLAHOMA

The Oklahoma Museum of Natural History, formerly the J. Willis Stovall Museum of the University of Oklahoma, is located in Norman, Oklahoma. It is authorized to maintain biological, archeological, paleontological, and some geological collections belonging to the state. The Oklahoma State Archaeological Survey office is also located at the university.

Annual permits for archeological "exploration or excavation" on state lands or lands of political subdivisions must be obtained from the state archeologist. As the permitee must donate all discoveries and field notes to the state, however, it will be interesting to see how much archeology is accomplished under this type of provision (OS T. 53 Sec. 361).In addition to working for free, the permittee is also granted the privilege of paying the state $50 for the permit.

Section 361 also makes it illegal to "intentionally and knowingly deface American Indian or aboriginal paintings, pictographs, petroglyphs or other marks or carvings on rock or elsewhere that are of archaeological interest and pertain to early American Indian or aboriginal habitation of the country."

Contacts: State Archeologist, Oklahoma State Archaeological Survey, University of Oklahoma, 1808 Newton Drive, Norman, OK 73019; Oklahoma Museum of Natural History, University of Oklahoma, Norman, OK 73019; Oklahoma Historical Society, Wiley Post Building, Oklahoma City, OK 73105.

OREGON

A person may not knowingly and intentionally excavate, injure, destroy, or alter an archeological site or object or remove an object located on public or private land without a permit issued by the Oregon State Parks and Recreation Department under ORS 390.235 (ORS Sec. 358.920). An exception to the rule is that arrowheads lying on the surface may be collected without a permit if it can be accomplished without a tool.

Permits may only be issued to "qualified archeologists" and materials recovered must generally be donated to the Oregon State Museum of Anthropology. Any excavation of a Native American cairn or burial must be cleared through the state historic preservation officer and the appropriate tribe (ORS Sec. 97.750).

41

A person may not sell, trade, barter such objects, or offer to do so, without a Certificate of Origin indicating, among other things, that the object was acquired prior to 1983, if from public land. If the object was obtained after 1983 it belongs to the state, with the exception that some collections may be retained by the owner under certain conditions specified in ORS 358.923.

Contacts: State Historic Preservation Officer, Oregon State Parks and Recreation Department, 1115 Commercial Street Northeast, Salem, OR 97310; Oregon State Museum of Anthropology, Salem, OR 97310.

PENNSYLVANIA

Pennsylvania's Historic Preservation Act is an archeologist's welfare act, reserving to the state the exclusive right to conduct archeological investigations upon state lands (PS 37 PCSA 506). Permits may be granted to outsiders by the Pennsylvania Historical and Museum Commission, but all specimens collected under the permit remain the exclusive property of the state. Hence, the state will usually rely upon paid employees or contractors to get any work done. The act has no doubt had an inflationary effect on highway and other government construction because contractors whose activities could affect archeological sites must build the estimated cost of archeological surveys into their bid (Sec. 507). These surveys, again, give contract archeologists jobs. Those who violate the act suffer onerous fines of up to $2,500 or one year in jail or both (Sec. 511).

Contacts: Pennsylvania Historical and Museum Commission, P.O. Box 1026, Harrisburg, PA 17108, Carnegie Museum of Natural History, 4400 Forbes Avenue, Pittsburgh, PA 15213; and Academy of Natural Sciences, 1900 Benjamin Franklin Parkway, Philadelphia, PA 19103.

RHODE ISLAND

The legislative purpose of Rhode Island's Antiquities Act is that "the public has an interest in the identification, interpretation, preservation, and protection of the state's archaeological resources" (General Laws of Rhode Island, 42-45.1-2). Consequently, the "state of Rhode Island

and Providence Plantations" reserves the exclusive right to conduct archeological field investigations on state lands and exclusive dominion over "underwater historic properties" found in navigable waters of the state, including the sea (RIGL 42-45.1-4).

The State Historical Preservation Commission may issue permits for field archeology and even pay "fair compensation" for recovered underwater artifacts. Since all items recovered are retained by the state, however, there is little incentive for the private archeologist to cooperate with the state (RIGL 42-45.1-5).

The commission is also in charge of designating State Archaeological Landmarks which, if on private land, must have the written consent of the owner. Once private land is designated, no person may conduct field investigations without the permission of the owner *and* the commission (RIGL 42-45.1-10). The commission may attempt to intervene in archeological work on private lands to encourage people to report archeological finds to the commission (RIGL 42-45.1-11).

Contacts: Rhode Island Historical Preservation Commission, 150 Benefit Street, Providence, RI 02903.

SOUTH CAROLINA
The custodian of submerged archeological resources from navigable waters and one league seaward is the South Carolina Institute of Archeology and Anthropology (South Carolina Underwater Antiquities Act of 1991, Title 54, Chap. 7, Sec. 54-7-640). The custodian of submerged paleontological material is the South Carolina Museum Commission (Sec. 54-7-640). However, the Institute of Archeology and Anthropology issues regulations regarding submerged paleontology.

South Carolina retains title to all archeological and paleontological property recovered from submerged lands within the state's control, but may be conveyed to licensees (Sec. 54-7-630). There appears to be no authority over terrestrial archeology and paleontology.

Any person desiring to conduct activities which may remove, displace, or destroy submerged archeological or paleontological properties must obtain a license from the institute (Sec. 54-7-650A). A person may not "knowingly recover, collect, excavate, or disturb" a submerged property without a license (Sec. 54-7-650G). However, licenses are not required for one who plans to "inspect, study, explore, photograph, measure, record, conduct a reconnaissance survey, use magnetic or acoustic detection devices" without "excavation, destruction, substantive injury, or disturbance" (Sec. 54-7-660). All licensees must furnish the institute with a report and inventory of objects recovered (Sec. 54-7-670G). Violations are misdemeanors with fines of not more than $100 (Sec. 54-7-810). A further advantage of having a license is that title to recovered property may be transferred to the licensee (Sec. 54-7-630). The institute may enter into agreements with licensees for the disposition of recovered property, including division of the property with the licensee, and all agreements must give "fair treatment" to the licensee (Sec. 54-7-650B,C,D).

The most available form of license is called a "hobby license" for a person desiring to conduct "temporary, intermittent, recreational, small scale, noncommercial search and recovery" of submerged properties, including from the river banks and beaches below the mean low watermark (Sec. 54-7-670). Hobby licenses are individual or instructional (for skuba clubs, etc.). The license fee is only $5 for residents and $10 for nonresidents for a six-month hobby license. Hobby licenses may not be used in waters for which exclusive licenses have been issued. Hobby licenses are also extremely limited in the type of equipment that may be used, and the number and type of artifacts that may be collected. However, the hobbyist can obtain title to recovered property.

An "instructional license" is available under a separate provision for dive clubs and charter businesses. These licenses may be renewed upon a six-month or two-year basis (Sec. 54-7-680).

A third type of license is called "an intensive survey license" or "data recovery license" intended for serious amateurs and professionals (Sec. 54-7-690). Such a license is exclusive for its duration, and for the purpose of "delineating the boundaries of a specific location which the applicant believes may contain submerged properties." A license will be issued only to those meeting certain professional standards, including research plan, techniques, and methodology. The license will not be issued to a person seeking title or commercial salvage of a submerged property except under certain conditions.

Contacts: Institute of Archeology and Anthropology, University of South Carolina, Columbia, SC 29208; South Carolina Museum Commission, 301 Gervis Street, P.O. Box 100107, Columbia, SC 29201; South Carolina Department of Archives and History, P.O. Box 11669, Capitol Station, Columbia, SC 29211.

SOUTH DAKOTA

The state of South Dakota reserves to itself the exclusive right to conduct field investigations on sites owned or controlled by the state or its political subdivisions in order to "preserve archeological and scientific information" (SDCL 1-20-25). The State Historical Society designates archaeological sites of significance, but may not designate private lands without the express written consent of the owner (SDCL 1-20-30).

The state archeologist, who is employed by the secretary of Education and Cultural Affairs, determines who is qualified for permits to explore on state lands or designated state archeological register sites. However, the permittee must be a "reputable museum, university, college, or other historical, scientific or educational institution or society" not necessarily public, "with a view toward disseminating the knowledge gained" (SDCL 1-20-32).

All specimens collected under permit remain the permanent property of the state, except that the state archeologist may make prior arrangements for the disposition of the specimens in an "appropriate institution of the state or for the loan of such specimens to qualified institutions in or out of the state" (SDCL 1-20-34). Thus, it is important for out-of-state museums or collectors to agree on the disposition of objects prior to or as part of obtaining the permit.

It is a Classs 2 misdemeanor to conduct field investigations on public lands or to remove antiquities or artifacts from private land without consent of the owner (SDCL 1-20-36). The statute does not specify what control the state may exert once private lands are designated, so owners are cautioned to obtain independent legal advice before agreeing to designation.

Contacts: State Archeologist, Department of Education and Cultural Affairs, Office of History, 900 Governors Drive, Pierre, SD 57501; State Historical Society, Box 5005, Rapid City, SD 57701.

TENNESSEE

The Tennessee Historical Commission maintains a register of historical "sites" (TCA 4-11-201). A "site" is defined as "any location of historic or prehistoric human activity such as, but not restricted to, mounds, forts, earthworks, burial grounds, structures, villages, mines, caves, and all locations which are or may be sources of paleontological remains" (TCA 11-6-102). It is a misdemeanor to carve upon, paint, deface, or otherwise injure artifacts, Native American paintings or "sites" (TCA

11-6-106). It is also illegal to "excavate upon any site" without a permit from the state archeologist which, in cases of $5,000 in damage, constitute Class E felony (TCA 11-6-105).

All artifacts and materials excavated under permit or otherwise belong to the state of Tennessee but may be loaned to nonprofit scientific organizations, public agencies, museums, and institutions of higher learning (TCA 11-6-104). The Division of Archeology also regulates paleontological sites associated with archeological sites (TCA 11-6-101).

Contacts: State Archeologist, Division of Archeology, Department of Environment and Conservation, 701 Broadway, Nashville, TN 37219.

TEXAS

The Texas Antiquities Code is administered by the Antiquities Committee that issues permits to qualified private firms for the "survey and discovery, excavation, demolition, or restoration of, or the conduct of scientific or educational studies" on public land (TNR Sec. 191.054). The Antiquities Committee may also contract with qualified private firms for the "discovery and scientific investigation of sunken or abandoned ships or wrecks of the sea or . . . archeological deposits or treasure imbedded in the earth" (TNR Sec. 191.053). However, all objects recovered are retained by the state unless released by the committee.

Only pre-twentieth-century shipwrecks are declared to be archeological landmarks. Also landmarks are "sites, objects, buildings, artifacts, implements, and locations of historical, archaeological, scientific or educational interest" including prehistoric and historical aboriginal campsites, dwellings, habitation sites, and their artifacts and implements of culture, on state lands or those of its political subdivisions (TNR Sec. 191.091, 092).

Contacts: Texas Antiquities Committee, P.O. Box 12276, Capitol Station, Austin, TX 78711; General Land Office, Stephen F. Austin State Office Building, Austin, TX 78711.

UTAH

Title 9, Chapter 8, Part 3 of the 1953 Utah Code covers "antiquities" including archeological, anthropological, and critical paleontological resources on institutional trust lands and school and institutional land grants. Materials recovered from these lands cannot be sold and remain the property of the state. The State Antiquities Section of the Utah

Division of State History sets the permit requirements for surveying or excavating on state-controlled lands (UCA 1953, Sec. 9-8-305). All archeological work must be carried out under the supervision of the state archeologist. Archeological discoveries on private lands also must be reported to the antiquities section (UCA 1953, Sec. 9-8-402).

46

Contacts: State Archeologist, Utah Division of State History, Antiquities Section, 300 Rio Grande, Salt Lake City, UT 84101.

VERMONT

The Vermont Division of Historic Preservation regulates "historic resources" through a state archeologist (1975 Vermont Historic Preservation Act, Title 22, Chap. 14, Secs. 701-791). An historical resource is defined as a "building, structure, object, district, area, or site that is significant in the history, architecture, archeology or culture of this state," clearly excluding paleontology.

The state reserves the exlusive right to perform field investigation on sites owned or controlled by the state, and all information and objects derived from state lands remain the property of the state (Sec. 762). No private land may be designated an archeological landmark without the owner's permission (Sec. 763). The director of the division, with the advice of the state archeologist, issues permits to qualified amateurs or professionals who must submit a summary report and all the collected specimens to the state (Sec. 764). Section 764 is not designed to encourage field investigation by outsiders if all specimens must be turned over to the state.

Separate sections regulate underwater archeology. The permit process is the same as with terrestrial archeology, except that the permittee may receive "fair compensation" in terms of a "percentage of the reasonable cash value of the objects recovered or a fair share of the objects recovered" (Sec. 782). A person who conducts field investigation activities on or under land owned by the state or within a state archeological landmark, or who "defaces, destroys, or otherwise alters any archaeological site or specimen" without a permit, may suffer a fine up to $1,000 or a jail sentence up to six months, or both.

Contacts: State Archeologist, Division of Historic Preservation, Pavilion Office Building, 135 State Street, Drawer 33, Montpelier, VT 05676.

VIRGINIA

The Virginia Antiquities Act (Sec. 10.1-2302) is administered by the

Virginia Department of Historic Resources. The department issues permits for any archeological field investigation on state-controlled lands or state archeological sites. Permit applicants, including amateurs, must demonstrate archeological qualifications. It is a Class I misdemeanor "to intentionally deface, damage, destroy, displace, disturb or remove any object of antiquity on any designated state archaeological site or state-controlled land" (Sec. 10.1-2306).

47

Underwater archeology is managed by the Virginia Institute of Marine Science and the Virginia Marine Resources Commission. All underwater materials remain the property of the Commonwealth. No underwater recovery operations are allowed except by permit from the Virginia Marine Resources Commission (Sec. 62.1-3). Permits are issued after the commission, institute and other concerned state interests conclude it is in the Commonwealth's interest to issue the permit. The applicant may receive a fair share of the objects or a reasonable percentage of the cash value of the objects that are recovered, depending upon negotiations.

Cave archeology is treated in the Virginia Cave Protection Act and administered by the Department of Conservation and Recreation that issues permits. Approval of the Department of Historic Resources is also required to conduct excavations in a cave. The Cave Protection Act also includes paleontological materials, cave deposits, and minerals. Failure to obtain a permit is a Class I misdemeanor. Violating the reporting requirements is a Class 3 misdemeanor.

Contacts: Virginia Department of Historic Resources, 221 Governor Street,Richmond, VA 23219.

WASHINGTON

The state of Washington has established the Washington Archeological Research Center to "discover, identify, excavate, and study" the archeological resources of the state, and serve as a repository (Washington Code, Sec. 27.53.020). The state reserves title to all "sites, objects, structures, artifacts, implements, and locations of prehistorical or archaeological interest" located in, on, or under the surface of lands or waters owned or controlled by the state or its political subdivisions (Sec. 27.53.040). These include prehistoric and historic Native American burials, campsites, dwellings, habitation sites, rock shelters, caves, and their artifacts (Sec. 27.53.040). In fact, all "historic archeological· resources abandoned for thirty years or more" on public lands, such as ships, aircraft, and treasure trove are also included(Sec. 27.53.045).

48

Archeological investigation is prohibited on all private and public lands within the state without a permit from the director of the Department of Community Development through its Office of Acheology and Historic Preservation (Sec. 27.53.060). It is a misdemeanor to "knowingly remove, alter, dig into, or excavate by use of any mechanical, hydraulic, or other means, or to damage, deface, or destroy any historic or prehistoric archaeological resource or site, or remove any archaeological object from such site" without a written permit from the director. It is a Class C felony to excavate "Indian graves or cairns, or any glyptic or painted record of any tribe or peoples, or historic graves as defined in chapter 68.05 RCW." The provisions of the section do not apply, however, to artifacts found exposed on the surface which are not "historic archaelogical resources or sites."

"Qualified or professional" archeologists are authorized to enter public lands for the limited purposes of archeological "resource location and evaluation studies, including site sampling activities" (Sec. 27.53.080). However, scientific excavations may be carried out only after appropriate agreement is made between the professional archeologist or institution of higher education and the appropriate agency or political subdivision. Notice of the agreement must be filed with the Archeological Reserach Center.

Amateur societies may be approved by the supervising state agency based on a written proposal detailing the scope and duration of the activity. The Archeological Research Center must also approve the proposals. The permittee must complete an extensive environmental checklist, and ensure that the proposed archeological work will be consistent with the state Environmental Policy Act (EPA). The state may require that artifacts collected on public land stay in Washington, but not those from private land.

The property owner is free to deny access, or to enter into a separate agreement, including charging a fee for the activities. However, the 1989 amendments which do not allow landowners to perform excavation, or permit excavation, on their own land (Sec. 27.53060[2]) may be subject to constitutional challenge.

Washington takes a more pragmatic view of its underwater archeology and may contract with private persons and institutions for the discovery and salvage of submerged artifacts in exchange for "fair" compensation, not less than ninety percent of the appraised value of the objects recovered (Sec. 27.53.110). In fact, the person or entity who first discovers a previously unreported historical archeological resource on state-owned submerged lands, and reports the site or location, shall have the right of first refusal for future salvage permits (Sec. 27.53.100). Of course, the salvor must mitigate any archeological damage that occurs during the operation (Sec. 27.53.120). We recommend that this potentially contentious provision be neutralized in the written contract by limiting the salvor's monetary liability for "failure to mitigate" to a percentage of his net recovery, so that such an adventure does not lead to liability over and above the value of the contract.

49

Contacts: Office of Archeology and Historic Preservation, Department of Community Development, 111 West 21st Avenue, KL-11, Olympia, WA 98504.

WEST VIRGINIA

West Virginia is especially concerned about the safety of unmarked human graves of "earlier West Virginians," but does not intend to "interfere with the normal activities of private property owners" (West Virginia Code, Sec. 29-1-8a). No person may "excavate, remove, destroy, or otherwise disturb any historic or prehistoric ruins, burial grounds, archeological site, or human skeletal remains, unmarked grave, grave artifact or grave marker of historical significance" without a valid permit from the West Virginia Historic Preservation Section of the Division of Culture and History.

The statute penalizes unauthorized excavation of "human skeletal remains of historical significance," and failure to comply with the terms of a permit for disinterment or displacement of human skeletal remains, as a felony subject to imprisonment for two to five years. Illegal excavation of lesser items is a misdemeanor, subject to fines of $100 to $500, a jail sentence of up to six months, or both. The statute does not restrict permits to any particular class of person.

Contacts: West Virginia Historic Preservation Section, Division of Culture and History, Capital Complex, Charleston, WV 25305.

WISCONSIN

Wisconsin's Historic Preservation Act gives the state the exclusive right and privilege of field archeology on state lands, and establishes regulations for field archeology on sites owned by political subdivisions (Wisconsin Statutes Annotated, Sec. 44.47). The state archeologist, through the director of the State Historical Society, is responsible for approving permits to "qualified natural persons" for field archeology on state sites and sites owned by political subdivisions (Sec. 44.47[4][a]). All objects discovered on state sites are owned by the State Historical Society as trustee for the state (Sec. 44.47[5]), although a permit may name another custodian. The type of acceptable custodian is not defined in the statute.

Contacts: Wisconsin State Historical Society, 816 State Street, Madison, WI 53706.

WYOMING

The Wyoming State Board of Land Commissioners requires a permit for the excavation of "prehistoric ruins, pictographs, hieroglyphics, or any other ancient markings, or writing or archeological and paleontological deposits" on state or federal public lands (Wyoming Statutes 1977, Title 36, Public Lands, Sec. 36-1-114). The board is also authorized to protect "natural bridges, natural scenic features and formations." Violations are misdemeanors.

Contacts: Wyoming State Board of Land Commissioners, Herschler Building, 122 West 25th Street, Cheyenne, WY 82002; Wyoming State Historic Preservation Officer, Department of Commerce, Barrett Building, Cheyenne, WY 82002.

CHAPTER 3

FEDERAL LAWS AND AGENCIES AFFECTING PALEONTOLOGICAL AND GEOLOGICAL COLLECTING

When Are You Doing Paleontological Collecting?

Paleontology is the study of ancient life. Over the last several years, paleontology has become the most popular of geological sciences. Paleontology is concerned with fossils, the actual or altered remains or traces of once-living organisms preserved in rocks. Most major cities have a regional museum or historical center that displays geological exhibits or fossil collections. Similarly, amateur clubs and organizations are active in many parts of the country. Fossils are actively bought and sold throughout the world and fossil collecting, preparation, and display also provides business opportunities.

Originally the word "fossil" referred to anything "dug up" out of the ground. A fossil may be the actual remains of a complete organism, such as an insect or bacterium preserved in amber or chert, a fish preserved in a limy concretion, a baby mammoth preserved in ice, or a fossil leaf preserved in mudstone. Fossils may also be parts of organisms such as isolated bones, teeth, shells, or wood that are altered to varying degrees by the removal or addition of organic or mineral matter. All of the original matter comprising the organism may have decayed or eroded away and the fossil is the mold or cast of the organism. Fossils can also consist of traces of animal activities such as burrows, tracks, or trails.

Paleontology Distinguished From Archeology

Paleontology is not the same as archeology although the two sciences are frequently confused. Paleontology is a natural science allied with geology and biology. Archeology is a social science, a subspecialty of either anthropology or classics, ancient history, or art history. Paleontology is concerned with the evolution of life on this planet as revealed by the fossil record; archeology is concerned with the evolution of human cultures as revealed by their artifacts.

52

The distinction between paleontology and archeology is not always sharp. For example, the evolution of primates, especially higher primates (monkeys, apes, and humans) is a subspecialty called paleoanthropology. Similarly, fossil animals are frequently found at ancient archeological sites where animal remains represent the food items of the primitive people at the site. For example, mammoths were hunted by early inhabitants of North America and their remains are found associated with spear points and other tools. Sometimes human remains represent the prey of predators. These are examples of the overlap between archeology and paleontology. Consequently, laws and regulations that concern archeology also apply to fossils occurring at archeological sites. These laws are discussed later in this book.

The State of Paleontology Today

To paraphrase from Dickens' *A Tale of Two Cities*, it is the best of times, and the worst of times, in paleontology. It is the best of times because now, more than ever before, the general public is interested in fossils and ancient life. It supports museums, reads books about fossils, buys fossils from dealers, and goes out and collects fossils! Paleontology may well be the most popular science today. Newspapers, magazines, television, and feature films have made just about every household in the United States aware of fossils. Interestingly enough, the demise of the Soviet Union and its allies has opened new opportunities to collect or purchase fossils from more parts of the world than ever before. This new awareness is very sophisticated. Allie Oop, King Kong, Creature from the Black Lagoon, and Godzilla have given way to Steve Gould's popular books about evolution and the fossil-rich Burgess Shale fauna, Bob Bakker's face in Sega ads, and Michael Crichton's book and movie, *Jurassic Park*.

It is the worst of times because academic jobs and graduate programs in paleontology have almost disappeared. At the same time, fossils once viewed as scientific curiosities to public land managers are now viewed as priceless commodities, and fossil collectors are now viewed as greedy gold-rushers. National and state pride also play a part, as it has in archeology, in obstructing free commerce in display or scientific specimens.

The Case Of Sue, the Only Dinosaur Ever Arrested by the FBI

A perfect example of government's overreaction to the problem is the case of Pete and Neil Larson. As kids on their parents' ranch in South

Dakota , they collected and curated fossils and dreamed of having a museum. As adults, they earned college degrees in geology and established the Black Hills Institute of Geological Research in tiny Hill City, South Dakota. Their business excavates and sells superbly prepared fossil specimens to museums, including the Smithsonian in Washington, D.C., the American Museum of Natural History in New York, the Carnegie in Pittsburgh, and the Sorbonne in Paris.

In 1990, they made the discovery of a lifetime, the tenth *Tyrannosaurus rex* skeleton in the world, as well as the largest and most complete. They paid Maurice Williams, the owner of the 30,000-acre ranch where it was discovered, the sum of $5,000 for the right to the fossil. Ordinarily, an oral agreement is just as legal as a written agreement. However, the Larsons should have checked the status of Mr. Williams' title. Hence, a $150 visit to an attorney could have saved what later became millions in legal fees.

The Larsons named the female dinosaur Sue. They excavated Sue and moved her in large crates to their Black Hills museum. In 1992, after BHIGR employees had spent hundreds of hours chipping away rock from her bones, exposing her five-foot head with its complete jaw, the FBI seized Sue without notice, along with most of the Larsons' business records. The Larsons were never charged with stealing Sue, but the U.S. attorney used their records to charge them with 154 other crimes. After a lengthy trial and $1 million in attorney's fees, a federal jury refused to convict the Larsons on any fossil-stealing counts, convicting them only on three customs violations, one count of receiving stolen property worth under $100, and one count of obstruction of justice, a misdemeanor. The customs violations involved failure to declare traveler's checks because they were issued by a Japanese bank, and the failure to declare a sum of $10,000 or more in cash in leaving the country, even though no individual in the group carried that sum. We sincerely doubt that anyone else in the country is doing time for such crimes.

In civil litigation over Sue, the federal government argued that it owned Sue. The same federal judge who had issued the search warrant for Sue ruled that she belonged to Maurice Williams. It seems Maurice Williams held title to the land by "trust deed" from the BIA. Hence, until the trust matured in 1994, Mr. Williams could not sell any "part of his land" without BIA approval. In short, because Maurice Williams was a Native American, Judge Battey treated him as incompetent to contract, and voided his contract with the Larsons as we do minors who may renounce their contracts made before the age of eighteen. We beg to differ with Judge Battey. In real estate law, Mr. Williams is not incompetent to contract merely because he may not have good title. Rather, if he agrees to sell something he doesn't own, he is obligated to cure the title or return the money, neither of which Maurice Williams did!

54

Now, oddly, the government has given approval for Maurice Williams to sell Sue to the highest bidder through a New York auction house! As for Judge Battey, he will remain infamous for his ingenious fiction that an unexcavated dinosaur is "part of the realty," unlike other commodities such as timber, crops, or even gold which could be sold by the owner under trust deed. Sue has been in storage since the FBI seized her in 1992, unavailable to science or the public. Pete Larson is in a federal prison for two years. His incarceration orders read that he is in prison with hardened felons for "failure to fill out forms."

The Black Hills Institute of Geological Research filed a "mechanic's lien" against any present or future owners of Sue for $212,000 in labor and expenses incurred in her restoration. In most states, a mechanic's lien is valid against real estate and personal property repaired or improved at the request of the owner. Not surprisingly, Judge Battey denied the lien.

In a Sylvia Chase CBS *Primetime Live* documentary in December 1992, the landowner admitted that he and the Cheyenne River Sioux tribe brought in the feds because they wanted more money for Sue. So, the acting U.S. attorney, and his successor, spent millions of taxpayer dollars, not in the interest of science, but so that one party in a civil dispute could make more money. It reminds one of the greed and power plays that withheld the Dead Sea Scrolls from public access for many years.

Thus, collecting fossils has become a complicated exercise, not because of the difficulty of finding and taking fossils, but because of all the rules, regulations, and laws the collector needs to know. People who have collected fossils have been charged with crimes by federal and state agencies. People collecting fossils on private land, thinking they had the landowner's authorization, have been accused of various offenses. Not only do different rules apply to invertebrate, vertebrate, and plant fossils, but they also vary according to the age of the rocks in which the fossils are found, and the ownership of the land. For example, there are more than fifty federal agencies that manage public lands; in theory each one can issue its own rules for fossil collecting. Moreover, certain lands may have special designations and restrictions such as ACEC (Area of Critical Environmental Concern), WSA (Wilderness Study Area), and RNA (Research Natural Area), each being treated differently although all are within Bureau of Land Management jurisdiction.

Getting On The Land

At the time of writing, at least two federal laws are being proposed that deal with collecting fossils on lands managed by the federal government. These proposals are worlds apart in terms of who is or isn't a professional paleontologist and what can or can't be done with fossils collected on public lands. To complicate matters, there are state-owned lands as well as federally-owned lands, and states may impose rules and regulations for fossil collecting on state lands. Similarly, there are laws that apply when you want to export fossils from one country to another.

Collecting on private lands also requires special precautions, as the case of Sue demonstrates. Unless the landowner on whose land you want to collect fossils is a close relative (and almost certainly if the landowner is a close relative), one simply must have a signed agreement that protects the interest of the collector and landowner. You should also request documentation by deed (and survey if possible) that the landowner owns the rights to the subsurface as well as the surface. This juncture would be the appropriate time to consult an attorney. See Appendix C for sample lease forms.

It is simply not enough to have a permit to collect fossils. More and more, some method of reporting is required in order to satisfy the requirements of the permits. This includes documenting what was found where, when, and by whom.

Chapters 3 and 4 attempt to explain to the fossil collector how to safely negotiate through the minefields awaiting him and will be of use to the academic paleontologist wanting to increase research collections, commercial paleontologists trying to find fossils to sell, and amateur paleontologists continuing an avocation.

Who Is A Paleontologist?

In our book, professional paleontologists include those employed by government, museums, universities, and industry, such as oil companies or fossil-collecting companies that sell fossils to museums and schools. This is a broader definition than readers will have seen elsewhere, but it does reflect reality.

56

Paleontology and the collection of fossils have had a commercial aspect almost as long as the profession has existed. Various individuals and firms have operated over the years and in fact have made substantive contributions to the science and provided important fossils to museums, colleges, and universities. There is a tendency to pay attention to the spectacular fossils that commercial paleontologists sell, such as complete mounted dinosaur skeletons or dinosaur eggs, or magnificent ammonite shells with complicated suture patterns and glossy luster. We tend to forget about the humble (but no less important) snail shells, brachiopods, and bryozoans needed for classrooms and paleontology laboratories in our schools and colleges.

The diversity of living organisms in the world today, from the microscopic to the gigantic, provides a hint of the range of different organisms preserved as fossils in the rocks of the Earth. Because of this diversity, most paleontologists tend to specialize in the fossils that they collect or study. The main divisions of paleontology include vertebrate paleontology, invertebrate paleontology, paleobotany, and micropaleontology. Vertebrate paleontology deals with the fossil record of backboned animals, invertebrate paleontology with the fossil record of invertebrates, paleobotany with the fossil record of plants, and micropaleontology with the fossil record of very small organisms. Within any of these subdisciplines are still more specialized areas of study. As might be expected, the distinctions between different specialties are frequently not clear-cut.

This book suggests that modern paleontology is a very broad continuum in which there are no longer clear distinctions between academic paleontology, amateur/hobbyist paleontology, or commercial paleontology. An interest in fossils unites all of these perspectives. Especially with the attrition of university-level positions, paleontologists are moving between being academic, amateur, and commercial collectors, in order to support themselves and still stay with the discipline they love.

Important questions have been raised by paleontologists and lawmakers regarding the different collecting goals among academic, commercial, and amateur paleontologists. Collecting fossils can involve exploring for fossils, surface collecting of exposed fossils such as shark's teeth or petrified wood, excavating sediments containing fossils, preparing the fossil by patiently chipping away its rock matrix and gluing disjoined pieces together, or obtaining fossils by purchase or trade. In the broadest terms, the distinctions between the groups of people who collect fossils are more illusory than real, as all paleontologists employ the same methods to obtain the same result. There are then four different reasons why people collect fossils:

1. Collecting as part of a research design.
2. Making representative collections of one kind or another.
3. Salvage paleontology; collecting to save fossils.
4. Collecting complete andor well-preserved fossils for display.

57

Collecting as Part of a Research Design

Collecting activities can be directed towards specific goals. A paleontologist attempting to understand particular environments will concentrate on collecting fossils from rocks preserving that environment. The study of how a particular fossil species grew would require the collection of large numbers of individuals of the species for analysis.

Making Representative Collections of One Kind or Another

Representative collections attempt to be diverse in coverage but limited in size. Thus, a collection may attempt to include examples of all major groups of brachiopods, or fossils from all the sedimentary units in a region, or all the Mesozoic mammal localities in the Western Interior. The intent of representative collections is to provide limited examples of a large number of fossils or fossil localities.

Salvage Paleontology

Development activities such as mining, building construction, dam construction, airport expansion, and many more activities all share one common characteristic: lands are disturbed. In the process of removing some materials and exposing others, fossil-bearing rocks or sediments may be encountered. The salvage of fossils uncovered by development has had a spotty past. Some important discoveries have been made, but these have been by chance rather than the result of an organized survey and mitigation effort.

Collecting Complete or Well Preserved Fossils for Display

Fossils are not rare. Most sedimentary rocks contain fossils of some kind. Of course, most fossils are very small and cannot be seen without a microscope, such as fossil pollen, spores, or foraminifera. Certain rocks formed in particular environments contain abundant fossils, such as brachiopods in Devonian silty limestones. Yet few brachiopod shells are required to meet the demand for specimens for museum exhibition, and fossil pollen is rarely exhibited at all.

When organisms die, most decay or are eaten by scavengers and are not fossilized. Most organisms that are fossilized are usually damaged to some extent and are only partially preserved. In general, it is comparatively rare for fossils to be exceptionally well-preserved. This is especially true for complex organisms consisting of many parts or of large size. However, it is not true that well-preserved and even superbly well-preserved, display-quality fossils are rare in the sense of total numbers. This paradox is the result of a numbers game. Even if only one of every ten thousand of a species is fossilized, so many tens of millions of individuals existed over such a long period of time, across so many thousands of miles, that many more well-preserved fossils exist than can ever be collected. For example, in the four corners area of New Mexico alone, there is more fossil-bearing rock from the age of dinosaurs than there is total land area in the state of Indiana. At most, one or two paleontologists and an equal number of hobbyists will visit the area in one year. The famous fossilfish-bearing Green River Formation covers thousands of square miles over large portions of Wyoming and Utah, and probably contain 5,000 fossils (the actual number can be as small as 1,000 or as much as 10,000) for every man, woman, and child alive on the Earth today.

The chances of being fossilized increase if the organism has sturdy hard parts such as a shell, external skeleton, teeth, or bones. The chances of being preserved also increase if the animal or plant existed in large numbers. Thus, there are many more fossil shark teeth, Green River fishes, brachiopods, and ammonites than can ever be collected by all the fossil collectors in the world, including academic, commercial and hobbyist.

Because of the relative scarcity of display-quality specimens, however, complete and well-preserved fossils have commercial value. Display-quality fossils may end up in private collections, especially if they are of "manageable" size, but most find their way into museum collections or colleges and universities. A large proportion of the display fossils in the museums of the world were discovered or collected by commercial or amateur paleontologists. In fact museums and scientific institutions rely heavily on commercial paleontologists for both scientific and display specimens, and institutions routinely sell and barter between themselves. In all of these transactions, the market place determines the price, and the value of display-quality fossils naturally falls as their number increases.

Purchasing, Selling, Trading or Donating Fossils

Apart from collecting your own fossils, there are four ways to obtain or dispose of fossils: purchase, sale, trade, or donation. Although anyone is free to purchase fossils without a critical eye, it is potentially foolhardy. Not only might you be spending money for something that is being misrepresented, you could be accused of receiving illegally gotten property if the fossil was improperly acquired by the seller. We recommend that everyone have a basic understanding of fossils, especially the fossils you buy. It is also very important that you only make purchases from reputable dealers, whether the dealer is the collector, or only the retailer. The reputation of dealers can be verified in several ways. You can consult with your Better Business Bureau, ask the dealer for references, or determine whether the dealer is a member of a trade association that maintains standards of business ethics and conduct.

Assuming that these requirements have been met, there are certain other minimum standards that both seller and buyer should meet. The fossil should be accompanied by data indicating where it was collected, including township, range, and section coordinates and other details that would allow the locality to be found again. Geological data that identifies the rock formation that hosts the fossil should also be included. If the fossil was collected in the United States, there should be data that indicates the fossil was collected on private land with the owner's permission or from a licensed quarry on state land. This should be in the form of a certificate of verification issued by the seller that every fossil he sells is from private or licensed lands, or a separate document that lists the specific locality for your purchase as being privately owned, including the name of the owner, or from a licensed locality with the permit number under which the fossil was collected.

Some states do not require permits for collecting fossils. It is just as important for the dealer to certify that fact, together with locality data to the purchaser. This protects both parts of the transaction, and there is simply no reason for a dealer not to provide this information to a purchaser. Similarly, there is no reason for the buyer not to demand this information.

It is important to bear in mind that at the time of this writing, no commercial collection of any fossils is allowed from public lands managed by the federal government. This rule applies to dinosaurs, clam shells, ammonites, and brachiopods alike. It applies to all fossils from federally managed lands whether or not they were originally collected with no intention of sale. State policy can be quite different, and commercial collection of fossils is an activity regulated by license or permit in some states. The collection of fossils for sale is a permitted, licensed, or otherwise regulated activity in some foreign countries as well.

Since museums and universities have always transacted sales or trades of fossils collected on federally managed public lands, they are potentially liable for these transactions. At the time of this writing, no museum or university has even been prosecuted for such activities.

Most paleontologists, whether they are academic, amateur, or commercial, believe that unique, rare, or otherwise significant fossil specimens should be available for scientific study. In fact, privately-held specimens have been described in scientific journals. Others have been donated to scientific collections. Collections have been transferred to an appropriate institution as gifts while the donor was alive, or as bequests. Both instances may have positive tax advantages as donations. Significant fossils have been purchased from commercial dealers by donors and presented to museums and universities. These too have carried tax advantages. Dealers routinely make an earnest effort to find educational institutions that will purchase their scientifically significant specimens.

Navajo Nation Policy

Nation policy maintains that fossils found on lands of the Navajo Nation are the property of the Navajo Nation. Fossils from the Navajo Nation that are maintained elsewhere can be recalled at any time.

Archeological and environmental clearance(s) may be required before paleontological collection can proceed.

A federal antiquities permit has been required in the past prior to beginning any excavation for collection. Such permits were previously issued by the National Park Service. A copy of the approved federal permit was to be filed with the Tribal Minerals Department. It is likely that if a federal permit were to be required again, it would be issued by the Bureau of Land Management, the lead agency in issuing such permits now.

Prior to publication of any report containing data gathered on the specimens and the associated geological formations, the report will be reviewed and approved by the Tribal Minerals Department. A copy of the final report will be provided to the Minerals Department for its permanent record. Advance notification of project commencement and completion must be given to the Minerals Department.

Rights of local Navajo people are protected and respected. Personnel of the Minerals Department will have the option of monitoring the field work of the permittee. Recent policy would seem to indicate that only the Minerals Department has the authority to issue permits to collect fossils on Navajo lands. BIA involvement is restricted to allotted lands. Reliance is placed on OSM for coal producing lands. This reliance would open the way for assessment via FLPMA, NEPA, and SMCRA.

61

Current Federal Laws Affecting Fossil Collecting

Petrified Wood Act of 1962

The Petrified Wood Act of 1962 originated as an amendment to the 1872 Mining Act so that petrified wood deposits were not considered valuable minerals within the meaning of the 1872 law. The Petrified Wood Act directs the Secretary of the Department of the Interior "to provide by regulation that limited quantities of petrified wood may be removed without charge from those public lands which he shall specify."

Present rules allow petrified wood to be collected for non-commercial purposes without a permit, but quantities are limited to twenty-five pounds plus a piece per day and not more than 250 pounds per person each year. A specimen weighing more than 250 pounds requires a permit. Specimens obtained under the free use provision may not be sold or bartered to commercial dealers. Commercial collection is governed by the Materials Act of 1947 and regulations dealing with mineral material sales.

No specific regulation applies to collecting petrified wood on Navajo lands except those that apply to fossils in general, and also ARPA.2.

Antiquities Act of 1906

The Antiquities Act of 1906 prohibits the appropriation, taking, excavating, injuring, or destroying of any "historic or prehistoric ruin or monument, or any object of antiquity, situated on lands owned or controlled by the government of the United States," without permission from the federal land manager concerned with the lands involved. The details of this legislation, including how it impacts fossil collection, are discussed in Chapter I.

Federal Land Policy Management Act of 1976 (FLPMA)

FLPMA authorizes the Bureau of Land Management, created in 1946, to manage the public lands for the expressed purposes of "multiple use and sustained yield" and to prevent "its unnecessary or undue degradation." Multiple use is defined as "balanced and diverse resource uses that takes into account the long-term needs of future generations for renewable and nonrenewable resources, including, but not limited to, recreation, range, timber, minerals, watershed, wildlife and fish, and natural, scenic, scientific, and historical values." The BLM may employ "permits, leases, licenses, published rules, or other instruments" to achieve these purposes.

The BLM controls 270 million acres, or approximately one-eighth of our country's surface, as well as the mineral rights underlying 570 million acres. These statistics are more meaningful in the western states, where the BLM controls great galloping chunks, including eighty-three percent of the land surface of Nevada, and close to half of the states of Utah, Wyoming, Idaho, Oregon, Colorado, and New Mexico.

BLM lands represent "leftovers" from federal sale of various homestead and mining patents, and gifts of certain sections to the states. There is no demonstrated design to preserve these lands as permanent sanctuaries. Rather, Congress intended BLM lands to serve as an economic and recreational resource and reserve. BLM rules, then, should be very different from those that apply to our national parks and wilderness areas. It is also significant that Congress used the word "public" rather than "federal" or "national," further emphasizing the difference between "national" parks and "public" lands held in trust for use by the public. Conceivably, BLM lands could serve in the future to relieve population pressure, as public lands have done in the past.

Although fossils are not specifically mentioned in FLPMA, "scientific values" are interpreted by the BLM to include fossil resources on a par with other scientific values.

In 1982, the BLM began making rules for fossils, geological materials, and hobby mineral materials. In the absence of formally adopted rules at the national level, the BLM informally regulates fossil collecting at the state office level. The general rule is that a permit from the BLM is required to remove vertebrate fossils and scientifically significant invertebrate and plant fossils. Three types of permits are issued: (1) noncollection reconnaissance permits for surveying and mapping, (2) collection and limited removal permits that allow for surface collection and limited testing, and (3) excavation permits. Permits are issued only to "academic, scientific, governmental, or other qualified institutions or individuals or companies," and materials recovered under a permit must be deposited in an institution with public access.

We emphasize that the above are merely recommendations of the BLM and do not constitute formal rules. Formal rulemaking requires a series of public hearings before formal adoption. Thus, we maintain that the BLM continues to act illegally in enforcing rules that do not exist.

BLM administers the leasing of oil, gas, coal, and minerals. Leases frequently contain stipulations that protect other resources that might be impacted by the development activities. The oil and gas lease form provides that the "areas to be administered may require inventories or special studies to determine the extent of impacts to other resources. . . . If in the conduct of operations, threatened or endangered species, objects of historic or scientific interest, or substantial unanticipated environmental effects are observed, lessee shall immediately contact lessor. Lessee shall cease any operations that would result in the destruction of such species or objects."

FLPMA should not apply to fossils found on Navajo lands unless the Navajo choose to delegate authority for regulating fossil resources. In fact, the BLM has been asked to intercede in paleontological matters on Navajo lands in previous fossil cases. BLM enforcement officers have investigated fossil collectors and prosecuted certain sales of fossils from Navajo lands in New Mexico.

An interesting case involved Mr. M., a commercial dealer in Santa Fe who bought fragmentary dinosaur material from amateur collectors in Farmington, New Mexico. Mr. Brad Archer, Curator, Arizona State University Geology Museum, and a serious amateur collector from Arizona, Mr. John Babiarz, intended the material for a public museum in Arizona. They had also identified a large part of a dinosaur skeleton in the field from the localities indicated by the original collectors. The Arizona individuals applied for Navajo collecting permits but the permit application was denied. The Arizona individuals stabilized the purchased fossils and invested several hundred hours of preparation.

The Farmington collectors also provided Mr. M. with some Native American artifacts and other fossils. Some of the fossils consisted of mammal teeth from the period of time soon after the demise of the dinosaurs known as the "Dawn of Mammals." The dealer had shown these fossils to the curator at the Museum of Natural History in

Albuquerque, and discussed whether they were legally acquired. Unbeknownst to Mr. M., the curator then notified BLM officials who charged Mr. M. with theft and other federal crimes. They also confiscated M's business records that referred to the dinosaur fossils sold to the Arizona collectors.

64

The BLM then investigated Archer and Babiarz in Arizona. Although no charges were ever brought, their records and fossils were confiscated and eventually were placed in the custody of the Navajo Tribal Police. Officials at the BLM maintained they were requested to intervene by BIA and tribal officials, but could show no authority under FLPMA for interfering on non-BLM lands, even if requested. The Arizona individuals were later contacted by the New Mexico Museum of Natural History and requested to share their knowledge of the confiscated fossil material! The New Mexico Museum of Natural History then acquired the fossil dinosaur material from the custody of the Navajo Tribal Police and placed the material on exhibit without acknowledging the preparation of the fossils by the Arizona individuals or their publication of the fossil in *The Journal of Paleontology*. Enough for a Tony Hillerman novel?

National Forest Management Act

The United States Department of Agriculture controls 200 million acres, or twenty-five percent of all public lands, in the nation's 155 national forests, through the U.S. Forest Service. Unlike the Department of the Interior and its agency, the BLM, the Department of Agriculture has promulgated formal regulations that prohibit "excavating, damaging, or removing any vertebrate fossil or removing any paleontological resource for commercial purposes without a special use authorization" (36 CFR Sec. 261.9[I]). "Excavating, damaging, or removing any cave resource without a special use authorization" is also prohibited (36 CFR Sec. 261.9[j]). The present rules are more user-friendly than those in effect prior to 1986, when collection of any "paleontological resource" whatsoever required a permit. Two primary reasons were stated for the rule change, that should be of interest to fossil initiatives now before the federal or state governments (51 Federal Register 30355, August 26, 1986).

The distinction made by Congress between archeological and paleontological resources in the Archeological Resources Protection Act of 1979 (ARPA) implies that federal land management agencies need not exercise the same degree of protection for the two resources. The collection of paleontological objects on National Forest lands is "a legitimate scientific and educational pursuit and there is no evidence of widespread conflicts or problems that would require a blanket prohibition" but vertebrate fossils "have traditionally been accorded special significance and will remain subject to regulation."

Regardless, land managers may issue special closure orders to protect "objects or areas of historical, archeological, geological, or paleontological interest" or for "scientific experiments or investigations."

Presumably, one may collect invertebrate fossils for noncommercial purposes without a permit. A strict reading of the law would require that permits be granted for commercial collection of invertebrate fossils as well, but we have heard from collectors that no such permits are being issued.

National Environmental Policy Act of 1969 (NEPA)

The National Environmental Policy Act (NEPA) was enacted in 1969. NEPA requires federal agencies to prepare an Environmental Impact Statement (EIS) for any major federal action that significantly affects the quality of the human environment, including natural aspects of our national heritage. Although NEPA only constrains federal agencies, the need for these agencies to address impacts on fossil resources may result from the EIS process. The details of this legislation are discussed more thoroughly in Chapter I.

Surface Mining Control and Reclamation Act of 1977 (SMCRA)

The Surface Mining Control and Reclamation Act of 1977 (SMCRA) was the first comprehensive federal statute to regulate the environmental impacts of coal mining on a national scale. The primary purpose of SMCRA is to force mine operators to mitigate surface damage from coal mining by requiring them to return mined areas to their approximate original appearance and contours. For practical reasons, SMCRA disregards coal itself as a fossil resource. However, mine operators are restrained from harming significant paleontological localities: "Operators shall not knowingly disturb, alter, injure, or destroy any scientifically important paleontological remains or any historical or archeological site, structure, building or object on Federal lands. Operators shall immediately bring to the attention of the authorized officer any cultural and/or paleontological resources that might be altered or destroyed on

Federal lands by his/her operations, and shall leave such discovery intact until told to proceed by the authorized officer."

U. S. Geological Survey Enabling Legislation

The U.S. Geological Survey is authorized to collect and study the nation's fossil resources. Paleontology has always been viewed as a tool for interpreting the age of rocks, the correlation of rocks from one area to another, depositional environments, and potentially valuable minerals and energy resources contained in the rocks. Native American tribes could maintain that all fossils found on reservations remain their property and request return of all fossils collected by U.S. Geological Survey geologists and paleontologists from its lands. U.S. Bureau of Land Management geologists and paleontologists have also made collections from Navajo lands, although the reason for these collections and possible benefits to the tribes are less clearly defined.

The Historic Sites Act of 1935 and the National Historic Preservation Act of 1966

These acts provide for the preservation of historic sites, buildings, and objects of national significance for the inspiration and benefit of the people of the United States. The Landmarks (NNL) program clearly requires the National Park Service to set aside a paleontogical site as a national landmark if it is "an outstanding representative example of the nation's natural heritage, including geological features . . . or fossil evidence of the development of life on earth". The details of this legislation are described in Chapter I.

The Mineral Leasing Act of 1920

The Mineral Leasing Act of 1920 requires that the Secretary of the Department of the Interior must review the environmental impacts to an area before issuing a coal lease. Any lease issued must address those impacts deemed significant, and the lease holder may be required to submit an appropriate plan of operation and reclamation to mitigate those impacts. Impacts can be seen as affecting cultural, historic or scientific resources.

The Mining Law of 1872

The Mining Law of 1872 provides for the location and patent of certain mineral deposits, generally hard-rock deposits such as gold,

66

silver, lead, and zinc not treated by the 1920 Mineral Leasing Act or the 1947 Materials Act. Petrified wood and fossils cannot be claimed under the 1872 Mining Law under existing precedent, but Congress could easily legislate otherwise.

In 1913, Earl Douglas, collecting for the Carnegie Museum, attempted to acquire rights to dinosaur-bearing rocks near Vernal, Utah by staking placer mining claims under the 1872 Mining Law. The Interior Department denied the claim, maintaining that fossils "are not mineral within the meaning of the United State mining laws, and lands containing such remains are not subject to entry under such laws." The department reasoned that fossils did not "possess economic value for use in trade, manufacture, the sciences, or in mechanical or ornamental arts," a premise that is no longer true. See Earl Douglas, 44 Pub. Lands Dec. 325 (1915), as cited in David Lazerwitz's "Bones of Contention," *Indiana Law Journal*, Vol. 69, No. 2, Spring 1994.

Because we now know that fossils possess economic value and are sold, bartered, and traded in commerce and between museums and scientific institutions, and do contain minerals, Congress should reconsider whether we should simply include them under the 1872 Mining Law. We often hear that fossils are a valuable and nonrenewable commodity. If so, then they should be treated the same as we do precious metals. Using the 1872 Mining Law as a model, or at least the salvaging laws of the federal and state governments, would encourage exploration, discovery, and systematic, scientific excavation. Paleontologists who make valuable discoveries could use the protection that any miner has against claim-jumping. Also one who invests in discovering and preparing fossils needs some incentive other than a government paycheck, or fossils will go uncollected and erode away, lost forever to the public.

Two federal departments regulate the impacts of development activities and exploration under the 1872 Mining Law: the Department of the Interior, through the Bureau of Land Management, and the Department of Agriculture, through the U.S. Forest Service. Both agencies require mining operators to protect fossils. For example, BLM policy states: "Operators shall not knowingly disturb, alter, injure, or destroy any scientifically important paleontological remains or any historical or archeological site, structure, building or object on Federal lands. Operators shall immediately bring to the attention of the authorized officer any cultural and/or paleontological resources that might be altered or destroyed on Federal lands by his/her operations, and shall leave such discovery intact until told to proceed by the authorized officer." The policy doesn't explain how an operator is to recognize a "scientifically important" fossil. The BLM policy toward fossils is different from its policy toward mining in general that requires no permit or notice for "casual use" or "activities ordinarily resulting in only negligible disturbance" (43 C.F.R. Sec. 3809.0-5[b]).

The Materials Act of 1947

The Materials Act of 1947 authorizes the U.S. Department of Interior, through the BLM, and the Department of Agriculture, through the U.S. Forest Service, to dispose of materials such as common varieties of sand, stone, gravel, pumice, pumicite, cinders, and clay. These materials are differentiated from "valuable mineral deposits" subject to the Mining Act of 1872. The act does not apply to national parks or Native American lands.

The Materials Act appears to be the only statutory authority for disposal of fossils for commercial uses. However, removal of materials under the act must be done with agency authority and by paying "adequate compensation." Obviously, if one has not paid adequate compensation and does not have agency authority, one can be charged with theft. The Materials Act was the basis for the Mr. M. prosecution mentioned previously.

The Reservoir Salvage Act of 1960

The Reservoir Salvage Act of 1960 is intended to provide protection for archeological and historical data potentially impacted by federal dam construction. Paleontology would qualify under "scientific or prehistorical" values. Further details are discussed in Chapter I.

Archeological Resources Protection Act of 1979 (ARPA)

Fossils are excluded from ARPA except when they occur in an archeological context. However, ARPA controls who can conduct field studies, as well as the collection and disposition of fossils thus covered. ARPA is discussed in detail in Chapter I as it applies to archeology.

National Park Service

Under the U.S. Department of Agriculture, the National Park Service manages eighty-three million acres, or eleven percent of public lands. Of these, national parks consume fifty-one million acres, and national preserves the rest.

Bureau of Indian Affairs

The BIA, under the Secretary of the Department of Interior, acts as trustee of Indian-owned lands amounting to fifty-five million acres, or seven percent of the total territory under federal stewardship. The 300 reservations, home to more than 500 tribes, are governed by elected leaders who determine activities on their land, including camping, hunting, fishing, and collecting of archeological, botanical, geological, and paleontological specimens. However, as we saw in the case of Sue, the dinosaur, BIA approval may be required prior to collecting where the landowner's title has not matured into complete title because of the trust relationship with the BIA.

Department of Defense

Military reservations and bases consume twenty-seven million acres, chiefly in the west and south. The Department of Defense regulates access to these lands. There are more than 220 endangered or threatened species and 100,000 archeological sites on military reservations.

Department of Commerce

The National Oceanic and Atmospheric Administration regulates the national estuarine research reserves and national marine sanctuaries. Estuarine research reserves are located on state-owned lands and are co-regulated by the department and the state involved. There are twelve national marine santuaries for those interested in coral reefs, kelp, and other saltwater habitats.

Department of Energy

The DOE manages fifty sites totalling 2.4 million acres, including the WIPP underground nuclear waste site in Carlsbad, New Mexico. There is some public access to these sites, should you find fossils you want to collect.

Pending Federal Legislative Initiatives
Vertebrate Paleontological Resource Preservation Act (VPRPA)

The bill known as the Baucus Bill is sponsored by Senator Max Bachus (D-Montana). This is a very restrictive bill with a Draconian penalty structure of thousands of dollars in fines. This bill carries stiff penalties for unpermitted collection of vertebrate fossils on public lands. Although the bill does not specifically cover Native American lands, it could be adopted by tribal governments if they wished.

This bill (VPRPA) includes the following:

1. Federal lands are a valuable resource of the people of the United States;

2. Each individual who uses federal lands is (a) exercising both a right and a priceless privilege; and (b) must accept the responsibility of careful stewardship of the lands so that the privilege can be exercised by future generations;

3. Vertebrate paleontological resources on federal lands and Native American lands are an accessible and irreplaceable part of the heritage of the United States and offer significant educational opportunities to all citizens;

4. Vertebrate paleontological resources are increasingly endangered because of their commercial attractiveness and because many are rare or unique;

5. Vertebrate paleontological resources are (a) nonrenewable resources; (b) are natural aspects of the national heritage of the United States; (c) have scientifically significant value; and (d) have important educational value;

6. (a) Federal laws in effect prior to the date of enactment of this act do not provide adequate protection to prevent the loss and destruction of vertebrate paleontological resources and sites on federal lands resulting from uncontrolled excavations and pillage; and (b) there is no consistent federal policy for comprehensive management of the resources and sites;

7. Amateur collectors are a valuable part of the scientific and educational communities;

8. (a) There is a wealth of paleontological information that has been legally obtained by private individuals for noncommercial purposes and that has been voluntarily made available to the scientific community; and (b) this information has been an invaluable contribution to the advancement of paleontological science in the United States;

9. The activities described in paragraph (8) by private individuals, particularly amateur collectors, should be encouraged and facilitated;

10. (a) Reasonable access to vertebrate paleontological resources on federal lands should be provided to professional and amateur vertebrate paleontologists for scientific, educational and recreational purposes; (b) a mechanism to encourage cooperation and to exchange information among the professional and amateur communities and the general pub-

lic should also be adopted; and (c) increased awareness and enjoyment of the resources by children and young adults should be fostered;

11. Those resources that are of scientific significance belong in the public trust and should be placed in suitable repositories, including museums, universities, colleges, and other educational institutions; and

12. If housed in the repositories, the resources should be available for study and public educational purposes (including public display).

71

Paleontological Resource Preservation Act (PRPA)

This proposed bill was developed by the American Lands Access Association (ALAA) in response to what it viewed as the very restrictive Baucus Bill. The PRPA, if submitted to Congress, will be introduced by Representative Joe Skeen (R-New Mexico) and Tim Johnson (D-South Dakota).

Important sections of the draft legislation state:

1. Significant paleontological resources on public lands are an accessible and important part of the education and heritage of the United States;

2. Scientifically significant resources on public lands are increasingly endangered and must be preserved by encouraging their timely collection in order to prevent their destruction by weathering, and other natural causes and pillage;

3. Federal laws in existence on the date of enactment of this act do not provide protection to prevent the loss and destruction of these paleontological resources;

4. Amateur, commercial, academic, and museum paleontologists and collectors are all a vital part of the scientific and educational communities;

5. (a) There is a wealth of paleontological information that has been largely obtained by private individuals, amateur and professional, for noncommercial purposes and that has been voluntarily made available to the scientific community; and (b) this information has been an invaluable contribution to the advancement of paleontology in the United States;

6. The activities described in paragraph (5) by private individuals, particularly amateur collectors, should be encouraged and facilitated;

7. Paleontological resources, though nonrenewable; are (a) for practical purposes, recurring resources due to the continuing action of natural erosion on the geologic formations containing the resources; (b)

are natural aspects of our national heritage; (c) have important educational value and often have significant scientific value; (d) need to be preserved by collection prior to their loss to either natural forces or pillage; and (e) have important aesthetic and commercial value.

72

8. (a) Access to paleontological resources on public lands should be provided to professional and amateur paleontologists for scientific and educational purposes and to commercial entities under proper guidelines pursuant to this act; and (b) a mechanism to exchange scientific information between the professional, amateur, and commercial communities should be adopted;

9. Those resources that are scientifically significant should be placed in suitable repositories, including museums, universities, colleges, other educational institutions, and recorded in the United States Geological Survey data bank;

10. When housed in repositories, the resources should be available for scientific study and educational purposes;

11. Each federal agency should adopt a uniform national policy on paleontological collecting on federal lands that is consistent with (a) the specific federal mandate of the agency; and (b) the protection of scientifically significant paleontological resources pursuant to this act;

12. Each state should (a) adopt a uniform policy on paleontological collecting on state-owned lands; (b) appoint a designated state paleontologist;

13. Each Native American tribe should adopt a uniform policy on paleontological collecting on the lands of the tribe;

14. Paleontological societies and institutions in the United States and federal land management agencies should develop permanent and broadly based educational programs to share information with landowners and commercial and amateur collectors of paleontological resources regarding (i) significant paleontological resources; (ii) the research needs of professional and amateur paleontologists; (iii) the needs for care and curation of collections; (iv) the legitimate role of commercial collectors on public and private lands; and, fostering scientific education at all educational levels;

15. Commercial collection and sale of vertebrate and invertebrate fossils to the public as well as educational institutions, contributes to the overall appreciation of our fossil heritage and to the educational, economic, and career interest in paleontology if done ethically so as not to reduce the scientific and educational value of paleontological discoveries;

16. Collecting that separates fossils from their geological and paleoecological contexts, or that removes rare and important fossils from the realm of public education and scientific study, or that interferes with ongoing excavation by researchers engaged in permitted studies or excavation, decreases the benefit of public lands for the people of the United States; and

17. Commercial activity has historically been a source of significant scientific paleontological discovery and for materials for scientific and educational study.

Paleontological Resource Act (PRA)

This bill will be sponsored in the Senate by Senator Tom Daschle (D-South Dakota) and possibly others. This bill is an alternative to the two draft bills noted above. The spirit of the bill is more in keeping with the ALAA Bill and it is possible that, in the House, sponsors will include Representatives Joe Skeen (R-New Mexico) and Tim Johnson (D-South Dakota), who will give up support for the ALAA Bill and support the Daschle initiative. This bill deals with all fossils and is generally less onerous than the Baucus Bill. However, it does regulate paleontology on public lands. Although not inclusive of Native American lands, once again, there is no provision that would restrict the application of the bill's measures to such lands if requested by tribal government authorities. This bill was obviously developed from the earlier legislation with a good deal of appreciation of the National Academy of Science study. It can be viewed as moderate simplification of the previous bills.

Important sections of this draft legislation includes the following:

1. Significant paleontological resources on public lands are accessible and in addition to their commercial and scientific value, are useful for earth science education;

2. Federal laws in existence on the date of enactment of this act do not provide uniform regulations for the collection of paleontological resources on public land;

3. Paleontological resources should be collected for commercial, scientific, and educational purposes;

4. Collecting that separates scientifically significant fossils from their geological and paleontological contexts, that removes rare and significant fossils from the realm of public education or scientific study, or that interferes with ongoing excavation by researchers engaged in permitted studies or excavations, decreases the benefit of public lands for the people of the United States;

74

5. Access to paleontological resources on public lands should be provided to casual collectors, commercial entities, research scientists, and educators under proper guidelines pursuant to this act;

6. Fossils that are scientifically significant should be placed in suitable repositories, including museums, universities, colleges, or other nonprofit educational institutions in order to be available for scientific study and educational purposes; and

7. A uniform national policy on paleontological collecting on federal lands should be adopted by all federal land management agencies and should be consistent with the specific federal mandate of the agency and the protection of scientifically significant paleontological resources pursuant to this act.

NAS Committee on Guidelines for Paleontological Collecting

In 1987, the National Academy of Sciences convened a Committee on Guidelines for Paleontological Collecting, that published its findings in the same year. The conclusions of the committee were embodied in the following ten recommendations:

1. A uniform national policy on paleontological collecting should be adopted by all federal agencies. Existing statutory authority is adequate for implementation of such a policy.

2. Each state should adopt a uniform paleontological policy for state-owned lands.

3. All public lands should be open to fossil collecting for scientific purposes. Except in cases involving quarrying for commercial collecting, collecting fossils on public land should not be subject to permit requirements or other regulation.

4. Fossils of scientific significance should be deposited in institutions where there are established research and educational programs in paleontology. These repositories will ensure that specimens are accessioned, maintained, and remain available for study and education. There is no justification for requiring that fossils be deposited in an institution in the same state in which they are found; such requirements discourage paleontological research.

5. Commercial collecting of fossils from public lands should be regulated to minimize the risk of losing fossils and data of importance to paleontology. Permit applications must be subject to review by paleontologists qualified to assess the projects' potential impact on related research programs. Applications must receive the endorsement of a pale-

ontologist who is willing to supply guidance to the commercial operation. Specimens deemed to be of special scientific interest must be deposited in a public institution, such as a museum, college, or university.

6. Private landowners should follow the guideline that commercial collecting of fossils be undertaken with thorough scientific oversight to ensure that the scientific usefulness of specimens is not impaired.

7. Blanket paleontological inventories, mitigation, or salvage activities should not be undertaken, funded, or required by government agencies as a routine part of environmental assessment, impact analysis, permitting, land management, or similar programs.

8. Land managers or developers who require scientific guidance on perceived paleontological problems should initially seek advice from the U. S. Geological Survey, or appropriate state geological surveys, which in turn may wish to contact appropriate paleontological organizations.

9. The Department of the Interior, in cooperation with the professional paleontological community, should identify and evaluate potential paleontological localities of national significance (both on public and private lands) for designation as National Natural Landmarks (NNLs), pursuant to the existing National Natural Landmark Program administered by the National Park Service (36 CFR 62).

10. The paleontological societies of the nation should develop permanent and broadly-based educational programs to inform landowners and commercial and amateur collectors of the research needs of professional paleontology.

In the absence of a leading role by the federal government, only a smattering of states have adopted legislation expressly regulating fossil and mineral collection on state lands. Unfortunately, fossils are often lumped together with human artifacts as part of the state's "historic preservation" effort, without concern for the differences between the two sciences.

There is a fairly standard "Cave Protection Act" in many states that protects archeology, fossils, and geologic formations in publicly or privately owned caves.

ALABAMA
Alabama has a state Museum of Natural History, but no apparent laws regulating paleontological and geological collecting on state land as of this writing.

ALASKA
Paleontology is treated together with archeology in Alaska. See the discussion in Chapter 2.

ARIZONA
Paleontology and archeology are treated under one regulatory scheme in Arizona. See the discussion in Chapter 2.

ARKANSAS
Arkansas has adopted a Cave Resources Protection Act that appears to be fairly uniform in all the states that have adopted it (Title 15, Chap. 20, Subchap. 6, Arkansas Code of 1987 Annotated). These acts outlaw vandalizing natural cave formations, or man-made material or structures in the caves.

Contacts: Arkansas State Parks, One Capitol Mall, Little Rock, AR 72201; Arkansas Geological Commission, 3815 West Roosevelt,

Fayetteville, AR 72704; Arkansas Archeological Survey, P.O. Box 1249, Fayetteville, AR 72702.

CALIFORNIA

The Department of Natural Resources regulates state park activities, and twenty-eight state parks are accessible to rock-hounds. Mineral collectors are limited to "not more than one specimen plus 15 pounds of mineralogical materials" (Sec. 4610.3). However, "Indian arrowheads, Indian stone tools, or other archeological specimens" may not be collected (Sec. 4610.9). Again, "qualified institutions and individuals" may collect under specific authorization of the director of the California State Lands Commission, 1807 13th Street, Sacramento, CA 95814.

Where mineral prospectors once wandered across our public lands, armed only with pick, shovel, and mule, California now requires that prospectors carry a permit as well. The State Lands Commission issues prospecting permits, under its own rules and regulations, for lands that "are not known mineral lands," to "any qualified applicant" upon payment of a reasonable fee as determined by the commission, of not less than one dollar per acre for each acre described in the permit (Public Resources Code, Sec. 6891). However, no permit may be issued for lands "containing commercially valuable mineral deposits" or "known mineral lands." Permits can be extended for up to three years to prospect for minerals (excluding oil, gas, or other hydrocarbon substances) "upon lands wherein the mineral deposits belong to the state." Contrary to the U.S. Mining Law of 1872, California law has virtually destroyed prospecting on any lands not being currently mined, because ninety percent of new prospecting takes place in old mines, placer sites, or claims.

California has adopted cave protection laws that generally prohibit breaking, altering, or disturbing anything, natural or man-made, found in either public or privately owned caves. Section 623 of the penal code makes it a misdemeanor, punishable by imprisonment for up to one year and/or a fine of $1,000, to violate a cave. The following is from the California Cave Protection Act:

> (A) Except as otherwise provided in this Section, any
> person who, without the prior written permission of
> the owner of a cave, intentionally and knowingly does

78

any of the following acts is guilty of a misdemeanor punishable by imprisonment in the county jail not exceeding one year, or by a fine not exceeding one thousand dollars, or both.

(1) Breaks, breaks off, cracks, carves upon, paints, writes or otherwise marks upon or in any manner destroys, mutilates, injures, defaces, mars, or harms any natural material found in any cave.

(2) Disturbs or alters any archeological evidence of prior occupation in any cave.

(3) Kills, harms, or removes any animal or plant life found in any cave.

(4) Burns any material which produces any smoke or gas which is harmful to any plant or animal found in any cave.

(5) Removes any material found in any cave.

(6) Breaks, forces, tampers with, removes or otherwise disturbs any lock, gate, door, or any other structure or obstruction designed to prevent entrance to any cave, whether or not entrance is gained.

COLORADO

Geological materials and quarries on state land are regulated by the State Board of Land Commissioners through permits or special mining leases (Colorado Revised Statutes Annotated, Title 34 and Title 36). In fact, the state's expressed policy is "to permit the extraction and exploration of minerals" from "mineral resource areas," unless extraction and exploration "cause significant danger to public health and safety" (Sec. 24-65.1-202).

See Chapter 2 on archeology for the treatment of fossils.

Contacts: Office of the State Archeologist, 1300 Broadway, Denver, CO 80203; Colorado Division of Parks and Outdoor Recreation, 1313 Sherman Street, Room 618, Denver, CO 80203; Colorado Division of Wildlife, 6060 Broadway, Denver, CO 80216; Colorado Department of Highways, 4201 East Arkansas Avenue, Denver, CO 80222.

CONNECTICUT

Fossil and mineral specimens are regulated on state-owned lands by the Department of Environmental Protection. Dinosaur State Park has been set aside as a reserve for Triassic dinosaur track-ways and other paleontological materials.

Contacts: Parks and Recreation Unit, Department of Environmental Protection, State Office Building, Room 267, Hartford, CT 06106; Office of State Archeology, Connecticut State Museum of Natural History, U-23, University of Connecticut, Storrs, CT 06269; and Dinosaur State Park, West Street, Rocky Hill, CT 06067.

DELAWARE

Delaware has no explicit statutes governing the collection of geological and paleontological materials for personal use. However, the Department of Natural Resources and Environmental Control issues agency regulations covering public lands, parks, and memorials (Title 29, Sec. 8008). The department requires a permit for scientific, educational, or research activities on these lands, so it can be inferred that the state would prosecute collection for personal use. Anyone violating the "rules and regulations promulgated" by the department "shall be fined not less than $25 nor more than $250 or imprisoned not more than thirty days, or both." Always obtain written permission from the appropriate agency. But, again, lack of notice that certain activities constitute a crime may be a defense to any prosecution.

Contacts: Public Lands Commission, Department of Natural Resources and Environmental Control, Richardson Robbins Building, 89 Kings Highway, P.O. Box 1401, Dover, DE 19903; Division of Parks and Recreation, Department of Natural Resources and Environmental Control, Richardson Robbins Building, 89 Kings Highway, P.O. Box 1401, Dover, DE 19903; Division of Historical and Cultural Affairs, Hall of Records, Dover, DE 19903; Bureau of Archeology and Historic Preservation, 15 The Green, P.O. Box 1401, Dover, DE 19901.

DISTRICT OF COLUMBIA

The district has no regulation governing the collection of geological, paleontological, or archeological materials. Parks within the district are controlled by the National Park Service and thus are subject to federal regulation. One should assume, to be on the safe side, that federal laws and policies would be brought into play and the prudent action would be to contact appropriate federal agencies.

FLORIDA

Under Title XVI, Chapter 240, all vertebrate fossils on state land are the property of the state, with title vested in the Florida Museum of Natural History (Sec. 240.516[3]). It is the declared intention of the legislature that vertebrate paleontological sites be protected and preserved and "field investigation activities, including, but not limited to, collection, excavation, salvage, restoration, and cataloguing of fossils be discouraged." Accordingly, the Museum of Natural History may designate "state vertebrate paleontological sites" that are "areas of great and continuing significance to the scientific study and public understanding of the faunal history of the state" (Sec. 240.5161[7]). No privately owned site may be designated without the owner's express written consent. However, upon designation, "no person may conduct paleontological field investigation activities on the site without first securing a permit for such activities as provided in Sec. 240.5162." Penalties for "destruction, defacement, purchase, and sale of vertebrate fossils found on or under land owned or leased by the state" or on "vertebrate paleontological sites" without a permit are fines up to $500 or county jail for up to six months, or both, plus forfeiture of materials and records (Sec. 240.5162).

81

The Florida Museum of Natural History, though, may sell vertebrate fossils, and defines the rules by which "nonessential vertebrate fossils" may be sold or disposed of by a person holding a permit (Sec. 240.5162[1]). Florida's permitting system is more reasonable than most, requiring only a $5 fee and no onerous qualifications for the collector or destination requirements (Sec. 240.5162[1]). However, consult the current regulations to see whether they comport with the statute. If not, they may be challenged.

Commercial mining and quarrying are, of course, exempt from permit requirements, but mine operators are "encouraged" to cooperate with the state by notifying the Florida Museum of Natural History whenever vertebrate fossils are discovered (Sec. 240.516[1]).

Contacts: Department of Natural Resources, Division of Recreation and Parks, 3900 Commonwealth Boulevard, Tallahassee, FL 32399; Department of Natural Resources, Bureau of State Lands, 3900 Commonwealth Boulevard, Tallahassee, FL 32399; Department of State, Division of Historical Resources, R.A. Gray Building, Room 305, 500 South Bronough Street, Tallahassee, FL 32399; Florida Museum of Natural History, University of Florida, Gainesville, FL 32611.

GEORGIA
Georgia's Department of Natural Resources regulates collection on state lands (Official Code of Georgia Annotated, Sec. 12-3-52). It is illegal to dig, excavate, or remove "any material" from state land, including

state parks, without written permission from the department's commissioner. Thus a permit is required for any archeological, paleontological, or gem and mineral collecting.

The Department of Natural Resources also licenses surface mining under Title 12, "Conservation and Natural Resources," and Chapter 4, "Mineral Resources and Caves" (Sec. 12-4-74). Even gold panners who "discover phosphate rock or phosphatic deposit in the navigable streams or waters of this state or in any public land on their banks or margins, and files with the Secretary of State notice of such discovery" is entitled to a license from the secretary of state. The license gives the licensee "or his assigns" the exclusive right, for ten years, of "digging, mining, and removing from such location and from any areas for a distance of five miles in any or all directions therefrom the phosphate rock and phosphatic deposits that may be found therein" (Sec. 12-4-100). The annual mining fees for phosphates and gold recovered under the previous section are $1.00 per ton due on October 1 of each year for the previous year, and the initial license fee is $100. However, the licensee must also post a bond with the Office of Treasury and Fiscal Services in the "penal sum of $20,000," that is held to ensure "true and faithful reports" to the Office of Treasury and Fiscal Services on or before October 1 of each year (Sec. 12-4-101). Licenses may lapse if good faith work is not commenced within three years (Sec. 12-4-102).

Any person who "digs, mines, removes, or cleanses phosphate rock or phosphatic deposits from the beds of the navigable streams" of the state or from any public lands without a license, or is not engaged in the "prosecution of lawfully authorized searches," is guilty of a misdemeanor (Sec. 12-4-103). Since the statute uses the term "authorized searches," we suggest obtaining permission before you even prospect for the subject minerals. Moreover, we would like to draw to Georgia's attention that it is difficult to prospect for gold without some actual "removing or cleansing."

Dealers must beware that any person who purchases "native gold, gold bullion, gold dust, gold nuggets, or gold amalgam" and fails to show that the source was licensed (as required under Sec. 12-4-120), is guilty of a misdemeanor (Sec. 12-4-122).

Georgia's Cave Protection Act is similar to that of California's, but adds its own embellishments (Sec. 12-4-141 et seq). Its legislative purpose is so common to many other states that it bears quotation in full:

The State of Georgia finds that caves are uncommon geologic phenomena and that the minerals deposited therein may be rare and occur in unique forms of great beauty which are irreplaceable if destroyed. It is also found that the wildlife which have evolved to live in caves are unusual and of limited numbers, and many are rare and endangered species, and that caves are a natural conduit for ground-water flow and are highly subject to water pollution, which has far-reaching effects transcending man's property boundaries. It is, therefore, declared to be the policy of this state and the intent of this article to protect these unique natural resources (Sec. 12-4-141). It is unlawful for any person to willfully or knowingly. without the express, written permission of the owner, to: 1. Break, break off, crack, carve upon, write upon, burn, or otherwise mark upon, remove, or in any manner destroy, disturb, deface, mar, or harm the surfaces of any cave or any natural or archeological material therein, including speleotherms; 2. Disturb or alter in any manner the natural condition of any cave; 3. Break, force, tamper with, or otherwise disturb a lock, gate, door, or other obstruction designed to control or prevent access to any cave, even though entrance thereto may not be gained; or 4. Enter a cave posted against trespassing or a cave with a lock, gate, door, or other obstruction designed to control or prevent access to the cave (Sec. 12-4-143[4]).

It is also illegal to sell, offer to sell, or export speleotherms without written consent of the owner of the cave (Sec. 12-4-144).

Contacts: State Archeologist, Department of Natural Resources, 270 Washington Street Southwest, Atlanta, GA 30334

HAWAII

In a refreshingly simply scheme, Hawaii's Department of Land and Natural Resources administers all public lands, water, minerals, parks, historical sites, forests, and forest reserves (Hawaii Revised Statutes, Sec. 171-3). The department generally prohibits collecting of mineral or fossil materials without permit, or mining license, if applicable, under HRS Sec. 182-1 et seq.

Contacts: Hawaii Department of Land and Natural Resources, 1151 Punchbowl Street, Honolulu, Hawaii 96813.

84

IDAHO

Commercial mining of minerals and gems is regulated by the Idaho Department of Lands (Idaho Code, Title 47, Chap. 13 and 15). Lands not already leased are open to casual exploration (Sec. 47-702), but a lease is necessary if minerals are to be removed in commercial quantities (Sec. 47-717). If collectors want to protect a "claim" to either a prospecting area or a mineral discovery, they are required to post an "exploration certificate of location" conspicuously on each 20-acre tract or one-half river mile, according to the requirements the Board of Land Commissioners (Sec. 47-703). These mining "locations" protect your site from third parties for two years, subject to the requirement that you perform at least $100 in "work" on the claim in each year (Sec. 47-703[5]).

Idaho protects caves and caverns under its criminal code (Sec. 18-7035). As in most states, the general criminal code protects all state lands from damage by "trespass," including cutting or carrying off wood, trees, topsoil, or dumping trash (Sec. 6-211). Collectors must be aware of these laws as they go about their business.

The Idaho Bureau of Mines and Geology maintains records of mineral and fossil deposits. The state fossil is the Hagerman horse fossil (Sec. 67-4507).

Contacts: Bureau of Minerals, Department of Lands, State House, Room 121, Boise, ID 83702; Idaho Historical Society, 610 North Julia Davis Drive, Boise, ID 83702; Department of Parks and Recreation, 2177 Warm Springs Avenue, Boise, ID 83720.

ILLINOIS

The Illinois Archaeogical and Paleontological Resources Protection Act (20 ICS 3435) protects archeological sites and "significant fossil or material remains on public lands." Such remains include "traces or impressions of animals or plants that occur as part of the geological record that are known and are included in the files maintained by the Illinois State Museum under Section 10" (20 ICS 3435/.02). The Illinois State Museum certifies "known archeological and paleontological sites" and maintains files on these sites, "whether on state-controlled or privately owned property" (20 ICS 3435/10).

The Illinois Historic Preservation Agency is charged with issuing permits for "exploration, excavation, and collection" of paleontological and archeological materials in consultation with the head of the land-managing agency. The agency will require a report, and all recovered materials belong to the state. It is unclear if the act requires permits on private lands that are "known sites" as certified by the state. If so, this part of the Act is in conflict with Section 3435/1 that gives the state the exclusive right to regulate, explore, excavate, or survey resources "found upon or within any public lands." Collectors should first receive written permission from the landowner, then apply for a permit from the appropriate state agency. If refused, based on the vagueness of the statute and the constitutionality of asserting state control over private land, they should bring injunctive action before risking prosecution.

> Nature preserves are closely regulated and one may not:Cut, break, injure, destroy, take or remove any tree, shrub, timber, flower, plant, or other natural object including rocks, soil, or water from, or to conduct scientific research on, a dedicated nature preserve, except that small quantities of such materials may be collected and removed for scientific or educational purposes by written permit from the owner, the Department of Conservation and the Illinois Natures Preserves Commission (17 Illinois Administrative Code 510.10[d]).

The Illinois state park system also protects historic sites, geologic formations, and natural, forested areas, through regulations regarding camping, vehicles, and collecting natural resources (20 ICS 835 et seq.). Even the Illinois Department of Agriculture has duties concerning conservation easements (505 ICS 35 et seq.). As in most states, metal detectors and other devices may not be used in state parks or preserves without permission.

Contacts: Field Museum of Natural History, Roosevelt Road at Lake Shore Drive, Chicago, IL 60605-2496; Illinois State Museum, 1920 10th Street South, Springfield, IL 62704; Illinois Department of Conservation, 524 South Second Street, Springfield, IL 62706; Illinois

Nature Preserves Commission, 600 North Grand West, Springfield, IL 62706; and Illinois Historic Preservation Agency, Preservation Services Division, Old State Capitol, Springfield, IL 62701.

INDIANA

The Indiana Department of Natural Resources may issue a permit to "any person" to take "sand, gravel, stone, or other mineral or substance" from or under the bed of any of the *navigable waters* of the state (Indiana Statutes 14-3-1-14.5). The fee for collecting from navigable water courses is only $50, but the permittee must pay the state a "reasonable value" for the material and meet certain other conditions. Taking the material without a permit is a Class B infraction. According to the geological survey, though, casual collecting is otherwise liberally allowed on *land*, and no formal permit is required.

Indiana caves contain some archeological and fossil material, but are most popular for geologic formations such as stalagmites. It is illegal on private or public land to "knowingly and without the express consent of the cave owner," disfigure, remove mineral deposits or archeological or paleontological artifacts, or destroy, remove, or harass cave-dwelling animals for "other than scientific purposes" (IS 35-43-1-3[b]). It is also illegal to break locks, gates, fences, or deposit trash, no matter what your purpose. Scientific purpose is defined as "exploration and research conducted by persons affiliated with recognized scientific organizations with the intent to advance knowledge and with the intent to publish the results of said exploration or research in an appropriate medium." The standard "scientific exemption" in this and other statutes should be read as allowing amateurs to collect, as long as they are properly affiliated or have their own cultural or educational organization that publishes research.

In the absence of legislation affecting minerals and fossils on most lands, individual departments such as Parks and Highways should be consulted regarding the lands within their jurisdictions.

Contacts: Indiana Geological Survey, University of Indiana, Bloomington, IN 46204; Ronald Richards, Indiana State Museum, 202 North Alabama, Indianapolis, IN, 46204; Indiana Department of Natural Resources, including Division of Nature Preserves, Division of Fish and Wildlife, Division of Forestry, and Division of Parks, Government Center, 402 West Washington Street, Indianapolis, IN 46204; Dr. James (Rick) Jones, Division of Historic Preservation and Archeology, Government Center, 402 West Washington Street, Indianapolis, IN 46204.

IOWA

Paleontology is combined with archeology, so refer to the Iowa archeology section in Chapter 2. We do note that Iowa counties are permitted to own limestone quarries for use in paving roads and in fertilizer production. We suggest that collectors who wish to find mineral or fossil specimens in quarries approach county government or private owners rather than state government agencies (ICA Section 353.1).

87

Contacts: Iowa State Geologist, Geological Survey, University of Iowa, 109 Trowbridge Hall, Iowa City, IA 52242-1319; Iowa Department of Natural Resources, Wallace State Office Building, Des Moines, IA 50319-0034.

KANSAS

Kansas does not yet have any formal legislation concerning collecting fossils and mineral specimens on state land. Fossils narrowly missed being included with artifacts in the state Antiquities Act introduced during the 1995 legislative session, according to Chris Maples, paleontologist at the Kansas Geological Survey.

Furthermore, many federal land agencies manage lands in Kansas, including the BLM, the Bureau of Reclamation, certain military reservations, reservoirs, Native American reservations, and national grasslands. Federal law as discussed elsewhere in this book should be consulted. Kansas does not have a specific cave protection act or casual prospecting act. Any questions should be referred to the USGS at (913) 842-9909, or the Kansas State Geological Survey.

Contacts: Dr. Larry Martin, vertebrate paleontologist, and Dr. Roger Kaesler, invertebrate paleontologist, Natural History Museum, 321C Dych Hall, University of Kansas, Lawrence, Kansas 66045; Museum of Natural History, University of Kansas, Lawrence, KS 66045; Kansas Geological Survey, University of Kansas, Campus West, 1930 Constant Avenue, Lawrence, KS 66044; Department of Wildlife and Parks, 900 Jackson, Room 502, Topeka, KS 66612.

KENTUCKY

Kentucky has no formal legislation regarding rock collecting, so collectors should consult the Kentucky Department of Mines and Minerals in Lexington regarding casual prospecting on state lands. Do not bother with the Department of Natural Resources in Frankfort whose jurisdiction is solely coal mine reclamation.

The brachiopod as the official state fossil of Kentucky is the only reference to fossils in the Kentucky Code (KRS Sec. 2.082). Since Kentucky has marvelous sedimentary exposures in quarries, lake bluffs, and road-cuts, collectors should consult the appropriate state agency, such as Parks or Highways. We know that the Department of State Parks, that manages forty-nine parks, will not allow mineral, fossil, or plants for that matter, without a special permit. Although there are no official regulations, we are told that the state highway patrol may ticket collectors who stop along a public highway, as a safety violation only.

Kentucky has a more comprehensive cave protection act with more stringent permit requirements than many other states (KRS Sec. 433.871). In addition to written permission from the owner of the cave, a permit from the state archeologist is required prior to excavating or removing any "archeological, paleontological, prehistoric or historic feature of any cave," even on private property (KRS Sec. 433.879). Field investigations and recovery operations, if approved, are then carried out under the supervision of the state archeologist and the Kentucky Heritage Council. There is no specific requirement that objects recovered must remain in Kentucky or become the property of Kentucky, only that the operations are carried out in a manner "to ensure that the maximum amount of historic, scientific, archaeologic, and educational information may be recovered and preserved in addition to the physical recovery of objects."

Contacts: Legal Counsel, Henry Curtis, Kentucky Department of Parks, 500 Mero Street, Capitol Parkway Tower, Room 10, Frankfort, KY 40601. The Kentucky Geological Survey at 228 MMR Building, University of Kentucky, Lexington, KY 40506-0107, should have publications for sale on fossil collecting and will soon be on the Internet, according to Dr. Don Chesnut, a paleontologist at the survey. G. Dever at the survey has knowledge of the various quarries in the state.

LOUISIANA

Louisiana's state fossil is petrified palmwood, and is used on official documents and insignia (LRS 49:162). However, collection of geological and paleontological materials on state lands does not appear to be regulated. In fact, fossils were specifically removed from the Archeological Resources Act by amendment in 1989 (LRS 41:1601-1614).

The State Mineral Board leases public lands for mineral production, including road beds and water bottoms (LRS 30:124) and regulates prospecting and mining. For example, prospecting by means of "torsion balance, seismograph explosions, mechanical device, or otherwise" is not allowed on highway easements or other public land without providing a list of the abutting land owners (LRS 30:210). It is recommended that one confirm whether casual collecting is subject to the mining regulations of the State Mineral Board.

Contacts: Louisiana Department of Natural Resources, State
Mineral Board, P.O. Box 2827, Baton Rouge, LA 70821-2827; Louisiana Geology Museum, Louisiana State University, Baton Rouge, LA 70804.

89

MAINE

The Maine Geological Survey and the agencies having jurisdiction over state-owned land co-regulate commercial prospecting and "mineral development" on state-owned lands and may make appropriate rules (Maine Revised Statutes Annotated, Title 12, Sec. 549). Exploration permits from such agencies are usually on such good terms that serious mineral collectors should take advantage of the protection provided.

For those interested in casual collection, Maine's Bureau of Public Lands manages all state-owned lands, including school lands (MRSA Title 12, Sec. 585). The commissioner is entitled to the cooperation of the Maine Geological Survey, the Department of Inland Fisheries and Wildlife, the Bureau of Parks and Recreation, Maine Land Use Regulation Commission, and the State Planning Office in compiling an inventory of state land. The director of the Bureau may grant permits and enter into contracts to cut timber, harvest grass and wild foods, tap maple trees for sap, and cultivate and harvest crops, sell gravel, and lease campsites on state land.

Casual collection of natural science specimens is specifically regulated in state parks and historic sites only. The "removal, molesting, injury or damage of anything natural, physical or historical" and the use of metal detectors is illegal within those areas except by special permit. However, it would be prudent for the collector to ask the director of the Bureau of Public Lands whether collection without a permit on most state lands is still allowed. Archeological permits on state land are issued by the Maine Historic Preservation Commission.

Contacts: Maine Bureau of Public Lands, P.O. Box 327, Farmington, ME 04938; Maine Geological Survey, State House Station 22, Augusta, ME 04333; Maine Bureau of Parks and Recreation, State House Station 22, Augusta, ME 04333; Maine Historic Preservation

Commission, 55 Capitol Street, Station 65, Augusta, ME 04333; Maine Department of Inland Fisheries and Wildlife, 284 State Street, Augusta, ME 04333.

MARYLAND

90

No person may conduct surface mining in the state without first obtaining a surface mining license from the Department of Natural Resources (Md. Nat. Res., Sec. 7-6A-06). Since the license fee is only $300, the serious mineral collector or researcher should look into this option in every state that does not specifically regulate casual collection. Although a surface mining license may have the disadvantage of requiring approval from state and local regulatory agencies responsible for "air and water pollution, sediment control, and zoning," a surface mining license would give the serious collector substantial security against intruders. In fact, some activities such as "removal of overburden" and "limited mining" for purposes of prospecting may not require a license at all. However, we always recommend having written permission because penalties for violating state law are as steep as $10,000. Prospecting for coal or on coal lands is viewed differently from other minerals, and may require more paperwork, such as a "plan for reclamation" (Sec. 7-514.6). So we do not recommend seeking a license to mine or prospect for coal!

The Maryland Department Natural Resources regulates geological, paleontological, and archeological collecting on state lands. Natural science specimens may not be removed from state parks without a permit from the Forest, Park, and Wildlife Service, and metal detectors and relic hunting are limited.

The Department of Natural Resources is specifically authorized by statute to regulate caves, and geological, paleontological, and archeological remains found in caves. Under Title 5, Forests and Parks, Subtitle 14, a person may not "excavate, remove, destroy, injure, deface, or in any manner disturb any paleontological site, including saltpeter workings, fossils, bones, and paleontological features found in any cave" without a permit from the secretary of the department (Sec. 5-1405). Permittees must "have a knowledge of paleontology" and permits are good for two years.

Archeology and paleontology still coexist in Section 5-628, as we have seen, but legislative surgery happily separated them in Section 5-1405, placing paleontology under the Department of Natural Resources, Forests and Parks, and archeology under the jurisdiction of the Division of Historical and Cultural Programs, Maryland Historical Trust. Although greatly improved, Section 5-1405 is still confusing as to whether it covers all paleontology, or only paleontological finds in caves.

Contacts: Maryland Department of Natural Resources, Division of Mines and Mining, Annapolis, MD 21401; Maryland Geological Survey, 2300 St. Paul Street, Baltimore, MD 21218; Maryland Historical Trust, Division of Historical and Cultural Programs, Department of Housing and Community Development, 45 Calvert Street, Annapolis, MD 21401; Maryland Department of Natural Resources, Forest, Parks, and Wilderness Service, Tawes State Office Building, Annapolis, MD 21401.

MASSACHUSETTS

Geological collecting on state lands does not appear to be regulated. In such cases, we recommend contacting the state agency that manages the particular tract sought to be explored or collected.

Permits for paleontological exploration, field investigation, and collecting on all state, county, or municipal lands and designated archeological landmarks must be obtained from the state archeologist (Massachusetts General Laws Annotated, Chap. 9, Art. 27). The permit request should address a research plan, qualifications of the permittee, and a description of the extent of surface disturbance expected. All objects recovered belong to the state unless a different agreement is reached in writing prior to the excavation. Discovery of any archeological or paleontological site must be reported to the State Archeologist, as well (MGLA, Chap. 9, Art. 27C).

Contacts: State Archeologist, Massachusetts Historical Commission, 80 Boyleston Street, Boston, MA 02116.

MICHIGAN

The State Owned Lands Protection Act prohibits injury to or removal of forest products, buildings, improvements, "sand, gravel, marl or other minerals," or other property on state-owned land without written permission from the Department of Natural Resources (MCLA Sec. 322.143). Purchasing objects illegally removed may also subject you to prosecution. However, the department has regulations for goldpanning and nondestructive rock and mineral collecting that may not require permits, so consult them regarding rock and fossil collecting on public lands. State parks are more restrictive, of course. Thus, it is unlawful to "destroy, damage or remove any tree, shrub, wildflower, or other vegetation, or to destroy, damage, deface or remove any state or publicly owned property" in state or public parks or recreation areas (MCLA 318.251).

The state of Michigan also protects private property by punishing willful trespass as a misdemeanor, punishable by up to thirty days, or a $50 fine, or both.

92

Contacts: Michigan Parks Division and Forest Management Division, Department of Natural Resources, Box 30028, Lansing, MI 48909; Michigan State Geologist, Department of Natural Resources, P.O. Box 30028, Lansing, MI 48909; State Archeologist, Bureau of History, Department of State, 208 North Capital Avenue, Lansing, MI 48918.

MINNESOTA

In Minnesota, the definition of real property *for purposes of taxation* includes the land itself, and all *mines, quarries, fossils, and trees* (MSA Sec. 272.03). Similar laws in South Dakota helped form Judge Battey's decision in the case of the *Tyrannosaurus rex* named Sue. See our discussion of *United States of America vs. Black Hills Institute of Geological Research, Inc., Peter Larson; Neal Larson; Robert Farrar; Terry Wertx; Jun Schmizu; and Edwin Allen Cole,* CR 93-50066, U.S. District Court for the District of South Dakota, in Chapter 3. The distinction made by Judge Battey between the dinosaur, and trees and minerals that have been severed from the real estate, was that she was *not yet excavated* when the deal was struck with the landowner.

The Department of Natural Resources' Division of Minerals issues permits for prospecting and leases for mining "gold, silver, copper, cobalt, coal, graphite, petroleum, sand, gravel, stone, natural gas, and all minerals, excepting iron ore, under the waters of any public lake or stream" (MSA Sec. 93.08). There is no statutory authority for regulation of fossil and mineral collecting on state lands, and the Division of Minerals does not require permits for casual or recreational rock collecting, except for gold. However, one must consult the state agency actually managing the collection site, as their regulations may be more restrictive. This rule should be followed in any state where the law does not clearly delineate authority.

For example, the Minnesota Division of Parks and Recreation requires permits for the collection of archeological, botanical, geological, and paleontological specimens from state parks. The Division is considering establishing a lapidary site in one park where permits will not be required. In Minnesota, counties manage their own tax-forfeited lands, so county government should be consulted on county land. Collectors are already familiar with the county clerk's and tax assessor's offices where one can obtain information on land ownership.

Contacts: Minnesota Department of Natural Resources, Division of Minerals, Box 45, 500 Lafayette Road, St. Paul, MN 55155; Minnesota Department of Natural Resources, Division of Parks and Recreation, Box 39, 500 Lafayette Road, St. Paul, MN 55155; Minnesota Department of Natural Resources, Bureau of Real Estate Management, Box 31, 500 Lafayette Rd, St. Paul, MN. 55155; Minnesota Science Museum, 30 East Tenth Street, St. Paul, MN 55101; Bell Museum of Natural History, University of Minnesota, Minneapolis, MN 55455.

MISSISSIPPI

Mineral leases on state lands are issued by the Mississippi Commission on Natural Resources (Sec. 29-7-1). However, permits for casual collecting of minerals and fossils are issued by the state agency with oversight of the land to be explored. Mississippi's public policy encourages economic development through the "wise use" of its natural resources (Sec. 57-23-3). Specifically, the state encourages the study of its animal, vegetable, and mineral resources that might be suitable as natural drug products for the industrial pharmaceutical markets. So stop looking at those rocks as just pretty faces!

Contacts: Mississippi Bureau of Geology, P.O. Box 5348, Jackson, MS 39205.

MISSOURI

The only statutory prohibition against geological or paleontological collecting on public lands appears to be Missouri State Section 577.073 that prohibits damage to state parks, including to any "object of archeological or historical value or interest." Special permits are available from the Department of Natural Resources for scientific research (10 CSR 90-2.040).

The Missouri Department of Conservation issues permits for collecting geological and paleontological materials on lands designated as "Natural Areas" and on state forest lands.

As to private lands, collecting without the owner's express written permission could cost treble damages for injury or removal of "stones, ore or mineral, gravel, clay or mold" or "other substance or material being part of the realty" (MS 537.340).

Missouri's Cave Resources Act regulates the use of caves, both public and private (MS Sec. 578.201 et seq.). Caves held open to the public are required to be inspected for safety once a year by the Division of Mine Inspection (MS Sec. 293.620).

94

Contacts: Missouri Department of Natural Resources, Division of Parks, Recreation, and Natural History Program, P.O. Box 176, Jefferson City, MO 65102; Missouri Department of Conservation, Forestry Division, P.O. Box 180, Jefferson City, MO 65102.

MONTANA

The Montana Bureau of Mines and Geology collects mineral specimens and deposits them in the state museums or in the Montana College of Mineral Sciences and Technology. Montana has adopted its own law concerning locating and protecting private claims to "gold, silver, cinnabar, lead, tin, copper, or other valuable deposits" on public land, very much like the U.S. Mining Law of 1872 (Montana Code Annotated, Sec. 82-2-101 et seq.).

The Montana Department of State Lands regulates the collection of gems, minerals, and rocks on state land and intended for sale for more than $100. The collector must have permission from the surface lessee, and a land use license from the department, that is available for a small processing fee. The landowner is free to assess his own fees on specimens removed from his property. The collector may also be responsible for reclamation, unless otherwise agreed with the landowner. The department is not authorized to regulate casual collecting, however, the collector is advised to consult with the agency with oversight over the land to be explored.

Montana also has a typical cave protection law that protects the archeological, paleontological, and geological features of caves from destruction or removal (MCA Sec. 23-2-900 et. seq.).

Paleontology and archeology are both managed under the Montana State Antiquities Act, reviewed in the Montana section of Chapter 2.

Contacts: Montana Department of State Lands, 1625 Eleventh Avenue, Capitol Station, Helena, MT 59620; Montana Bureau of Mines and Geology, Montana Tech of the University of Montana, 1300 West Park Street, Butte, MT 59701; Museum of the Rockies,

Montana State University, Bozeman, MT 95717; Montana Department of Fish, Wildlife, and Parks, 1420 East Sixth Avenue, Helena, MT 59620; Montana Department of Highways, 2701 Prospect Avenue, Helena, MT 59620.

NEBRASKA

The Nebraska Board of Educational Lands and Funds regulates mineral extraction and exploration on state school lands (Nebraska Revised Statutes, Sec. 72-269). Waste or trespass on educational lands of the state constitute a Class 2 misdemeanor. Although there is no statutory authority to require permits for casual collecting of fossils and minerals, the trespass statute could be interpreted to include removal of fossils or minerals without permission, and so we recommend asking for permits on school lands.

The Nebraska Game and Parks Commission regulates mineral, rock, and fossil collecting on state park lands (NRS Sec. 39-663, 39-667, and 81-805. Their regulations make it illegal to "possess, destroy, injure, deface, remove, or disturb" any "animal or plant matter and direct or indirect parts thereof, including but not limited to petrified wood, flower, cane or other fruit, egg, nest or nesting site, or of any soil, rock, or mineral formation, artifact, relic, historic or prehistoric feature, or of any other public property of any kind without prior permission of the Superintendent [of Parks]." Regulation 001.07A employs similar language and applies to nonpark lands managed by the Game and Parks Commission, particularly wildlife management and special recreation areas.

Contacts: Nebraska Board of Educational Lands and Funds, 555 North Cotner Boulevard, Lincoln, NE 68505; Nebraska Game and Parks Commission, 2200 North 33rd Street, P.O. Box 30370, Lincoln, NE 68503; Nebraska State Museum, University of Nebraska, 307 Morrill Hall, Lincoln, NE 68588-0338; Conservation and Survey Division of the University of Nebraska, Lincoln, NE 68588.

NEVADA

Geological collecting in state parks or preserves is controlled by the Division of State Parks. There appears to be no other statutory regulation of casual collecting, but the state agency with jurisdiction over the land to be entered should be consulted. The state precious gemstone is the Virgin Valley black fire opal. As in Nebraska, gemstones are defined as commodities (Nevada Revised Statutes, Sec. 91.050). Collections of minerals, art curiosities, and paleontological remains are considered important enough to be exempt from seizure for judgment liens (NRS Sec. 21.100).

Collection of minerals and fossils in state parks and preserves is naturally regulated by the Division of State Parks, along with the State Historic Preservation Office, and is much more limited than on other state and federal lands (NRS Sec. 407.130). Paleontology on state land in general is intertwined with archeology and is also reviewed in Chapter 2.

Contacts: Nevada State Museum, Capitol Complex, Carson City, NV 89701; Nevada Historic Preservation and Archeology Office, Nye Building, Room 113, 201 South Fall Street, Carson City, NV 89710; Nevada Division of State Parks, 1923 North Carson Street, Capitol Complex, Carson City, NV 89710.

NEW HAMPSHIRE
All geological and paleontological collecting on nonpark state lands is regulated by the Department of Resources and Economic Development, Division of Forests and Lands (Sec. 218:5). The Commissioner of Forests and Lands issues prospecting permits and mining permits (Sec. 12-E:8), and leases state lands for mineral production (Sec. 12-E:9). In fact, prospecting permits may be essential even to casual collectors under the terms of Section 12-E:3.

The Division of Parks and Recreation, of course, regulates state parks and recreational areas and preserves where collecting minerals and fossils is generally prohibited without special permission.

Contacts: New Hampshire Department of Resources and Economic Development, Division of Forests and Lands, P.O. Box 856, Concord, NH 03301; New Hampshire Department of Resources and Economic Development, Division of Parks and Recreation, Concord, NH 03301.

NEW JERSEY
The New Jersey Department of Conservation and Economic Development is not authorized except by special legislation to sell or lease timber or mineral resources, and the mining of fissionable materials is specifically prohibited (NJS 13:1B-15.12a7 and 13:1J-1). On state park and forest lands, no person may mutilate, destroy, alter or move "historical, pre-historical, or geological" materials without permission of the Department of Parks and Forestry (NJS 13:1L-10). As is common

in many state and federal parks, the use of metal detectors is restricted (NJS 7:2-2.17).

Contacts: New Jersey State Division of Parks and Forestry, P.O. Box 1420, Trenton, NJ 08625; New Jersey State Museum, 205 West State Street, Trenton, NJ 08625.

NEW MEXICO

Historically, the United States government granted Sections 16 and 36 of each township to the Territory of New Mexico, and, when it became a state, granted Sections 2 and 32 of each township in addition, or their equivalents, for the support of common schools (Enabling Act, Sec. 6). Thus, New Mexico's State Land Office, through its independently elected public lands commissioner, administers vast tracts of public land and its timber permits, mining leases, grazing leases, and recreational permits (NMSA 1978, Sec. 19-1-1 et. seq.). The Commercial Division of the land office regulates recreational use on public lands, and permits are generally recommended for fossil and mineral collection. New Mexico has a Division of Forestry, but its purpose is primarily fire suppression, there being no official state forests.

The second largest land use agency is the State Park and Recreation Division of the Department of Energy, Minerals, and Natural Resources. As with parks in other states, it is illegal to "cut, break, destroy, take or remove any tree, shrub , timber, plant or natural object in any state park or recreation area" (NMSA 1978, Sec. 16-2-32). A permit from the division is required to collect fossils and mineralogic specimens, except for Rockhound State Park at Deming where tourists may remove rock and mineral material on a limited basis. Elephant Butte State Park boasts some large fossil mammals such as camel and mammoth and good swimming and boating as well. Some of these fossils are on display at the Geronimo Springs Museum in Truth or Consequences.

The Museum of Natural History in Albuquerque, and the New Mexico Bureau of Mines and Mineral Resources in Socorro, are sources for information on localities.

Contacts: State Land Office, Assistant Commissioner of Commercial Section, 310 Old Santa Fe Trail, Santa Fe, NM 87501, (505) 827-5760; State Park and Recreation Division of New Mexico Department of Energy, Minerals and Natural Resources, 2040 South Pacheco, Santa Fe, NM 87501, (505) 827-7173; Bureau of Mines and Mineral Resources, Campus Station, Socorro, NM 87801, (505) 835-5420.

NEW YORK

New York's regulatory process is confusing. Paleontology is interleaved with archeology in the regulatory process, and there are too many agencies involved. The Commissioner of Education regulates archeological and paleontological collecting on state-owned lands generally, with permits issued by the director of the New York State Museum.

The Department of Environmental Conservation, Division of Lands and Forests, however, regulates geological and paleontological collecting on state forests and preserves. The Office of Parks, Recreation, and Historic Preservation regulates geological collecting on state park lands, and must be consulted by the commissioner of education on archeological and paleontological collecting on state park lands.

All deposits of gold and silver are owned by the state whether or not these minerals occur "in or upon private lands" (NYRS Sec. 801). This is largely a moot point because there is so little gold and silver in New York. All mineral deposits found on state lands belong to the state, of course. The Department of Environmental Conservation, Division of Mineral Resources, regulates mineral exploration and mining. New York also declares ownership of all fossils *ever discovered* on state lands.

Contacts: Division of Mineral Resources, and Division of Lands and Forests, New York State Department of Environmental Conservation, 50 Wolf Road, Albany, NY 12233; New York State Museum, Empire State Plaza, CEC 3140, Albany, NY 12230; New York State Office of Parks, Recreation and Historic Preservation, Empire State Plaza, Agency Building I, Albany, NY 12231; Paleontological Research Institute, 1259 Trumansburg Road, Ithaca, NY 14850; American Museum of Natural History, Central Park West at 79th Street, New York, NY 10024-5192.

NORTH CAROLINA

The North Carolina Department of Administration may sell, lease, or dispose of mineral rights or deposits in the vacant and unappropriated lands, swamplands, and lands acquired by the state by virtue of being sold for taxes (NCS 146-9). Minerals are defined as "soil, clay, coal, stone, gravel, sand, phosphate, rock, metallic ore, and any other solid material or substance of commercial value found in natural deposits on or in the earth." Serious mineral collectors and even paleontologists are urged to take advantage of such lease provisions, as the scope of the law applies.

North Carolina also has a Mining Commission, under the Department of Environment, Health, and Natural Resources (NCS 143B-290) and the Mining Act of 1971 (NCS 74-49).

North Carolina has no statutory prohibition against casual collecting. However, the Department of Natural Resources and Community Development, Division of Parks and Recreation, governs state parks, forests, and recreational areas. Collection of minerals and fossils in those areas is allowed for scientific purposes upon application and permit. The North Carolina Geological Survey and the State Mineral Museum should have information on localities concerning geological and paleontological collecting.

Contacts: North Carolina Department of Administration, Office of State Property, 116 West Jones Street, Raleigh, NC 27611; North Carolina Department of Natural Resources and Community Development, Division of Parks and Recreation, P.O. Box 27687, Raleigh, NC 27611; North Carolina Geological Survey, P.O. Box 27687, Raleigh, NC 27611.

NORTH DAKOTA

North Dakota's Paleontological Resource Protection Act is patterned after the federal Baucus Bill discussed in Chapter 3, that has never gotten out of committee in Congress. Under the North Dakota act, it is illegal to destroy, deface, alter, remove or dispose of any "paleontological resource" found or located upon any land owned by the state or its political subdivisions, including counties and municipalities, without approval of the state geologist (NDS 54-17.3-01 et seq.). Even private lands may be subject to the act if they were sold by the state or a county or municipality reserving title to archeological or paleontological resources (NDS 54-17.3-06).

The act is enforced by the North Dakota Industrial Commission, acting through the state geologist, who decides whether a paleontological resource is significant to understanding the "geologic history of North Dakota." The state geologist may issue permits, upon payment of a fee, to "investigate, excavate, collect, or record" paleontological resources. The state geologist also monitors the permittee's activities to ensure the "careful preservation and conservation" of the resource (NDS 54-17.3-03 and 04). Violators are guilty of a Class B misdemeanor and shall forfeit all paleontological specimens discovered (NDS 54-17.3-08). Therefore, one must first seek a permit to investigate paleontological sites, and then ask approval of the State Geologist before excavating or removing specimens. Even then, you are well advised to obtain a written agreement up front as to what class of specimens you may keep, or you may walk away with no specimens after an expensive undertaking. As is common in other states, the North Dakota Geological Survey is charged with preserving fossils, and normally geological surveys will give you information on the best localities (NDS 54-17.4-02).

100

The North Dakota Industrial Commission, through the state geologist, also regulates mineral explorations on state lands. Casual collection of minerals and gems is not addressed in the statutes, so we recommend that you consult with the state geologist regarding any administrative regulations that apply.

Contacts: State Geologist, North Dakota Industrial Commission, University Station, Grand Forks, ND 58202; North Dakota Geological Survey, 600 East Boulevard Avenue, Bismarck, ND 58505-0840.

OHIO

It is illegal to collect on archeological, geological, or paleontological sites found in a cave without the express written permission of the owner (Ohio Revised Code, Sec. 1517). Minerals taken from the bed of Lake Erie are regulated (ORC 1505.7).

The Department of Natural Resources prohibits geological and paleontological collecting on all state lands, including state parks and nature preserves (ORC Sec. 1501.41-3-11), except in designated areas. The Department of Transportation should be consulted regarding roadside collecting.

Contacts: Ohio Department of Natural Resources, Division of Parks and Recreation and Division of Natural Areas and Preserves, Fountain Square Building F-1, Columbus, OH 43224; Ohio Geological Survey, Fountain Square Building 9, Columbus, OH 43224; Ohio Department of Transportation, 25 South Front Street, Columbus, OH 43215.

OKLAHOMA

The Oklahoma Tourism and Recreation Department is authorized to create a State Register of Natural Heritage Areas (Oklahoma Statutes, Title 74, Sec. 1841). The sites may be "above or below the surface" and must have unique ecological, geological, or other special natural characteristics of scientific, educational, or passive recreational value. Private property may be listed as long as the natural owner's rights are not abridged. The register should include most important fossil and mineral localities in the state.

The department prohibits archeological, geological, and paleontological collecting in natural heritage areas and state parks. Other state agencies, such as the State Lands Department, the State Historical Society (that controls state historic sites) and the State Highway Department, must be consulted for their respective regulations.

Contacts: Oklahoma Tourism and Recreation Department, Division of State Parks, 500 Will Rogers Building, Oklahoma City, OK 73105; Oklahoma Museum of Natural History, University of Oklahoma, Norman, OK 73019; Oklahoma State Lands Department, 5801 North Broadway, Oklahoma City, OK 73105; Oklahoma Department of Transportation, 200 NE 21st, Oklahoma City, OK 73105; Oklahoma Historical Society, Wiley Post Building, Oklahoma City, OK 73105.

OREGON

The Oregon Department of Geology and Mineral Industries serves as the state geological survey and maintains collections and lists of localities (Oregon Revised Statutes, Sec. 516.010). The Oregon State Museum of Natural History houses geological and paleontological collections as well.

The Oregon Division of State Lands regulates geological and paleontological collecting on state lands. Rocks, minerals, semiprecious gems, and petrified wood may be collected on state lands without permit except when in quantities sufficient for commercial purposes and having a value of $500 or more (ORS Sec. 273.715). Special agreements are required for removal of precious stones (ORS Sec. 273.775-790), as well as meteorites.

Fossil collecting is regulated by the Division of State Lands under ORS Section 273.705 as either "archeological, anthropological, or prehistoric" materials. The State Parks and Recreation Department, however, will have some control over permits issued in state parks and preserves.

Contacts: Oregon Division of State Lands, 1445 State Street, Salem, OR 97310; Oregon State Department of Geology and Mineral Industries, 800 Northeast Oregon Street, #28, Portland, OR 97232; Pacific Northwest Museum of Natural History, 1500 East Main Street,

Portland, OR 97520; State Parks and Recreation Department, 1115 Commercial Street Northeast, Salem, OR 97310.

PENNSYLVANIA

Pennsylvania's Department of Environmental Resources administers mining of rocks, ores, and minerals in commercial quantities on state lands and the use of state-owned forest lands. A prospecting permit good for one year may be obtained for only $25, good for any state lands except state parks, historical parks, picnic and monument areas, and specially restricted areas (Pennsylvania Statutes, Sec. 144). The department also regulates collecting on state forest lands.

Casual collecting of minerals and fossils is not covered by statute. However, the Department of Environmental Resources and its divisions should be consulted regarding all state lands except those managed by the State Game Commission. Pennsylvania has a typical cave protection act that prohibits archeological, geological, and paleontological collecting without special permit from the Department of Environmental Resources (32 PS Sec. 5603).

Contacts: Academy of Natural Sciences, 1900 Benjamin Franklin Parkway, Philadelphia, PA 19103; Carnegie Museum of Natural History, 4400 Forbes Avenue, Pittsburgh, PA 15213; Pennsylvania Game Commission, 2001 Elmerton Avenue, Harrisburg, PA 17108; Pennsylvania Department of Environmental Resources, P.O. Box 8552, Harrisburg, PA 17105.

RHODE ISLAND

Regulation of gems, minerals, and fossils is by the particular state agency having control of the property in question, such as Parks, Highways, or the State Properties Committee.

Contact: Rhode Island State Properties Committee, Department of Environmental Management, 83 Park Street, Providence, RI 02903.

SOUTH CAROLINA

The South Carolina Department of Parks, Recreation, and Tourism regulates mineral collecting through South Carolina Code Annotated, Sec. 51-3-145 that prohibits "destroying, cutting, breaking, removing defacing, mutilating, injuring, taking, or gathering any tree, shrub, plant, rock, mineral, or geological feature except by permit issued by the Department." The department issues permits for scientific purposes only.

The state geologist and the Geological Mapping Division of the Department of Natural Resources do not have regulatory duties, but should have helpful information on the distribution of mineral resources in the state (SCRA Sec. 48-22-30).

Other state agencies that administer fossil and mineral collecting on state lands are the Public Service Authority, the State Budget and Control Board, the Highway Department, and the Wildlife and Marine Resources Department. Minerals are defined as "soil, clay, stone, gravel, sand, phosphate, rock, metallic ore, and any other solid material or substance found in natural deposits on or in the earth" (Sec. 48-20-40[4]). The South Carolina Coastal Tidelands and Wetlands Act also permits scientific collecting in its protected areas (Sec. 48-39-260).

Contacts: South Carolina Department of Parks, Recreation and Tourism, 1205 Pendleton Street, Suite 113, Edgar Brown Building, Columbia, SC 29201; South Carolina Wildlife and Marine Resources Department, P.O. Box 167, Columbia, SC 29202; South Carolina Geodetic Survey, 5 Geology Road, Columbia, SC 29210-4089.

SOUTH DAKOTA

South Dakota requires a permit from the Commissioner of School and Public Lands to either "survey or excavate" paleontological resources on any lands under jurisdiction of the commissioner, commonly called "school lands" (Laws, 1996). A $25 fee for a survey permit and a $250 fee for an excavation permit must be paid.

Permit requirements include establishment of minimum qualifications for the permittee, duration of the permit, approval by the property's lessee if any, and a research design that provides for the recovery of the maximum amount of scientific, paleontological, and educational information. In addition, a qualified paleontologist must be consulted for approval of curation plans for collected specimens.

No specimens may be removed from the state without permission of the commissioner, and any *scientifically significant paleontological collections* recovered from school lands belong to the state. The resulting law was improved quite a bit over its first draft, by limiting the cost of permits and reserving only scientifically significant specimens for the state, as opposed to all specimens recovered. Also, the first draft required consultation as to curation and proper repository with the state archeologist, and that provision was improved to consultation with a "qualified paleontologist." We are told that other improvements will be made in 1997.

Violation is considered a Class I misdemeanor and can result in forfeiture of paleontological materials discovered. Any person who discovers a scientifically significant fossil on lands under the jurisdiction of the commissioner is also required to report it.

The South Dakota Department of Game, Fish, and Parks also prohibits archeological, botanical, geological, and paleontological collecting on parks, lake-access, game preserves, and recreation areas without permission. Mineral collection is not prohibited on state school or forest lands, however.

Contacts: South Dakota Commissioner of School and Public Lands, 500 East Capital Avenue, Pierre, SD 57501; South Dakota Department of Game, Fish and Parks, Foss Building, Pierre, SD 57501.

TENNESSEE

Tennessee's Department of Environment and Conservation administers its Natural Areas Preservation Act that is more comprehensive than most (Tennessee Code Annotated, Sec. 11-14-101 et seq). Protected natural areas are divided into two classifications for the convenience of visitors: Class I that are scenic-recreational areas, and Class II that are natural-scientific areas, associated with "floral assemblages, forest types, fossil assemblages, geological phenomena, hydrological phenomena, swamplands, and other similar features" (TCA Sec. 11-14-106). Class II areas of special interest to readers would be: Virgin Falls Pocket Wilderness, containing caves; Morril's Cave, containing eight to ten miles of passages and interesting rock formations; Colditz Cave, containing a seventy-five-foot waterfall and interesting rock formations; Bone Cave, containing significant archeological finds; and Lost Cove Cave. Removal of "plants, animals, or geological specimens" is prohibited in natural areas except by permit from the commissioner of the Department (TCA Sec. 11-14-106). Collecting of plants, rocks, minerals, animal life, and other natural objects is also prohibited in state parks without a permit from the superintendent of State Parks.

With all of its caves, Tennessee has naturally adopted a cave protection act that makes it illegal to "break, break off, crack, carve upon, write or otherwise mark upon, or in any manner destroy, mutilate, injure, deface, mar or harm" any "stalactites, stalagmites, helictites, anthodites, gypsum flowers or needles, flowstone, draperies, columns or other similar crystalline material formations" (TCA Sec. 11-5-108). The state also has a geological division that should be a good resource for information on rock and fossiliferous formations.

Contacts: Tennessee Department of Environment and Conservation, 701 Broadway, Nashville, TN 37219; Tennessee Division of Parks and Recreation, 701 Broadway, Nashville, TN 37219.

TEXAS

The Texas General Land Office regulates mineral rights on public lands, including the beds of rivers, islands, lakes, reefs, that part of the Gulf of Mexico within the state's territorial jurisdiction, and unsold public school land. These lands are open to prospecting for minerals that are not subject to lease or permit under any other statute (Texas Nat Res. Sec. 53.011). Royalties are one-sixteenth of the value of the minerals produced, and leases are issued immediately (Sec. 53.018) if the applicant shows that the mineral is located on a state tract subject to prospecting (Sec. 53.023). In-kind royalties may be accepted. Except for state parks, there is no reference to casual collecting of gems, minerals, or fossils on public lands and, therefore, these subjects must fall under the general leasing provisions above. The Texas State Parks and Wildlife Department does prohibit geological and paleontological materials in the state parks without a permit.

Contacts: Commissioner, General Land Office, Stephen Austin State Office Building, Austin, TX 78711; Texas Parks and Wildlife Department, 4200 Smith School Road, Austin, TX 78744.

UTAH

Utah has no specific statutory coverage of mineral collecting. Hence, we recommend consulting with the state agency having jurisdiction over the site.

In 1995, the responsibility for preservation and protection of fossils was transferred from the Utah Department of Community and Economic Development, Division of State History, to the Utah Department of Natural Resources and the Utah Geological Survey (SB No. 108). Permits are still issued by the School and Trust Lands Administration, and may be delegated at a later time to the Utah Geological Survey.

Getting a permit requires the approval of the land manager for the fossil locality, a screening of the permit application by the survey director or designee; meeting qualifications required for a permit and submitting data, consulting with a designated museum representative on matters of curation of collections, and providing any other required information.

Collected fossils may only be removed from Utah with permission from the School and Institutional Trust Lands Administration, after consulting with the Utah Geological Survey. Specimens remain the property of the State of Utah and cannot be sold (UC, Sec. 63-73-12 and 13). Violation of these requirements constitute a Class B misdemeanor (UC Sec. 63-73-14). Utah also requires that anyone who discovers fossils on private lands promptly report the discovery to the survey (UC Sec. 63-73-17). However, it is unclear whether the state intends to assume ownership of such finds, that would no doubt be unconstitutional.

Contacts: Utah Geological Survey, 1594 West North Temple, Suite 3410, Salt Lake City, UT 84114-6100; Utah Department of Natural Resources, 1594 West North Temple, Suite 300, Salt Lake City, UT 84114-6100; Utah School and Institutional Trust Lands Administration, 675 East 500 South, Suite 500, Salt Lake City, UT 84102.

VERMONT

Vermont's Agency of Natural Resources consists of various departments that regulate collecting in one way or the other, such as the Department of Forests, Parks, and Recreation, Department of Fish and Wildlife, Department of Environmental Conservation (replacing the Water Resources Board), and Division of Geology and Mineral Resources. The Agency of Transportation also administers some state lands. Since most lands are owned privately, these are protected from collectors by the trespass laws (13 Vermont Statutes Annotated, Chap. 81, Sec. 3833 and 3834) and treble damages for conversion of trees or defacing marks on logs (13 VSA Chap. 77, Sec. 3606).

Vermont is one of a few states that provides permits for recreational goldpanning (10 VSA Chap. 41, Subchap. 2) and other mining activities in state waters (10 VSA Chap. 47, Subchap. 1). A citizen of the United States who discovers a valuable "mine or quarry" upon state lands may still work such mine or quarry exclusively, upon paying two percent royalty to the state and other acts of compliance (29 VSA Chap. 9, Sec. 302, V.S. 1947). The foregoing provision does not apply to state parks and forests (Sec. 308). One can also relocate claims defaulted on by prior claimants (Sec. 307).

Any mining activity usually requires the permission of the Department of Environmental Conservation, but not casual collecting.

The state geologist, through the Division of Geology and Mineral Resources, has no regulatory authority regarding collecting activity, but may have useful information.

Contacts: Vermont Agency of Natural Resources, Department of Forest, Parks, and Recreation, 103 South Main Street, Center Building, Waterbury, VT 05676; State Geologist, Vermont Agency of Natural Resources, Division of Geology and Mineral Resources, 103 South Main Street, Center Building, Waterbury, VT 05676.

VIRGINIA

There does not appear to be any clear mandate to regulate either geological or paleontological collecting on state-controlled lands. Thus, the state agency managing the land regulates collecting. Large landholding agencies are the Department of Conservation and Recreation, Department of Forestry, Division of State Parks, and Department of Game and Inland Fisheries. These agencies issue permits for scientific or educational purposes only.

Virginia also has a cave protection act that prohibits archeological, botanical, geological, and paleontological collecting in caves without a permit from the Department of Conservation and Recreation (Virginia Code, Sec. 10.1-1003). Permits are issued only for scientific investigation and excavation.

Contacts: Virginia Department of Conservation and Recreation, 203 Governor Street, Suite 302, Richmond, VA 23219; Virginia Department of Forestry, P.O. Box 3758, Alderman and McCormick Road, Charlottesville, VA 22903; Virginia Commission of Game and Inland Fisheries, 4010 West Broad Street, Richmond, VA 23230; Virginia Division of State Parks, 203 Governor Street, Suite 306, Richmond, VA 23219.

WASHINGTON

The Washington Department of Natural Resources regulates mining and collecting of geological and paleontological specimens on state land, studies mineral resources, and prepares mineral exhibits (Washington Revised Codes, Sec. 43.30.138). The Green River Gorge alone contains two miles of Eocene fossils open to recreation.

Washington allows the sale of public lands, "whenever it appears to the board of county commissioners that it is for the best interests of the county . . . that any part . . . of property . . . belonging to the county . . . should be sold, the board shall sell and convey such property," including "any timber, mineral, or other resources on any land owned by the county." The county may, however, reserve for itself oil, gas, coal, ores, minerals, gravel, timber, and fossils with the intention of exploring or, "opening, developing, and working mines, thereon, and taking out and removing . . . oils, gases, coal, ores, minerals, gravel, timber and fossils." It is laudable that Washington considers fossils to be a marketable commodity, thus ensuring their preservation, rather than secret shrines to be left in the ground to erode (Sec. 36.34.010).

Washington also allows for the sale of resources from tax-forfeited lands. "Any moneys derived from the lease of such land or from the sale of forest products, oils, gases, coal, minerals, or fossils therefrom, shall be distributed as follows" (Sec. 76.12.030). Thus, if the locality is on county land, the county board should be consulted for possible lease of mineral and paleontological resources, and if on state land, the Department of Natural Resources.

Contacts: Washington Department of Natural Resources, Division of Lands and Minerals, Olympia, WA 98504.

WEST VIRGINIA

The director of the Department of Natural Resources regulates the West Virginia Cave Protection Act (West Virginia Code, Chap. 20). No person may "excavate, remove, destroy, injure or deface any historic or prehistoric ruins, burial grounds, archeological or paleontological site including saltpeter workings, relics or inscriptions, fossilized footprints, bones or any other such features" found in a cave without a permits from the director (WVC Sec. 20-7A-5). Permittees must provide a detailed statement giving the reasons and objectives, provide data and results, and obtain the prior written permission of the director if the site is state-owned, or the landowner if the site is privately owned. There are no restrictions on the qualifications of persons who may be issued permits.

Other than caves, there is no specific regulation of casual collecting of geological material in West Virginia. The West Virginia Public Lands Corporation manages most of the land (WVC Sec. 20-1-15) and may lease lands to which it holds title for the "development of minerals, gas or oil" (WVC Sec. 20-1A-6). Otherwise, the particular state agency or political subdivision having title to the land should be consulted. Counties in West Virginia may lease their lands for oil, gas, or other mineral production, and should be consulted regarding mineral collection or even paleontology (WVC Sec. 7-3-4). Furthermore, leasing and conveyance of mineral interests owned by missing, unknown, or abandoning owners is made easy through the circuit court under Section 55-12A-I, et seq.

West Virginia does not have a central authority in charge of paleontological collection. However, the Public Lands Corporation should be consulted for collecting on its land, as well as the Department of Commerce in charge of state parks, and other state agencies such as Highways, or political subdivisions.

109

Contacts: West Virginia Department of Natural Resources, Office of Real Estate Management (including old Public Lands Corporation), Building 3, Room 643, 1900 Kanawha Boulevard East, Charleston, WV 25305; West Virginia Division of Parks and Recreation, Department of Commerce, Capital Complex, Charleston, WV 25305; West Virginia Public Lands Corporation, Charleston, WV 25305.

WISCONSIN

The Wisconsin Department of Natural Resources issues prospecting and mining permits for both public and private lands (Wisconsin Statutes Annotated, Sec. 144.80 to 144.94). Unlicensed explorations can cost an operator from $100 to $1,000 per parcel. Unlicensed prospecting and mining can cost substantially more. The department may also lease state park and forest lands (Sec. 26.08).

Although we can find no statutory regulations against casual collecting, the Department of Natural Resources prohibits collection of specimens on state lands except for research and scientific purposes, museums, and academics. However, one should check with local counties who manage their own tax-forfeited lands and often own or lease quarries for road construction as well.

The Wisconsin Geological and Natural History Survey, like many state geological surveys, is a good place to start in asking what permits are required. It is also a place to look for field reports, and topographic and geological maps, that may lead to landowners more easily than records of the local county tax assessor.

Contacts: Wisconsin Department of Natural Resources, P.O. Box 7921, Madison, WI 53707; Wisconsin Geological and Natural History Survey, 3817 Mineral Point Road, Madison, WI 53705.

WYOMING

Casual collecting of rocks, minerals, and common invertebrate fossils is legal on most state lands without a permit from the State Board of Land Commissioners, provided that there is no excavation or disturbance of the surface (Wyoming Statutes, Sec. 36-1-114-116). Otherwise, the collection of fossils, rocks, and minerals is unlawful in state parks, campgrounds, historic sites and other recreational areas under the jurisdiction of the Wyoming Recreation Commission and other state agencies (WS Sec. 36-8-103 and 105).

All fossils and traces are owned by the state (WS Sec. 36-1-114) and discoveries must be disclosed to the curator of the University of Wyoming Geological Museum. The State Board of Land Commissioners controls permits under statutory conditions (WS Sec. 36-1-114-116). The permittee must provide a notarized inventory of fossils collected by May 31st of each year. Although the state has the right to retain all fossils, the Board of Land Commissioners may agree to loan fossils permanently to scientific institutions under two types of fossil removal permits:

(a) Nonexclusive, scientific fossil removal permit that covers the collection of specimens for incorporation into research collections, for public museums, and for teaching purposes. Such specimens may not be sold.

(b) Exclusive commercial fossil removal permit for the collection of specimens to be sold.

Such permits authorize only the sale of common types of fossils, as defined in the permit. The commissioner of Public Lands or his designated representative, the state geologist, and the curator or designated representative of the Museum, have the right to inspect all commercial fossil-collecting sites and examine collected material at any time.

The board also leases state land for quarrying or mining of gem-quality rock, including jade. All mining permits must be approved by the Wyoming Department of Environmental Quality.

Contacts: Wyoming Recreation Commission, State Parks Division, Herschler Building, 122 West 25th Street, Cheyenne, WY 82002; University of Wyoming Geological Museum, P.O. Box 3006, University Station, Laramie, WY 82071; Geological Survey of Wyoming, University of Wyoming, Box 3008, University Station, Laramie, WY 82071.

CHAPTER 5

FEDERAL AGENCIES AND LAWS REGULATING PLANT AND ANIMAL COLLECTING

United States Fish and Wildlife Service
The U.S. Congress passed the Federal Endangered Species Act in 1973 and again in 1988. The U.S. Fish and Wildlife Service, under the Department of Agriculture, enforces the act and is responsible for deciding which species are listed. Although the USFWS must conduct formal hearings on pro- posed listings or delistings, their decisions can be made without approval by Congress.

This important legislation attempts to protect animal and plant species that are considered to be threatened or endangered and likely to become extinct if no protective actions are taken. The act prohibits the importation or exportation of endangered species and actions that might jeopardize designated species in the United States or its territorial waters. The act precludes "collecting" activities involving endangered species except by special permit. Such activities include pursuing, enticing, harassing, wounding, trapping, or capturing endangered wildlife, or their eggs or young, and possessing, selling, bartering, or purchasing protected wildlife, or any bodily part of such wildlife, such as feathers, fur, or bones. Hence, one must be careful to avoid picking up scattered feathers, bones, or eggshells in the outdoors, as they may belong to an endangered species.

Penalties associated with conviction of violating the act can be ruinous. Penalties can be imposed up to $100,000 in fines for individuals and one year in prison, and $200,000 for organizations, including forfeiture of associated equipment. Rewards are offered for information provided that leads to convictions.

Most states have adopted the federal act by reference, in addition to more stringent laws of their own, for flora or fauna of special interest to that state (see Chapter 6). Appendix I contains a copy of the Federal Endangered Species Act and current lists of designated organisms.

The U.S. Forest Service
Collection of plant and wildlife specimens may be prohibited or con- trolled regardless of whether they are endangered or threatened, if they are located on public land managed by a federal agency. If a specimen is found on national forest lands, for example, collectors will need to consult with the local U.S. Forest Service (USFS) office.

The Department of Agriculture directs the USFS, and has broad authority to restrict use of the forests under the National Forest

Management Act and the Forest Service General Provisions (16 USC Sec. 551-580). The USFS normally requires a permit and a fee for removal of natural resources from the forest, including firewood and live trees. Damaging or removing any plant that is "classified as a threatened, endangered, sensitive, rare, or unique species" is illegal (36 CFR Sec. 261.9). Hunting, trapping, fishing, molesting, killing, or having in your possession any kind of wild animal, bird, fish, eggs of such bird, firearm, unleashed dog, or other implement capable of taking animal life is also illegal, but only "to the extent federal or state law is violated."

Hence, the USFS does not appear to have independent prohibitions against taking plants and animals, but has merely adopted and enforced the laws of other agencies and of the state, including the Endangered Species Act. However, the following regulation is unique in that it attempts to suspend the laws of nature: It is illegal to "curtail the free movement of any animal or plant life into or out of a cave" (36 CFR, Sec. 261.8[e]).

As in any park system, there are extensive regulations concerning the handling of garbage, glass bottles, fires, and off-road vehicles. In 1994, the Forest Service considered a general prohibition against alcohol use on forest lands, but dropped the idea because it was so unpopular. Violations of regulations are punishable by fines of up to $500, incarceration up to six months, or both.

The USFS motto, "If you pack it in, you can pack it out" has been interpreted to apply to horse dung, although it does not apply to droppings of forest animals or cattle grazing under permit (See 36 CFR Sec. 261.11). It also prohibits "possessing or leaving refuse, debris, or litter in an exposed or unsanitary condition." This is especially hard on professional outfitters, as they must either bury horse droppings or bag them and carrying them to the nearest receptacle, as well as any unused hay or feed.

Bureau of Land Management
The Federal Land Policy Management Act of 1976 (FLPMA) is the organic act giving the BLM management of public lands for the express purposes of "multiple use and sustained yield" and to prevent "its unnecessary or undue degradation" (43 USC Sec. 1732). Multiple use is defined as "balanced and diverse resource uses that takes into account the long-term needs of future generations for renewable and nonrenewable resources, including, but not limited to, recreation, range, timber, minerals, watershed, wildlife and fish, and natural, scenic, scientific, and historical values." The BLM may employ "permits, leases, licenses, published rules, or other instruments" to achieve these purposes.

The BLM controls 270 million acres under U.S. Department of the Interior stewardship, or approximately one-eighth of our country's surface, as well as the mineral rights underlying 570 million acres. These statistics are more meaningful in the western states, where the BLM controls great galloping chunks, including eighty-three percent of the land surface of Nevada, and close to half of the states of Utah, Wyoming, Idaho, Oregon, Colorado, and New Mexico.

BLM lands represent "leftovers" from Department of the Interior sales of various homestead and mining patents, and gifts of certain sections to the states. There is no demonstrated design to preserve these lands as permanent sanctuaries. Rather, Congress intended BLM lands to serve as an economic and recreational resource and reserve. BLM rules, then, should be very different from those that apply to our national parks and wilderness areas. It is also significant that Congress used the word "public" rather than "federal" or "national," further emphasizing the difference between "national" parks and "public" lands held in trust for use by the public. Conceivably, BLM lands could serve in the future to relieve population pressure, as public lands have done in the past.

Whereas the BLM prohibits acts that "willfully deface, remove or destroy any plants or their parts, soil, rocks or minerals, or cave resources," it is permissible to "collect from the public lands reasonable amounts" of certain commodities in designated areas for "noncommercial purposes." The collectible items include "commonly available renewable resources such as flowers, berries, nuts, seeds, cones and leaves" or "forest products for use in campfires." The operative phrase seems to be "commonly available," not "renewable," because the same section makes even nonrenewable resources such as rocks, minerals, and *common* invertebrate fossils and semiprecious gemstones collectible. Thus, common plants, butterflies and wildlife would seem to be collectible, but one should check with the local BLM office.

A contract or permit may be issued for collection of renewable or nonrenewable resources for commercial purposes (43 CFR 8365.1-5). Always ask your local BLM office to see the formal regulation supporting any restrictions. For example, Towner Seed Company of Socorro, New Mexico, one of the few wholesalers of wild seed, should not have been turned down under the CFR regulation just cited. Towner Seed Company collects wild seed and sells it, often to the government, to be planted along highways and elsewhere on public land for erosion control and wildlife browse. Rather than consuming the resource, as in the case of lumber, seed-pickers actually propagate the spread of plants. The parent plants that contributed the seed also double and triple as a result of the accidental fertilization caused by the seed-pickers dropping seed and stomping it.

In addition to the environmental benefits of seed-picking, one can see from 43 CFR Section 8365.1-5 that seeds are "renewable resources" suitable for a commercial collection permit. However, in the past, BLM and USFS officials denied seed-pickers access to good seed-picking on public land. The USFS wanted to charge a fee of $2 a pound. This was technically legal, but unreasonable, as it would automatically inflate the price to other government agencies buying the seed. The BLM denied access totally. When management changed, the policy changed, conceding that seeds were a renewable resource.

National Park Service
Under the U.S. Department of Agriculture, the National Park Service manages eighty-three million acres, or eleven percent of public lands. Of these national parks comprise fifty-one million acres, and national preserves the rest.

Bureau of Indian Affairs
The BIA, under the Secretary of the Department of Interior, acts as trustee of Indian-owned lands amounting to fifty-five million acres, or seven percent of the total territory under federal stewardship. The 300 reservations, home to more than 500 tribes, are governed by elected leaders who determine activities on their land, including camping, hunting, fishing, and collecting of archeological, botanical, geological, and paleontological samples. However, as we saw in the case of Sue, the dinosaur, BIA approval may be required prior to collecting where the landowner's title has not matured into complete title because of the trust relationship with the BIA.

Department of Defense
Military reservations and bases consume twenty-seven million acres, chiefly in the West and South. The Department of Defense regulates access to these lands. There are more than 220 endangered or threatened species and 100,000 archeological sites on military reservations.

Department of Commerce
The National Oceanic and Atmospheric Administration regulates the national estuarine research reserves and national marine sanctuaries. Estuarine research reserves are located on state-owned lands and are co-regulated by the department and the state involved. There are twelve national marine sanctuaries for those interested in coral reefs, kelp, and other saltwater habitats.

Department of Energy
The DOE manages fifty sites, totalling 2.4 million acres, including the WIPP underground nuclear waste site in Carlsbad, New Mexico. There is some public access to these sites, should you find flora and fauna you want to collect.

REFERENCES
Federal Lands in the Fifty States, produced by the cartographic division of the National Geographic Society, Washington, D.C.

CHAPTER 6

STATE LAWS AFFECTING
PLANT AND ANIMAL COLLECTING

ALABAMA

The Alabama Department of Conservation and Natural Resources regulates natural resources, including fish and game, protected species, state parks, monuments, and historical sites (Code of Alabama, Sec. 9-2-I). As with most states, Alabama protects certain natural areas having unique "geological formations, wildlife habitats, and and recreational values," especially wetlands and coastal areas (Sec. 9-7-I0 and Amendment 543 to the Constitution of Alabama, I90I). Unlike most states, Alabama does not have a separate Endangered Species Act.

  Contacts: Alabama Department of Conservation and Natural Resources, State Lands Division, 64 North Union Street, Montgomery, AL 36I30.

ALASKA

Alaska outlaws the importation, possession, transportation, and release of live venomous reptiles, live venomous insects, or their eggs, but a permit may be granted by the commissioner of Fish and Game (Alaska Statutes Annotated, Sec. I6.05.92I). One also commits a misdemeanor who "harvests, injures, imports, exports, or captures a species or subspecies of fish or wildlife" listed under AS I6.20.I90, Alaska's strict Endangered Species Act. The commissioner of the Fish and Game Department determines and publishes a protected species list every two years. Hence, anyone interested in collecting should obtain a current list from the commissioner. The commissioner may issue a special permit for "scientific or educational purposes, or for propagation in captivity for the purpose of preservation" (see Sec. I6.20.I95). The phrase "fish and wildlife" includes "birds" (AS Sec. I6.20.2I0).

  As in most states, Alaska protects "fish, game, and aquatic plant resources" not on the endangered list through seasonal hunting, fishing, or harvest licenses (Sec. I6.05.020 through I6.05. 25I). Again, one should check with the Fish and Game Commissioner, who may issue a permit for "scientific or educational purposes, or for propagation or exhibition purposes" (Sec. I6.05.930).

Beware that serious penalties, such as forfeiture of one's vehicle and equipment, are routinely inflicted on those who violate state game laws (AS Sec. 16.05.190). On the other hand, Alaska, as with most states, protects a hunter's rights from those who would "intentionally obstruct or hinder" lawful hunting, fishing, trapping, or viewing of fish or game (AS Sec. 16.05.790).

As for damage to plants not on the endangered list, Alaska and many other states have codified the ancient and respected tort of trespass. Thus, Alaska prohibits "cutting or injuring trees or shrubs" on "(1) the land of another person or on the street or highway in front of a person's house, or (2) a village or municipal lot, or cultivated grounds, or the commons or public land of a village or municipality, or (3) the street or highway in front of land described in (2)" (AS Sec. 09.45.730). The remedy for trespass is damages, even for an unintentional act. Always seek permission from a private or government landowner before digging or cutting plant species.

Contacts: Alaska Department of Fish and Game, Wildlife Conservation Division, 333 Raspberry Road, Anchorage, AK, 99518 (907) 267-2180; Alaska Department of Natural Resources, Division of Land and Water Management, 400 Willoughby Avenue, Anchorage, Juneau, AK 99801.

ARIZONA

Arizona is unusual because it has a very restrictive Native Plants Act, aimed at preserving the popular saguaro and other cacti used in landscaping. Under Title 3, Chapter 7, Article I, no person or common carrier may transport a protected plant, or receive or possess a protected native plant without a permit (Sec. 3-909).

It is also unlawful to "destroy, dig up, mutilate, collect, cut, harvest or take any living highly safeguarded native plant or the living parts of any highly safeguarded native plant, including seeds or fruit" from state or public land without a permit, tags, seals, or receipts from the Department of Agriculture, or from private land without the written permission of the landowner, and any required permits, tags, seals, or receipts (Sec. 3-908).

Naturally, landowners who must destroy protected native plants in clearing land or canals, etc., are exempted so long as the plants are not transported from the land or offered for sale (Sec. 3-904), but the landowner must give up to sixty days notice to the Department of Agriculture.

Arizona is also unusual because it permits its agents to go upon private land in order to conduct native plant surveys (Sec. 3-910), with or without the owner's permission.

Arizona's Game and Fish Commission should be consulted regarding regulation of seasons, bag limits, and possession limits for wildlife, including birds (Title 17 Chap. 2, Art. 3). An unusual provision makes it unlawful to "take or injure any bird or harass any bird upon its nest, or remove the nests or eggs of any bird, except as may occur in normal horticultural and agricultural practices and except as authorized by commission order" (Sec. 17-236). Permits may be issued for scientific purposes.

Contacts: Arizona Department of Agriculture, 1688 West Adams, Phoenix, AZ 85007; Arizona Department of Game and Fish, 2221 West Greenway Road, Phoenix, AZ 85023.

ARKANSAS

Arkansas does not have an endangered species act. The Natural Resources and Economic Development Department acquires and protects habitats of endangered species (Sec. 15-20-308). The Arkansas Game and Fish Commission administers some bewildering and conflicting laws concerning wildlife. For example, the trapping or capturing of wild bear, deer, wild turkey, wild pheasant, grouse, prairie chicken, partridge, quail, turtle dove, or robin redbreast, is prohibited at any season of the year (Sec. 15-43-230). Yet some of these species are subject to being hunted seasonally, so apparently capturing them is worse than killing them! (Perhaps Arkansas has experienced a problem with mistreatment of wildlife in captivity.)

In addition, it is illegal to "catch, kill, injure, pursue, or have in your possession, either dead or alive, or purchase, expose for sale, transport, or ship, or receive or deliver for transportation" any species of wild fowl except blackbirds, crows, and starlings (Sec. 15-45-210). Apparently, most pigeons and sparrows are also exempted. However, any person desiring to collect wild birds, their nests, or eggs for scientific study, school instruction, or other educational use, may obtain a permit from the director of the Arkansas State Game and Fish Commission (Sec. 15-45-210). The same permit process applies for certain animals and propagating species (Sec. 15-41-106). State parks are totally off limits for collecting (Sec. 15-45-211). The Game and Fish Commission should be consulted regarding particular species and issues.

Contacts: Arkansas Game and Fish Commission, 2 Natural Resources Drive, Little Rock, AR 72201.

CALIFORNIA

California's Fish and Game Commission regulates the taking of "birds, mammals, fish, amphibia, and reptiles," anywhere in the state, through its Fish and Game Department. The Commission lacks jurisdiction over commercial harvesting of "fish, amphibia, kelp, or other aquatic plants" (Fish and Game Code, Division 1: "Fish and Game Commission," Sec. 200). The Fish and Game Department issues all necessary certificates, licenses, and tags for hunting and harvesting wildlife, including permits to take wildlife or fish for "scientific, educational or propagation purposes" (Division 2, Sec. 1002).

The department may also sell wild aquatic plants or animals, except "rare, endangered, or fully protected species, for aquaculture use at a price approximating the administrative cost to the department for the collection or sale" (Div. 12, Chap. 4, Sec. 15301). If you are a "registered aquaculturist," you may receive written approval of the department to collect your own (Sec. 15301). The department even designates public clam-digging areas (Div. 12, Chap. 5, Sec. 15401). Anyone who violates the Fish and Game Code, or regulations thereunder, may be fined not more than $5,000 or incarcerated for up to one year, or both (Div. 9, Chap. 1, Sec. 12008). The department has also set guidelines for civil damages for poaching and illegal sales of wildlife, that "may not exceed $10,000" (Div. 1, Chap. 6, Sec. 500).

California law does not set forth a list of protected plant species, but the Fish and Game Code refers to permits to collect aquatic plants. Although the jurisdiction of the Fish and Game Department is expressly limited to wildlife and fish by Section 200 above, one should check with them to see if they have attempted to adopt any regulations on collecting plant species. One instance where the Fish and Game Department has been granted jurisdiction over plants is in "ecological reserves" where it is unlawful to trespass, or to "take therein any bird or the nest or eggs thereof, or any mammal, fish, mollusks, crustaceans, amphibia, reptiles, or any other form of plant or animal life" (Fish and Game Code, Div. 2, Chap. 5, Art. 4, Sec. 1583). California also makes it illegal to "possess with the intent to sell, or to sell, within the state, the dead body, or any part or product thereof, of any species or subspecies of any fish, bird, mammal, amphibian, reptile, mollusk, invertebrate, or plant" that may not be imported under the Federal Endangered Species Act of 1973 (Title 16, USC 1531), the Marine Mammal Protection Act of 1972 (16 USC 1361), or species listed in the Federal Register by the Secretary of the Interior (California Penal Code, Part 1, Title 15, Chap. 2, Sec. 653p). Thus, any horticulturist collecting wild plants in California and seeking to sell them, or propagate them to sell, should check the federal listings. Beware that collecting regulated or endangered California-grown plants will subject you to arrest: "possession" is the offending act. However, one may argue that the law is unconstitutionally vague because it appears to punish only the act of importing federally protected plants into California.

119

In general the California code is poorly indexed, poorly organized, and too numerous and verbose. Section numbers should incorporate title, division, and chapter, as they do in Colorado's below, to simplify reference.

Contacts: State Lands Commission, State of California, 1807 13th Street, Sacramento, CA 95814.

COLORADO

Colorado's express policy is to "manage all nongame wildlife, recognizing the private property rights of individual property owners" (Sec. 33-2-102 of the Colorado Non-Game and Endangered Species Conservation Act). The Colorado Division of Wildlife and Parks and Division of Outdoor Recreation administer the act and publishes a list of endangered or threatened species. It is illegal to "take, possess, transport, export, process, sell or offer for sale, or ship" these animals (Sec. 33-2-105). The list is reviewed once every five years, starting back on July 1, 1986 (Sec. 33-2-105[a]).

However, as in many states, Colorado has gone beyond endangered species and declared its ownership of all wildlife under Sec. 33-1-101. Hence, the penal section of the Wildlife Act (Sec. 33-6-109) makes it a misdemeanor to "hunt, take, or have in such person's possession" any wildlife, except as licensed under Article 106 of the act.

Violations are punished with fines, incarceration, and "points or suspension or revocation of license privileges." Fines for taking any animal on the state's endangered or threatened species list range from $2,000 to $100,000. For example, taking a golden eagle, rocky mountain goat, or bighorn sheep can carry a fine between $1,000 and $100,000. Raptors and wild turkeys not on the list carry fines of $200, and "all fish, mollusks, crustaceans, amphibians, and reptiles" not on the list carry fines of $35! The fine for any animal not covered by specific provisions in the act is $50. Fines are compounded and incarceration added for multiple violations or specimens.

The act expressly covers capturing or killing of any nongame wildlife species in the state. Hence, one must apply to the Division of of Wildlife and Parks for a permit under Section 33-2-106(3) for the "taking, possession, transportation, exportation, or shipment" of species or subspecies on the state's endangered or threatened species lists, and, presumably, any other nongame wildlife as well. Permits may be granted for "scientific, zoological, or educational purposes, for propagation in captivity, or for other special purposes."

Game species, of course, are regulated by the Colorado Fish and Game Department under normal hunting and fishing license jurisdiction. Migratory game birds are specially regulated by the Wildlife and Parks Division under Sec. 33-1-115(1) that adopts the same open season as the federal Migratory Bird Treaty Act. As with many states, the commission also issues licenses for the possession of raptors for falconry and captive breeding purposes (Sec. 33-1-112[2]). Finally, conducting or even attending blood sports between animals is illegal (Sec. 18-9-204).

Contacts: Denver Museum of Natural History, 2001 Colorado Boulevard, Denver, CO 80205; Colorado Division of Parks and Outdoor Recreation, 1313 Sherman Street, Rm 618, Denver, CO 80203; Colorado Division of Wildlife, 6060 Broadway, Denver, CO 80216; Colorado Department of Highways, 4201 East Arkansas Avenue, Denver, CO 80222.

CONNECTICUT

Connecticut's policy is to protect a system of "natural area preserves" that offer outstanding "scientific, educational, biological, geological, paleontological, or scenic value" (Sec. 23-5[a]). The Fisheries and Game Commissioner regulates licenses and permits for taking game and nongame wildlife, including threatened or endangered species (Sec. 26-303, 26-312, 26-40[d]).

It is unlawful, even for the owner on whose property the species occurs, to "willfully take any endangered or threatened species for the purpose of selling, offering for sale, transporting for commercial gain or exporting such specimen" or to take such species from public or private property without the written consent of the owner (Sec. 26-311). However, the act does not prevent "a person from performing any legal activities on his own land that may result in the incidental taking of endangered or threatened animal and plant species or species of special concern" (Sec. 26-311[b]).

Contacts: Parks and Recreation Unit, Department of Environmental Protection, State Office Building, Room 267, Hartford, CT 06106; Connecticut Department of Fisheries and Game, Hartford, CT 06106.

DELAWARE

The Department of Natural Resources and Environmental Control, through the Division of Fish and Wildlife, regulates the fish and game laws (Title 7, Chap. 5), and the Endangered Species Act (Title 7, Chap. 6 and 7).

Contacts: Department of Natural Resources and Environmental Control, Division of Fish and Wildlife, Richardson Robbins Building, 89 Kings Highway, P.O. Box 1401, Dover, DE 19903; Department of Natural Resources and Environmental Control, Division of Parks and Recreation, Richardson Robbins Building, 89 Kings Highway, P.O. Box 1401, Dover, DE 19903.

FLORIDA

Florida's Department of Agriculture, Horticulture, and Animal Industry protects "native flora" under Title 35, Chapter 581. The department lists "endangered", "threatened," or "commercially exploited" species on a regulated plant index.

It is unlawful for any person to "willfully destroy or harvest" any such plant on private property belonging to another or on public property without permission from the landowner, and, in the case of endangered species and commercially exploited plants, without a special permit from the department (Sec. 581.185). However, permits for species also listed on the federal Endangered Species List must comport with federal permit requirements.

Title 28, "Natural Resources, Conservation, Reclamation, and Use," regulates endangered or threatened wildlife and fish. The Florida Game and Fresh Water Fish Commission has jurisdiction over freshwater and upland species, while the Florida Department of Environmental Protection oversees marine species (Sec. 372.072[4][a]).

It is unlawful, for example, to sell, possess, or transport alligator skins (Sec. 372.662). It is also unlawful to "intentionally kill, injure possess, or capture, or attempt to kill" an alligator or other crocodilian, or eggs of same (Sec. 372.663). Marine turtles rate their own protection act (Sec. 370.12[1]), as do sea cows under the Florida Manatee Sanctuary Act (Sec. 370.12[2]). Consult the appropriate agency before pursuing any plant or wildlife collecting in Florida.

122

   Contacts: Department of Agriculture, Horticulture, and Animal Industries, Mayo Building, Tallahassee, FL 32399; Department of Game and Fresh Water Fish, 3620 South Meridian Street, Tallahassee, FL 32399-1600.

GEORGIA

The Georgia Department of Game and Fish regulates both game and nongame species. Georgia has an endangered species act under which the Department of Game and Fish issues regulations for the protection of certain species, but may not affect rights on private property or in public or private streams (Sec. 27-3-130). However, the general policy of the state is that it is illegal to "hunt, trap, fish, take, possess, or transport any nongame species of wildlife" except rats, mice, coyotes, armadillos, groundhogs, beaver, freshwater turtles, poisonous snakes, frogs, spring lizards, fiddler crabs, freshwater crayfish, freshwater mussels, and nutria" (Sec. 27-1-28).

   As in many states, it is illegal to capture or possess falcons or golden eagles without a permit (Sec. 27-2-17). Hunters must obtain permission from landowners before entering their lands (Sec. 27-3-1).

   Contacts: Georgia Department of Natural Resources, Game and Fisheries Division, 2123 U.S. Highway, Social Circle, GA 30279.

HAWAII

The Hawaii Department of Land and Natural Resources regulates wildlife and issues permits for scientific studies of aquatic and other life forms for scientific, educational, or propagation purposes (HRS Sec. 187A-6).

   Contacts: Department of Land and Natural Resources, 1151 Punchbowl Street, Honolulu, HI 96813.

IDAHO

The Idaho Fish and Game Department regulates all wildlife issues. Idaho does not have a specific endangered species act or endangered plants act. However, it prohibits miscellaneous activities such propagating or holding in captivity "big game" animals without permit (Sec. 36-

701). The state refers to the federal Endangered Species Act in an apparent attempt to wrest "state control" of some issues, such as declaring that wolf/dog hybridizations are known to exist in Idaho and are not protected species under the act (Sec. 36-715). Other animals are regulated as far as possession, sale, or importation as part of disease suppression among livestock, including the fox, skunk, and raccoon (Sec. 25-236).

123

Contacts: Idaho Fish and Game Commission, P.O. Box 25, Boise, ID 83707.

ILLINOIS

Illinois has enacted its own Endangered Species Protection Act (520 ICS 10 et seq.), separate from its Wildlife Code (520 ICS 5 et seq.). The Department of Natural Resources, Endangered Species Division, regulates nongame wildlife, and the Department of Natural Resources, Wildlife Division, regulates game. The Department of Natural Resources, Office of Land Management regulates the state park system. The Department of Natural Resources recently reorganized and replaced the Department of Conservation, so a complete listing of its subagencies and statutory dominion was not available upon request. For example, it appears to regulate varied species under varied acts, such as wild ginseng (525 ICS 20/2e) and fish and aquatic life that are not considered endangered (515 ICS 5/10-55), as well as mineral and mining resources. Therefore, the Department of Natural Resources should be consulted directly to ascertain the appropriate subagency that concerns you. Illinois' Cave Protection Act (525 ICS 5 et seq.) is similar to California's and others cited herein.

Illinois has also followed the trend toward conservation easements (765 ICS 120 et seq.). Officially named the Real Property Conservation Rights Act, Illinois' law permits a private landowner to burden his property by deeding a "conservation right" to an agency of the government in trust to protect existing open space, natural areas, native plants, animals, geographic formations, or even buildings and historical sites. Although these easements must be rare, it is conceivable that a government agency may have a legitimate objection to collection or excavation on a parcel of private land even though you may have the permission of the current landowner. As discussed elsewhere regarding Native American lands, it is always wise to insist on an abstract of title and to ask an experienced attorney for an opinion as to who has authority to grant permission before you engage in serious collection on private lands.

Contacts: Department of Natural Resources (Endangered Species Division, Wildlife Division, and Office of Land Management), 524 South Second Street, Springfield, IL 62701-1787.

INDIANA

124

The Department of Natural Resources, Division of Fish and Wildlife, regulates the state's endangered species act (Chap. 8.5). The act adopts the federal Endangered Species List and the federal Migratory Waterfowl Act. But Indiana's department may augment its list of endangered species with indigenous species and subspecies, and also designate additional species as "in need of management." The department reviews its list of endangered species every two years, so the department should always be consulted regarding its current list and regulations.

It is illegal to "take, possess, transport, export, process, sell or offer for sale or ship" nongame species deemed by the director to be in need of management without a permit from the Department of Natural Resources (IS 14-2-8.5-4). As with other endangered species acts, permits may be granted for "scientific, zoological, or other special purpose" (IS 14-2-8.5-10).

The department of Natural Resources also regulates and licenses hunting, fishing, trapping, and propagating game species (IS 14-2-3-3, 14-2-7-8). The department should always be consulted, not only regarding the season, but the method of capture, as certain snares and nets are outlawed. On the other hand, it is also illegal to "harass" or "interfere with" hunters and trappers in their lawful activities (IS 14-2-11-2).

Contacts: Indiana Department of Natural Resources, Division of Fish and Wildlife, Government Center, 402 West Washington Street, Indianapolis, IN 46204; Indiana Department of Natural Resources, Division of Nature Preserves, Division of Parks, and Division of Forests, 402 West Washington Street, Indianapolis, IN 46204.

IOWA

Iowa can claim to be the Big Brother of all wildlife protection schemes. First, it is illegal to "disturb, pursue, shoot, kill, take, or attempt to take or have in possession" certain game birds or animals except in season, specifically gray or fox squirrels, bobwhite quail, cottontail or jack rabbit, duck, snipe, pheasant, goose, woodcock, partridge, coot, rail, ruffed rouse, wild turkey, pigeons, or deer (ICA Sec. 481A.48). The same prohibitions apply to nongame wildlife, including wild fish, birds, bats, reptiles, and amphibians, except turtles and frogs, and including "an egg, a nest, a dead body, or part of a dead body" (ICA Sec. 481A.42). In addition to the foregoing "protected" species, there are also "endangered species" under Iowa's Endangered Plants and Wildlife Act (Chap. 481B).

We cannot advise collectors to take photographs or otherwise "disturb" Iowa wildlife except insecta, turtles, and frogs that are not on the endangered list at the time. Since the Iowa Department of Natural Resources regulates all wildlife in Iowa, we advise consulting them before proceeding to photograph or capture wildlife in Iowa.

Contacts: Iowa Department of Natural Resources, Wallace State Office Building, Des Moines, Iowa 50319-0034.

KANSAS

Kansas boasts a nongame and endangered species conservation act regulated by its Department of Wildlife and Parks (KSA Sec. 32-957). The act is not comprehensive, however, and relies upon regulations issued by the secretary for its implementation in listing endangered species and in issuing special permits authorized under KSA Section 32-961. Thus, consultation with the secretary of the department is necessary.

Of special interest is a criminal act called "commercialization of wildlife." Under KSA Section 32-1005, the state sets forth minimum values for certain wildlife and demands reimbursement accordingly when wildlife is "illegally harvested" for commercial purposes. The law would not apply to animals taken under legal hunting or fishing licenses. Middlemen and consumers of illegally harvested wildlife or fish can also be liable, however, the values range from $500 for an eagle to $2 for a bullfrog. Thus, one would not be able to capture falcons for training and resale, for example, without paying the state of Kansas $125 each. Furthermore, possession of wildlife valued at more than $500 *in the aggregate* is a Class E felony, and possession under $500 *in the aggregate* is a Class A misdemeanor, with their attendant fines, and you could have all of your equipment confiscated.

Contacts: Kansas Department of Wildlife and Parks, 900 Southwest Jackson, Suite 502, Topeka, Kansas 66612-1233.

KENTUCKY

The Kentucky Department of Fish and Wildlife Resources regulates hunting and fishing licenses and permits for holding or propagation of wildlife (KRS Sec. 150.280). The department also decides which wildlife are endangered or protected (KRS Sec. 150.183).

In addition, all lands controlled by the Department of Parks are designated wildlife sanctuaries, and no animals or even plants may be taken or disturbed without a permit from the Department of Parks (KRS Sec. 148.029). Requests for permits should be directed to Mr. Carey Tichenor, State Naturalist, at (502) 564-2172, extension 246, fax (502) 564-6100, at the Department of Parks address given below.

The Kentucky Nature Preserves Commission regulates the state's Endangered and Threatened Plants Act (KRS Sec. 146.605). Although the commission lists endangered or threatened plants, its enforcement appears to be limited to making the lists public and educating the public. However, nature preserves, such as the Robison Forest in eastern Kentucky, would be off-limits to collecting without a permit. Requests for permits should be directed to the commission.

Contacts: Kentucky Nature Preserves Commission, Capitol Plaza Tower, 5th Floor, 500 Mero Street, Frankfort, KY 40601; Kentucky Department of Fish and Wildlife Resources, 1 Game Farm Road, Frankfort, KY 40601; Kentucky Department of Parks, 500 Mero Street, Capitol Parkway Tower, Room 10, Frankfort, KY 40601.

LOUISIANA

Louisiana's Department of Wildlife and Fisheries regulates a comprehensive endangered species act with rather severe penalties (LRS 56:1907). As with similar acts in other states, the department may issue special permits for "scientific purposes" as exceptions to the prohibitions in the act (LRS 56:1904).

The department may also issue special licenses and permits for nonendangered wildlife, to certain government and academic institutions, a "recognized scientist, or to any other responsible person" to take, possess, and transport at any time wild birds or the plumage, skins, nests, eggs, or young thereof, and wild quadrupeds, the skins or young thereof (LRS 56:105). The department must be satisfied that the wildlife are to be taken or possessed for "scientific, educational, experimental, or breeding purposes only and are not to be sold or otherwise disposed of by the permittee for profit." Inquiries may be made of Secretary Joe Herring, (504) 765-2800 or fax (504) 765-2607.

Contacts: Louisiana Department Wildlife and Fisheries, Baton Route, LA 70804.

MAINE

The Maine Department of Inland Fisheries and Wildlife regulates licensing and registration for hunters and fishermen (Chap. 702, Sec. 7011 et seq), as well as Maine's Endangered Species Act (Subchap. V, Sec. 7751 et seq.). It does not have jurisdiction over plants.

The act sets out the interesting crime of "misuse of an endangered or threatened species" (Chap. 713, Sec. 7756). Misuse consists of possessing, selling, hunting, trapping, or exporting endangered or threatened species, or even "deliberately feeding, setting bait, or harassing" said species. So all of you wildlife photographers and artists had better consult with the department before setting up your blind.

Contacts: Maine Department of Inland Fisheries and Wildlife, 284 State Street, Augusta, ME 04333.

MARYLAND

The Maryland legislature protects endangered wildlife and plants through its Nongame and Endangered Species Conservation Act (MNR Sec. 10, Subtitle 2A). A person may not export, take, possess, process, sell, offer for sale, deliver, carry, transport, or ship listed species without a permit from the Secretary of the Division of Forest, Park, and Wildlife Services .

As in other states, permits may be issued for otherwise prohibited acts for "scientific purposes or to enhance the propagation or survival of the affected species" (Sec. 10-2A-05). Penalties for violating the act may be as high as $1,000 or one year in jail, and forfeiture of equipment and vehicles (Sec. 10-2A-07).

As with the federal government, the Maryland legislature has delegated *carte blanche* power over the actual listing or unlisting of species to the secretary of the Division of Forest, Park, and Wildlife Services (Sec. 10-2A-04). Since the secretary is not elected or otherwise directly accountable to the people or to the legislature, the only remedy for those aggrieved may be a court challenge regarding the accuracy of the "best scientific, commercial, and other data" that the secretary must rely upon under Section 10-2A-04(c).

Beware of the treacherous scope of common words under endangered species acts, which often make it just as illegal to take dead animals, or parts of animals, as the whole animal. Maryland's act, for example, defines "plant" as "seeds, roots, and other parts of the plant" and "take" as "harass, harm, pursue, hunt, shoot, wound, kill, trap, capture, or collect, or an attempt to engage in any such conduct".

Contacts: Maryland Department of Natural Resources, Division of Forest, Park and Wildlife Services, Tawes State Office Building, Annapolis, MD 21401.

128

MASSACHUSETTS

Massachusetts has adopted its own endangered species act and also enforces the Federal Endangered Species Act by reference (MGLA 131A Sec. 2). The Department of Inland Fisheries and Game determines which species are listed for the state. Therefore, one must consult both lists if one doesn't want to "take, possess, transport, export, process, sell or offer for sale, buy or offer to buy, or act as a common carrier transporting or receiving for shipment any plant or animal species listed as endangered, threatened or of special concern." In addition, Massachusetts prohibits "altering significant habitat" of any protected species.

A person may possess or propagate plants listed, provided that the sources for such propagation or possession shall not be taken from the wild (MGLA 131A Sec. 3). Fines for violating the act can range from $500 to $20,000 (MGLA 131A Sec. 6).

Contacts: Massachusetts Department of Inland Fisheries and Game, 100 Cambridge Street, Boston, MA 02125.

MICHIGAN

Violating Michigan's Endangered Species Act could send you to jail for up to ninety days, or cost you between $100 and $1,000, or both (MCLA, 299.228), a moderate to severe penalty as compared to other states. As with other states, it is illegal to "take, possess, transport, import, export, process, sell or offer for sale, buy, or offer to buy, nor shall a common carrier ship" species of fish, plants or wildlife listed by the state or federal governments as endangered (MCLA 299.226).

Wildlife sanctuaries such as Pine Lake are, of course, more restrictive. It is illegal to hunt, trap, capture, kill, or molest wild game or song birds or wild game animals, or their nests and homes (MCLA 317.222). Permits may be granted to use carnivorous birds (falcons) or animals to hunt in sanctuaries.

Contacts: Michigan Department of Natural Resources, Division of Game and Fish, Box 30028, Lansing, MI 48909.

MINNESOTA

Cutting timber anywhere on state lands without a permit is, of course, trespass, with liability for damages double the value of the timber cut

(MSA, Sec. 90.301). One of us can remember cutting boughs and Christmas trees as a child for extra money at Christmas time, a time-honored tradition probably in jeopardy. There are also special rules and harvest permits for wild ginseng, wild rice, and certain aquatic vegetables (MSA Sec. 84.093, 84.091).

Minnesota owns all wildlife in the state, and people may not own them or destroy them, except as authorized under the game and fish laws (MSA Sec. 97A.025). It appears you have to buy a hunting license and kill a game animal first if you want to make it a pet. The Minnesota endangered species law also makes it illegal to "administer contraceptive chemicals to noncaptive wild animals without a permit" (MSA Sec. 84.0895). So, before you try to sterilize that bull moose, talk it over with the commissioner!

Minnesota has a rather standard endangered species act, patterned after the federal act (MSA Sec. 84.0895). However, enforcement and penalties for violations are the same as under the game and fish laws, that are likely less onerous than in some other states (MSA Sec. 84.0894). A person may not "take, buy, sell, transport, or possess a *protected* wild animal unless allowed by the game and fish laws." On the other hand, a person may not "take, import, transport, or sell an *endangered* species" at all, except by permit under the endangered species act. One may not sell, or possess with intent to sell, any article made from the parts of a wild animal (MSA 97A.501). The act is regulated by the Department of Natural Resources, and its updated lists should be consulted to determine which animals or plants are protected or endangered.

Contacts: Minnesota Department of Natural Resources, Division of Fish and Wildlife, Box 39, 500 Lafayette Road, St. Paul, MN 55155.

MISSISSIPPI

The state's endangered species act is enforced by the State Game and Fish Commission (Mississippi Statutes, Sec. 49-5-105). However, the commission also issues permits, revocable at their pleasure, to collect and possess wild animals, birds, birds' nests, or their eggs, for "scientific purposes," except for migratory birds named in the Migratory Bird Treaty Act (MS, Sec. 49-1-41).

Contacts: Mississippi Game and Fish Commission, 2906 North State Street, Jackson, MS 39205.

129

MISSOURI

All wildlife resources in Missouri are governed by a conservation commission consisting of four members (Mo. Constitution, Art. 4, Sec. 40a). It is illegal to sell, or possess with intent to sell, import, or transport any species, or its parts, designated by the Missouri Conservation Commission or the U.S. Department of the Interior, from the federal Endangered Species Act. The same is true of any article made in whole or in part from said species (MS 252.240). The same is true of the collecting, digging, or picking of any rare or endangered plant without the permission of the property owner.

It is a misdemeanor to have in one's possession or control *any* wildlife in Missouri except as permitted by the rules and regulations of the Conservation Commission (MS 252-190). Even plants along state and county roadways are protected under Missouri law, except by permission of the governmental entity responsible (MS 229.475).

Contacts: Missouri Department Conservation, P.O. Box 180, Jefferson City, MO 65102.

MONTANA

Montana has a very complete endangered species act, including a provision for falconry (Sec. 87-5-100 et. seq.). Wild buffalo, for example, are a managed species. First violations carry penalties of $250, second violations carry fines of $500 or jailtime up to thirty days, and subsequent convictions are between $500 and $1,000 and six months in jail (Sec. 87-5-111).

The Department of Fish, Wildlife and Parks that enforces the act does not have *carte blanche* authority to list species as endangered; it can only recommend listings to the legislature (Sec. 87-5-107). The department may also issue permits for taking fish and game for scientific purposes, even to individuals who are "investigating a scientific subject" (Sec. 87-2-806). Wetlands are established through a citizens' advisory council (Sec. 2-15-3405).

Contacts: Montana Department of Fish, Wildlife, and Parks, 1420 East Sixth Avenue, Helena, MT 59620.

NEBRASKA

The Nebraska Game and Parks Commission maintains a Natural Areas Register (Nebraska Revised Statutes, Sec. 37-1403). The commission also enforces the state's Nongame and Endangered Species Conservation Act (NRS Sec. 37-430-37-438). Nongame species are defined as mollusks, crustaceans, or vertebrate wildlife not legally classified as game or endangered species, and may include protected plants (Sec. 37-434).

Nebraska shares the dubious distinction with a few other states of delegating its unelected officials *carte blanche* authority over listing species, subject only to the minor nuisances of publishing the list and waiting thirty days for public comment. The commissioner may permit exceptions to the general prohibition against interfering with protected species, such as licenses for falcony or scientific study (Sec. 37-720).

131

Contacts: Nebraska Game and Parks Commission, 2200 North 33rd Street, P.O. Box 30370, Lincoln, NE 68503.

NEVADA

Contrary to New Mexico, Nevada delegates protection of federally listed endangered species to local counties where the population is in excess of 400,000 or more (Nevada Revised Statutes, 244.386). However, it is generally unlawful to "sell or expose for sale, to barter, trade or purchase" *any species of wildlife* or parts thereof without a permit or license from the State Wildlife Commission (NRS 501.379). The law does not apply to the protection of persons or property from "unprotected wild birds or mammals" on or in the immediate vicinity of home or ranch premises.

Wildlife is classified as either unprotected, protected, or game (NRS 501.110). There are no closed seasons for unprotected animals, no open seasons for protected wildlife, and limited open seasons for game, including fur-bearing mammals, game mammals, game birds, and game fish (NRS 501.015 and 501.065). Reptiles, amphibians, mollusks, and crustaceans must also be classified in the three-part system. Examples of protected wildlife include raptors (hawks and owls), bald and golden eagles, and some migratory waterfowl, for which capture permits may be issued for scientific purposes. Endangered species "in danger of extinction" appear to be a fourth category (NRS 503.585). Permits are available for falconry.

Contacts: Nevada State Wildlife Commission, 4600 Kietzke Lane, Suite 125C, Reno NV 89502.

NEW HAMPSHIRE

New Hampshire has a native plant protection act (New Hampshire Statutes Sec. 217-A:1 et. seq.), regulated by the commissioner of the Department of Resources and Economic Development. The commissioner publishes a "natural heritage inventory" listing plants in the state that are threatened. It is a violation for persons, other than the owner of private property on which the species listed is located, to export, import, transport, take, possess, sell, offer for sale, deliver, carry, transport or ship protected species. New Hampshire also has an endangered species conservation act for wildlife (NHS Sec. 212-A:1).

Contacts: New Hampshire Department of Resources and Economic Development, P.O. Box 856, Concord, NH 03301.

132

NEW JERSEY

The New Jersey Department of Environmental Protection is authorized, since 1994, to cooperate with the private Nature Conservancy organization , in inventorying "rare species and natural communities" (NJS 13:1B-15.146). Also in 1994, New Jersey enacted protective measures for freshwater wetlands in addition to the already protected coastal wetlands (NJS 13:9B-2). The Department of Environmental Protection issues permit for regulated activities (NJS 13:9B-9).

New Jersey also adopted an endangered plant species list act (NJS 13:1B-15.151) and an endangered and nongame species conservation act (NJS 23:2A-1), all in 1994. The Nongame Species Act is enforced by the Department of Environmental Protection and Energy, through its Division of Fish, Game, and Wildlife, with penalties for violators ranging from $20 to $5,000.

Contacts: New Jersey Department of Environmental Protection, 401 East State Street, Trenton, NJ 08625.

NEW MEXICO

New Mexico's Wildlife Conservation Act, enacted in 1974 and amended in 1995, is the vehicle by which the state protects endangered or threatened species (Chap. 17, Art. 2, Sec. 37-46). The legislative purpose of the act is to "maintain, and to the extent possible, enhance the numbers" of "wildlife indigenous to the state that may be found to be threatened or endangered" (NMSA 1978, Sec. 17-2-39).

State policy is also to protect species "deemed to be endangered elsewhere" by prohibiting the taking, possession, transportation, exportation, processing, sale or offering for sale or shipment" wildlife listed on the United States lists. In fiscal 1996, $450,000 was appropriated from the general fund to operate the Conservation Services Division of the Department of Fish and Game, of which $100,000 was intended for the conservation of endangered or threatened species.

The director of the Department of Game and Fish enforces the act and promulgates regulations concerning how species are listed or delisted (Sec. 17-2-40). To New Mexico's credit, the listing process, including "recovery plans," is similar to "environmental impact statements" required under NEPA. Public hearings are required, and the director must accept data on the "potential economic or social impacts or opportunities of a change in the legal status of the species" (Sec. 17-2-40E). Extensive public involvement in the listing process was not granted until 1995, when paragraphs B through M of Section 17-2-40 were added. The result was no doubt the outcome of lobbying by the Coalition of Counties, a national organization with its roots in New Mexico's Catron County and the writings of men such as Jim Catron of Socorro, New Mexico, and the county commissioners of Nye County, Nevada.

The coalition's goal is local pre-emption over federal and state actions, as in the case of the spotted owl, that can destroy local communities. Not surprisingly, local citizens feel they are treated as "colonies" unable to vote on their own future, because listing of endangered species is now performed almost exclusively by federal or state bureaucrats rather than our elected officials. The state attorney general has now sided with state government by issuing its opinion that county land use ordinances cannot restrict traditional federal and state regulatory authority (1994 Op. Atty Gen. 94-01). However, any person adversely affected by an administrative action has the right to appeal directly to the Court of Appeals (Sec. 17-2-43.1). As with all administrative appeals, the agency's action will be upheld unless it is shown to be (1) arbitrary, capricious, or an abuse of discretion; (2) not supported by substantial evidence in the record; or (3) otherwise not in accordance with law (i.e., exercising powers beyond those delegated by the legislature).

The state of New Mexico continues to be at the forefront of controversy in the battle over endangered species. When public hearings are held on these issues, one can determine the majority sentiment by whether the cowboy hats of the ranchers outnumber the green caps of the "treehuggers" as the ranchers call them. The latest battlegrounds are the Gila River over the Gila trout, the Mexican brown wolf that the U.S. Fish and Wildlife Service is "reintroducing" to south-central New Mexico, and the Rio Grande minnow that threatens irrigation of crops in the entire Rio Grande Valley. The last battle fought and lost by local government was that of the spotted owl, that closed lumber operations and a lumber mill that helped to support the citizens of Reserve, New Mexico, in Catron County.

Meanwhile, conservation officers, sheriffs, and state police will enforce the act against anyone who may "take, possess, transport, export, process, sell or offer for sale or ship any species of wildlife" on the federal or state lists (Sec. 17-2-41). The verb "take" also means to "harass, hunt, capture, or kill any wildlife or to attempt to do so" (Sec.17-2-38L). As in most states, conservation officers have broad powers of search and seizure, so one must not rely unduly upon Fourth Amendment rights.

Native Americans who are using wildlife for religious purposes may be exempted from the act, but this is not a blanket exemption if one's activities "materially and negatively affect" a protected species (Sec. 17-2-41D). One may also obtain a permit to take protected wildlife for "scientific, zoological, or educational purposes, for propagation in captivity, or to protect private property" or to prevent damage to property or protect human health (Sec. 17-2-42C and D).

The penalty for removing or destroying protected wildlife, without obtaining such a permit, even for such good reasons, is a fine of $50 to $300 or imprisonment of up to ninety days or both. On the other hand, taking wildlife for no such good reason subjects one to more serious penalties of a $1,000 fine or incarceration up to one year, or both (Sec. 17-2-45). Hence, one should always have a legitimate reason to take a specimen. However, even better than having a good reason is to obtain the latest listings and a permit from the director if your intended specimen is on the federal or state endangered or threatened lists.

The New Mexico State Game Commission regulates all wildlife in the state, not just endangered or threatened species. The New Mexico Hunting and Fishing Regulations (Chap. 17, Art. 2, Sec. 1-36) list game mammals, birds, and fish, that may not be hunted except under the season and license regulations of the commission (Sec. 17-2-3). It is this Section of Chapter 17 that protects songbirds (Sec. 17-2-13), bullfrogs (Sec. 17-2-4 and 16), hawks, vultures, and owls (Sec. 17-2-14), and horned toads (Sec. 17-2-15). As in most states, wildlife are considered to be free roaming and all wildlife belongs to the state.

As in most states, it matters not that the wildlife may be temporarily on private land. The only exception in New Mexico is that wild horses on the White Sands Missile Range fall under jurisdiction of the federal government, not the state, no doubt due to the federal government's ownership of the land. As a sidenote, the writers performed an unofficial audit of the Bureau of Land Management's adoption program for wild horses and burros. In the New Mexico, Texas, and Oklahoma area, we discovered that the program is costing the taxpayers $6,000 per animal, which is four to five times the value the market places on a blooded registered horse.

New Mexico also boasts an abbreviated endangered plants act (75-6-1, NMSA 1978). The act is administered by the New Mexico Department of Natural Resources that is also in charge of investigating and listing species determined to be endangered. Public involvement in the listing process for plants is not provided as it was in the case of wildlife. Perhaps it is an oversight that the legislature intends to cure in the near future. Since one can be fined from $300 to $1,000 or incarcerated for up to 120 days, or both, for picking or digging certain species of plants, one should check with the department to obtain a current listing before venturing forth.

Contacts: Conservation Services Division, Endangered Species Section of the New Mexico Department of Game & Fish, 408 Galisteo, P.O. Box 25112, Santa Fe, NM 87504, (505) 827-9904.

NEW YORK

New York retains ownership of "all fish, game, wildlife, shellfish, crustacea and protected insects in the state, except those legally acquired and held in private ownership" (NY Envir. Conser. Sec. 11-0105). The Fish and Wildlife Law divides wildlife, including insects, into protected and unprotected wildlife (Sec. 11-0107).

No person shall, at any time of the year, "pursue, take, wound or kill" protected wildlife, except by permit from the Department of Fish and Wildlife or in open season as set forth in Section 11-1103. There are very specific trapping restrictions, for example, such as the type of trap, the time of day and location, and no trapping within 100 feet of a dwelling, fifteen feet of a beaver dam, or five feet of a muskrat den (Sec. 11-1101). A person who gives aid to "wildlife in distress" is exempt from the prohibitions of the act (Sec. 11-0919). Wildlife may not be taken on or from any public highway except in forest preserve counties (Sec. 11-0901). However, falconry and breeding of game birds may be permitted by the department.

New York also has a rudimentary endangered or threatened plants act that authorizes permits and seasons for wild American ginseng, as an example.

New York has a biodiversity research institute (Sec. 235-a). The legislature found "the preservation of areas which are significant because of their scenic or natural beauty or wetland, shoreline, geological or ecological character, and the preservation of areas which are significant because of their historical, archeological, architectural or cultural amenities, is fundamental to the maintenance, enhancement and improvement of recreational opportunities, tourism, community attractiveness, balanced economic growth and the quality of life in all areas of the state" (Sec. 49-0301). New York also endorses "conservation easements," a form of restriction on private property that prevents future owners from affecting certain conservation values of the property (Sec. 49-0301).

136

Contacts: New York Department of Fish and Wildlife, 50 Wolf Road, Albany, NY 12233.

NORTH CAROLINA

North Carolina's endangered species act is enforced by its Wildlife Resources Commission (NCS 113-270.3-337). It is unlawful, as is common to these acts, to "take, possess, transport, sell, barter, trade, exchange, export, or offer for sale, or give away for any purpose including advertising or other promotional purpose" any "animal on a protected wild animal list" except as authorized by the commission. Actually, North Carolina's prohibitions are less onerous than the laws of some states that outlaw possessing various parts or byproducts of animals, such as feathers, hides, or eggs.

North Carolina's Plant Protection and Conservation Act is enforced by the Department of Agriculture through the North Carolina Plant Conservation Board (NCS 106-202). The act makes it unlawful to "uproot, dig, take or otherwise disturb or remove from the lands of another" any plant on a protected plant list without a written permit from the owner that is not valid for more than 180 days. The present "list" includes wild ginseng. Criminal penalties range from $100 to $1,000, and additional civil penalties up to $2,000 may be assessed by the board. As is common to all states with protected species lists, the act incorporates the federal Endangered Species List and add species important or native to North Carolina.

North Carolina's State Parks Act boasts that the state offers "unique archaeologic, geologic, biological, scenic, and recreational resources" (NCS 113-44.8). The North Carolina Department of Environment, Health, and Natural Resources administers the state parks, forests, and game refuges (NCS 14-131). It is criminal trespass to "cut, dig, break, injure or remove any timber, lumber, firewood, trees, shrubs or other plants" or to "pursue, trap, hunt or kill any bird or other wild animals or take fish" within these areas. Forestry, fish, and game wardens enforce the law. The department also administers an extensive trail system (NCS 113A-85).

Contacts: North Carolina Department of Environment, Health, and Natural Resources, Wildlife Resources Division, P.O. Box 27687, Raleigh, NC 27611; North Carolina Agriculture Department, Plant Conservation Board, 2 West Edenton, Raleigh, NC, 27611.

NORTH DAKOTA

North Dakota boasts a system of "nature preserves" for "scientific research in such fields as agriculture, ecology, forestry, genetics, geology, paleontology, pharmacology, soil science, taxonomy, and similar fields" (NDS 55-11-03). They are regulated, along with state parks, by the Parks and Recreation Department.

North Dakota's Game and Fish Department regulates hunting, fishing, and collecting of animal life, including nests and eggs of protected birds (Chapter 20 generally). Of special concern to the state are the golden eagle, the bald eagle, and raptors.

Contacts: North Dakota Game and Fish Department, 100 North Bismarck Expressway, Bismarck, ND; North Dakota Parks and Recreation Department, 1835 Bismarck Expressway, Bismarck, ND.

OHIO

Ohio's endangered plants are protected by Chapter 1518 of the Ohio Revised Code that empowers the chief of the Division of Natural Areas and Preserves to make rules setting forth criteria for identifying and designating native species. No one may "willfully root up, injure, destroy, remove, or carry away" protected plants from "public highways, public property, or waters of the state, or the property of another, without the written permission of the owner, lessee, or other person entitled to possession" (OS Sec. 1518.02).

Title to all wildlife found in the state of Ohio resides in the state, unless the animal is legally confined or held by private ownership legally acquired (OS Sec. 1531.02). Hunting and collection of wildlife, including aquaculture, are administered by the Department of Natural Resources, Division of Wildlife.

Contacts: Ohio Department of Natural Resources, Division of Wildlife, Fountain Square Building F-1, Columbus, OH 43224; Ohio Department of Natural Resources, Division of Natural Areas and Preserves, Fountain Square Building F-1, Columbus, OH 43224.

OKLAHOMA

The Oklahoma Wildlife Conservation Code is administered by the Department of Wildlife Conservation that is directed to print a list of endangered and threatened species along with its hunting regulations each year (OS T. 29 Sec. 5-412). The penalties for "possessing, hunting, chasing, harassing, capturing, shooting at, wounding, or killing, taking or attempting to take, trapping or attempting to trap" endangered or threatened species are fines of $100 to $1,000 or jail up to thirty days or both (OS T. 29 Sec. 5-412). The penalties for possessing "protected" wildlife are separate and somewhat less severe (OS T. 29 Sec. 7-503).

In addition, Oklahoma has a biological survey office under the direction and supervision of the Board of Regents of the University of Oklahoma (OS T. 70 Sec. 3314). Mounted specimens of deer and turkey may not be used to entice or enforce violations of the law (Sec. 5-413). In addition to normal hunting regulations, falconer's licenses may be obtained from the department (Sec. 4-108).

Oklahoma's Cave Protection Act takes special care to protect any plant or animal life found in any cave or cavern, especially salamanders and fish of the genera *chologaster, typhlicthys* or *amblyopsis* (commonly known as cavefish) (OS T. 21 Sec. 1789).

Contacts: Oklahoma Department of Wildlife Conservation, 500 Will Rogers Building, Oklahoma City, OK 73105.

OREGON

Oregon has enacted both a threatened or endangered wildlife act (ORS 496.172) and a threatened or endangered plants act (ORS 564.120). As is typical in other such states, plants are regulated by the state Department of Agriculture and wildlife is regulated by the state Department of Fish and Wildlife.

Contacts: Oregon Department of Fish and Wildlife, 2501 Southeast First, Portland, OR; Oregon Department of Agriculture, 635 Capitol Northeast, Portland, OR.

PENNSYLVANIA

Pennsylvania protects threatened and endangered plants through its Department of Environmental Resources (PS 32 PS 5311). The way the law is written, it may be unlawful to "disturb, pick or take" *any* wild plant from state lands and only threatened and endangered plants from private land, without the permission of the owner.

Pennsylvania protects endangered wildlife through its Game and Fish Commission (PS 34 PCSA 2167). One should obtain the list from them and inquire about collecting permits under Section 2922. Persons of "known scientific attainment in ornithology or mammalogy or agents of public museums or institutions of learning" are eligible for permits. For you wild meat gourmets, it is unlawful to buy or sell game or edible parts of game in Pennsylvania, or to import it from another state without certain certification (Sec. 2312). Also, wildlife lawfully taken during the open season may only be retained by residents until the end of the license year in which taken, so one should consume any meat in the freezer with haste (Sec. 2307).

Contacts: Pennsylvania Department of Environmental Resources, P.O. Box 8552, Harrisburg, PA 17105; Pennsylvania Game Commission, 2001 Elmerton Avenue, Harrisburg, PA 17110.

RHODE ISLAND
Rhode Island has an endangered species act covering both plants and wildlife (RIGL 20-37-1). The act is administered by the Department of Environmental Management that may issue "special permits to traffic in protected plants or wildlife (RIGL 20-37-3)." Penalties for violating the act run from $500 to $5,000.

Contacts: Rhode Island Department of Environmental Management, 83 Park Street, Providence, RI 02903.

SOUTH CAROLINA
South Carolina has a lengthy nongame and endangered species conservation act (Title 50, Chap. 15), regulated by the Department of Wildlife and Marine Resources. Violations are punishable as misdemeanors with fines up to $500 or imprisonment up to six months, or both (Sec. 50-15-50[d]). One who commits the "gross destruction of or injury to wildlife, aquatic life, endangered or threatened species, or lands or waters" can be liable for treble damages for "deliberate or grossly negligent" acts.

Exceptions to the act are activities licensed for scientific purposes (Sec. 50-17-50). As in most states, "wildlife" is broadly defined as mammal, fish, bird, amphibian, reptile, mollusk, crustacean, arthropod, or other invertebrate. Thus, the department should be consulted for the list of protected plants and animals, that we know includes the horseshoe crab, that may only be harvested with a permit within certain hours for trawling (Sec. 50-17-165).

Contacts: South Carolina Department of Wildlife and Marine Resources, Division of Wildlife and Freshwater Fisheries, P.O. Box 167, Columbia, SC 29202.

SOUTH DAKOTA
South Dakota has enacted an extensive endangered species act, covering

both plants and wildlife (SDCL 34A-8-1 et seq). The act is adminis-tered by the Department of Game, Fish, and Parks.

The secretary of the department, together with the secretary of agriculture, may issue permits for taking or transporting protected species of plants or wildlife if for "scientific, zoological, or educational purposes, or for propagation in captivity" (SDCL 34A-8-8). Otherwise, it is illegal to take, possess, transport, import, export, process, sell or offer for sale, buy or offer to buy any species appearing on the federal lists or those maintained by the South Dakota Commission of Game, Fish and Parks. Protected species may also be captured or killed if they are dangerous to human health or property (SDCL 34A-8-11). This is a provision fairly typical to all state endangered species laws.

Contacts: South Dakota Department of Game, Fish, and Parks, Anderson Building, Pierre, SD 57501.

TENNESSEE

Tennessee's Department of Environment and Conservation administers the state's Natural Areas Preservation Act of 1971. The act protects areas possessing "scenic, scientific including biological, geological and/or recreational values" from activities such as dumping, commercialization, construction, and changing populations (TCA Sec. 11-14-101 et seq.).

Tennessee's "natural areas" are divided into "scenic-recreation-al areas" and "natural-scientific areas," the latter associated with floral assemblages, fossil assemblages, geological phenomena, or other features unique in natural or scientific value. Natural areas may be developed with foot trails, foot bridges, overlooks, and primitive campgrounds helpful to tourists.

Removal of plants, animals or geological specimens is not per-mitted except by permits from the department. Violations are punishable by fines of "not less than" $100 per day of such violation.

Tennessee's Nongame and Endangered or Threatened Wildlife Species Conservation Act of 1974 protects "species or subspecies" of wildlife indigenous to the state that may be "endangered or threatened" (TCA Sec. 70-8-101 et seq). Under a rather odd provision, the Tennessee Wildlife Resources Commission may treat a species as an endangered or threatened species merely because it *resembles an endangered species* (TCA Sec. 70-8-112). Tennessee also makes it illegal to sell, prop-agate, or transfer "exotic animals" not indigenous to the state without documentary evidence showing the supplier and date of acquisition.

The Tennessee Wildlife Resources Commission must review its list of protected species every two years (TCA Sec. 70-8-105). Unlike New Mexico's process, Tennessee's regulatory agency is not accountable for the economic and social impact of its decisions regarding endangered species.

It is unlawful to "take, attempt to take, possess, transport, export, process, sell or offer for sale or ship nongame wildlife" listed by the commission. As in many states, "take" means to "harass, hunt, capture, or kill or attempt to harass, hunt, capture, or kill wildlife." Violation of the act is a misdemeanor and the violator may forfeit merchandise and equipment such as vehicles, and searches by law enforcement agencies may be warrantless (TCA Sec. 70-8-108).

Tennessee also boasts a rare plant protection and conservation act that is administered by the Department of Agriculture (TCA Sec. 70-8-301 et seq). It is unlawful under the act for anyone other than the landowner, lessee, or other person entitled to possession, or manager in case of public land, or a person with written permission from the owner or manager, to "uproot, dig, take, remove, damage, destroy, possess, or otherwise disturb for any purpose" any endangered plants listed by the department. Nursery farmers must obtain a license from the department to purchase up to ten plants in each calendar year, or to sell or export endangered species. The department must review its endangered species list every three years.

Contacts: Tennessee Wildlife Resources Commission, 701 Broadway, Nashville, TN 37219.

TEXAS

Texas has an extensive system of protected sand dunes, coastal areas, historic areas, parks, barrier islands, preserves, and wildlife refuges managed by the Texas Department of Parks and Wildlife. Texas has an extensive wildlife protection act as well, but permits are available from the Department of Parks and Wildlife to take wildlife for scientific, rehabilitation, or propagation purposes (Texas Parks & Wildlife, Sec. 43.027) Even falconry permits are available.

Texas also has an endangered plants act (TPW Sec. 88.001 et seq). A permit from the department is required even though one is taking or transporting protected plants from private land (Sec. 88.0081).

Contacts: Texas Department of Parks and Wildlife, 4200 Smith School Road, Austin, TX 78744.

UTAH

The Division of Wildlife Resources within the Department of Natural Resources is the wildlife authority for Utah and the trustee and custodian of protected wildlife (UCA 1953 23-14-1 as amended in 1995). The state's definitions of endangered and threatened wildlife appears to apply only to wildlife already designated by the federal Endangered Species Act (UCA 1953 23-13-2 as amended).

142

A person who is adjudged guilty of "illegal taking, illegal possession, or wanton destruction" of wildlife may be ordered to pay restitution (UCA 1953 23-20-4.5). Taking protected animals in Utah such as bison, bighorn sheep, rocky mountain goat, moose, bear, cougar or an endangered animal on the federal list can cost you $1,000, elk and threatened animals on the federal list $750, golden eagle or river otter $500, pronghorn antelope or deer $400, and so on.

Contacts: Utah Department of Natural Resources, Division of Wildlife, 1594 West North Temple, Suite 3410, Salt Lake City, UT 84114-6100.

VERMONT

Vermont has a protection of endangered species act, covering both wildlife and plants, that is regulated by the Agency of Natural Resources (10 VSA, Chap. 123, Sec. 5401-5408). Any such agency must be consulted regarding its listing of endangered species and its rules that change from year to year.

As in a few other states, the unelected head of the agency determines which species are listed, subject to using the "best scientific, commercial, and other data available," but subject to no higher authority than the secretary's decision (Sec. 5402). It is illegal under the act to "take, possess, or transport wildlife or plants" that are listed as endangered or threatened, subject to fines up to $1,000 for endangered species (no less than $500 for the second offense), and up to $500 for a threatened species (no less than $250 for the second offense) (Sec. 5403).

Contacts: Agency of Natural Resources, 103 South Main Street, Waterbury, VT 05676.

WASHINGTON

The director of the Game and Fish Commission is mandated to "investigate the habits and distribution of the various species of wildlife native to or adaptable to the habitats of the state," and can recommend what species can or cannot be hunted, fished, or which should be protected (Sec. 77.12.020).

It is unlawful to traffic in wildlife or articles made from wildlife designated as endangered species and conviction is as a gross misdemeanor with a fine of not less than $250 nor more than $1000 and/or imprisonment in the county jail for not less than thirty days nor more than one year (Sec. 77.21.010). The penalties increase for each subsequent violation within a five-year period and can be prosecuted as a Class C felony.

It is also unlawful to bring into Washington and "offer for sale, sell, possess, exchange, buy, transport, or ship wildlife or articles made from an endangered species." A common carrier cannot knowingly ship or receive wildlife or articles made from wildlife considered to be endangered species (Sec. 77.16.040).

Washington also follows a very pragmatic approach towards the protection of plants and animals. The director of agriculture, "may declare ladybugs or other insects to be beneficial insects and necessary to maintain a beneficial biological balance." (Sec. 15.61.010).

The Parks and Recreation Commission oversees parks and recreational areas (Sec. 43.51.180). Any person commits a misdemeanor who "cuts, breaks, injures, destroys, takes or removes any tree, shrub, timber, plant, or natural object in any park or parkway." The same is true for any person who "kills, or pursues with intent to kill, any bird or animal in any park or parkway." Fishes cannot be taken "from the waters of any park or parkway, except in conformity with such general rules as the commission may prescribe." Collection of specimens of wildlife considered endangered is only by authorization of the commission.

Washington has also taken upon itself the task of protecting carrier and racing pigeons from harm. "It is a class I civil infraction for any person, other than the owner thereof or his authorized agent, to knowingly shoot, kill, maim, injure, molest, entrap, or detain any Antwerp Messenger or Racing Pigeon, commonly called 'carrier or racing pigeons,' having the name of its owner stamped upon its wing or tail. . . . " (Sec. 9.61.190).

Contacts: Department of Natural Resources, Division of Lands and Minerals, Olympia, WA 98504.

WEST VIRGINIA

West Virginia does not have an endangered species act, but regulates its wildlife in the normal fashion through the Department of Natural Resources, Division of Wildlife Resources (West Virginia Code 1966, Chap. 20, Art. 2). Licenses can be obtained for unusual activities, including roadside menageries (Sec. 20-2-52), private propagation of fish and aquatic life (Sec. 20-2-48), and hunting or taking wildlife for "scientific or propagation" purposes (Sec. 20-2-50). However, the major duties of the division appears to be routine handling of hunting and fishing licenses and regulating hunting seasons.

Contacts: Department of Natural Resources, Division of Wildlife Resources, Capital Complex, Charleston, WV 25305.

144

WISCONSIN

Wisconsin does not have an endangered species act, but simply regulates the hunting, fishing, trapping, and taking of all wildlife through its Fish and Game Code, Wisconsin Statutes Annotated, Chapter 29. The harvest of wild and domestic ginseng is also regulated under the Fish and Game Code (Sec. 29.547), as well as wild rice, title to all rice being "vested" in the state (Sec. 29.544).

Contacts: Wisconsin Fish and Game Commission, Madison, WI.

WYOMING

Wyoming does not have an endangered species act. Rather, its Game and Fish Commission licenses hunting, fishing, trapping, and taking of wildlife in the normal fashion (Sec. 23-1-302). However, the commission does protect "nonpredacious" birds such as eagles and their nests and eggs from destruction (Sec. 23-3-101 and 108). The commission may grant licenses for "scientific or educational purposes to capture, take, or ship out of Wyoming" such wildlife or nests or eggs of nonpredacious birds as the commission may deem proper. Wyoming also makes it illegal to maintain fighting dogs or fowls, or to commit other acts of cruelty to animals (Sec. 6-3-203). We can find no attempt to regulate endangered plants.

Contacts: Wyoming Game and Fish Commission, Herschler Building, 122 West 25th Street, Cheyenne, WY 82002.

ALABAMA

Alabama has designated the following state symbols: flower, camellia (1959); bird, yellowhammer (1927); tree, southern pine (longleaf) (1949); saltwater fish, tarpon (1955); freshwater fish, largemouth bass (1975); mineral, hematite (1967); rock, marble (1969); fossil, *Basilosaurus cetoides* (1984); butterfly, eastern tiger swallowtail (1989); insect, monarch butterfly (1989); reptile, Alabama red-bellied turtle (1990); gemstone, star blue quartz (1990); shell, *Scaphella junonia johnstoneae* (1990).

ALASKA

Alaska has designated the following state symbols: flower, forget-me-not; tree, sitka spruce (1962); bird, willow ptarmigan (1955); gem, jade (1968); fish, king salmon (1962); marine mammal, bowhead whale (1983); fossil, woolly mammoth, (1986); mineral, gold (1968).

ARIZONA

Arizona has designated the following state symbols: flower, flower of the saguaro cactus (1931); bird, cactus wren (1931); tree, palo verde (1954); fossil, petrified wood (1988); gemstone, turquoise (1974); animals, ringtail (mammal), Arizona ridgenose rattlesnake (reptile), Arizona tree frog (amphibian), Arizona trout (fish) (1986).

ARKANSAS

Arkansas has designated the following state symbols: flower, apple blossom (1901); tree, pine (1939); bird, mockingbird (1929); insect, honeybee (1973).

CALIFORNIA

California has designated the following state symbols: flower, golden poppy (1903); tree, California redwoods *Sequoia sempervirens* (1937) and *Sequoia gigantea* (1953); bird, California valley quail (1931); animal, California grizzly (1953); fish, California golden trout (1947).

COLORADO

Colorado has designated the following as symbols: flower, Rocky Mountain columbine (1899); tree, Colorado blue spruce (1939); bird, lark bunting (1931); animal, Rocky Mountain bighorn sheep (1961); fossil, *Stegosaurus* (1991), gemstone, aquamarine (1971).

CONNECTICUT

Connecticut has designated the following state symbols: flower, mountain laurel (1907); tree, white oak (1947); animal, sperm whale (1975); bird, American robin (1943); insect, praying mantis (1977); mineral, garnet (1977); shellfish, eastern oyster (1989); fossil, *Eubrontes giganteus* (1991).

DELAWARE

Delaware has designated the following state symbols: flower, peach blossom (1895); tree, American holly (1939); bird, blue hen chicken (1939); insect, ladybug (1974); fish, weakfish, *Cynoscion regalis* (1981).

FLORIDA

Florida has designated the following state symbols: flower, orange blossom (1909); bird, mockingbird (1927).

GEORGIA

Georgia has designated the following state symbols: flower, cherokee rose (1916); tree, live oak, (1937); bird, brown thrasher (1935).

HAWAII

Hawaii has designated the following state symbols: flower, yellow hibiscus (1988); tree, candlenur (Kukui) (1959).

IDAHO

Idaho has designated the following state symbols: flower, syringa (1931); tree, white paloosa (1975); gem, star garnet (1967); fish, cutthroat trout (1990); fossil, Hageman fossil horse (1988).

ILLINOIS

Illinois has designated the following state symbols: flower, violet (1908); tree, white oak (1973); bird, cardinal (1929); animal, white-tailed deer (1982); fish, bluegill (1987); insect, monarch butterfly (1975); mineral, fluorite (1965).

INDIANA

Indiana has designated the following state symbols: flower, peony (1957); tree, tulip tree (1931); bird, cardinal (1933).

IOWA

Iowa has designated the following state symbols: flower, wild rose (1897); bird, eastern goldfinch (1933).

KANSAS

Kansas has designated the following state symbols: flower, sunflower (1903); tree, cottonwood (1937); bird, western meadowlark (1937); animal, buffalo (1955).

KENTUCKY

Kentucky has designated the following as state symbols: flower, goldenrod; tree, tulip poplar; bird, Kentucky cardinal.

LOUISIANA

Louisiana has designated the following state symbols: flower, magnolia (1900); tree, bald cypress (1963); bird, pelican (1958).

MAINE

Maine has designated the following state symbols: flower, white pine cone and tassel (1895); tree, white pine tree (1945); bird, chickadee (1927); fish, landlocked salmon (1969); mineral, tourmaline (1971).

MARYLAND

Maryland has designated the following state symbols: flower, black-eyed Susan (1918); tree, white oak (1941); insect, Baltimore checkerspot butterfly (1973); crustacean, Maryland blue crab (1989); fish, rockfish (1965); fossil shell, *Ecophora gardnerae gardnerae* (Wilson) (1994).

MASSACHUSETTS

Massachusetts has designated the following state symbols: flower, mayflower (1918); tree, American elm (1941); bird, chickadee (1941); insect, ladybug (1974).

MICHIGAN

Michigan has designated the following state symbols: flower, apple blossom (1897); tree, white pine (1955); fishes, trout (1965), brook trout (1988); bird, robin (1931); stone, petoskey stone (1965); gem, Isle Royal greenstone, chlorastrolite (1972).

MINNESOTA

Minnesota has designated the following state symbols: flower, showy lady slipper (1902); mushroom, morel (1964); tree, red or norway pine (1953); bird, common loon (1961); fish, walleye (1965).

MISSISSIPPI

Mississippi has designated the following state symbols: flower, flower or bloom of the magnolia or evergreen magnolia (1952); tree, magnolia (1938); insect, honeybee (1980); shell, oyster shell (1974); fish, large-mouth or black bass (1974); bird, mockingbird (1944); waterfowl, wood duck (1974); water mammal, bottlenosed dolphin or porpoise (1974); land mammal, white-tailed deer (1974); fossil, prehistoric whale (1981); stone, petrified wood (1976).

MISSOURI

Missouri has designated the following state symbols: flower, hawthorne (1923); tree, flowering dogwood (1955); tree nut, black walnut (1990); insect, honeybee (1985); bird, bluebird (1927); fossil, crinoidea (1989); mineral, galena (1967); rock, mozarkite (1967).

MONTANA

Montana has designated the following symbols: flower, bitterroot (1985); tree, ponderosa pine (1949); bird, western meadowlark (1981); stones, sapphire and agate (1969).

NEBRASKA

The state of Nebraska has designated the following state symbols: flower, goldenrod (1895); tree, cottonwood (1972); insect, honeybee (1975); bird, western meadowlark (1929); mammal, white-tailed deer (1981); fossil, mammoth (1967); rock, prairie agate (1967); gemstone, blue agate (1967).

NEVADA

Nevada has recognized the following state symbols: flower, sagebrush (1959); trees, singing-leaf pinon (1953) and bristlecone pine (1987); grass, Indian ricegrass (1977); fish, Lahontan cutthroat trout (1981);

reptile, desert tortoise (1989); animal, desert bighorn sheep (1973); fossil, ichthyosaur (1977); precious gemstone, Virgin Valley black fire opal (1987); semiprecious gemstone, Nevada turquoise (1987); metal, silver (1977); rock, sandstone (1987).

NEW HAMPSHIRE

New Hampshire has designated the following state symbols: flower, purple lilac (1919); tree, white birch (1947); bird, purple finch (1957).

NEW JERSEY

New Jersey has designated the following state symbols: flower, purple violet (1913); tree, red oak (1950); insect, honeybee (1974); bird, eastern goldfinch (1935); animal, horse (1977).

NEW MEXICO

New Mexico has designated the following state symbols: flower, yucca (1927); grass, blue gramma (1989); tree, pinon (1949); insect, tarantula hawk wasp (1989); fish, cutthroat trout (1955); bird, roadrunner (1949); fossil, *Coelophysis* (1989); gem, turquoise (1967).

NEW YORK

New York has designated the following state symbols: flower, rose (1955); tree, sugar maple (1956); insect, ladybug (1989); fish, brook trout (1975); bird, bluebird (1970); gem, garnet (1969).

NORTH CAROLINA

North Carolina has designated the following state symbols: flower, dogwood (1941); tree, pine (1963); insect, honeybee (1973); reptile, eastern box turtle (1979); bird, cardinal (1943); mammal, gray squirrel (1969); shell, scotch bonnet (1965); rock, granite (1979).

NORTH DAKOTA

North Dakota has designated the following as state symbols: flower, wild prairie rose (1907); grass, western wheatgrass (1977); tree, American elm (1947); fish, northern pike (1969); bird, western meadowlark (1947); fossil, Teredo petrified wood (1967).

OHIO

Ohio has designated the following state symbols: flower, scarlet carnation (1904); tree, buckeye (1953); insect, ladybug (1975); bird, cardinal (1933); gemstone, flint (1965).

OKLAHOMA

Oklahoma has designated the following state symbols: flower, mistletoe (1893); tree, redbud (1937); reptile, mountain boomer lizard (1969); bird, scissor-tailed flycatcher (1951); animal, bison (1972); stone, rose rock (barite rose) (1968).

OREGON

Oregon has designated the following state symbols: flower, Oregon grape (1899); tree, Douglas fir (1939); insect, swallowtail butterfly (1979); fish, chinook salmon (1961); bird, western meadowlark (1927); animal, beaver (1969); rock, thunderegg (1965); gemstone, sunstone (1987).

PENNSYLVANIA

Pennsylvania has designated the following state symbols: flower, mountain laurel (1933); tree, hemlock (1931); bird, ruffed grouse (1931).

RHODE ISLAND

Rhode Island has designated the following state symbols: flower, violet (1968); tree, red maple (1954); shell, quahog; bird, Rhode Island red (1954); mineral, bowenite; stone, cumberlandite.

SOUTH CAROLINA

South Carolina has designated the following state symbols: flower, Carolina yellow jessamine (1924); tree, palmetto tree (1939); bird, Carolina wren (1948).

SOUTH DAKOTA

South Dakota has designated the following state symbols: flower, American pasqueflower (1903); tree, Black Hills spruce (1947); insect, honeybee (1978); fish, walleye (1982); bird, ringnecked pheasant (1943); animal, coyote (1949); mineral, rose quartz (1966); gemstone, Fairburn agate (1966).

TENNESSEE

Tennessee has designated the following state symbols: flower, iris (1933); wild flower, passion flower (1973); tree, tulip poplar (1947); animal, raccoon (1971).

TEXAS

Texas has designated the following state symbols: flower, bluebonnet (1901); grass, sideoats gramma (1971); tree, pecan (1919); seashell, lightning whelk (1987); fish, Guadalupe bass (1989); reptile, horned lizard (1993); gem, Texas blue topaz; stone, petrified palmwood (1969).

UTAH

Utah has designated the following state symbols: flower, sego lily (1911); grass, Indian rice grass (1990); tree, blue spruce (1933); insect, honeybee (1983); fish, rainbow trout (1971); bird, California gull (1955); animal, rocky mountain elk (1971); fossil, *Allosaurus* (1988); gem, topaz (1971);

VERMONT

Vermont has designated the following state symbols: flower, red clover (1894); tree, sugar maple (1949); insect, honeybee (1978); bird, hermit thrush (1941).

VIRGINIA

Virginia has designated the following state symbols: flower, American dogwood (1918); bird, cardinal (1950); shell, oyster shell (1974).

WASHINGTON

Washington has designated the following state symbols: flower, coast rhododendron (1949); tree, western hemlock (1947); fish, steelhead trout (1969); bird, willow goldfinch (1951); gem, petrified wood (1975).

WEST VIRGINIA

West Virginia has designated the following state symbols: flower, rhodo-dendron (1903); tree, sugar maple (1949); bird, cardinal (1949); animal, black bear (1973).

WISCONSIN

Wisconsin has designated the following state symbols: flower, wood violet (1949); tree, sugar maple (1949); insect, honeybee (1977); fish, muskellunge (1955); bird, robin (1949); animal, white-tailed deer (1957); mineral, galena (1971); rock, red granite (1971); fossil, trilobite (1985).

WYOMING

Wyoming has designated the following state symbols: flower, Indian paintbrush (1917); tree, cottonwood (1947); bird, meadowlark (1927); gemstone, jade (1967).

APPENDIX B

USEFUL ADDRESSES

ALABAMA
Department of Conservation
and Natural Resources
64 North Union Street
Montgomery, Alabama 36130

Department of Archives and History
624 Washington Avenue
Montgomery, Alabama 36130

State Historic Preservation Officer
Alabama Historical Commission
468 South Perry Street Street
Montgomery, Alabama 36130-0900

ALASKA
Division of Parks and
Outdoor Recreation
Office of History and Archeology
P. O. Box 107001
Anchorage, Alaska 99510

Department of Natural Resources
Division of Land and Water Management
400 Willoughby Avenue
Juneau, Alaska 99801

AMERICAN SAMOA
Territorial Historical Preservation Officer
Department of Parks and Recreation
America Samoa Government
Pago Pago, American Samoa 96799

ARIZONA
Director
Arizona State Museum
University of Arizona
Tucson, Arizona 85721

Office of State Historic
Preservation
Arizona State Parks
1300 West Washington
Phoenix, Arizona 85007

ARKANSAS
Arkansas Historic Preservation
Program
1500 Tower Building
323 Center Street
Little Rock, Arkansas 72201

Arkansas State Parks
One Capitol Mall
Little Rock, Arkansas 72704

Arkansas Archaeological Survey
P. O. Box 1249
Fayetteville, Arkansas 72702

Arkansas Geological Commission
3815 West Roosevelt
Fayetteville, Arkansas 72704

CALIFORNIA
Director
California State lands Commission
1807 13th Street
Sacramento, California 95814

California Department of Fish
and Game
1416 Ninth Street
Sacramento, California 95814

California Department of Parks
and Recreation
P.O. Box 942896
Sacramento, California 94296

State Historic Preservation Officer
Office of Historic Preservation
Department of Parks and Recreation
P.O. Box 942896
Sacramento, California 94296-0001

COLORADO
Office of the State Archeologist
1300 Broadway
Denver, Colorado 80203

Colorado Division of Parks and
Outdoor Recreation
1313 Sherman Street, Room 618
Denver, Colorado 80216

Colorado Division of Wildlife
6060 Broadway
Denver, Colorado 80216

Colorado Department of Highways
4201 East Arkansas Avenue
Denver, Colorado 80222

Denver Museum of Natural History
2001 Colorado Boulevard
Denver, Colorado 80205

State Historic Preservation Officer
Colorado History Museum
1300 Broadway
Denver, Colorado 80203-2137

CONNECTICUT
Office of State Archaeology
Connecticut State Museum of
Natural History
U-23
University of Connecticut
Storrs, Connecticut 06269

Department of Environmental
Protection
Parks and Recreation Unit
State Office Building, Room 267
Hartford, Connecticut 06106

Dinosaur State Park
West Street
Rocky Hill, Connecticut 06067

State Historic Preservation Officer
Connecticut Historical Commission
59 Prospect Street
Hartford, Connecticut 06106

DELAWARE
Public Lands Commission,
Department of Natural Resources,
and Environmental Control
Richardson Robbins Building
89 Kings Highway, P. O. Box 1401
Dover, Delaware 19903

Division of Parks and Recreation
Richardson Robbins Building
89 Kings Highway
P. O. Box 1401
Dover, Delaware 19903

Division of Historical and
Cultural Affairs
Hall of Records
Dover, Delaware 19903

Bureau of Archaeology and
Historic Preservation
15 The Green
P. O. Box 1401
Dover, Delaware 19903

Division of Fish and Wildlife
P. O. Box 1401
Dover, Delaware 19903

DISTRICT OF COLUMBIA
State Historic Preservation Officer
Suite 1120
614 H Street Northwest
Washington, D. C. 20001

**FEDERATED STATES OF
MICRONESIA**
Historic Preservation Officer
Office of Administrative Services
Division of Archives and Historic
Preservation
FSM National Government
P.O. Box PS 35
Palikir, Pohnpei 96941

FLORIDA
Department of Natural Resources
Division of Recreation and Parks
3900 Commonwealth Boulevard
Tallahassee, Florida 32399

Department of Natural Resources
Bureau of State Lands
3900 Commonwealth Boulevard
Tallahassee, Florida 32399

State Historic Preservation Officer
Department of State
Division of Historical Resources
R.A. Gray Building, Room 305
500 South Bronough Street
Tallahassee, Florida 32399

155

Florida Museum of Natural History
University of Florida
Gainesville, Florida 32611

GEORGIA
Georgia Department of
Natural Resources
State Archaeologist
270 Washington Street, Southwest
Atlanta, Georgia 30334

Georgia Department of Natural
Resources
Game and Fisheries Division
2123 U.S. Highway
Social Circle, Georgia 30279

Director
Historic Preservation Division
Department of Natural Resources
205 Butler Street, Southeast
Suite 1462
Atlanta, Georgia 30334

GUAM
State Historic Preservation Officer
Department of Parks and Recreation
Division of Historic Resources
490 Naval Hospital Road
Agana Heights, Guam 96910

HAWAII
Hawaii Department of Land
and Natural Resources
1151 Punchbowl Street
Honolulu, Hawaii 96813

156

Hawaii State Historic
Preservation Division
Department of Land and
Natural Resources
33 South King Street
Honolulu, Hawaii 96813

IDAHO
Department of Lands
Bureau of Minerals
Statehouse, Room 121
Boise, Idaho 83702

State Historical Preservation
Officer
Idaho Historical Society
210 Main Street
Boise, Idaho 83702

Department of Parks
and Recreation
2177 Warm Springs Avenue
Boise, Idaho 83720

ILLINOIS
Field Museum of Natural History
Roosevelt Road at Lake Shore Drive
Chicago, Illinois 60605-2496

Illinois State Museum
1920 Tenth Street South
Springfield, Illinois 62704

Illinois Department of Conservation
524 South Second Street
Springfield, Illinois 62706

Illinois Nature Preserves Commission
600 North Grand West
Springfield, Illinois 62706

Illinois Historic Preservation Agency
Preservation Services Division
Old State Capitol
Springfield, Illinois 62701

INDIANA
Indiana Department of
Natural Resources
Government Center
402 West Washington Street
Indianapolis , Indiana 46204
same address for the:
State Historic Preservation Officer
Division of Fish and Wildlife
Division of Nature Preserves
Division of Parks
Division of Historic Preservation
and Archaeology

Indiana Geological Survey
University of Indiana, Bloomington
Bloomington, Indiana 46204

Indiana State Museum
202 North Alabama
Indianapolis, Indiana 46204

IOWA
Iowa Department of Natural
Resources
Wallace State Office Building
Des Moines, Iowa 50319-0034

Iowa State Geologist
Geological Survey
University of Iowa
109 Trowbridge Hall
Iowa City, Iowa 52242-1319

State Archaeologist
Eastlawn Building
University of Iowa
Iowa City, Iowa 52242

State Historical Preservation
Officer
State Historical Society of Iowa
Capitol Complex
East Sixth and Locust Streets
Des Moines, Iowa 50319

KANSAS
State Archaeologist
Kansas State Historical Society
120 West Tenth Street
Topeka, Kansas 66612

Kansas Department of Wildlife
and Parks
900 Southwest Jackson
Suite 502
Topeka, Kansas 66612-1233

Museum of Natural History
University of Kansas
Lawrence, Kansas 66045

Kansas Geological Survey
University of Kansas
Campus West
1930 Constant Avenue
Lawrence, Kansas 66044

KENTUCKY
State Archaeologist
439 Pennsylvania Avenue
Lexington, Kentucky 40506

Department of Parks
500 Mero Street
Capitol Parkway Tower
Room 10
Frankfurt, Kentucky 40601

Kentucky Geological Survey
University of Kentucky
228 MMR Building
Lexington, Kentucky 40506-0107

Kentucky Department of Fish and
Wildlife Resources
1 Game Farm Road
Frankfort, Kentucky 40601

Kentucky Nature Preserves
Commission
Capitol Plaza Tower
500 Mero Street
Frankfort, Kentucky 40601

State Historic Preservation Officer
300 Washington Street
Frankfort, Kentucky 40601

LOUISIANA
Louisiana Department of Culture,
Recreation and Tourism
Division of Archeology
P.. Box 44247
Baton Rouge, Louisiana 70804

Geology Museum
Louisiana State University
Baton Rouge, Louisiana 70803

State Historic Preservation Officer
Office of Cultural Development
P.O. Box 44247
Baton Rouge, Louisiana 70804

MAINE
State of Maine
Department of Inland Fisheries
and Wildlife
284 State Street

Augusta, Maine 04333

Historic Preservation Commission
55 Capitol Street
Station 65
Augusta, Maine 04333

Maine Geological Survey
State House Station 22
Augusta, Maine 04333

Maine Bureau of Parks and
Recreation
State House Station 22
Augusta, Maine 04333

REPUBLIC OF THE MARSHALL ISLANDS
Secretary of Interior Affairs and
Historic Preservation
P.O. Box 18
Majuro
Marshall Islands 96960

MARYLAND
Maryland Division of Historical
and Cultural Programs
100 Community Place
Crownsville, Maryland 21032

MASSACHUSETTS
State Archeologist
Massachusetts Historical
Commission
80 Boylston Street
Boston, Massachusetts 02116

State Historic Preservation Officer
Massachusetts Historical Commission
Massachusetts Archives Facility
220 Morrissey Boulevard
Boston, Massachusetts 02125

MICHIGAN
Michigan Geological Survey
Department of Natural Resources
P.O. Box 30028
Lansing, Michigan 48909

State Archeologist
Michigan Bureau of History
Department of State
208 North Capitol Avenue
Lansing, Michigan 48918

Supervisor of the State Historic
Preservation Office
Bureau of Michigan History
Department of State
717 West Allegan
Lansing, Michigan 48918

MINNESOTA
Minnesota Science Museum
30 East Tenth Street
St. Paul, Minnesota 55101

Minnesota Historical Society
Historic Sites and Archeology Division
Fort Snelling History Center
Fort Snelling, Minnesota 55111

Minnesota Department of
Natural Resources
Division of Minerals
Box 45
500 Lafayette Road
St. Paul, Minnesota 55155

Bell Museum of Natural History
University of Minnesota
Minneapolis, Minnesota 55455

State Historic Preservation Officer
Minnesota Historical Society
345 Kellogg Boulevard West
St. Paul, Minnesota 55102

MISSISSIPPI
Mississippi Bureau of Geology
P.O. Box 5348
Jackson, Mississippi 39296

State Historic Preservation Officer
Mississippi Department of Archives
and History
P. O. Box 571
Jackson, Mississippi 39205

MISSOURI
Missouri Department of Natural
Resources
Division of Parks, Recreation and
Historic Preservation
Historic Preservation Program
Natural History Program
P. O. Box 176
Jefferson City, Missouri 65102

MONTANA
Museum of the Rockies
Montana State University
Bozeman, Montana 95717

Montana Historical Society
1410 Eighth Avenue
P.O. Box 201202
Helena, Montana 59620

Montana Department of
State Lands
1625 Eleventh Avenue
Capitol Station
Helena, Montana 59620

Montana State Historic
Preservation Officer
Montana Historical Society
225 North Roberts Street
Helena, Montana 59620

Montana Department of Fish,
Wildlife and Parks
1420 East Sixth Avenue
Helena, Montana 59620

Montana Department of Natural
Resources and Conservation
32 South Ewing
Helena, Montana 59620

NEBRASKA
Nebraska State Museum
University of Nebraska
Lincoln, Nebraska 68588

Nebraska Game and Parks
Commission
2200 North 33rd Street
Lincoln, Nebraska 68503

Nebraska State Historical Society
1500 R Street
P.O. Box 82554
Lincoln, Nebraska 68501

NEVADA
Nevada State Historic Preservation
Officer
100 Stewart Street
Capital Complex
Carson City, Nevada 89710

Nevada State Museum
State Capitol
Carson City, Nevada 89710

NEW HAMPSHIRE
New Hampshire State Historic
Preservation Office
Division of Historical Resources
P.O. Box 2043
Concord, New Hampshire 03302

NEW JERSEY
New Jersey State Museum
205 West State Street
Trenton, New Jersey 08625

State Historic Preservation Officer
Department of Environmental
Protection
CN-402
401 East State Street
Trenton, New Jersey 08625

New Jersey Division of Parks
and Forestry
P.O. Box 1420
Trenton, New Jersey 08625

NEW MEXICO
New Mexico Energy, Minerals and
Natural Resources Department
State Park and Recreation Division
P.O. Box 1147
Santa Fe, New Mexico 87503

New Mexico Bureau of Mines and
Mineral Resources
Campus Station
Socorro, New Mexico 87801

New Mexico State Historic
Preservation Officer
La Villa Rivera
228 East Palace Drive
Santa Fe, New Mexico 87503

Laboratory of Anthropology
Museum of New Mexico
113 Lincoln Avenue
Santa Fe, New Mexico 87503

NEW YORK
Paleontological Research Institution
1259 Trumansburg Road
Ithaca, New York 14850

American Museum of Natural History
Central Park West at 79th Street
New York, New York 10024-5192

New York State Museum
Empire State Plaza
CEC 3140
Albany, New York 12230

New York State Departmental of
Environmental Conservation
50 Wolf Road
Albany, New York 12233

New York State
Office of Parks, Recreation and
Historic Preservation
Empire State Plaza
Agency Building 1
Albany, New York 12231

NORTH CAROLINA

North Carolina Geological Survey
P.O. Box 27687
Raleigh, North Carolina 27611

North Carolina Department of
Administration
Office of State Property
116 West Jones Street
Raleigh, North Carolina 27601

North Carolina Division of Archives
and History
Department of Cultural Resources
Office of State Archeology
109 East Jones Street
Raleigh, North Carolina 27611

North Carolina Department of
Natural Resources and Community
Development
Division of Parks and Recreation
P.O. Box 27687
Raleigh, North Carolina 27611

NORTH DAKOTA

North Dakota Geological Survey
600 East Boulevard Avenue
Bismarck, North Dakota 58505-0840

North Dakota Historical Society
University of North Dakota
Grand Forks, North Dakota 58202

State Historic Preservation Officer
State Historical Society of North
Dakota
North Dakota Heritage Center
Bismarck, North Dakota 58505

COMMONWEALTH OF THE NORTHERN MARIANA ISLANDS

Historic Preservation Officer
Department of Community and
Cultural Affairs
Commonwealth of the Northern
Mariana Islands
Saipan, Mariana Islands 96950

OHIO

Ohio Geological Survey
Fountain Square Building 9
Columbus, Ohio 43224

Ohio Historical Society
1985 Velma Avenue
Columbus, Ohio 43211

Ohio Division of Natural Areas
and Preserves
Foundation Square Building F-1
Columbus, Ohio 43224

OKLAHOMA

Oklahoma Archaeological Survey
University of Oklahoma
1808 Newton Drive
Norman, Oklahoma 73019

Oklahoma Museum of
Natural History
University of Oklahoma
Norman, Oklahoma 73019

Oklahoma Division of State Parks
500 Will Rogers Building
Oklahoma City, Oklahoma 73105

Oklahoma Historical Society
Wiley Post Building
Oklahoma City, Oklahoma 73105

OREGON

State Historic Preservation Office
525 Trade Street Southeast
Salem, Oregon 97310

Oregon Division of State Lands
1445 State Street
Salem, Oregon 97310

State Historic Preservation Officer
State Parks and Recreation Department
1115 Commercial Street Northeast
Salem, Oregon 97310

REPUBLIC OF PALAU

Historic Preservation Officer
Ministry of Social Services
Division of Cultural Affairs
P.O. Box 100
Government of Palau
Koror, Republic of Palau 96940

PENNSYLVANIA

Academy of Natural Sciences
1900 Benjamin Franklin Parkway
Philadelphia, Pennsylvania 19103

Carnegie Museum of Natural History
4400 Forbes Avenue
Pittsburgh, Pennsylvania 15213

Pennsylvania Game Commission
2001 Elmerton Avenue
Harrisburg, Pennsylvania 17110

Pennsylvania Historical and Museum
Commission
P.O. Box 1026
Harrisburg, Pennsylvania 17108

Pennsylvania Department of
Environmental Resources
P.O. Box 8552
Harrisburg, Pennsylvania 17105

COMMONWEALTH OF
PUERTO RICO

State Historic Preservation Officer
La Fortaleza
P.O. Box 82
San Juan, Puerto Rico 00901

RHODE ISLAND

Rhode Island Historical Preservation
Commission
150 Benefit Street
Providence, Rhode Island 02903

Rhode Island Department of
Environmental Management
83 Park Street Providence
Providence, Rhode Island 02903

SOUTH CAROLINA

South Carolina Museum Commission
301 Gervis Street
P.O. Box 100107
Columbia, South Carolina 29201

South Carolina Wildlife and Marine
Resources Department
Division of Wildlife and Freshwater
Fisheries
P.O. Box 167
Columbia, South Carolina 29202

South Carolina Department of
Archives and History
P.O. Box 11669, Capitol Station
Columbia, South Carolina 29211

SOUTH DAKOTA

State Historical Preservation Center
South Dakota State Historical Society
900 Governors Drive
Pierre, South Dakota 57501

South Dakota Department of Game,
Fish and Parks
Foss Building
Pierre, South Dakota 57501

TENNESSEE

Tennessee Department
of Conservation
Division of Archaeology
701 Broadway
Nashville, Tennessee 37219

State Historic Preservation Officer
Department of Environment
and Conservation
701 Broadway
Nashville, Tennessee 37243

TEXAS

State Historic Preservation Office
Texas Historical Commission
Capitol Station
P.O. Box 12276
Austin, Texas 78711

Texas Antiquities Committee
P.O. Box 12276
Austin, Texas 78711

Texas Parks and Wildlife Department
4200 Smith School Road
Austin, Texas 78744

General Land Office
Stephen F. Austin State
Office Building
Austin, Texas 78711

UTAH

Utah Division of State History
Antiquities Section
300 Rio Grande
Salt Lake City, Utah 84101

VERMONT

Vermont Agency of Natural Resources
Department of Forest, Parks
and Recreation
103 South Main Street
Waterbury, Vermont 05676

Vermont Division for
Historic Preservation
135 State Street, Drawer 33
Montpelier, Vermont 05633

Vermont Agency of Natural Resources
Division of Geology and
Mineral Resources
103 South Main Street
Center Building
Waterbury, Vermont 05676

VIRGIN ISLANDS
State Historic Preservation Officer
Department of Planning and
Natural Resources
Nisky Center, Suite 231
No. 45A Estate Nisky
Charlotte Amalie, St. Thomas
Virgin Islands 00830

VIRGINIA
Virginia Department of
Historic Resources
221 Governor Street
Richmond, Virginia 23219

Virginia Department of
Conservation and Recreation
203 Governor Street
Suite 302
Richmond, Virginia 23219

Virginia Museum of Natural History
1001 Douglas Avenue
Martinsville, Virginia 24112

Virginia Department of Forestry
P.O. Box 3758
Alderman and McCormick Road
Charlottesville, Virginia 22903

Virginia Marine Resources
Commission
P.O. Box 756
Newport News, Virginia 23607

WASHINGTON
State Historic Preservation Officer
Community Preservation and
Development Division
Department of Community
Development
111 West 21st Avenue, KL-11
Olympia, Washington 98504

WEST VIRGINIA
West Virginia Department
of Commerce
Division of Parks and Recreation
Capital Complex
Charleston, West Virginia 25305

Virginia Department of
Culture and History
Capital Complex
Charleston, West Virginia 25305

West Virginia Department of
Natural Resources
Capital Complex
Charleston, West Virginia 25305

WISCONSIN
Wisconsin State Historical Society
816 State Street
Madison, Wisconsin 53706

Wisconsin Geological and
Natural History Survey
3817 Mineral Point Road
Madison, Wisconsin 53705

Wisconsin Department of
Natural Resources
P.O. Box 7921
Madison, Wisconsin 53707

WYOMING
Geology Museum
University of Wyoming
Laramie, Wyoming 82070

Wyoming Geological Survey
Box 3008
University Station
Laramie, Wyoming 82071

State of Wyoming
Commissioner of Public Lands
Herschler Building
122 West 25th Street
Cheyenne, Wyoming 82002

State Historic Preservation Officer
Department of Commerce
Barrett Building
Cheyenne, Wyoming 82002

APPENDIX C

USING BASIC INSTRUMENTS, MAPS, AND LEASES

Using Basic Instruments and Maps

We live in a remarkable age. Satellites orbiting the Earth provide virtually instant communication anywhere in the world. Weather forecasting and analysis is now carried out with observations made on a global scale from space. In addition, it is possible for anyone with the necessary electronic equipment to tie into specially equipped satellites and locate their actual position on the ground within a few meters. Of course these space-age applications are expensive. The cost of purchasing and using global positioning systems (GPS) is thousands of dollars and beyond the reach of most of us. Yet, accurately locating oneself is of great importance in collecting specimens of any type. Apart from being able to locate yourself in rural or "wild" areas and not get lost, accurate locality data is critical to both the legality and marketability of your specimens. Fortunately, there are reasonably priced alternatives to expensive hardware. While the information in this appendix was designed for fossil collectors, it is equally applicable to other collectors as well. An excellent guide to geo-positioning techniques is published by the Bureau of Land Management (B.L.M.) for public dissemination.

Why Care Where Your Specimen Is From?

Information about where your specimens are from is very important, just about as important as the specimens themselves. It is absolutely imperative to know where your specimens were found, and in what rocks. Let's look at two inappropriate examples of recording locality data: Ralph Smith's farm, near Peoria, Illinois, and the Pierre Shale, northeastern New Mexico.

Although it may be possible to locate Ralph Smith's farm now, and we all hope Ralph has a long life, there is no certainty Ralph will always own the particular farm where you found the specimens. Also, no information has been conveyed regarding where on the farm the specimens were found or in what rock unit. In the second example, the rock unit, the Pierre Shale has been identified, as a geographic region in northeastern New Mexico. However, northeastern New Mexico is a very large region, larger than many states! The description omits information as to who owns the land, and if it is important to determine the age of the specimen, the Pierre Shale is not the same age everywhere. If you purchase your specimens, you should be equally dissatisfied with such vague locality information.

Adequate Locality Data

In a real sense, specimens have four addresses and each address is really a different dimension. First, the geographic address of the specimens. This should be detailed enough to allow you to relocate your collecting site, as well as for any specimens you purchase or for which you trade.

Data should be reproducible. Any other scientist should be able to find the location your specimens are from and possibly find more specimens. The second address after the location is the stratigraphic address of your specimens and this is in part determined by the geographic address. Your specimens are from a particular layer of rock, called a formation, or part of a formation. The third address of your specimen is the address of your specimen in time, or how old your specimen is. It is useful to know where the specimen is found relative to specimens higher and lower in the rock record, and how old your specimen is in terms of years. The fourth address is the ownership of the land on which the specimen was found and the ownership of the specimen itself. We discuss land ownership and specimen collecting throughout this book and point out the difficulties that might be encountered by collecting on nonprivate land, specially designated public lands, public lands with the approval of the land managing agency, or only after the necessary permits had been secured.

In rural or remote areas, there are no signs that let you know whether you are on private or public lands. Ignorance is no defense, especially since there are adequate records to help you determine landownership or management. Any of the local land managing agencies, state, Native American or federal, will have maps that show the distribution and ownership of private and public lands. The local court house will have records dealing with the ownership of private lands. It is up to you to be able to interpret and use these and other maps when you are collecting specimens. It is up to you to always contact the landowner or manager and let them know what your intentions are.

It is not impossible that if you sell or trade specimens, inquiries might be made by government agents as to whether your specimens were

168

acquired in an appropriate manner from private lands or with the necessary permits if they are from public lands. Obviously, if you can demonstrate that you have adequate records for each of your specimens or specimen collections, many of the questions from government officials will
be easily addressed. In the event there is any further doubt, you should
be able to direct or take the official to the locality and demonstrate that
there is no problem with your specimens.

Kinds of Maps

Just about any map is much, much better than no map at all, or just rely-
ing on memory and landmarks, which may change greatly over time.
Standard road maps available at just about any gasoline station are generally very well done and a good place to start with as you record your
specimen hunting expeditions. In rural areas, using these maps with a
ruler will be accurate enough to locate you within a mile or two of where
you actually are.

Occasionally, maps are printed on the backs of ordinary state
road maps that may surprise you in terms of their usefulness. If you are
collecting specimens near or in urban areas (still possible in some
places), street maps found on the backs of these road maps may well be
the best map you can have. Similarly, if you are collecting within a city
or town, the maps in the local telephone book may help locate your
specimen collection areas to within an accuracy of feet. Also look for
survey monuments or ribbons tied on a bush to help you determine
property boundaries.

Other sorts of maps that are available include county highway
maps, often published by state highway departments. These maps are
done for individual counties and are very accurate with a great deal of
detail. They show individual houses, other man-made structures, and all
paved and unpaved roads, but do not show topographic features.
Another drawback of these maps is that they are frequently of a large
size and cumbersome.

Topographic Maps

The preceding examples of maps are planimetric maps: they only show
distances along or between discrete locations and are basically plans of
the area. Missing from these maps is the dimension of relief, or the differences in elevation between different parts of the area. It is possible to
show relief or topography, on a two-dimensional map by using contours,

lines along which every point is at the same elevation. The United States Geological Survey publishes topographic maps that systematically cover the country in a regular manner. These maps cover rectangular segments called quadrangles that are bounded by latitude and longitude. The top of all topographic maps is geographic north, the bottom south, the right side east, and the left side west.

Each topographic map is named for a prominent feature in the area covered by the map. You can also find useful features such as different classes of roads, tracks and trails to power lines, property and park boundaries, stock tanks, ponds, wooded areas, and marshes. The U.S. Geological Survey publishes a circular that explains the symbols used on these maps.

In general, topographic maps are published in two sizes: 15-minute quadrangle that are 15 minutes of latitude by 15 minutes of longitude in area, and 7 1/2-minute quadrangles that are 7 1/2 minutes of latitude by 7 1/2 minutes of longitude in area. The United States Public Land Survey System established north-south principal meridians and east-west base lines that intersect to form a grid of regularly numbered townships and ranges. Townships are numbered north and south of the base line and ranges are numbered east and west of the principal meridian. The smallest division, a section, covers one square mile (640 acres). Each township and range square is divided into 36 sections. Sections can be further subdivided into quarter sections (areas of 160 acres) and quarter sections even further divided into halves or quarters, consisting of 80 or 40 acres each, respectively. Thus, the geographic address for a specimen locality could be designated within a 40-acre tract as Township 41N, Range 36E, the NE 1/4 of the SW 1/4 of Section 16.

Topographic maps are published at various scales: 1:1,000,000, 1:250,000, 1:62,500, and 1:24,000. A 7 1/2-minute map is at a scale of 1:24,000, meaning one inch on the map equals 24,000 inches on the ground, or 2000 feet. A location is most accurate when it can be in related to some feature shown on the topographic map such as a stream, wind mill, hill, or road. It can also be determined by taking bearings or determining the direction from some known point to a locality using a compass, and measuring the distance.

Available now for some parts of the United States are *orthophoto quadrangles*. These are aerial photographs that have been transposed on conventional 7 1/2-minute topographic maps. Orthophoto quadrangles are particularly useful for locating yourself, and are handy for mapping geologic units.

Geologic Maps

Geologic map are the basic tools of all geologic work, regardless of the specialty. Geologic maps depict the rock surface of an area as if the surficial deposits were removed. Different kinds of rock are shown in different colors and/or overprinted patterns. Color is usually an indication of origin and age. For example, igneous rocks are usually shown in red colors; green colors indicate rocks of Cretaceous age. From the geology of an area depicted on a map, it is possible to determine not only the location of a specimen or a specimen bed, but also the age of the specimen. When the geology of a map area is superimposed on the topography, it is relatively easy to locate the rock unit on the ground, its thickness, and whether it is flat-lying or inclined.

Basic Instruments

With only four, easily available and inexpensive tools, a topographic map will provide a great deal of useful information to the specimen collector. These tools are a ruler, simple calipers or dividers, a protractor, and a compass.

The ruler will allow you to measure straight line distances between points on the topographic map, and help in reconstructing topographic cross-sections. The calipers will help measure more complex distances. The protractor will enable you to measure angles and take bearings or directions from your maps. It can also be used to measure dip or attitude of a stratum. The compass will allow you to determine bearings, directions from one point to another. A simple compass will allow you to take bearings without using the topographic map or as an enhancement to using the map. It will also enable you to determine the strike direction of the rocks containing the specimens you are collecting. Of course if you have available funds, a $100 Brunton compass, or a $45 Silva Ranger compass, would be well worth the expenditure. We also recommend practicing these methods before you venture into the unknown.

Private Land and Getting on the Land

The premise of this section may not sit well with some readers. The premise of this section is that any agreement, understanding, or "deal," is only worth the paper it is written on. We know that some readers have used the time-honored "handshake" as the only contract or understanding they need. We also know that this method of conducting a business relationship can easily fail. As we have repeatedly emphasized elsewhere in this book, the first step in formalizing any business relationship is to secure appropriate legal advice. This suggestion applies to both parties involved, the owner of the land, and the collector. Private agreements are not binding, of course, where government has pre-empted rights to the specimen, as in the case of wildlife, archeological antiquities, and in the bizarre case of *Black Hills Institute of Geological Research, Inc. v. United States,* recounted in Chapter 3.

Sample Lease Form
<u>LEASE AGREEMENT</u>
THIS AGREEMENT, made this _____ day of_____, 199__, between _____, whose post office address is _____, herein referred to as Lessor(s), and _____, whose post office address is _____ _____, herein referred to as Lessee.
PURPOSE: The following described real property owned by the Lessor(s) is hereby leased and let to the Lessee for the purpose of collecting, preparing and selling fossil vertebrates.
LEGAL DESCRIPTION: The Lessor(s) lease and let to the Lessee the following described real property, to-wit:_____

_____

_____

located in _____ County, State of _____.
TERM OF LEASE: This lease shall be for a term of ____ years, commencing the date hereof. Such lease will be renewable by the Lessee on the same terms and conditions or an additional like term by the Lessee giving Lessor(s) written notice thereof prior to the termination of this lease.
RENT: Lessee will pay to the Lessor(s) ten (10%) percent of the actual selling price of any fossils collected from the Lessor(s) property and which are sold by the Lessee for a sum exceeding One Thousand ($1,000.00) and No/100 Dollars. Lessee will pay such sum to Lessor(s) within thirty (30) days of such sale and receipt of the pur-

chase price by Lessee.

TITLE TO SPECIMENS: Legal title to fossil specimens located and/or collected by the Lessee on the Lessor(s) property shall be in the Lessee, whether or not removed from the property.

INGRESS AND EGRESS: The Lessee, his employees or agents, shall have the right to ingress and egress to any of the above described property for his purposes.

EXCLUSIVE LEASE: This is an exclusive lease and the Lessor(s) will not lease the above described property to any other commercial fossil collector or to anyone else for similar purposes during the term of the lease.

DONATION OF CASTS: In the event the Lessee molds or casts any specimen collected on Lessor(s)'s property, Lessee will prepare one (I) cast that he will donate to the museum or institution of Lessor(s)'s choice, on behalf of the Lessor(s), or give to Lessor(s) to dispose of at Lessor(s)'s discretion.

LIABILITY: Lessee agrees to hold the Lessor(s) safe and harmless from any and all claims rising from any act or negligence of the Lessee or his agents, contractors, employees, or licensees, in the use and occupancy of the above premises.

OTHER:_____

IN WITNESS WHEREOF, The parties have signed this Agreement the day and year first above written,

LESSOR_____

LESSEE_____
WITNESSES:_____

   _____

   _____

NOTARY ACKNOWLEDGEMENT

APPENDIX D

BUREAU OF INDIAN AFFAIRS
(BIA) AREA OFFICES

Aberdeen Area Office
(Nebraska, North Dakota,
and South Dakota)
Bureau of Indian Affairs
115 4th Avenue Southeast
Aberdeen, South Dakota 37401
(605) 226-7343

Albuquerque Area Office
(Colorado and New Mexico)
Bureau of Indian Affairs
615 First Street Northwest
P.O. Box 26567
Albuquerque, New Mexico 87125
(505) 766-3170

Anadarko Area Office
(Kansas and West Oklahoma)
Bureau of Indian Affairs
WCD-Office Complex
P.O. Box 368
Anadarko, Oklahoma 73005
(405) 247-6673

Billings Area Office
(Montana and Wyoming)
Bureau of Indian Affairs
316 North 26th Street
Billings, Montana 59101
(406) 657-6315

Eastern Area Office
(New York, Maine,Louisiana, Florida,
North Carolina and Mississippi)
Bureau of Indian Affairs
1951 Constitution Avenue,

Northwest
Washington, D.C. 20245
(703) 235-2571

Juneau Area Office
(Alaska)
Bureau of Indian Affairs
Federal Building
P.O. Box 3-8000
Juneau, Alaska 99802
(907) 586-7177

Minneapolis Area Office
(Minnesota, Iowa, Michigan,
and Wisconsin)
Bureau of Indian Affairs
Chamber of Commerce Building
15 South Fifth Street, 6th Floor
Minneapolis, Minnesota 55402
(612) 349-3631

Muskogee Area Office
(East Oklahoma)
Bureau of Indian Affairs
Old Federal Building
Muskogee, Oklahoma 74401
(918) 687-2296

Navajo Area Office
(Navajo Reservation only,
Arizona and New Mexico)
Bureau of Indian Affairs
P.O. Box M
Window Rock, Arizona
(602) 871-5151

Phoenix Area Office
(Arizona, Nevada, Utah,
California, and Idaho)
Bureau of Indian Affairs
No. 1 North First Street
P.O. Box 10
Phoenix, Arizona 850
(602) 379-6600

Portland Area Office
(Oregon, Washington)
1425 Irving Street
P.O. Box 3785
Portland, Oregon 972
(503) 231-6702

Sacramento Area Office
(California)
2800 Cottage Way
Sacramento, California
(916) 978-4691

APPENDIX E

Antiquities Act of 1906
(16 USC 431-433)

Be it enacted by the Senate and House of Representatives of the United States of America in Congress assembled, That any person who shall appropriate, excavate, injure, or destroy any historic or prehistoric ruin or monument, or any object of antiquity, situated on lands owned or controlled by the Government of the United States, without the permission of the Secretary of the Department of the Government having jurisdiction over the lands on which said antiquities are situated, shall, upon conviction, be fined in a sum of not more than five hundred dollars or be imprisoned for a period of not more than ninety days, or shall suffer both fine and imprisonment, in the discretion of the court.

Sec. 2. That the President of the United States is hereby authorized, in his discretion, to declare by public proclamation historic landmarks, historic and prehistoric structures, and other objects of historic or scientific interest that are situated upon the lands owned or controlled by the Government of the United States to be national monuments, and may reserve as a part thereof parcels of land, the limits of which in all cases shall be confined to the smallest area compatible with proper care and management of the objects to be protected: Provided, That when such objects are situated upon a tract covered by a bona fide unperfected claim or held in private ownership, the tract, or so much thereof as may be necessary for the proper care and management of the object, may be relinquished to the Government, and the Secretary of the Interior is hereby authorized to accept the relinquishment of such tracts in behalf of the Government of the United States.

Sec. 3. That permits for the examination of ruins, the excavation of archaeological sites, and the gathering of objects of antiquity upon the lands under their respective jurisdictions may be granted by the Secretaries of the Interior, Agriculture, and War to institutions which they may deem properly qualified to conduct such examination, excavation, or gathering, subject to such rules and regulation as they may prescribe Provided, That the examinations, excavations, and gatherings are undertaken for the benefit of reputable museums, universities, colleges, or other recognized scientific or educational institutions, with a view to increasing the knowledge of such objects, and that the gatherings shall be made for permanent preservation in public museums.

176   Sec. 4. That the Secretaries of the Departments aforesaid shall make and publish from time to time uniform rules and regulations for the purpose of carrying out the provisions of this Act.

Approved, June 8, 1906

APPENDIX F

List of National Parks and Monuments
and when established under (16 USC Section 431)

The Organic Act

President Woodrow Wilson signed the "Organic Act" on August 25, 1916 (39 Stat. F35) which created the National Park Service:

> "The service thus established shall promote and regulate the use of Federal areas known as national parks, monuments and reservations if by such means and measures as conform to the fundamental purpose of the said parks, monuments and reservations, which purpose is to conserve the scenery and the natural and historic objects and the wild life therein and to provide for the enjoyment of the same in such manner and by such means as will leave them unimpaired for the enjoyment of future generations."

Ackia Battleground National Monument, Mississippi (see section 450r of this title). - Proc. No. 2307, Oct. 25, 1938, 53 Stat. 2494.

Admiralty Island National Monument, Alaska (Monument established within Tongass National Forest by Pub. L. 96-487, title V, Sec. 503(b), Dec. 2, 1980, 94 Stat. 2399). - Proc. No. 4611, Dec. 1, 1978, 93 Stat. 1446.

Andrew Johnson National Monument, Tennessee (Monument redesignated Andrew Johnson National Historical Site, see section 450o of this title). - Proc. No. 2554, Apr. 27, 1942, 56 Stat. 1955.

Aniakchak National Monument, Alaska (Monument established as unit of National Park System, see section 410hh(1) of this title). Proc. No. 4612, Dec. 1, 1978, 93 Stat. 1448.

Arches National Monument, Utah (Monument abolished and funds made available to Arches National Park, see section 272 of this title). - Proc. No. 1875, Apr. 12, 1929, 46 Stat. 2988; Proc. No. 2312, Nov. 25, 1938, 53 Stat. 2504; Proc. No. 3360, July 22, 1960, 74 Stat. c79; Proc. No. 3887, Jan. 20, 1969, 83 Stat. 920.

Aztec Ruins National Monument, New Mexico. - Proc. No. 1650, Jan. 24, 1923, 42 Stat. 2295; Proc. No. 1840, July 2, 1928, 45 Stat. 2954; Proc. No. 1928, Dec. 19, 1930, 46 Stat. 3040; Proc. No. 2787, May 27, 1948, 62 Stat. 1513; Pub. L. 100-559, title VI, Sec. 601-604, Oct. 28, 1988, 102 Stat. 2800.

Badlands National Monument, South Dakota (Monument redesignated *Badlands National Park,* see section 441e-1 of this title). - Proc. No. 2320, Jan. 25, 1939, 53 Stat. 2521.

Bandelier National Monument, New Mexico. - Proc. No. 1322, Feb. 11, 1916, 39 Stat. 1764; Proc. No. 3388, Jan. 9, 1961, 75 Stat. 1014; Proc. No. 3539, May 27, 1963, 77 Stat. 1006.

Becharof National Monument, Alaska. - Proc. No. 4613, Dec. 1, 1978, 93 Stat. 1450.

Bering Land Bridge National Monument, Alaska. - Proc. No. 4614, Dec. 1, 1978, 93 Stat. 1451.

Big Hole Battlefield National Monument, Montana (Monument redesignated *Big Hole National Battlefield,* see section 430uu of this title). - Ex. Ord. No. 1216, June 23, 1910; Proc. No. 2339, June 29, 1939, 53 Stat. 2544.

Black Canyon of the Gunnison National Monument, Colorado. - Proc. No. 2033, Mar. 2, 1933, 47 Stat. 2558; Proc. No. 2286, May 16, 1938, 52 Stat. 1548; Proc. No. 2372, Oct. 28, 1939, 54 Stat. 2669; Proc. No. 3344, Apr. 8, 1960, 74 Stat. c56; Pub. L. 98-357, July 13, 1984, 98 Stat. 397.

Bryce Canyon National Monument, Utah. - Proc. No. 1664, June 8, 1923, 43 Stat. 1914; Proc. No. 1930, Jan. 5, 1931, 46 Stat. 3042; Proc. No. 1952, May 4, 1931, 47 Stat. 2455.

Buck Island Reef National Monument, Virgin Islands. - Proc. No. 3443, Dec. 28, 1961, 76 Stat. 1441, Proc. No. 4346, Feb. 1, 1975, 89 Stat. 1237; Proc. No. 4359, Mar. 28, 1975, 89 Stat. 1254.

Cabrillo National Monument, California. - Proc. No. 1255, Oct. 14, 1913, 38 Stat. 1965; Proc. No. 3273, Feb. 2, 1959, 73 Stat. c19; Proc. No. 4319, Sept. 28, 1974, 88 Stat. 2514.

Canyon De Chelly National Monument, Arizona (see section 445 of this title). - Proc. No. 1945, Apr. 1, 1931, 47 Stat. 2448; Proc. No. 2036, Mar. 3, 1933, 47 Stat. 2562.

Cape Krusenstern National Monument, Alaska (Monument established as unit of National Park System, see section 410hh(3) of this title). - Proc. No. 4615, Dec. 1, 1978, 93 Stat. 1453.

Capitol Reef National Monument, Utah (Monument abolished and funds made available to Capitol Reef National Park, see section 273 of this title). - Proc. No. 2246, Aug. 2, 1937, 50 Stat. 1856; Proc. No. 3249, July 2, 1958, 72 Stat. c48; Proc. No. 3888, Jan. 20, 1969, 83 Stat. 922.

Capulin Volcano National Monument, New Mexico (see section 460uu-46(g) of this title). - Proc. No. 1340, Aug. 9, 1916, 39 Stat. 1792.

Carlsbad Cave National Monument, New Mexico (Monument redesignated *Carlsbad Caverns National Park,* see section 407 of this title). Proc. No. 1679, Oct. 25, 1923, 43 Stat. 1929.

Casa Grande National Monument, Arizona. - Proc. No. 1470, Aug. 3, 1918, 40 Stat. 1818.

Castillo de San Marcos National Monument, Florida (Monument changed from Fort Marion National Monument by act June 5, 1942, ch. 337, 56 Stat. 312). - Proc. No. 1713, Oct. 15, 1924, 43 Stat. 1968.

Castle Pinckney National Monument, South Carolina. - Proc. No. 1713, Oct. 15, 1924, 43 Stat. 1968.

Cedar Breaks National Monument, Utah. - Proc. No. 2054, Aug. 22, 1933, 48 Stat. 1705.

Chaco Canyon National Monument, New Mexico (Monument abolished and funds made available to Chaco Culture National Historical Park, see section 410ii-I(a) of this title). - Proc. No. 740, Mar. 11, 1907, 35 Stat. 2119; Proc. No. 1826, Jan. 10, 1928, 45 Stat. 2937.

Channel Islands National Monument, California (Monument abolished and incorporated in Channel Islands National Park, see section 410ff of this title). - Proc. No. 2281, Apr. 26, 1938, 52 Stat. 1541; Proc. No. 2825, Feb. 9, 1949, 63 Stat. 1258.

Chesapeake and Ohio Canal National Monument, Maryland. - Proc. No. 3391, Jan. 18, 1961, 75 Stat. 1023.

Chiricahua National Monument, Arizona. - Proc. No. 1692, Apr. 18, 1924, 43 Stat. 1946; Proc. No. 2288, June 10, 1938, 52 Stat. 1551.

Cinder Cone National Monument, California. - Proc. No. 753, May 6, 1907, 35 Stat. 2131.

Colonial National Monument, Virginia (Monument redesignated Colonial National Historical Park, see section 81 of this title). - Proc. No. 1929, Dec. 30, 1930, 46 Stat. 3041; Proc. No. 2055, Aug. 22, 1933, 48 Stat. 1706.

Colorado National Monument, Colorado. - Proc. No. 1126, May 24, 1911, 37 Stat. 1681; Proc. No. 2037, Mar. 3, 1933, 47 Stat. 2563; Proc. No. 3307, Aug. 7, 1959, 73 Stat. c69.

Craters of the Moon National Monument, Idaho. - Proc. No. 1694, May 2, 1924, 43 Stat. 1947; Proc. No. 1843, July 23, 1928, 45 Stat. 2959; Proc. No. 1916, July 9, 1930, 46 Stat. 3029; Proc. No. 2499, July 18,

1941, 55 Stat. 1660; Proc. No. 3506, Nov. 19, 1962, 77 Stat. 960.

Death Valley National Monument, California and Nevada. - Proc. No. 2028, Feb. 11, 1933, 47 Stat. 2554; Proc. No. 2228, Mar. 26, 1937, 50 Stat. 1823; Proc. No. 2961, Jan. 17, 1952, 66 Stat. c18.

Denali National Monument, Alaska. - Proc. No. 4616, Dec. 1, 1978, 93 Stat. 1455.

Devil Postpile National Monument, California. - Proc. No. 1166, July 6, 1911, 37 Stat. 1715.

Devils Tower National Monument, Wyoming. - Proc. No. 658, Sept. 24, 1906, 34 Stat. 3236; act Aug. 9, 1955, ch. 647, 69 Stat. 575.

Dinosaur National Monument, Utah-Colorado. - Proc. No. 1313, Oct. 4, 1915, 39 Stat. 1752; Proc. No. 2290, July 14, 1938, 53 Stat. 2454; Pub. L. 100-701, Sec. 2-4, Nov. 19, 1988, 102 Stat. 4641.

Edison Laboratory National Monument, New Jersey (Monument and Edison Home National Historic Site together with certain adjacent lands redesignated Edison National Historic Site by Pub. L. 87-628, Sec. 1, Sept. 5, 1962, 76 Stat. 428). - Proc. No. 3148, July 14, 1956, 70 Stat. c49.

Effigy Mounds National Monument, Iowa. - Proc. No. 2860, Oct. 25, 1949, 64 Stat. a371.

El Morro National Monument, New Mexico. - Proc. No. 695, Dec. 8, 1906, 34 Stat. 3264; Proc. No. 1377, June 18, 1917, 40 Stat. 1673.

Fort Jefferson National Monument, Florida (Monument abolished and incorporated in Dry Tortugas National Park, see section 410xx of this title). - Proc. No. 2112, Jan. 4, 1935, 49 Stat. 3430; Pub. L. 96-287, title II, June 28, 1980, 94 Stat. 600; Pub. L. 102-525, title II, Sec. 201(c), Oct. 26, 1992, 106 Stat. 3440.

Fort Laramie National Monument, Wyoming (Monument redesignated Fort Laramie Historic Site by Pub. L. 86-444, Sec. 3, Apr. 29, 1960, 74 Stat. 84). - Proc. No. 2292, July 16, 1938, 53 Stat. 2461.

Fort Marion National Monument, Florida (Monument redesignated Castillo de San Marcos National Monument by act June 5, 1942, ch. 337, 56 Stat. 312). - Proc. No. 1713, Oct. 15, 1924, 43 Stat. 1968.

Fort Matanzas National Monument, Florida. - Proc. No. 1713, Oct. 15, 1924, 43 Stat. 1968; Proc. No. 2114, Jan. 9, 1935, 49 Stat. 3433; Proc. No. 2773, Mar. 24, 1948, 62 Stat. 1491.

Fort Niagara National Monument, New York. - Proc. No. 1745, Sept. 5, 1925, 44 Stat. 2582.

Fort Pulaski National Monument, Georgia. - Proc. No. 1713, Oct. 15, 1924, 43 Stat. 1968.

Fort Wood National Monument, New York. - Proc. No. 1713, Oct. 15,1924, 43 Stat. 1968.

Fossil Cycad National Monument, South Dakota. - Proc. No. 1641, Oct. 21, 1922, 42 Stat. 2286.

Gates of the Arctic National Monument, Alaska. - Proc. No. 4617, Dec. 1, 1978, 93 Stat. 1457.

Gila Cliff-Dwellings National Monument, New Mexico. -Proc. No. 781, Nov. 16, 1907, 35 Stat. 2162; Proc. No. 3467, Apr. 17, 1962, 76 Stat. 1465.

Glacier Bay National Monument, Alaska (Monument redesignated Glacier Bay National Park, see section 410hh-1(1) of this title). - Proc. No. 1733, Feb. 26, 1925, 43 Stat. 1988; Proc. No. 2330, Apr. 18, 1939, 53 Stat. 2534; Proc. No. 3089, Mar. 31, 1955, 69 Stat. c27; Proc. No. 4618, Dec. 1, 1978, 93 Stat. 1458.

Grand Canyon National Monument, Arizona. - Proc. No. 794, Jan. 11, 1908, 35 Stat. 2175; Proc. No. 2022, Dec. 22, 1932, 47 Stat. 2547; Proc. No. 2393, Apr. 4, 1940, 54 Stat. 2692.

Gran Quivira National Monument, New Mexico (Monument abolished and funds made available to Salinas National Monument by Pub. L. 96-550, title VI, Sec. 601(b), Dec. 19, 1980, 94 Stat. 3231.

Salinas National Monument redesignated Salinas Pueblo Missions National Monument by Pub. L. 100-559, title I, Sec. 101, Oct. 28, 1988, 102 Stat. 2797). - Proc. No. 882, Nov. 1, 1909, 36 Stat. 2503; Proc. No. 1545, Nov. 25, 1919, 41 Stat. 1778.

Great Sand Dunes National Monument, Colorado. - Proc. No. 1994, Mar. 17, 1932, 47 Stat. 2506; Proc. No. 2681, Mar. 12, 1946, 60 Stat. 1339; Proc. No. 3138, June 7, 1956, 70 Stat. c31.

Holy Cross National Monument, Colorado (Monument abolished by act Aug. 3, 1950, ch. 530, 64 Stat. 404). - Proc. No. 1877, May 11, 1929, 46 Stat. 2993.

Hovenweep National Monument, Colorado-Utah. - Proc. No. 1654, Mar. 2, 1923, 42 Stat. 2299; Proc. No. 2924, Apr. 26, 1951, 65 Stat. c8; Proc. No. 2998, Nov. 20, 1952, 67 Stat. c21; Proc. No. 3132, Apr. 6, 1956, 70 Stat. c26.

Jackson Hole National Monument, Wyoming (Monument abolished and incorporated in Grand Teton National Park, see section 406d-1 of this title). - Proc. No. 2578, Mar.
15, 1943, 57 Stat. 731.

Jewel Cave National Monument, South Dakota. - Proc. No. 799, Feb. 7, 1908, 35 Stat. 2180.

Joshua Tree National Monument, California (see section 450ii of this title). - Proc. No. 2193, Aug. 10, 1936, 50 Stat. 1760.

Katmai National Monument, Alaska (Monument redesignated Katmi National Park, see section 410hh-1(2) of this title). - Proc. No. 1487, Sept. 24, 1918, 40 Stat. 1855; Proc. No. 1950, Apr. 24, 1931, 47 Stat. 2453; Proc. No. 2177, June 15, 1936, 49 Stat. 3523;

Proc. No. 2564, Aug. 4, 1942, 56 Stat. 1972; Proc. No. 3890, Jan. 20, 1969, 83 Stat. 926; Proc. No. 4619, Dec. I, 1978, 93 Stat. 1460.

Kenai Fjords National Monument, Alaska. - Proc. No. 4620, Dec. I, 1978, 93 Stat. 1462.

Kobuk Valley National Monument, Alaska. - Proc. No. 4621, Dec. I, 1978, 93 Stat. 1463.

Lake Clark National Monument, Alaska. - Proc. No. 4622, Dec. I,1978, 93 Stat. 1465.

Lassen Peak National Monument, California. - Proc. No. 754, May 6, 1907, 35 Stat. 2132.

Lava Beds National Monument, California. - Proc. No. 1755, Nov. 21, 1925, 44 Stat. 2591;i Proc. No. 2925, Apr. 27, 1951, 65 Stat. c9.

Lehman Caves National Monument, Nevada (Monument abolished and lands incorporated in, and funds made available for, Great Basin National Park, see section 410mm(d) of this title). - Proc. No. 1618, Jan. 24, 1922, 42 Stat. 2260.

Lewis and Clark Cavern National Monument, Montana. - Proc. No. 807, May 11, 1908, 35 Stat. 2187; Proc. No. 1123, May 16, 1911, 37 Stat. 1679.

Marble Canyon National Monument, Arizona. - Proc. No. 3889, Jan. 20, 1969, 83 Stat. 924.

Meriwether Lewis National Monument, Tennessee (Monument included in Natchez Trace Parkway, see section 460-I of this title). - Proc. No. 1730, Feb. 6, 1925, 43 Stat. 1986; Proc. No. 1825, Dec. 6, 1927, 45 Stat. 2935.

Misty Fjords National Monument, Alaska (Monument established within Tongass National Forest by Pub. L. 96-487, title V, Sec. 503(b), Dec. 2, 1980, 94 Stat. 2399). - Proc. No. 4623, Dec. I, 1978, 93 Stat. 1466.

Montezuma Castle National Monument, Arizona. - Proc. No. 696, Sept. 8, 1906, 93 Stat. 3265; Proc. No. 2226, Feb. 23, 1937, 50 Stat. 1817.

Mound City Group National Monument, Ohio (Monument redesignated Hopewell Culture National Historic Park, see section 401uu of this title). - Proc. No. 1653, Mar. 2, 1923, 42 Stat. 2298; Pub. L. 96-607, title VII, Sec. 701, Dec. 28, 1980, 94 Stat. 3540.

Mount Olympus National Monument, Washington (Monument abolished and lands incorporated in Mount Olympus National Park, see section 251 of this title). - Proc. No. 869, Mar. 2, 1909, 35 Stat. 2247; Proc. No. 1191, Apr. 17, 1912, 37 Stat. 1737; Proc. No. 1293, May 11, 1915, 39 Stat. 1726; Proc. No. 1862, Jan. 7, 1929, 45 Stat. 2984.

Muir Woods National Monument, California. - Proc. No. 793, Jan. 9, 1908, 35 Stat. 2174; Proc. No. 1608, Sept. 22, 1921, 42 Stat. 2249; Proc. No. 2122, Apr. 5, 1935, 49 Stat. 3443; Proc. No. 2932, June 26, 1951, 65 Stat. c20; Proc. No. 3311, Sept. 8, 1959, 73 Stat. c76.

Mukuntuweap National Monument, Utah (Monument redesignated Zion National Monument by Proc. No. 1435, Mar. 18, 1918, 40 Stat. 1760, and later redesignated Zion National Park, see section 344 of this title). - Proc. No. 877, July 31, 1909, 36 Stat. 2498.

Natural Bridges National Monument, Utah. - Proc. No. 804, Apr. 16, 1908, 35 Stat. 2183; Proc. No. 881, Sept. 25, 1909, 36 Stat. 2502; Proc. No. 1323, Feb. 11, 1916, 39 Stat. 1764; Proc. No. 3486, Aug. 14, 1962, 76 Stat. 1495.

Navajo National Monument, Arizona. - Proc. No. 873, May 20, 1909, 36 Stat. 2491; Proc. No. 1186, Mar. 14, 1912, 37 Stat. 1733.

Noatak National Monument, Alaska. - Proc. No. 4624, Dec. 1, 1978, 93 Stat. 1468.

Ocmulgee National Monument, Georgia (see section 447a of this title). - Proc. No. 2212, Dec. 23, 1936, 50 Stat. 1798; Proc. No. 2493, June 13, 1941, 55 Stat. 1654; Pub. L. 102-67~ July 9, 1991, 105 Stat. 325.

Old Kasaan National Monument, Alaska (Monument abolished and incorporated in Tongass National Forest by act July 26, 1955, ch. 387, 69 Stat. 380). - Proc. No. 1351, Oct. 25, 1916, 39 Stat. 1812.

Oregon Caves National Monument, Oregon. - Proc. No. 876, July 12, 1909, 36 Stat. 2497.

Organ Pipe Cactus National Monument, Arizona. - Proc. No. 2232, Apr. 13, 1937, 50 Stat. 1827.

Papago Saguaro National Monument, Arizona. - Proc. No. 1262, Jan. 31, 1914, 38 Stat. 1991.

Perry's Victory and International Peace Memorial National Monument, Ohio. - Proc. No. 2182, July 6, 1936, 50 Stat. 1734.

Petrified Forest National Monument (Monument disestablished on establishment of Petrified Forest National Park, see sections 119 and 444 of this title). - Proc. No. 697, Dec. 8, 1906, 34 Stat. 3266; Proc. No. 1167, July 31, 1911, 37 Stat. 1716; Proc. No. 1927, Nov. 14, 1930, 46 Stat.

3040; Proc. No. 1975, Nov. 30, 1931, 47 Stat. 2486; Proc. No. 2011, Sept. 23, 1932, 47 Stat. 2532.

Pinnacles National Monument, California. - Proc. No. 796, Jan. 16, 1908, 35 Stat. 2177i Proc. No. 1660, May 7, 1923, 43 Stat. 1911. Proc. No. 1704, July 2, 1924, 43 Stat. 1961; Proc. No. 1948, Apr. 13, 1931, 47 Stat. 2451; Proc. No. 2050, July 11, 1933, 48 Stat. 1701; Proc. No. 2528, Dec. 5, 1941, 55 Stat. 1709.

Pipe Spring National Monument, Arizona. - Proc. No. 1663, May 31, 1923, 43 Stat. 1913.

Port Chicago National Memorial, California. - Pub. L. 102-562, title II, Oct. 28, 1992, 106 Stat. 4235.

Rainbow Bridge National Monument, Utah. - Proc. No. 1043, May 30, 1910, 36 Stat. 2703.

Russell Cave National Monument, Alabama. - Proc. No. 3413, May 11, 1961, 75 Stat. 1058.

Saguaro National Monument, Arizona. - Proc. No. 2032, Mar. 1, 1933, 47 Stat. 2557; Proc. No. 3439, Nov. 15, 1961, 76 Stat. 1437; Pub. L. 102-61, June 19, 1991, 105 Stat. 303.

Santa Rosa Island National Monument, Florida. - Proc. No. 2337, May 17, 1939, 53 Stat. 2542; Proc. No. 2659, Aug. 13, 1945, 59 Stat. 877.

Scotts Bluff National Monument, Nebraska. - Proc. No. 1547, Dec. 12, 1919, 41 Stat. 1779; Proc. No. 1999, June 1, 1932, 47 Stat. 2512; Proc. No. 2391, Mar. 29, 1940, 54 Stat. 2690.

Shoshone Cavern National Monument, Wyoming (Monument abolished by act May 17, 1954, ch. 203, 68 Stat. 98). - Proc. No. 880, Sept. 21, 1909, 36 Stat. 2501.

Sieur de Monts National Monument, Maine. - Proc. No. 1339, July 8, 1916, 39 Stat. 1785.

Sitka National Monument, Alaska (Monument redesignated Sitka National Historical Park by Pub. L. 92-501, Oct. 18, 1972, 86 Stat. 904). - Proc. No. 959, Mar. 23, 1910, 36 Stat. 2601; Proc. No. 2965, Feb. 25, 1952, 66 Stat. c22.

Statue of Liberty National Monument. - Proc. No. 1713, Oct. 15, 1924, 43 Stat. 1968; Proc. No. 2250, Sept. 7, 1937, 51 Stat. 393; Proc. No. 3656, May 11, 1965, 79 Stat. 1490.

Sunset Crater Volcano National Monument, Arizona (Monument changed from Sunset Crater National Monument by Pub. L. 101-612, Sec. 15, Nov. 16, 1990, 104 Stat. 3222). - Proc. No. 1911, May 26, 1930, 46 Stat. 3023.

Timpanogos Cave National Monument, Utah. - Proc. No. 1640, Oct. 14, 1922, 42 Stat. 2285; Proc. No. 3457, Mar. 27, 1962, 76 Stat. 1457.

Tonto National Monument, Arizona. - Proc. No. 787, Dec. 19, 1907, 35 Stat. 2168; Proc. No. 2230, Apr. 1, 1937, 50 Stat. 1825.

Tumacacori National Monument, Arizona (Monument abolished and lands incorporated in, and funds made available for, Tumacacori National Historical Park, see section 410ss of this title). - Proc. No. 821, Sept. 15, 1908, 35 Stat. 2205; Proc. No. 3228, Mar. 28, 1958, 72 Stat. c30.

Tuzigoot National Monument, Arizona. - Proc. No. 2344, July 25, 1939, 53 Stat. 2548.

Verendrye National Monument, North Dakota. - Proc. No. 1380, June 29, 1917, 40 Stat. 1677.

Walnut Canyon National Monument, Arizona. - Proc. No. 1318, Nov. 30, 1915, 39 Stat. 1761; Proc. No. 2300, Sept. 24, 1938, 53 Stat. 2469.

Wheeler National Monument, Colorado (Monument abolished by act Aug. 3, 1950, ch. 534, 64 Stat. 405). - Proc. No. 831, Dec. 7, 1908, 35 Stat. 2214.

White Sands National Monument, New Mexico. - Proc. No. 2025, Jan. 18, 1933, 47 Stat. 2551; Proc. No. 2108, Nov. 28, 1934, 49 Stat. 3426; Proc. No. 2295, Aug. 29, 1938, 53 Stat. 2465; Proc. No. 3024, June 24, 1953, 67 Stat. c53.

Wrangell-St. Elias National Monument, Alaska. - Proc. No. 4625, Dec. 1, 1978, 93 Stat. 1470.

Wupatki National Monument, Arizona. - Proc. No. 1721, Dec. 9, 1924, 43 Stat. 1977; Proc. No. 2243, July 9, 1937, 52 Stat. 1841; Proc. No. 2454, Jan. 20, 1941, 55 Stat. 1608.

Yucca House National Monument, Colorado. - Proc. No. 1549, Dec. 19, 1919, 41 Stat. 1781.

Yukon-Charley National Monument, Alaska. - Proc. No. 4626, Dec. 1, 1978, 93 Stat. 1472.

Yukon Flats National Monument, Alaska. - Proc. No. 4627, Dec. 1, 1978, 93 Stat. 1473.

Zion National Monument, Utah (Monument combined with Zion National Park into a single National park unit, see section 346b of this title. A prior Zion National Monument, formerly Mukuntuweap National Monument, Proc. No. 877, July 31, 1909, 36 Stat. 2498, and Proc. No. 1435, Mar. 18, 1918, 40 Stat. 1760, was redesignated Zion National Park, see section 344 of this title). - Proc. No. 2221, Jan. 22, 1937, 50 Stat. 1809.

Miscellaneous National Monuments

Agate Fossil Beds National Monument, Nebraska. - Pub. L. 89-33, June 5, 1965, 79 Stat. 123.

Alibates Flint Quarries National Monument, Texas. - Pub. L. 89-154, Aug. 31, 1965, 79 Stat. 587. Name changed from Alibates Flint Quarries and Texas Panhandle Pueblo Culture National Monument by Pub. L. 95-625, title III, Sec. 321(c), Nov. 10, 1978, 92 Stat. 3488.

Congaree Swamp National Monument, South Carolina. - Pub. L. 94-545, Oct. 18, 1976, 90 Stat. 2517, as amended by Pub. L. 100-524, Sec. 5, 6, Oct. 24, 1988, 102 Stat. 2607.

El Malpais National Monument, New Mexico. - Pub. L. 100-225, title I, Sec. 101-104, Dec. 31, 1987, 101 Stat. 1539 (16 U.S.C. 460uu et seq.).

Florissant Fossil Beds National Monument, Colorado. - Pub. L. 91-60, Aug. 20, 1969, 83 Stat. 101.

Fossil Butte National Monument, Wyoming. - Pub. L. 92-537, Oct. 23, 1972, 86 Stat. 1069.

Hagerman Fossil Beds National Monument, Idaho. - Pub. L. 100-696, title III, Sec. 301-308, Nov. 18, 1988, 102 Stat. 4575, as amended by Pub. L. 101-512, title I, Nov. 5, 1990, 104 Stat. 1923.

Hohokam Pima National Monument, Arizona. - Pub. L. 92-525, Oct. 21, 1972, 86 Stat. 1047.

John Day Fossil Beds National Monument, Oregon. - Pub. L. 93-486, title I, Sec. 101(a)(2), Oct. 26, 1974, 88 Stat. 1461.

Kill Devil National Monument, North Carolina. - Act Mar. 2, 1927, ch. 251, 44 Stat. 1264. Name change to Wright Brothers National Memorial, Dec. 1, 1953.

Little Bighorn Battlefield National Monument, Montana. - Pub. L. 102-201, titles I, II, Dec. 10, 1991, 105 Stat. 1631.

Mount St. Helens National Volcanic Monument, Washington. - Pub. L. 97-243, Aug. 26, 1982, 96 Stat. 301.

Newberry National Volcanic Monument, Oregon. - Pub. L. 101-522, Nov. 5, 1990, 104 Stat. 2288.

Pecos National Monument, New Mexico (included in Pecos National Historical Park by Pub. L. 101-313, title II, Sec. 202(b), June 27, 1990, 104 Stat. 278 (16 U.S.C. 410rr-1(b))). - Pub. L. 89-54, June 28, 1965, 79 Stat. 195; repealed by Pub. L. 101-313, title II, Sec. 202(c), June 27, 1990, 104 Stat. 278 (16 U.S.C. 410rr-1(c)).

Petroglyph National Monument, New Mexico. - Pub. L. 101-313, title I, June 27, 1990, 104 Stat. 272, as amended by Pub. L. 103-50, ch. IV, Sec.

401, July 2, 1993, 107 Stat. 252.

Poverty Point National Monument, Louisiana. - Pub. L. 100-560, Oct. 31, 1988, 102 Stat. 2803.

Salinas Pueblo Missions National Monument, New Mexico. - Pub. L. 96-550, title VI, Sec. 601, Dec. 19, 1980, 94 Stat. 3231, as amended by Pub. L. 100-559, title I, Sec. 101, Oct. 28, 1988, 102 Stat. 2797.

National Memorials

Arkansas Post National Memorial, Arkansas. - Pub. L. 86-595, July 6, 1960, 74 Stat. 333.

Astronauts Memorial, John F. Kennedy Space Center, Florida. Recognized as national memorial to astronauts who die in line of duty by Pub. L. 102-41, May 8, 1991, 105 Stat. 242.

Benjamin Franklin National Memorial, Pennsylvania. - Designation of Benjamin Franklin Memorial Hall as National Memorial by Pub. L. 92-551, Oct. 25, 1972, 86 Stat. 1164.

Chamizal National Memorial, Texas. - Pub. L. 89-479, June 30, 1966, 80 Stat. 232.

Coronado National Memorial, Arizona. - Acts Aug. 18, 1941, ch. 365, Sec. 1, 55 Stat. 630, and July 9, 1952, ch. 610, 66 Stat. 510 (16 U.S.C. 450y); Proc. No. 2995, Nov. 5, 1952, 67 Stat. c18.

Custis-Lee Mansion National Memorial, Virginia. - Act Mar. 4, 1925, ch. 562, 43 Stat 1356. Made permanent memorial by act June 29, 1955, ch. 223, 69 Stat. 190.

David Berger Memorial, Ohio. - Pub. L. 96-199, title I, Sec. 116, Mar. 5, 1980, 94 Stat. 71.

Disabled American Veterans Vietnam Veterans National Memorial, New Mexico. - Recognized as a memorial of national significance by Pub. L. 100-164, Nov. 13, 1987, 101 Stat. 905.

Father Marquette National Memorial, Michigan. - Pub. L. 94-160, Dec. 20, 1975, 89 Stat. 848.

Federal Hall National Memorial, New York. - Designated May 26, 1939. Designation changed from Federal Hall Memorial Historic Site by act Aug. 11, 1955, ch. 779, 69 Stat. 632.

Fort Caroline National Memorial, Florida. - Act Sept. 21, 1950, ch. 973, 64 Stat. 897. Established Jan. 16, 1953.

Franklin Delano Roosevelt National Memorial, District of Columbia. - Pub. L. 97-224, July 28, 1982, 96 Stat. 243.

Hamilton Grange National Memorial, New York. - Pub. L. 87-438, Apr. 27,

1962, 76 Stat. 57, as amended by Pub. L. 100-701, Sec. 1, Nov. 19, 1988, 102 Stat. 4640.

House Where Lincoln Died National Memorial, District of Columbia. Act June 11, 1896, ch. 420, 29 Stat. 439.

Johnstown Flood National Memorial, Pennsylvania. - Pub. L. 88-546, Aug. 31, 1964, 78 Stat. 752.

Lincoln Boyhood National Memorial, Indiana. - Pub. L. 87-407, Feb. 19, 1962, 76 Stat. 9.

Lincoln Museum National Memorial, District of Columbia. - Act Apr. 7, 1866, ch. 28, Sec. 1, 14 Stat. 23.

Lincoln National Memorial, District of Columbia. - Act Feb. 9, 1911, ch. 42, 36 Stat. 898.

Mount Rushmore National Memorial, South Dakota. - Act Feb. 25, 1929, ch. 315, 45 Stat. 1300.

National Fallen Firefighters' Memorial, Maryland. - Pub. L. 101-347, Aug. 9, 1990, 104 Stat. 398.

Patrick Henry National Memorial, Virginia. - Pub. L. 99-296, May 12, 1986, 100 Stat. 429.

Seabees of the United States Navy Memorial. - Pub. L. 92-422, Sept. 18, 1972, 86 Stat. 678.

Signers of the Declaration of Independence Memorial, District of Columbia. - Pub. L. 95-260, Apr. 17, 1978, 92 Stat. 197.

Thomas Jefferson National Memorial, District of Columbia. - Act June 26, 1934, ch. 763, 48 Stat. 1243.

United States Marine Corps Memorial, Virginia. - Act July 1, 1947, ch. 196, 61 Stat. 242, as amended July 7, 1952, ch. 585, 66 Stat. 441; June 16, 1953, ch. 120, 67 Stat. 64.

United States Navy Memorial, District of Columbia. - Pub. L. 96-199, title I, Sec. 113, Mar. 5, 1980, 94 Stat. 70.

U.S.S. Indianapolis Memorial, Indiana. - Pub. L. 103-160, div. A, title XI, Sec. 1165, Nov. 30, 1993, 107 Stat. 1765.

Vietnam Veterans Memorial, District of Columbia. - Pub. L. 96-297, July 1, 1980, 94 Stat. 827.

Washington Monument National Memorial, District of Columbia. - Act Aug. Z. 1876, ch. 250, Sec. 1, 19 Stat. 123.

Wright Brothers National Memorial, North Carolina. - Kill Devil Hill National Monument authorized by act Mar. 2, 1927, ch. 251, 44 Stat. 1264. Name changed to Wright Brothers National Memorial, Dec. 1, 1953.

ALBERT EINSTEIN MEMORIAL
Conveyance of property to National Academy of Sciences for erection and maintenance of a Memorial to Albert Einstein on south side of Square Numbered 88 between 21st Street, 22d Street, and Constitution Avenue, District of Columbia, with reverter of title when no longer used for memorial purposes or public access is restricted, was authorized by Pub. L. 95-625, title VI, Sec. 612, Nov. 10, 1978, 92 Stat. 3521, as amended Pub. L. 96-87, title IV, Sec. 401(o), Oct. 12, 1979, 93 Stat. 666.

STUDY TO ADD ALASKA AND HAWAII TO LINCOLN NATIONAL MEMORIAL
Pub. L. 94-556, Oct. 19, 1976, 90 Stat. 2632, directed Secretary of the Interior to study feasibility of and make recommendations for recognition at an appropriate place at Lincoln National Memorial of the addition to the Union of the States of Alaska and Hawaii, directed that recommendations, after review and approval by Commission of Fine Arts, National Capital Planning Commission, and Advisory Council on Historic Preservation, be submitted to Committees on Interior and Insular Affairs of the Senate and the House of Representatives, and, if neither committee adopted a resolution of disapproval, directed Secretary to carry out recommendations.

CROSS REFERENCE
National Capital memorials and commemorative works, see section 1001 et seq. of Title 40, Public Buildings, Property, and Works.

SECTION REFERRED TO IN OTHER SECTIONS
This section is referred to in sections 407, 410mm, 432, 434, 470cc, 470dd, 1133 of this title; title 43 section 1714.

APPENDIX G

(USC Title 16, Section 1)
Historic Sites Act of 1935
16 USC Sections 461-467

Sec. 461. Declaration of national policy
It is declared that it is a national policy to preserve for public use historic sites, buildings, and objects of national significance for the inspiration and benefit of the people of the United States. (Aug. 21, 1935, ch 593, sec. 1,49 Stat. 666.)

Sec. 462. Administration by Secretary of the Interior; powers and duties enumerated
The Secretary of the Interior (hereinafter in sections 461 to 467 of this title referred to as the Secretary), through the National Park Service, for the purpose of effectuating the policy expressed in section 461 of this title, shall have the following powers and perform the following duties and functions:
(a) Secure, collate, and preserve drawings, plans, photographs, and other data of historic and archaeologic sites, buildings, and objects.
(b) Make a survey of historic and archaeologic sites,
buildings, and objects for the purpose of determining which possess exceptional value as commemorating or illustrating the history of the United States.
(c) Make necessary investigations and researches in the United States relating to particular sites, buildings, or objects to obtain true and accurate historical and archaeological facts and information concerning the same.
(d) For the purpose of sections 461 to 467 of this title, acquire in the name of the United States by gift, purchase, or otherwise any property, personal or real, or any interest or estate therein, title to any real property to be satisfactory to the Secretary: Provided, That no such property which is owned by any religious or educational institution, or which is owned or administered for the benefit of the public shall be so acquired without the consent of the owner: Provided further, That no such property shall be acquired or contract or agreement for the acquisition thereof made which will obligate the general fund of the Treasury

for the payment of such property, unless or until Congress has appropriated money which is available for that purpose.

(e) Contract and make cooperative agreements with States, municipal subdivisions, corporations, associations, or individuals, with proper bond where deemed advisable, to protect, preserve, maintain, or operate any historic or archaeologic building, site, object, or property used in connection therewith for public use, regardless as to whether the title thereto is in the United States: Provided, That no contract of cooperative agreement shall be made or entered into which will obligate the general fund of the Treasury unless or until Congress has appropriated money for such purpose.

(f) Restore, reconstruct, rehabilitate, preserve, and maintain historic or prehistoric sites, buildings, objects, and properties of national historical or archaeological significance and where deemed desirable establish and maintain museums in connection therewith.

(g) Erect and maintain tablets to mark or commemorate historic or prehistoric places and events of national historical or archaeological significance.

(h) Operate and manage historic and archaeologic sites, buildings, and properties acquired under the provisions of sections 461 to 467 of this title together with lands and subordinate buildings for the benefit of the public, such authority to include the power to charge reasonable visitation fees and grant concessions, leases, or permits for the use of land, building space, roads, or trails when necessary or desirable either to accommodate the public or to facilitate administration: Provided,

That the Secretary may grant such concessions, leases, or permits and enter into contracts relating to the same with responsible persons, firms, or corporations without advertising and without securing competitive bids.

191

APPENDIX H

Archaeological Resources Protection Act of 1979 (ARPA)

AN ACT To protect archaeological resources on public lands and Indian lands, and for other purposes. Be it enacted of the Senate and the house of Representatives of the United States of America in Congress assembled,

SHORT TITLE
Section I. This Act may be cited as the "Archaeological Resources Protection Act of 1979."

FINDINGS AND PURPOSE
SEC. 2 (a) The Congress finds that (1) archaeological resources on public lands and Indian lands are an accessible and irreplaceable part of the Nation's heritage, (2) these resources are increasingly endangered because of their commercial attractiveness, (3) existing Federal laws do not provide adequate protection to prevent the loss and destruction of these archaeological resources and sites resulting from uncontrolled excavations and pillage; and (4) there is a wealth of archaeological information which has been legally obtained by private individuals for noncommercial purposes and which could voluntarily be made available to professional archaeologists and institutions.

(b) The purpose of this Act is to secure, for the present and future benefit of the American people, the protection of archaeological resources and sites which are on public lands and Indian lands, and to foster increased cooperation and exchange of information between governmental authorities, the professional archaeological community, and private individuals having collections of archaeological resources and data which were obtained before the date of the enactment of this Act.

DEFINITIONS
SEC. 3. As used in this Act—

(1) The term "archaeological resource" means any material remains of past human life or activities which are of archaeological interest, as determined under the uniform regulations promulgated pursuant to this Act. Such regulations containing such determination shall include, but

not be limited to: pottery, basketry, bottles, weapons, weapon projectiles, tools, structures or portions of structures, pit houses, rock paintings, rock carvings, intaglios, graves, human skeletal materials, or any portion or piece of any of the foregoing items. Nonfossilized and fossilized paleontological specimens, or any portion or piece thereof, shall not be considered archaeological resources, under the regulations under this paragraph, unless found in an archaeological context. No item shall be treated as an archaeological resource under regulations under this paragraph unless such item is at least 100 years of age.

(2) The term "Federal land manager" means, with respect to any public lands, the Secretary of the department, or the head of any other agency or instrumentality of the United States, having primary management authority over such lands. In the case of any public lands or Indian lands with respect to which no department, agency, or instrumentality has primary management authority, such term means the Secretary of the Interior. If the Secretary of the Interior consents, the responsibilities (in whole or in part) under this Act of the Secretary of any department (other than the Department of the Interior) or the head of any other agency or instrumentality may be delegated to the Secretary of the Interior with respect to any land managed by such other Secretary or agency head, and in any such case, the term "Federal land manager" means the Secretary of the Interior.

(3) The term "public lands" means (A) lands which are owned and administered by the United States as part of (i) the national park system, (ii) the national wildlife refuge system, or (iii) the national forest system; and (B) all other lands the fee title to which is held by the United States, other than lands on the Outer Continental Shelf and lands which are under the jurisdiction of the Smithsonian Institution,

(4) The term "Indian lands" means lands of Indian tribes, or Indian individuals, which are either held in trust by the United States or subject to a restriction against alienation imposed by the United States, except for any subsurface interest in lands not owned or controlled by an Indian tribe or an Indian individual.

(5) The term "Indian tribe" means any Indian tribe, band, nation, or other organized group or community, including any Alaska Native village or regional or village corporation as defined in, or established pursuant to, the Alaska Native Claims Settlement Act (85 Stat. 688).

(6) The term "person" means an individual, corporation, partnership, trust, institution, association, or any other private entity or any officer,

employee, agent, department, or instrumentality of the United States, of any Indian tribe, or of any State or political subdivision thereof.

(7) The term "State" means any of the fifty States, the District of Columbia, Puerto Rico, Guam, and the Virgin Islands.

194

EXCAVATION AND REMOVAL

SEC. 4. (a) Any person may apply to the Federal land manager for a permit to excavate or remove any archaeological resource located on public lands or Indian lands and to carry out activities associated with such excavation or removal. The application shall be required, under uniform regulations under this Act, to contain such information as the Federal land manager deems necessary, including information concerning the time, scope, and location and specific purpose of the proposed work. (b) A permit may be issued pursuant to an application under subsection (a) if the Federal land manager determines, pursuant to uniform regulations under this Act, that- (I) the applicant is qualified, to carry out the permitted activity, (2) the activity is undertaken for the purpose of furthering archaeological knowledge in the public interest, (3) the archaeological resources which are excavated or removed from public lands will remain the property of the United States, and such resources and copies of associated archaeological records and data will be preserved by a suitable university, museum, or other scientific or educational institution, and (4) the activity pursuant to such permit is not inconsistent with any management plan applicable to the public lands concerned. (c) If a permit issued under this section may result in harm to, or destruction of, any religious or cultural site, as determined by the Federal land manager, before issuing such permit, the Federal land manager shall notify any Indian tribe which may consider the site as having religious or cultural importance. Such notice shall not be deemed a disclosure to the public for purposes of section 9. (d) Any permit under this section shall contain terms and conditions, pursuant to uniform regulations promulgated under this Act, as the Federal land manager concerned deems necessary to carry out the purposes of this Act. (e) Each permit under this section shall identify the individual who shall be responsible for carrying out the terms and conditions of the permit and for otherwise complying with this Act and other law applicable to the permitted activity. (f) Any permit issued under this section may be suspended by the Federal land manager upon his determination that the permittee has violated any provision of subsection (a), (b), or (c) of section 6. Any such permit may be revoked by such Federal land manager upon assessment of a civil penalty under section 7 against the permittee or upon the permittee's conviction under section 6.)(g)(1) No permit shall be required under this section or under the Act of June 8, 1906 (16 U.S.C. 431), for the excavation or removal by any Indian tribe or member thereof of any archaeological resource located on Indian lands of such Indian tribe, except that in the absence of tribal law regulating the excavation or removal of archaeological resources on Indian lands, an individual tribal member shall be required to obtain a permit under this section. (2) In the case of any permits for the excavation or removal of any archaeological resources located on Indian lands, the permit may be granted only after obtaining the consent of the Indian or Indian tribe owning or having jurisdiction over such lands. The permit shall include such terms and conditions as may be requested by such Indian or Indian tribe. (h)(1) No permit or other permission shall be required under the Act of June 8, 1906 (16 U.S.C. 431-433), for any activity for which a permit is issued under this section. (2) Any permit issued under the Act of June 8, 1906, shall remain in effect according to its terms and conditions following the enactment of this Act. No permit shall be required to carry out any activity under a permit issued under the Act of June 8, 1906, before the date of the enactment of this Act which remains in effect as provided in this paragraph, and nothing in this Act shall modify or affect any such permit. (i) Issuance of a permit in accordance with this section and applicable regulations shall not require compliance with section 106 of the Act of October 15, 1966 (80 Stat. 917, 16 U.S.C. 470f). (j) Upon the written request of the Governor of any State, the Federal land manager shall issue a permit, subject to the provisions of subsections (b)(3), (b)(4), (c), (e), (f), (g), (h), and (i) of this section for the purpose of conducting archaeological research, excavation, removal, and curation, on behalf of the State or its educational institutions, to such Governor or to such designee as the Governor deems qualified to carry out the intent of this Act.

CUSTODY OF RESOURCES

Sec. 5. The Secretary of the Interior may promulgate regulations providing for (1) the exchange, where appropriate, between suitable universities, museums, or other scientific or educational institutions, of archaeological resources removed from public lands and Indian lands pursuant to this Act, and (2) the ultimate disposition of such resources and other resources removed pursuant to the Act of June 27, 1960 (16 U.S.C. 469-469c) or the Act of June 8, 1906 (16 U.S.C. 431-433). Any exchange or ultimate disposition under such regulation of archaeological resources excavated or removed from Indian lands shall be subject to the consent of the Indian or Indian tribe which owns or has jurisdiction over such lands. Following promulgation of regulations, under this section, notwithstanding any other provision of law, such regulations shall govern the disposition of archaeological resources removed from public lands and Indian lands pursuant to this Act.

PROHIBITED ACTS AND CRIMINAL PENALTIES

Sec. 6. (a) No person may excavate, remove, damage, or otherwise alter or deface any archaeological resource located on public lands or Indian lands unless such activity is pursuant to a permit issued under section 4, a permit referred to in section 4(h)(2), or the exemption contained in section 4(g)(1). (b)No person may sell, purchase, exchange, transport, receive, or offer to sell, purchase, or exchange any archaeological resource if such resource was excavated or removed from public lands or Indian lands in violation of (1) the prohibition contained in subsection (a), or (2) any provision, rule, regulation, ordinance, or permit in effect under any other provision of Federal law. (c) No person may sell, purchase, exchange, transport, receive, or offer to sell, purchase, or exchange, in interstate or foreign commerce, any archaeological resource excavated, removed, sold, purchased, exchanged, transported, or received in violation of any provision, rule, regulation, ordinance, or permit in effect under State or local law. (d) Any person who knowingly violates, or counsels, procures, solicits, or employs any other person to violate, any prohibition contained in subsection (a), (b), or (c) of this section shall, upon conviction, be fined not more than $10,000 or imprisoned not more than one year, or both: Provided, however, That if the commercial or archaeological value of the archaeological resources involved and the cost of restoration and repair of such resources exceeds the sum of $5,000, such person shall be fined not more than $20,000 or imprisoned not more than two years, or both. In the case of a second or subsequent such violation upon conviction such person shall be fined not more than $100,000, or imprisoned not more than five years, or both. (e) The prohibitions contained in this section shall take effect on the date of the enactment of this Act. (f) Nothing in subsection (b)(1) of this section shall be deemed applicable to any person with respect to an archaeological resource which was in the lawful possession of such person prior to the date of the enactment of this Act. (g) Nothing in subsection (d) of this section shell be deemed applicable to any person with respect to the removal of arrowheads located on the surface of the ground.

CIVIL PENALTIES

Sec. 7. (a)(I) Any person who violates any prohibition contained in an applicable regulation or permit issued under this Act may be assessed a civil penalty by the Federal land manager concerned. No penalty may be assessed under this subsection unless such person is given notice and opportunity for a hearing with respect to such violation. Each violation shall be a separate offense. Any such civil penalty may be remitted or mitigated by the Federal land manager concerned. (2) The amount of such penalty shall be determined under regulation promulgated pursuant to this Act, taking into account, in addition to other factors-(A) the archaeological or commercial value of the archaeological resource involved, and (B) the cost of restoration and repair of the resource and the archaeological site involved. Such regulations shall provide that, in the case of a second or subsequent violation by any person, the amount of such civil penalty may be double the amount which would have been assessed if such violation were the first violation by such person. The amount of any penalty assessed under this subsection for any violation shall not exceed an amount equal to double the cost of restoration and repair of resources and archaeological sites damaged and double the fair market value of resources destroyed or not recovered. (3) No penalty shall be assessed under this section for the removal of arrowheads located on the surface of the ground. (b)(I) Any person aggrieved by an order assessing a civil penalty under subsection (a) may file a petition for judicial review of such order with the United States District Court for the District of Columbia or for any other district in which such a person resides or transacts business. Such a petition may only be filed within the 30-day period beginning on the date the order making such assessment was issued. The court shall hear such action on the record made before the Federal land manager and shall sustain his action if it is supported by substantial evidence on the record considered as a whole. (2) If any person fails to pay an assessment of a civil penalty (A) after the order making the assessment has become a final order and such person has not filed a petition for judicial review of the order in accordance with paragraph (I), or (B) after a court in an action brought under paragraph (I) has entered a final judgment upholding the assessment of a civil penalty, the Federal land managers may request the Attorney General to institute a civil action in a district court of the United States for any district in which such person is found, resides, or transacts business to collect the penalty and such court shall have jurisdiction to hear and decide any such action. In such action, the validity and amount of such penalty shall not be subject to review. (c) Hearings held during proceedings for the assessment of civil penalties authorized by subsection (a) shall be conducted in accordance with section 554 of title 5 of the United States Code. The Federal land manager may issue subpoenas for the attendance and testimony of witnesses and the production of relevant papers, books, and documents, and administer oaths. Witnesses summoned shall be paid the same fees and mileage that are paid to witnesses in the courts of the United States. In case of contumacy or refusal to obey a subpoena served upon any person pursuant to this paragraph, the district court of the United States for any district in which such person is found or resides or transacts business, upon application by the United States and after notice to such person, shall have jurisdiction to issue an order requiring such person to appear and give testimony before the Federal land manager or to appear and produce documents before the Federal land manager, or both, and any failure to obey such order of the court may be punished by such court as a contempt thereof.

REWARDS; FORFEITURE
Sec. 8. (a) Upon the certification of the Federal land manager concerned, the Secretary of the Treasury is directed to pay from penalties and fines collected under sections 6 and 7 an amount equal to one-half of such penalty or fine, but not to exceed $500, to any person who furnishes information which leads to the finding of a civil violation, or the conviction of criminal violation, with respect to which such penalty or fine was paid. If several persons provided such information, such amount shall be divided among such persons. No officer or employee of the United States or of any service in the performance of his official duties shall be eligible for payment under this subsection. (b) All archaeological resources with respect to which a violation of subsection (a), (b), or (c) of section 6 occurred and which are in the possession of any person, and all vehicles and equipment of any person which were used in con-

nection with such violation, may be (in the discretion of the court or administrative law judge, as the case may be) subject to forfeiture to the United States upon- (1) such person's conviction of such violation under section 6, (2) assessment of a civil penalty against such person under section 7 with respect to such violation, or (3) a determination of any court that such archaeological resources, vehicles, or equipment were involved in such violation. (c) In cases in which a violation of the prohibition contained in subsection (a), (b), or (c) of section 6 involve archaeological resources excavated or removed from Indian lands, the Federal land manager or the court, as the case may be, shall provide for the payment to the Indian or Indian tribe involved of all penalties collected pursuant to section 7 and for the transfer to such Indian or Indian tribe of all items forfeited under this section.

CONFIDENTIALITY
Sec. 9. (a) Information concerning the nature and location of any archaeological resource for which the excavation or removal requires a permit or other permission under this Act or under any other provision of Federal law may not be made available to the public under subchapter II of chapter 5 of title 5 of the United States Code or under any other provision of law unless the Federal land manager concerned determines that such disclosure would (1) further the purposes of this Act or the Act of June 27, 1960 (16 U.S.C. 469-469c), and (2) not create a risk of harm to such resources or to the site at which such resources are located. (b) Notwithstanding the provisions of subsection (a), upon the written request of the Governor of any State, which request shall state (1) the specific site or area for which information is sought, (2) the purpose for which such information is sought, (3) a commitment by the Governor to adequately protect the confidentiality of such information to protect the resource from commercial exploitation, the Federal land manager concerned shall provide to the Governor information concerning the nature and location of archaeological resources within the State of the requesting Governor.

REGULATIONS; INTERGOVERNMENTAL COORDINATION
Sec 10. (a) The Secretaries of the Interior, Agriculture and Defense and the Chairman of the Board of the Tennessee Valley Authority, after public notice and hearing, shall promulgate such uniform rules and regulations as may be appropriate to carry out the purposes of this Act. Such

rules and regulations may be promulgated only after consideration of the provisions of the American Indian Religious Freedom Act (92 Stat. 469, 42 U.S.C. 1996). Each uniform rule or regulation promulgated under this Act shall be submitted on the same calendar day to the Committee on Energy and Natural Resources of the United States Senate and to the Committee on Interior and Insular Affairs of the United States House of Representatives, and no such uniform rule or regulation may take effect before the expiration of a period of ninety calendar days following the date of its submission to such Committees. (b) Each Federal land manager shall promulgate such rules and regulations under subsection (a) as may be appropriate for the carrying out of his functions and authorities under this Act.

COOPERATION WITH PRIVATE INDIVIDUALS

Sec. 11. The Secretary of the Interior shall take such action as may be necessary, consistent with the purposes of this Act, to foster and improve the communication, cooperation, and exchange of information between-(1) private individuals having collections of archaeological resources and data which were obtained before the date of the enactment of this Act, and (2) Federal authorities responsible for the protection of archaeological resources on the public lands and Indian lands and professional archaeologists and associations of professional archaeologists. In carrying out this section, the Secretary shall, to the extent practicable and consistent with the provisions of this Act, make efforts to expand the archaeological data base for the archaeological resources of the United States through increased cooperation between private individuals referred to in paragraph (I) and professional archaeologists and archaeological organizations.

SAVINGS PROVISIONS

Sec. 12. (a) Nothing in this Act shall be construed to repeal, modify, or impose additional restrictions on the activities permitted under existing laws and authorities relating to mining, mineral leasing, reclamation, and other multiple uses of the public lands. (b) Nothing in this Act applies to, or requires a permit for, the collection for private purposes of any rock, coin, bullet, or mineral which is not an archaeological resource, as determined under uniform regulations promulgated under section 3(I). (c) Nothing in this Act shall be construed to affect any land other than public land or Indian land or to affect the lawful recovery, collection, or sale of archaeological resources from land other than public land or Indian land.

REPORT

Sec. 13. As part of the annual report required to be submitted to the specified committees of the Congress pursuant to section 5(c) of the Act of June 27, 1960 (74 Stat. 220, 16 U.S.C. 469-469a), the Secretary of the Interior shall comprehensively report as a separate component on the activities carried out under the provisions of this Act, and he shall make such recommendations as he deems appropriate as to changes or improvements needed in the provisions of this Act. Such report shall include a brief summary of the actions undertaken by the Secretary under section 11 of this Act, relating to cooperation with private individuals.

APPENDIX I

FEDERAL LAWS ON PLANTS AND ANIMALS OF THE UNITED STATES
and
FEDERAL ENDANGERED SPECIES ACT OF 1973 (16 USC 1531-1543)

LACEY ACT

Passed in 1900, the Lacey Act prohibits import, export, transportation, sale, receipt, acquisition, or purchase of fish, wildlife, or plants that are taken, possessed, transported or sold in violation of any Federal, State, tribal, or foreign law. The 1981 amendments to the act were designed to strengthen Federal laws and improve Federal assistance to States and foreign governments in enforcement of fish and wildlife laws. The act has become a vital tool in efforts to control smuggling and trade in illegally-taken fish and wildlife. Another aspect of the Lacey Act regulates the transportation of live wildlife, requiring that animals be transported into the United States under humane and healthful conditions. The act also allows the Interior Secretary to designate those wildlife species considered injurious to humans and prohibit their importation into the country.

Penalties

Individuals convicted of violating the Lacey Act may be sentenced up to $100,000 and one year in jail for misdemeanors and up to $250,000 and five years' imprisonment for felony violations. Fines for organizations in violation of the act are up to $250,000 and $500,000 for misdemeanor and felony violations, respectively. In addition, vehicles, aircraft, and equipment used in the violation as well as illegal fish, wildlife, and plants may be subject to forfeiture.

Rewards

Persons who provide information on violations of the Lacey Act may be eligible for cash rewards.

MIGRATORY BIRD TREATY ACT

This act, originally passed in 1918, provides protection for migratory birds. Under the Act, it is unlawful to take, import, export, possess, buy, sell, purchase, or barter any migratory bird. Feathers or other parts, nests, eggs, and products made from migratory birds are also covered by the act. Take is defined as pursuing, hunting, shooting, poisoning, wounding, killing, capturing, trapping, or collecting.

Exceptions

Migratory bird hunting regulations, established by the U.S. Fish and Wildlife Service, allow the taking, during designated seasons, of ducks, geese, doves, rail, woodcock, and some other species. In addition, permits may be granted for various non-commercial activities involving migratory birds and some commercial activities involving captive-bred migratory birds.

Penalties

Individuals or organizations may be fined up to $5,000 and $10,000, respectively, and may face up to six months imprisonment for misdemeanor violations of the act. Felony violations may result in fines of up to $250,000 for individuals, $500,000 for organizations, and up to two years imprisonment.

EAGLE PROTECTION ACT

Bald eagle protection began in 1940 with the passage of the Eagle Protection Act. Later amended to include the golden eagle, the act makes it unlawful to import, export, take, sell, purchase, or barter any bald eagle or golden eagle, their parts, products, nests, or eggs. Taking includes pursuing, shooting, poisoning, wounding, killing, capturing, trapping, collecting, molesting, or disturbing the eagles.

Exceptions

Permits may be granted for scientific or exhibition use, or for traditional and cultural use by Native Americans. However, no permits may be issued for import, export, or commercial activities involving eagles.

Penalties

Misdemeanor violations may result in fines of up to $100,000 for individuals and $200,000 for organizations and one year's imprisonment. Fines of up to $250,000 and $500,000 for individuals and organizations, respectively, may result from felony violations.

Rewards

Persons providing information leading to the conviction of Eagle Protection Act violators may be eligible for cash rewards.

204

MARINE MAMMAL PROTECTION ACT

Passed in 1972, the Act establishes a moratorium on taking and importing marine mammals, their parts, and products. The Act provides protection for polar bears, sea otters, walruses, dugongs, manatees, whales, porpoises, seals, and sea lions.

Under this act it is unlawful to:

Take any marine mammal on the high seas or in waters or on lands under U.S. jurisdiction. The prohibition applies to persons, vessels, or other conveyances.

Import any marine mammal or marine mammal product into the United States.

Use any port or harbor under U.S. jurisdiction for any purpose connected with unlawful taking or importation of any marine mammal.

Possess any unlawfully taken marine mammal, including parts and products. Transport, purchase, sell, or offer to purchase or sell any marine mammal, including parts and products.

Exceptions

Alaskan Aleuts, Indians, and Eskimos who reside in Alaska are permitted to take marine mammals for subsistence purposes or for use in the manufacture and sale of native hand crafts. The Secretaries of Interior and Commerce may grant permits for importation of marine mammals for scientific research or public display purposes.

Export is not prohibited, but for species listed under CITES (e.g. walrus), a "Certificate of Origin" is required prior to export of handcrafted parts, scientific specimens, or animals collected for public display.

Penalties

Violations of the Marine Mammal Protection Act may result in fines of up to $100,000 and one year's imprisonment for individuals and up to $200,000 for organizations. In addition, aircraft, vessels, or other conveyances used in violations may be required to forfeit their cargo.

THE AFRICAN ELEPHANT CONSERVATION ACT

To assist in the conservation and protection of the African elephant populations, the United States passed the African Elephant Conservation Act in 1988.

Prohibitions

The African Elephant Conservation Act specifically forbids:

Import of raw African elephant ivory from any country other than an ivory producing country (any African country that contains any part of the population range of African elephants).

U.S. export of African elephant raw ivory.

Import of African elephant raw or worked ivory that was exported from an ivory producing country in violation of that country's laws or of CITES.

Import of worked ivory from any country unless that country has certified that such ivory was derived from legal sources.

Import of raw or worked ivory from a country for which a moratorium is in effect. (Effective June 9, 1989, the U.S. established a moratorium on ivory imports from all countries except for ivory trophies from certain approved countries and ivory antiquities.)

Penalties

Criminal violations—Violators of the prohibited acts shall, upon conviction, be fined $100,000 per individual or $200.000 per organization, or imprisoned for not more than one year, or both.

Civil violations—Individuals convicted of violating the prohibited acts may be assessed a civil penalty by the Secretary of Interior of not more than $5,000 for each such violation.

Rewards

Persons who provide information on violations of the African Elephant Conservation Act may be eligible for cash rewards. NOTE: The African elephant is also listed in Appendix I, CITES, and, as such, any import or export of African elephants, including their products (ivory, skin, etc.) for commercial purposes is prohibited. Any import or export for other than commercial purposes must be accompanied by valid CITES documents.

WILD BIRD CONSERVATION ACT

In 1992 the United States passed the Wild Bird Conservation Act. By October 1993, the law prohibits the import of all CITES-listed birds— almost 1,000 species—except for those included in an approved list either by country of origin or wild-caught birds or by specific captive breeding facilities.

For wild-caught approved birds, a management plan that provides for conservation of the species and its habitat is required. In addition, the Service establishes a moratorium on trade of any non-CITES species. Exemptions include game birds and bird species indigenous to the fifty United States and the District of Columbia.

The Act establishes an Exotic Bird Conservation Fund, to be funded by penalties, fines, donations, and any additional appropriations. The Fund is to be used to assist exotic bird conservation projects in their native countries. Particular attention is given to species subject to an import moratorium or quota in order to assist those countries in developing and implementing conservation management programs, law enforcement programs, or both.

Penalties

Criminal violations—Violators of the prohibited acts shall, upon conviction, be fined, or imprisoned for not more than two years, or both. Civil violations—Violators of the prohibited acts shall, upon conviction, be fined not more than $25,000.

FEDERAL ENDANGERED SPECIES ACT OF 1973
(16 USC 1531-1543)
Table of Contents

FINDINGS, PURPOSES, AND POLICY
SEC. 2.
(a) FINDINGS.-The Congress finds and declares that-

(1) various species of fish, wildlife, and plants in the United States have been rendered extinct as a consequence of economic growth and development untempered by adequate concern and conservation;

(2) other species of fish, wildlife, and plants have been so depleted in numbers that they are in danger of or threatened with extinction;

(3) these species of fish, wildlife, and plants are of aesthetic, ecological, educational, historical, recreational, and scientific value to the Nation and its people;

(4) the United States has pledged itself as a sovereign state in the international community to conserve to the extent practicable the various species of fish or wildlife and plants facing extinction, pursuant to-

(A) migratory bird treaties with Canada and Mexico;

(B) the Migratory and Endangered Bird Treaty with Japan;

(C) the Convention on Nature Protection and Wildlife Preservation in the Western Hemisphere;

(D) the International Convention for the Northwest Atlantic Fisheries;

(E) the International Convention for the High Seas Fisheries of the North Pacific Ocean;

(F) the Convention on International Trade in Endangered Species of Wild Fauna and Flora; and

(G) other international agreements; and

(5) encouraging the States and other interested parties, through Federal financial assistance and a system of incentives, to develop and maintain conservation programs which meet national and international standards is a key to meeting the Nation's international commitments and to better safeguarding, for the benefit of all citizens, the Nation's heritage in fish. wildlife. and plants.

(b) PURPOSES.-The purposes of this Act are to provide a means whereby the ecosystems upon which endangered species and threatened species depend may be conserved, to provide a program for the conservation of such endangered species and threatened species, and to take such steps as may be appropriate to achieve the purposes of the treaties and conventions set forth in subsection (a) of this section.

(c) POLICY.-(1) It Is further declared to be the policy of Congress that all Federal departments and agencies shall seek to conserve endangered species and threatened species and shall utilize their authorities in furtherance of the purposes of this Act.

(2) It is further declared to be the policy of Congress that Federal agencies shall cooperate with State and local agencies to resolve water resource issues in concert with conservation of endangered species.

DEFINITIONS

208

SEC. 3. For the purposes of this Act-

(1) The term "alternative courses of action" means all alternatives and thus is not limited to original project objectives and agency jurisdiction.

(2) The term "commercial activity" means all activities of industry and trade, including, but not limited to, the buying or selling of commodities and activities conducted for the purpose of facilitating such buying and selling: Provided, however, that it does not include exhibitions of commodities by museums or similar cultural or historical organizations.

(3) The terms "conserve," "conserving," and "conservation" mean to use and the use of all methods and procedures which are necessary to bring any endangered species or threatened species to the point at which the measures provided pursuant to this Act are no longer necessary. Such methods and procedures include, but are not limited to, all activities associated with scientific resources management such as research, census, law enforcement, habitat acquisition and maintenance, propagation, live trapping, and transplantation, and, in the extraordinary case where population pressures within a given ecosystem cannot be otherwise relieved, may include regulated taking.

(4) The term "Convention" means the Convention on International Trade in Endangered Species of Wild Fauna and Flora, signed on March 3. 1973 and the appendices thereto.

(5)(A) The term "critical habitat" for a threatened or endangered species means-

(i) the specific areas within the geographical area occupied by the species, at the time it is listed in accordance with the provisions of section 4 of this Act, on which are found those physical or biological features (I) essential to the conservation of the species and (II) which may require special management considerations or protection; and

(ii) specific areas outside the geographical area occupied by the species at the time it is listed in accordance with the provisions of section 4 of this Act, upon a determination by the Secretary that such areas are essential for the conservation of the species.

(B) Critical habitat may be established for those species now listed as threatened or endangered species for which no critical habitat has heretofore been established as set forth in subparagraph (A) of this paragraph.

(C) Except in those circumstances determined by the Secretary, critical habitat shall not include the entire geographical area which can be occupied by the threatened or endangered species.

(6) The term "endangered species" means any species which is in danger of extinction throughout all or a significant portion of its range other than a species of the Class Insecta determined by the Secretary to constitute a pest whose protection under the provisions of this Act would present an overwhelming and overriding risk to man.

(7) The term "Federal agency" means any department, agency, or instrumentality of the United States.

(8) The term "fish or wildlife" means any member of the animal kingdom, including without limitation any mammal, fish, bird (including any migratory, nonmigratory, or endangered bird for which protection is also afforded by treaty or other international agreement), amphibian, reptile, mollusk, crustacean, arthropod or other invertebrate, and includes any part, product, egg, or offspring thereof, or the dead body or parts thereof.

(9) The term "foreign commerce" includes, among other things, any transaction

(A) between persons within one foreign country;

(B) between persons in two or more foreign countries;

(C) between a person within the United States and a person in a foreign country; or

(D) between persons within the United States, where the fish and wildlife in question are moving in any country or countries outside the United States.

(10) The term "import" means to land on, bring into, or introduce into, or attempt to land on, bring into, or introduce into, any place subject to the jurisdiction of the United States, whether or not such landing, bringing, or introduction constitutes an importation within the meaning of the customs laws of the United States.

(11) The term "permit or license applicant" means, when used with respect to an action of a Federal agency for which exemption is sought under section 7, any person whose application to such agency for a permit or license has been denied primarily because of the application of section 7(a) to such agency action.

(12) "The term person means an individual, corporation, partnership, trust, association, or any other private entity; or any officer, employee, agent, department, or instrumentality of the Federal Government, of any State, municipality, or political subdivision of a State, or of any foreign government; any State, municipality, or political subdivision of a State; or any other entity subject to the jurisdiction of the United States."

(13) The term "plant" means any member of the plant kingdom, including seeds, roots and other parts thereof.

(14) The term "Secretary" means, except as otherwise herein provided, the Secretary of the Interior or the Secretary of Commerce as program responsibilities are vested pursuant to the provisions of Reorganization Plan Numbered 4 of 1970; except that with respect to the enforcement of the provisions of this Act and the Convention which pertain to the importation or exportation of terrestrial plants, the term also means the Secretary of Agriculture.

(15) The term "species" includes any subspecies of fish or wildlife or plants, and any distinct population segment of any species or vertebrate fish or wildlife which interbreeds when mature.

(16) The term "State" means any of the several States, the District of Columbia, the Commonwealth of Puerto Rico. American Samoa. the Virgin Islands, Guam. and the Trust Territory of the Pacific Islands.

(17) The term "State agency" means any State agency, department, board, commission, or other governmental entity which is responsible for the management and conservation of fish, plant, or wildlife resources within a State.

(18) The term "take" means to harass, harm, pursue, hunt, shoot, wound, kill, trap, capture, or collect, or to attempt to engage in any such conduct.

(19) The term "threatened species" means any species which is likely to become an endangered species within the foreseeable future throughout all or a significant portion of its range.

(20) The term "United States," when used in a geographical context, includes all States.

DETERMINATION OF ENDANGERED SPECIES AND THREATENED SPECIES

SEC. 4.

(a) GENERAL.

(1) The Secretary shall by regulation promulgated in accordance with

subsection (b) determine whether any species is an endangered species or a threatened species because of any of the following factors:

(A) the present or threatened destruction, modification, or curtailment of its habitat or range;

(B) overutilization for commercial, recreational, scientific, or educational purposes;

(C) disease or predation;

(D) the inadequacy of existing regulatory mechanisms;

(E) other natural or manmade factors affecting its continued existence.

(2) With respect to any species over which program responsibilities have been vested in the Secretary of Commerce pursuant to Reorganization Plan Numbered 4 of 1970-

(A) in any case in which the Secretary of Commerce determines that such species should

(i) be listed as an endangered species or a threatened species, or

(ii) be changed in status from a threatened species to an endangered species, he shall so inform the Secretary of the Interior, who shall list such species in accordance with this section,

(B) in any case in which the Secretary of Commerce determines that such species should

(i) be removed from any list published pursuant to subsection (c) of this section, or

(ii) be changed in status from an endangered species to a threatened species, he shall recommend such action to the Secretary of the Interior, and the Secretary of the Interior, if he concurs in the recommendation, shall implement such action; and

(C) the Secretary of the Interior may not list or remove from any list any such species, and may not change the status of any such species which are listed, without a prior favorable determination made pursuant to this section by the Secretary of Commerce.

(3) The Secretary, by regulation promulgated in accordance with subsection (b) and to the maximum extent prudent and determinable-

(A) shall, concurrently with making a determination under paragraph (1) that a species is an endangered species or a threatened species, designate any habitat of such species which is then considered to be critical habitat: and

(B) may, from time-to-time thereafter as appropriate, revise such designation.

(b) BASIS FOR DETERMINATIONS.

(1)(A) The Secretary shall make determinations required by subsection (a)(I) solely on the basis of the best scientific and commercial data available to him after conducting a review of the status of the species and after taking into account those efforts, if any, being made by any State or foreign nation, or any political subdivision of a State or foreign nation, to protect such species, whether by predator control, protection of habitat and food supply, or other conservation practices, within any area under its jurisdiction, or on the high seas.

(B) In carrying out this section, the Secretary shall give consideration to species which have been

(i) designated as requiring protection from unrestricted commerce by any foreign nation, or pursuant to any international agreement; or

(ii) identified as in danger of extinction, or likely to become so within the foreseeable future, by any State agency or by any agency of a foreign nation that is responsible for the conservation of fish or wildlife or plants.

(2) The Secretary shall designate critical habitat, and make revisions thereto, under subsection (a)(3) on the basis of the best scientific data available and after taking into consideration the economic impact, and any other relevant impact, of specifying any particular area as critical habitat. The Secretary may exclude any area from critical habitat if he determines that the benefits of such exclusion outweigh the benefits of specifying such area as part of the critical habitat, unless he determines, based on the best scientific and commercial data available, that the failure to designate such area as critical habitat will result in the extinction of the species concerned.

(3)(A) To the maximum extent practicable, within 90 days after receiving the petition of an interested person under section 553(e) of title S, United States Code, to add a species to, or to remove a species from, either of the lists published under subsection (c), the Secretary shall make a finding as to whether the petition presents substantial scientific or commercial information indicating that the petitioned action may be warranted. If such a petition is found to present such information, the Secretary shall promptly commence a review of the status of the species concerned. The Secretary shall promptly publish each finding made under this subparagraph in the Federal Register.

(B) Within 12 months after receiving a petition that is found under subparagraph (A) to present substantial information indicating that the petitioned action may be warranted, the Secretary shall make one of the following findings:

(i) The petitioned action is not warranted, in which case the Secretary shall promptly publish such finding in the Federal Register.

(ii) The petitioned action is warranted in which case the Secretary shall promptly publish in the Federal Register a general notice and the complete text of a proposed regulation to implement such action in accordance with paragraph (5).

(iii) The petitioned action is warranted but that

(I) the immediate proposal and timely promulgation of a final regulation implementing the petitioned action in accordance with paragraphs (5) and (6) is precluded by pending proposals to determine whether any species is an endangered species or a threatened species, and

(II) expeditious progress is being made to add qualified species to either of the lists published under subsection (c) and to remove from such lists species for which the protections of the Act are no longer necessary, in which case the Secretary shall promptly publish such finding in the Federal Register, together with a description and evaluation of the reasons and data on which the finding is based.

(C)(i) A petition with respect to which a finding is made under subparagraph (B)(iii) shall be treated as a petition that is resubmitted to the Secretary under subparagraph (A) on the date of such finding and that presents substantial scientific or commercial information that the petitioned action may be warranted.

(ii) Any negative finding described in subparagraph (A) and any finding described in subparagraph (B) (i) or (iii) shall be subject to judicial review.

(iii) The Secretary shall implement a system to monitor effectively the status of all species with respect to which a finding is made under subparagraph (B)(iii) and shall make prompt use of the authority under paragraph 7 to prevent a significant risk to the well being of any such species.

(D)(i) To the maximum extent practicable, within 90 days after receiving the petition of an interested person under section 553(e) of title 5, United States Code, to revise a critical habitat designation, the Secretary shall make a finding as to whether the petition presents substantial scientific information indicating that the revision may be warranted. The Secretary shall promptly publish such finding in the Federal Register.

(ii) Within 12 months after receiving a petition that is found under clause (i) to present substantial information indicating that the requested revision may be warranted, the Secretary shall determine how he intends to proceed with the requested revision, and shall promptly publish notice of such intention in the Federal Register.

(4) Except as provided in paragraphs (5) and (6) of this subsection, the provisions of section 553 of title 5, United States Code (relating to rulemaking procedures), shall apply to any regulation promulgated to carry out the purposes of this Act.

(5) With respect to any regulation proposed by the Secretary to implement a determination, designation, or revision referred to in subsection (a) (I) or (3), the Secretary shall

(A) not less than 90 days before the effective date of the regulation

(i) publish a general notice and the complete text of the proposed regulation in the Federal Register, and

(ii) give actual notice of the proposed regulation (including the complete text of the regulation) to the State agency in each State in which the species is believed to occur, and to each county or equivalent jurisdiction in which the species is believed to occur, and invite the comment of such agency, and each such jurisdiction, thereon;

(B) insofar as practical, and in cooperation with the Secretary of State, give notice of the proposed regulation to each foreign nation in which the species is believed to occur or whose citizens harvest the species on the high seas, and invite the comment of such nation thereon;

(C) give notice of the proposed regulation to such professional scientific organizations as he deems appropriate;

(D) publish a summary of the proposed regulation in a newspaper of general circulation in each area of the United States in which the species is believed to occur; and

(E) promptly hold one public hearing on the proposed regulation if any person files a request for such a hearing within 45 days after the date of publication of general notice.

(6)(A) Within the one-year period beginning on the date on which general notice is published in accordance with paragraph (5)(A)(i) regarding a proposed regulation, the Secretary shall publish in the Federal Register-

(i) if a determination as to whether a species is an endangered species or a threatened species, or a revision of critical habitat. is involved. either-

(I) a final regulation to implement such determination,

(II) a final regulation to implement such revision or a finding that such revision should not be made,

(III) notice that such one-year period is being extended under subparagraph (B)(i), or

(IV) notice that the proposed regulation is being withdrawn under sub-paragraph (B)(ii). together with the finding on which such withdrawal is based; or

(ii) subject to subparagraph (C), if a designation of critical habitat is involved, either-

(I) a final regulation to implement such designation, or

(II) notice that such one-year period is being extended under such sub-paragraph.

(B)(i) If the Secretary finds with respect to a proposed regulation referred to in subparagraph (A)(i) that there is substantial disagreement regarding the sufficiency or accuracy of the available data relevant to the determination or revision concerned the Secretary may extend the one-year period specified in subparagraph (A) for not more than six months for purposes of soliciting additional data.

(ii) If a proposed regulation referred to in subparagraph (a)(i) is not promulgated as a final regulation within such one-year period (or longer period if extension under clause (i) applies) because the Secretary finds that there is not sufficient evidence to justify the action proposed by the regulation the Secretary shall immediately withdraw the regulation. The finding on which a withdrawal is based shall be subject to judicial review. The Secretary may not propose a regulation that has previously been withdrawn under this clause unless he determines that sufficient new information is available to warrant such proposal.

(iii) If the one-year period specified in subparagraph (A) is extended under clause (i) with respect to a proposed regulation. then before the close of such extended period the Secretary shall publish in the Federal Register either a final regulation to implement the determination or revision concerned, a finding that the revision should not be made, or a notice of withdrawal of the regulation under clause (ii), together with the finding on which the withdrawal is based.

(C) A final regulation designating critical habitat of an endangered species or a threatened species shall be published concurrently with the final regulation implementing the determination that such species is endangered or threatened, unless the Secretary deems that-

(i) it is essential to the conservation of such species that the regulation implementing such determination be promptly published; or

(ii) critical habitat of such species is not then determinable, in which case the Secretary, with respect to the proposed regulation to designate such habitat. may extend the one-year period specified in subparagraph (A) by not more than one additional year. but not later than the close of such additional year the Secretary must publish a final regulation, based on such data as may be available at that time, designating, to the maximum extent prudent, such habitat.

(7) Neither paragraph (4), (5), or (6) of this subsection nor section 553 of title 5, United States Code, shall apply to any regulation issued by the Secretary in regard to any emergency posing a significant risk to the well-being of any species of fish and wildlife or plants, but only if-

(A) at the time of publication of the regulation in the Federal Register the Secretary publishes therein detailed reasons why such regulation is necessary; and

(B) in the case such regulation applies to resident species of fish or wildlife, or plants, the Secretary gives actual notice of such regulation to the State agency in each State in which such species is believed to occur. Such regulation shall, at the discretion of the Secretary, take effect immediately upon the publication of the regulation in the Federal Register. Any regulation promulgated under the authority of this paragraph shall cease to have force and effect at the close of the 240-day period following the date of publication unless, during such 240-day period, the rulemaking procedures which would apply to such regulation without regard to this paragraph are complied with. If at any time after issuing an emergency regulation the Secretary determines, on the basis of the best appropriate data available to him. that substantial evidence does not exist to warrant such regulation, he shall withdraw it.

(8) The publication in the Federal Register of any proposed or final regulation which is necessary or appropriate to carry out the purposes of this Act shall include a summary by the Secretary of the data on which such regulation is based and shall show the relationship of such data to such regulation; and if such regulation designates or revises critical habitat, such summary shall, to the maximum extent practicable, also include a brief description and evaluation of those activities (whether public or private) which, in the opinion of the Secretary, if undertaken may adversely modify such habitat, or may be affected by such designation.

(c) LISTS.

(I) The Secretary of the Interior shall publish in the Federal Register a list of all species determined by him or the Secretary of Commerce to be endangered species and a list of all species determined by him or the Secretary of Commerce to be threatened species. Each list shall refer to the species contained therein by scientific and common name or names, if any, specify with respect to such species over what portion of its range it is endangered or threatened, and specify any critical habitat within such range. The Secretary shall from time to time revise each list published under the authority of this subsection to reflect recent determinations, designations, and revisions made in accordance with subsections (a) and (b).

(2) The Secretary shall

(A) conduct, at least once every five years, a review of all species included in a list which is published pursuant to paragraph (1) and which is in effect at the time of such review; and

(B) determine on the basis of such review whether any such species should

(i) be removed from such list;

(ii) be changed in status from an endangered species to a threatened species; or

(iii) be changed in status from a threatened species to an endangered species. Each determination under subparagraph (B) shall be made in accordance with the provisions of subsection (a) and (b).

(d) PROTECTIVE REGULATIONS.-Whenever any species is listed as a threatened species pursuant to subsection (c) of this section. the Secretary shall issue such regulations as he deems necessary and advisable to provide for the conservation of such species. The Secretary may by regulation prohibit with respect to any threatened species any act prohibited under section 9(a)(1). In the case of fish or wildlife, or section 9(a)(2), in the case of plants, with respect to endangered species; except that with respect to the taking of resident species of fish or wildlife, such regulations shall apply in any State which has entered into a cooperative agreement pursuant to section 6(c) of this Act only to the extent that such regulations have also been adopted by such State.

(e) SIMILARITY OF APPEARANCE CASES.-The Secretary may, by regulation of commerce or taking, and to the extent he deems advisable, treat any species as an endangered species or threatened species even though it is not listed pursuant to section 4 of this Act if he finds that-

(A) such species so closely resembles in appearance, at the point in question a species which has been listed pursuant to such section that enforcement personnel would have substantial difficulty in attempting to differentiate between the listed and unlisted species;

(B) the effect of this substantial difficulty is an additional threat to an

endangered or threatened species, and

(C) such treatment of an unlisted species will substantially facilitate the enforcement and further the policy of this Act.

(f)(1) RECOVERY PLANS.-The Secretary shall develop and implement plans (hereinafter in this subsection referred to as "recovery plans") for the conservation and survival of endangered species and threatened species listed pursuant to this section, unless he finds that such a plan will not promote the conservation of the species. The Secretary, in development and implementing recovery plans, shall, to the maximum extent practicable

(A) give priority to those endangered species or threatened species, with-, out regard to taxonomic classification, that are most likely to benefit from such plans, particularly those species that are, or may be, in conflict with construction or other development projects or other forms of economic activity;

(B) incorporate in each plan-

(i) a description of such site-specific management actions as may be necessary to achieve the plan's goal for the conservation and survival of the species;

(ii) objective, measurable criteria which, when met, would result in a determination, in accordance with the provisions of this section, that the species be removed from the list; and

(iii) estimates of the time required and the cost to carry out those measures needed to achieve the plan's goal and to achieve intermediate steps toward that goal.

(2) The Secretary, in developing and implementing recovery plans, may procure the services of appropriate public and private agencies and institutions, and other qualified persons. Recovery teams appointed pursuant to this subsection shall not be subject to the Federal Advisory Committee Act.

(3) The Secretary shall report every two years to the Committee on Environment and Public Works of the Senate and the Committee on Merchant Marine and Fisheries of the House of Representatives on the status of efforts to develop and implement recovery plans for all species listed pursuant to this section and on the status of all species for which such plans have been developed.

(4) The Secretary shall, prior to final approval of a new or revised recovery plan, provide public notice and an opportunity for public review and comment on such plan. The Secretary shall consider all information pre-

sented during the public comment period prior to approval of the plan. (5) Each Federal agency shall, prior to implementation of a new or revised recovery plan, consider all information presented during the public comment period under paragraph (4).

(g) MONITORING.-

(1) The Secretary shall implement a system in cooperation with the States to monitor effectively for not less than five years the status of all species which have recovered to the point at which the measures provided pursuant to this Act are no longer necessary and which, in accordance with the provisions of this section, have been removed from either of the lists published under subsection (c).

(2) The Secretary shall make prompt use of the authority under paragraph 7 of subsection (b) of this section to prevent a significant risk to the well being of any such recovered species.

(h) AGENCY GUIDELINES.-The Secretary shall establish, and publish in the Federal Register. agency guidelines to insure that the purposes of this section are achieved efficiently and effectively. Such guidelines shall include, but are not limited to-

(1) procedures for recording the receipt and the disposition of petitions submitted under subsection (b)(3) of this section,

(2) criteria for making the findings required under such subsection with respect to petitions;

(3) a ranking system to assist in the identification of species that should receive priority review under subsection (a)(l) of the section, and

(4) a system for developing and implementing, on a priority basis, recovery plans under subsection (f) of this section. The Secretary shall provide to the public notice of, and opportunity to submit written comments on, any guideline (including any amendment thereto) proposed to be established under this subsection.

(i) If, in the case of any regulation proposed by the Secretary under the authority of this section, a State agency to which notice thereof was given in accordance with subsection

(b)(5)(A)(ii) files comments disagreeing with all or part of the proposed regulation, and the Secretary issues a final regulation which is in conflict with such comments, or if the Secretary fails to adopt a regulation pursuant to an action petitioned by a State agency under subsection (b)(3), the Secretary shall submit to the State agency a written justification for his failure to adopt regulations consistent with the agency's comments or petition.

LAND ACQUISITION
SEC. 5.

(a) PROGRAM.-The Secretary, and the Secretary of Agriculture with respect to the National Forest System, shall establish and implement a program to conserve fish, wildlife, and plants, including those which are listed as endangered species or threatened species pursuant to section 4 of this Act. To carry out such a program, the appropriate Secretary-

(1) shall utilize the land acquisition and other authority under the Fish and Wildlife Act of 1956, as amended, the Fish and Wildlife Coordination Act, as amended, and the Migratory Bird Conservation Act, as appropriate, and

(2) is authorized to acquire by purchase, donation, or otherwise, lands, waters, or interest therein, and such authority shall be in addition to any other land acquisition vested in him.

(b) ACQUISITIONS.-Funds made available pursuant to the Land and Water Conservation Fund Act of 1965, as amended, may be used for the purpose of acquiring lands, waters, or interests therein under subsection (a) of this section.

COOPERATION WITH THE STATES
SEC. 6.

(a) GENERAL.-In carrying out the program authorized by this Act, the Secretary shall cooperate to the maximum extent practicable with the States. Such cooperation shall include consultation with the States concerned before acquiring any land or water, or interest therein, for the purpose of conserving any endangered species or threatened species.

(b) MANAGEMENT AGREEMENTS.-The Secretary may enter into agreements with any State for the administration and management of any area established for the conservation of endangered species or threatened species. Any revenues derived from the administration of such areas under these agreements shall be subject to the provisions of section 401 of the Act of June 15. 1935 (49 Stat. 383: 16 U.S.C 715s).

(c)(1) COOPERATIVE AGREEMENTS.-In furtherance of the purposes of this Act, the Secretary is authorized to enter into a cooperative agreement in accordance with this section with any State which establishes and maintains an adequate and active program for the conservation of endangered species and threatened species. Within one hundred and twenty days after the Secretary receives a certified copy of such a proposed State program, he shall make a determination whether such program is in accordance with this Act. Unless he determines, pursuant to this paragraph, that the State program is not in accordance with this Act, he shall enter into a cooperative agreement with the State for the purpose of assisting in implementation of the State program. In order for a State program to be deemed an adequate and active program for the conservation of endangered species and threatened species, the Secretary must find, and annually thereafter reconfirm such finding, that under the State program-

(A) authority resides in the State agency to conserve resident species of fish or wildlife determined by the State agency or the Secretary to be endangered or threatened;

(B) the State agency has established acceptable conservation programs, consistent with the purposes and policies of this Act, for all resident species of fish or wildlife in the State which are deemed by the Secretary to bc endangered or threatened and has furnished a copy of such plan and program together with all pertinent details, information, and data requested to the Secretary;

(C) the State agency is authorized to conduct investigations to determine the status and requirements for survival of resident species of fish and wildlife;

(D) the State agency is authorized to establish programs, including the acquisition of land or aquatic habitat or interests therein, for the conservation of resident endangered or threatened species of fish or wildlife; and

(E) provision is made for public participation in designating resident species of fish or wildlife as endangered or threatened. or that under the State program-

(i) the requirements set forth in paragraphs (3), (4), and (5) of this subsection are complied with, and

(ii) plans are included under which immediate attention will be given to those resident species of fish and wildlife which are determined by the Secretary or the State agency to be endangered or threatened and which the Secretary and the State agency agree are most urgently in need of conservation programs; except that a cooperative agreement entered into with a State whose program is deemed adequate and active pursuant to clause (i) and this clause and this subparagraph shall not affect the applicability of prohibitions set forth in or authorized pursuant to section 4(d) or section 9(a)(I) with respect to the taking of any resident endangered or threatened species.

(2) In furtherance of the purposes of this Act, the Secretary is authorized to enter into a cooperative agreement in accordance with this sec-

tion with any State which establishes and maintains an adequate and active program for the conservation of endangered species and threatened species of plants. Within one hundred and twenty days after the Secretary receives a certified copy of such a proposed State program, he shall make a determination whether such program is in accordance with this Act. Unless he determines, pursuant to this paragraph, that the State program is not in accordance with this Act, he shall enter into a cooperative agreement with the State for the purpose of assisting in implementation of the State program. In order for a State program to be deemed an adequate and active program for the conservation of endangered species of plants and threatened species of plants. the Secretary must find, and annually thereafter reconfirm such finding, that under the State program-

(A) authority resides in the State agency to conserve resident species of plants determined by the State agency or the Secretary to be endangered or threatened;

(B) the State agency has established acceptable conservation programs, consistent with the purposes and policies of this Act, for all resident species of plants in the State which are deemed by the Secretary to be endangered or threatened, and has furnished a copy of such plan and program together with all pertinent details, information, and data requested to the Secretary;

(C) the State agency is authorized to conduct investigations to determine the status and requirements for survival of resident species of plants, and

(D) provision is made for public participation in designating resident species of plants as endangered or threatened: or that under the State program-

(i) the requirements set forth in subparagraphs (C) and (D) of this paragraph are complied with, and

(ii) plans are included under which immediate attention will be given to those resident species of plants which are determined by the Secretary or the State agency to be endangered or threatened and which the Secretary and the State agency agree are most urgently in need of conservation programs; except that a cooperative agreement entered into with a State whose program is deemed adequate and active pursuant to clause (i) and this clause shall not affect the applicability of prohibitions set forth in or authorized pursuant to section 4(d) or section 9(a)(I) with respect to the taking of any resident endangered or threatened species

(d) ALLOCATION OF FUNDS.

(1) The Secretary is authorized to provide financial assistance to any State, through its respective State agency, which has entered into a cooperative agreement pursuant to subsection (c) of this section to assist in development of programs for the conservation of endangered and threatened species or to assist in monitoring the status of candidate species pursuant to subparagraph (C) of section 4(b)(3) and recovered species pursuant to section 4(g). The Secretary shall allocate each annual appropriation made in accordance with the provisions of subsection (i) of this section to such States based on consideration of-

(A) the international commitments of the United States to protect endangered species or threatened species;

(B) the readiness of a State to proceed with a conservation program consistent with the objectives and purposes of this Act;

(C) the number of endangered species and threatened species within a State;

(D) the potential for restoring endangered species and threatened species within a State;

(E) the relative urgency to initiate a program to restore and protect an endangered species or threatened species in terms of survival of the species;

(F) the importance of monitoring the status of candidate species within a State to prevent a significant risk to the well being of any such species; and

(G) the importance of monitoring the status of recovered species within a State to assure that such species do not return to the point at which the measures provided pursuant to this Act are again necessary.

So much of the annual appropriation made in accordance with provisions of subsection (i) of this section allocated for obligation to any State for any fiscal year as remains unobligated at the close thereof is authorized to fie made available to that State until the close of the succeeding fiscal year. Any amount allocated to any State which is unobligated at the end of the period during which it is available for expenditure is authorized to be made available for expenditure by the Secretary in conducting programs under this section.

(2) Such cooperative agreements shall provide for-

(A) the actions to be taken by the Secretary and the States;

(B) the benefits that are expected to be derived in connection with the conservation of endangered or threatened species;

(C) the estimated cost of these actions; and

(D) the share of such costs to be borne by the Federal Government and by the States; except that-

(i) the Federal share of such program costs shall not exceed 75 percent of the estimated program cost stated in the agreement; and

(ii) the Federal share may be increased to 90 percent whenever two or more States having a common interest in one or more endangered or threatened species, the conservation of which may be enhanced by cooperation of such States. enter jointly into agreement with the Secretary. The Secretary may, in his discretion, and under such rules and regulations as he may prescribe, advance funds to the State for financing the United States pro rata share agreed upon in the cooperative agreement. For the purposes of this section, the non-Federal share may, in the discretion of the Secretary, be in the form of money or real property, the value of which will be determined by the Secretary whose decision shall be final.

(e) REVIEW OF STATE PROGRAMS.-Any action taken by the Secretary under this section shall be subject to his periodic review at no greater than annual intervals.

(f) CONFLICTS BETWEEN FEDERAL AND STATE LAWS.-Any State law or regulation which applies with respect to the importation or exportation of, or interstate or foreign commerce in, endangered species or threatened species is void to the extent that it may effectively

(I) permit what is prohibited by this Act of by any regulation which implements this Act, or

(2) prohibit what is authorized pursuant to an exemption or permit provided for in this Act or in any regulation which implements this Act. This Act shall not otherwise be construed to void any State law or regulation which is intended to conserve migratory, resident, or introduced fish or wildlife, or to permit or prohibit sale of such fish or wildlife. Any State law or regulation respecting the taking of an endangered species or threatened species may be more restrictive than the exemptions or permits provided for in this Act or in any regulation which implements this Act but not less restrictive than the prohibitions so defined.

(g) TRANSITION.-

(I) For purposes of this subsection, the term "establishment period" means, with respect to any State, the period beginning on the date of enactment of this Act and ending on whichever of the following dates first occurs:

(A) the date of the close of the 120-day period following the adjournment of the first regular session of the legislature of such State which commences after such date of enactment, or

(B) the date of the close of the 15 month period following such date of enactment.

(2) The prohibitions set forth in or authorized pursuant to sections 4(d) and 9(a)(1)(B) of this Act shall not apply with respect to the taking of any resident endangered species or threatened species (other than species listed in Appendix I to the Convention or otherwise specifically covered by any other treaty or Federal law) within any State-

(A) which is then a party to a cooperative agreement with the Secretary pursuant to section 6(c) of this Act (except to the extent that the taking of any such species is contrary to the law of such State); or

(B) except for any time within the establishment period when-

(i) the Secretary applies such prohibition to such species at the request of the State. or

(ii) the Secretary applies such prohibition after he finds, and publishes his finding, that an emergency exists posing a significant risk tn the well-being of such species and that the prohibition must be applied to protect such species. The Secretary's finding and publication may be made without regard to the public hearing or comment provisions of section 553 of title 5, United States Code. or any other provision of this Act; but such prohibition shall expire 90 days after the date of its imposition unless the Secretary further extends such prohibition by publishing notice and a statement of justification of such extension.

(h) REGULATIONS.-The Secretary is authorized to promulgate such regulations as may be appropriate to carry out the provisions of this section relating to financial assistance to States.

(i) APPROPRIATIONS.

(1) To carry out the provisions of this section for fiscal years after September 30, 1988, there shall be deposited into a special fund known as the cooperative endangered species conservation fund, to be administered by the Secretary, an amount equal to five percent of the combined amounts covered each fiscal year into the Federal aid to wildlife restoration fund under section 3 of the Act of September 2, 1937, and paid, transferred, or otherwise credited each fiscal year to the Sport Fishing Restoration Account established under 1016 of the Act of July 18, 1984.

(2) Amounts deposited into the special fund are authorized to be appropriated annually and allocated in accordance with subsection (d) of this section.

INTERAGENCY COOPERATION
SEC. 7
(a) FEDERAL AGENCY ACTIONS AND CONSULTATIONS.

(1) The Secretary shall review other programs administered by him and utilize such programs in furtherance of the purposes of this Act. All other Federal agencies shall, in consultation with and with the assistance of the Secretary, utilize their authorities in furtherance of the purposes of this Act by carrying out programs for the conservation of endangered species and threatened species listed pursuant to section 4 of this Act.

(2) Each Federal agency shall, in consultation with and with the assistance of the Secretary, insure that any action authorized, funded, or carried out by such agency (hereinafter in this section referred to as an "agency action") is not likely to jeopardize the continued existence of any endangered species or threatened species or result in the destruction or adverse modification of habitat of such species which is determined by the Secretary, after consultation as appropriate with affected States, to be critical, unless such agency has been granted an exemption for such action by the Committee pursuant to subsection (h) of this section. In fulfilling the requirements of this paragraph each agency shall use the best scientific and commercial data available.

(3) Subject to such guidelines as the Secretary may establish a Federal agency shall consult with the Secretary on any prospective agency action at the request of, and in cooperation with, the prospective permit or license applicant if the applicant has reason to believe that an endangered species or a threatened species may be present in the area affected by his project and that implementation of such action will likely affect such species.

(4) Each Federal agency shall confer with the Secretary on any agency action which is likely to jeopardize the continued existence of any species proposed to be listed under section 4 or result in the destruction or adverse modification of critical habitat proposed to be designated for such species. This paragraph does not require a limitation on the commitment of resources as described in subsection (d).

(b) OPINION OF SECRETARY.

(1)(A) Consultation under subsection (a)(2) with respect to any agency action shall be concluded within the 90-day period beginning on the date on which initiated or, subject to subparagraph (B), within such other period of time as is mutually agreeable to the Secretary and the Federal agency;

(B) in the case of an agency action involving a permit or license applicant, the Secretary and the Federal agency may not mutually agree to conclude consultation within a period exceeding 90 days unless the Secretary, before the close of the 90th day referred to in subparagraph (A)-

(i) if the consultation period proposed to be agreed to will end before the 150th day after the date on which consultation was initiated, submits to the applicant a written statement setting forth-

(I) the reasons why a longer period is required;

(II) the information that is required to complete the consultation; and

(III) the estimated date on which consultation will be completed; or

(ii) if the consultation period proposed to be agreed to will end 150 or more days after the date on which consultation was initiated, obtains the consent of the applicant to such period. The Secretary and the Federal agency may mutually agree to extend a consultation period established under the preceding sentence if the Secretary, before the close of such period, obtains the consent of the applicant to the extension.

(2) Consultation under subsection (a)(3) shall be concluded within such period as is agreeable to the Secretary, the Federal agency, and the applicant concerned.

(3)(A) Promptly after conclusion of consultation under paragraph (2) or (3) of subsection (a), the Secretary shall provide to the Federal agency and the applicant, if any, a written statement setting forth the Secretary's opinion, and a summary of the information on which the opinion is based, detailing how the agency action affects the species or its critical habitat. If jeopardy or adverse modification is found, the Secretary shall suggest those reasonable and prudent alternatives which he believes would not violate subsection (a)(2) and can be taken by the Federal agency or applicant in implementing the agency action. (B) Consultation under subsection (a)(3), and an opinion based by the Secretary incident to such consultation, regarding an agency action shall be treated respectively as a consultation under subsection (a)(2), and as an opinion issued after consultation under such subsection, regarding that action if the Secretary reviews the action before it is commenced by the Federal agency and finds and notifies such agency, that no significant changes have been made with respect to the action and that no significant change has occurred regarding the information used during the initial consultation.

(4) If after consultation under subsection (a)(2) of this section, the Secretary concludes that-

(A) the agency action will not violate such subsection, or offers reasonable and prudent alternatives which the Secretary believes would not violate such subsection;

(B) the taking of an endangered species or a threatened species incidental to the agency action will not violate such subsection; and

(C) if an endangered species or threatened species of a marine mammal is involved, the taking is authorized pursuant to section 1371(a)(5) of this title; the Secretary shall provide the Federal agency and the applicant concerned, if any, with a written statement that-

(i) specifies the impact of such incidental taking on the species,

(ii) specifies those reasonable and prudent measures that the Secretary considers necessary or appropriate to minimize such impact,

(iii) in the case of marine mammals, specifies those measures that are necessary to comply with section 1371(a)(5) of this title with regard to such taking, and

(iv) sets forth the terms and conditions (including, but not limited to, reporting requirements) that must be complied with by the Federal agency or applicant (if any), or both, to implement the measures specified under clauses (ii) and (iii).

(c) BIOLOGICAL ASSESSMENT.

(I) To facilitate compliance with the requirements of subsection (a)(2) each Federal agency shall, with respect to any agency action of such agency for which no contract for construction has been entered into and for which no construction has begun on the date of enactment of the Endangered Species Act Amendments of 1978, request of the Secretary information whether any species which is listed or proposed to be listed may be present in the area of such proposed action. If the Secretary advises. based on the best scientific and commercial data available, that such species may be present, such agency shall conduct a biological assessment for the purpose of identifying any endangered species or threatened species which is likely to be affected by such action. Such assessment shall be completed within 180 days after the date on which initiated (or within such other period as is mutually agreed to by the Secretary and such agency, except that if a permit or license applicant is involved, the 180-day period may not be extended unless such agency provides the applicant, before the close of such period, with a written statement setting forth the estimated length of the proposed extension and the reasons therefore) and, before any contract for construction is entered into and before construction is begun with respect to such action. Such assessment may be undertaken as part of a Federal agency's compliance with the requirements of section 102 of the National Environmental Policy Act of 1969 (42 U.S.C. 4332).

(2) Any person who may wish to apply for an exemption under subsection (g) of this section for that action may conduct a biological assessment to identify any endangered species or threatened species which is likely to be affected by such action. Any such biological assessment must, however, be conducted in cooperation with the Secretary and under the supervision of the appropriate Federal agency.

(d) LIMITATION ON COMMITMENT OF RESOURCES.-After initiation of consultation required under subsection (a)(2), the Federal agency and the permit or license applicant shall not make any irreversible or irretrievable commitment of resources with respect to the agency action which has the effect of foreclosing the formulation or implementation of any reasonable and prudent alternative measures which would not violate subsection (a)(2).

(e)(1) ESTABLISHMENT OF COMMITTEE.-There is established a committee to be known as the Endangered Species Committee (hereinafter in this section referred to as the "Committee").

(2) The Committee shall review any application submitted to it pursuant to this section and determine in accordance with subsection (h) of this section whether or not to grant an exemption from the requirements of subsection (a)(2) of this action for the action set forth in such application.

(3) The Committee shall be composed of seven members as follows:

(A) The Secretary of Agriculture.

(B) The Secretary of the Army.

(C) The Chairman of the Council of Economic Advisors.

(D) The Administrator of the Environmental Protection Agency. Agency.

(E) The Secretary of the Interior.

(F) The Administrator of the National Oceanic and Atmospheric Administration.

(G) The President, after consideration of any recommendations received pursuant to subsection (g)(2)(B) shall appoint one individual from each affected State, as determined by the Secretary, to be a member of the Committee for the consideration of the application for exemption for an agency action with respect to which such recommendations are made, not later than 30 days after an application is submitted pursuant to this section.

(4)(A) Members of the Committee shall receive no additional pay on account of their service on the Committee.

(B) While away from their homes or regular places of business in the performance of services for the Committee, members of the Committee shall be allowed travel expenses, including per diem in lieu of subsistence, in the same manner as persons employed intermittently in the Government service are allowed expenses under section 5703 of title 5 of the United States Code.

(5)(A) Five members of the Committee or their representatives shall constitute a quorum for the transaction of any function of the Committee, except that, in no case shall any representative be considered in determining the existence of a quorum for the transaction of any function of the Committee if that function involves a vote by the Committee on any matter before the Committee.

(B) The Secretary of the Interior shall be the Chairman of the Committee.

(C) The Committee shall meet at the call of the Chairman or five of its members.

(D) All meetings and records of the Committee shall be open to the public.

(6) Upon request of the Committee, the head of any Federal agency is authorized to detail, on a nonreimbursable basis, any of the personnel of such agency to the Committee to assist it in carrying out its duties under this section.

(7)(A) The Committee may for the purpose of carrying out its duties under this section hold such hearings, sit and act at such times and places. take such testimony, and receive such evidence, as the Committee deems advisable.

(B) When so authorized by the Committee, any member or agent of the Committee may take any action which the Committee is authorized to take by this paragraph.

(C) Subject to the Privacy Act, the Committee may secure directly from any Federal agency information necessary to enable it to carry out its duties under this section. Upon request of the Chairman of the Committee, the head of such Federal agency shall furnish such information to the Committee.

(D) The Committee may use the United States mails in the same manner and upon the same conditions as a Federal agency.

(E) The Administrator of General Services shall provide to the

Committee on a reimbursable basis such administrative support services as the Committee may request.

(8) In carrying out its duties under this section, the Committee may promulgate and amend such rules, regulations, and procedures, and issue and amend such orders as it deems necessary.

(9) For the purpose of obtaining information necessary for the consideration of an application for an exemption under this section the Committee may issue subpoenas for the attendance and testimony of witnesses and the production of relevant papers, books, and documents.

(10) In no case shall any representative, including a representative of a member designated pursuant to paragraph (3)(G) of this subsection, be eligible to cast a vote on behalf of any member.

(f) REGULATIONS.-Not later than 90 days after the date of enactment of the Endangered Species Act Amendments of 1978 the Secretary shall promulgate regulations which set forth the form and manner in which applications for exemption shall be submitted to the Secretary and the information to be contained in such applications. Such regulations shall require that information submitted in an application by the head of any Federal agency with respect to any agency action include but not be limited to-

(1) a description of the consultation process carried out pursuant to subsection (a)(2) of this section between the head of the Federal agency and the Secretary; and

(2) a statement describing why such action cannot be altered or modified to conform with the requirements of subsection (a)(2) of this section.

(g) APPLICATION FOR EXEMPTION AND REPORT TO THE COMMITTEE.-

(1) A Federal agency, the Governor of the State in which an agency action will occur, if any, or a permit or license applicant may apply to the Secretary for an exemption for an agency action of such agency if, after consultation under subsection (a)(2), the Secretary's opinion under subsection (b) indicates that the agency action would violate subsection (a)(2). An application for an exemption shall be considered initially by the Secretary in the manner provided for in this subsection, and shall be considered by the Committee for a final determination under subsection (h) after a report is made pursuant to paragraph (5). The applicant for an exemption shall be referred to as the "exemption applicant" in this section.

(2)(A) An exemption applicant shall submit a written application to the Secretary, in a form prescribed under subsection (f), not later than 90 days after the completion of the consultation process; except that, in the case of any agency action involving a permit or license applicant, such application shall be submitted not later than 90 days after the date on which the Federal agency concerned takes final agency action with respect to the issuance of the permit or license. For purposes of the preceding sentence, the term "final agency action" means (i) a disposition by an agency with respect to the issuance of a permit or license that is subject to administrative review, whether or not such disposition is subject to judicial review; or (ii) if administrative review is sought with respect to such disposition, the decision resulting after such review. Such application shall set forth the reasons why the exemption applicant considers that the agency action meets the requirements for an exemption under this subsection.

(B) Upon receipt of an application for exemption for an agency action under paragraph (I), the Secretary shall promptly

(i) notify the Governor of each affected State, if any, as determined by the Secretary, and request the Governors so notified to recommend individuals to be appointed to the Endangered Species Committee for consideration of such application, and

(ii) publish notice of receipt of the application in the Federal Registers including a summary of the information contained in the application and a description of the agency action with respect to which the application for exemption has been filed.

(3) The Secretary shall within 20 days after the receipt of an application for exemption, or within such other period of time as is mutually agreeable to the exemption applicant and the Secretary

(A) determine that the Federal agency concerned and the exemption applicant have-

(i) carried out the consultation responsibilities described in subsection (a) in good faith and made a reasonable and responsible effort to develop and fairly consider modifications or reasonable and prudent alternatives to the proposed agency action which would not violate subsection (a)(2);

(ii) conducted any biological assessment required by subsection (c); and

(iii) to the extent determinable within the time provided herein, refrained from making any irreversible or irretrievable commitment of resources prohibited by subsection (d); or

(B) deny the application for exemption because the Federal agency concerned or the exemption applicant have not met the requirements set forth in subparagraph (A) (i), (ii), and (iii). The denial of an application under subparagraph (B) shall be considered final agency action for purposes of chapter 7 of title 5, United States Code.

(4) If the Secretary determines that the Federal agency concerned and the exemption applicant have met the requirements set forth in paragraph (3)(A) (i), (ii) and (iii) he shall, in consultation with the Members of the Committee, hold a hearing on the application for exemption in accordance with sections 554, 555, and 556 (other than subsection (b) (1) and (2) thereof) of title 5. United States Code. and prepare the report to be submitted pursuant to paragraph (5).

(5) Within 110 days after making the determinations under paragraph (3) or within such other period of time as is mutually agreeable to the exemption applicant and the Secretary, the Secretary shall submit to the Committee a report discussing-

(A) the availability of reasonable and prudent alternatives to the agency action, and the nature and extent of the benefits of the agency action and of alternative courses of action consistent with conserving the species of the critical habitat;

(B) a summary of the evidence concerning whether or not the agency action is in the public interest and is of national or regional significance;

(C) appropriate reasonable mitigation and enhancement measures which should be considered by the Committee; and

(D) whether the Federal agency concerned and the exemption applicant refrained from making any irreversible or irretrievable commitment of resources prohibited by subsection (d).

(6) To the extent practicable within the time required for action under subsection (g) of this section, and except to the extent inconsistent with the requirements of this section, the consideration of any application for an exemption under this section and the conduct of any hearing under this subsection shall be in accordance with sections 554. 555. and 556 (other than subsection (b)(3) of section 556) of title 5. United States Code.

(7) Upon request of the Secretary, the head of any Federal agency is authorized to detail, on a nonreimbursable basis, any of the personnel of such agency to the Secretary to assist him in carrying out his duties under this section.

(8) All meetings and records resulting from activities pursuant to this

subsection shall be open to the public.

(h) EXEMPTION.-

(1) The Committee shall make a final determination whether or not to grant an exemption within 30 days after receiving the report of the Secretary pursuant to subsection (g)(5). The Committee shall grant an exemption from the requirements of subsection (a)(2) for an agency action if, by a vote of not less than five of its members voting in person-

(A) it determines on the record based on the report of the Secretary, the record of the hearing held under subsection (g)(4), and on such other testimony or evidence as it may receive, that-

(i) there are no reasonable and prudent alternatives to the agency action;

(ii) the benefits of such action clearly outweigh the benefits of alternative courses of action consistent with conserving the species or its critical habitat, and such action is in the public interest;

(iii) the action is of regional or national significance; and

(iv) neither the Federal agency concerned nor the exemption applicant made any irreversible or irretrievable commitment of resources prohibited by subsection (d); and

(B) it establishes such reasonable mitigation and enhancement measures, including, but not limited to, live propagation, transplantation, and habitat acquisition and improvement, as are necessary and appropriate to minimize the adverse effects of the agency action upon the endangered species, threatened species, or critical habitat concerned. Any final determination by Committee under this subsection shall be considered final agency action for purposes of chapter 7 of title 5 of the United States Code.

(2)(A) Except as provided in subparagraph (B), an exemption for an agency action granted under paragraph (1) shall constitute a permanent exemption with respect to all endangered or threatened species for the purposes of completing such agency action-

(i) regardless whether the species was identified in the biological assessment; and

(ii) only if a biological assessment has been conducted under subsection (c) with respect to such agency action.

(B) An exemption shall be permanent under subparagraph (A) unless-

(i) the Secretary finds, based on the best scientific and commercial data available, that such exemption would result in the extinction of a species that was not the subject of consultation under subsection (a)(2) or was not identified in any biological assessment conducted under subsection

(c), and

(ii) the Committee determines within 60 days after the date of the Secretary's finding that the exemption should not be permanent.

If the Secretary makes a finding described in clause (i), the Committee shall meet with respect to the matter within 30 days after the date of the finding.

235

(i) REVIEW BY SECRETARY OF STATE.-Notwithstanding any other provision of this Act, the Committee shall be prohibited from considering for exemption any application made to it, if the Secretary of State, after a review of the proposed agency action and its potential implications, and after hearing, certifies, in writing, to the Committee within 60 days of any application made under this section that the granting of any such exemption and the carrying out of such action would be in violation of an international treaty obligation or other international obligation of the United States. The Secretary of State shall, at the time of such certification, publish a copy thereof in the Federal Register.

(j) Notwithstanding any other provision of this Act, the Committee shall grant an exemption for any agency action if the Secretary of Defense finds that such exemption is necessary for reasons of national security.

(k) SPECIAL PROVISIONS.-An exemption decision by the Committee under this section shall not be a major Federal action for purposes of the National Environmental Policy Act of 1969 (42 U.S.C. 4321 et seq.): Provided, That an environmental impact statement which discusses the impacts upon endangered species or threatened species or their critical habitats shall have been previously prepared with respect to any agency action exempted by such order.

(1) COMMITTEE ORDERS.

(1) If the Committee determines under subsection (h) that an exemption should be granted with respect to any agency action, the Committee shall issue an order granting the exemption and specifying the mitigation and enhancement measures established pursuant to subsection (h) which shall be carried out and paid for by the exemption applicant in implementing the agency action. All necessary mitigation and enhancement measures shall be authorized prior to the implementing of the agency action and funded concurrently with all other project features.

(2) The applicant receiving such exemption shall include the costs of such mitigation and enhancement measures within the overall costs of

continuing the proposed action. Notwithstanding the preceding sentence the costs of such measures shall not be treated as project costs for the purpose of computing benefit-cost or other ratios for the proposed action Any applicant may request the Secretary to carry out such mitigation and enhancement measures. The costs incurred by the Secretary in carrying out any such measures shall be paid by the applicant receiving the exemption. No later than one year after the granting of an exemption, the exemption applicant shall submit to the Council on Environmental Quality a report describing its compliance with the mitigation and enhancement measures prescribed by this section. Such report shall be submitted annually until all such mitigation and enhancement measures have been completed. Notice of the public availability of such reports shall be published in the Federal Register by the Council on Environmental Quality.

(m) NOTICE.-The 60-day notice requirement of section 11(g) of this Act shall not apply with respect to review of any final determination of the Committee under subsection (h) of this section granting an exemption from the requirements of subsection (a)(2) of this section.

(n) JUDICIAL REVIEW.-Any person, as defined by section 3(13) of this Act, may obtain judicial review, under chapter 7 of title 5 of the United States Code, of any decision of the Endangered Species Committee under subsection (h) in the United States Court of Appeals for

(1) any circuit wherein the agency action concerned will be, or is being, carried out, or

(2) in any case in which the agency action will be, or is being, carried out outside of any circuit, the District of Columbia, by filing in such court within 90 days after the date of issuance of the decision, a written petition for review. A copy of such petition shall be transmitted by the clerk of the court to the Committee and the Committee shall file in the court the record in the proceeding, as provided in section 2112, of title 28, United States Code. Attorneys designated by the Endangered Species Committee may appear for, and represent the Committee in any action for review under this subsection.

(o) EXEMPTION AS PROVIDING EXCEPTION ON TAKING OF ENDANGERED SPECIES.-Notwithstanding sections 1533(d) and 1538(a)(1)(B) and (C) of this title, sections 1371 and 1372 of this title, or any regulation promulgated to implement any such section-

(1) any action for which an exemption is granted under subsection (h)

of this section shall not be considered to be a taking of an endangered species or threatened species with respect to any activity which is necessary to carry out such action: and

(2) any taking that is in compliance with the terms and conditions specified in a written statement provided under subsection (b)(4)(iv) of this section shall not be considered to be a prohibited taking of the species concerned.

237

(p) EXEMPTIONS IN PRESIDENTIALLY DECLARED DISASTER AREAS. In any area which has been declared by the President to be a major disaster area under the Disaster Relief Act of 1974, the President is authorized to make the determinations required by subsections (g) and (h) of this section for any project for the repair or replacement of a public facility substantially as it existed prior to the disaster under section 401 or 402 of the Disaster Relief Act of 1974* and which the President determines

(1) is necessary to prevent the recurrence of such a natural disaster and to reduce the potential loss of human life, and

(2) to involve an emergency situation which does not allow the ordinary procedures of this section to be followed. Notwithstanding any other provision of this section, the Committee shall accept the determinations of the President under this subsection.

INTERNATIONAL COOPERATION
SEC. 8.

(a) FINANCIAL ASSISTANCE.-As a demonstration of the commitment of the United States to the worldwide protection of endangered species and threatened species, the President may, subject the provisions of section 1415 of the Supplemental Appropriation Act. 1953 (31 U.S.C. 724), use foreign currencies accruing to the United States Government under the Agricultural Trade Development and Assistance Act of 1954 or any other law to provide to any foreign country (with its consent) assistance in the development and management of programs in that country which the Secretary determines to be necessary or useful for the conservation of any endangered species or threatened species listed by the Secretary pursuant to section 4 of this Act. The President shall provide assistance (which includes, but is not limited to, the acquisition, by lease or otherwise. of lands. waters. or interests therein) to foreign countries under this section under such terms and conditions as he deems appropriate. Whenever foreign currencies are available for the provision of assistance under this section, such currencies shall be used in preference to funds appropriated under the authority of section 15 of this Act.

(b) ENCOURAGEMENT OF FOREIGN PROGRAMS.-In order to carry out further the provisions of this Act, the Secretary, through the Secretary of State shall encourage-

(1) foreign countries to provide for the conservation of fish or wildlife and plants including endangered species and threatened species listed pursuant to section 4 of this Act;

(2) the entering into of bilateral or multilateral agreements with foreign countries to provide for such conservation; and

(3) foreign persons who directly or indirectly take fish or wildlife or plants in foreign countries or on the high seas for importation into the United States for commercial or other purposes to develop and carry out with such assistance as he may provide, conservation practices designed to enhance such fish or wildlife or plants and their habitat.

(c) PERSONNEL.-After consultation with the Secretary of State, the Secretary may-

(1) assign or otherwise make available any officer or employee of his department for the purpose of cooperating with foreign countries and international organizations in developing personnel resources and programs which promote the conservation of fish or wildlife or plants, and

(2) conduct or provide financial assistance for the educational training of foreign personnel, in this country or abroad, in fish, wildlife, or plant management, research and law enforcement and to render professional assistance abroad in such matters.

(d) INVESTIGATIONS.-After consultation with the Secretary of State and the Secretary of the Treasury, as appropriate, the Secretary may conduct or cause to be conducted such law enforcement investigations and research abroad as he deems necessary to carry out the purposes of this Act.

CONVENTION IMPLEMENTATION

SEC. 8A.

(a) MANAGEMENT AUTHORITY AND SCIENTIFIC AUTHORITY.-The Secretary of the Interior (hereinafter in this section referred to as the "Secretary") is designated as the Management Authority and the Scientific Authority for purposes of the Convention and the respective functions of each such Authority shall be carried out through the United States Fish and Wildlife Service.

(b) MANAGEMENT AUTHORITY FUNCTIONS.-The Secretary shall do all things necessary and appropriate to carry out the functions of the Management Authority under the Convention.

(c) SCIENTIFIC AUTHORITY FUNCTIONS.

(1) The Secretary shall do all things necessary and appropriate to carry out the functions of the Scientific Authority under the Convention.

(2) The Secretary shall base the determinations and advice given by him under Article IV of the Convention with respect to wildlife upon the best available biological information derived from professionally accepted wildlife management practices; but is not required to make, or require any State to make, estimates of population size in making such determinations or giving such advice.

(d) RESERVATIONS BY THE UNITED STATES UNDER CONVENTION.-If the United States votes against including any species in Appendix I or II of the Convention and does not enter a reservation pursuant to paragraph (3) of Article XV of the Convention with respect to that species, the Secretary of State, before the 90th day after the last day on which such a reservation could be entered, shall submit to the Committee on Merchant Marine and Fisheries of the House of Representatives, and to the Committee on the Environment and Public Works of the Senate, a written report setting forth the reasons why such a reservation was not entered.

(e) WILDLIFE PRESERVATION IN WESTERN HEMISPHERE.-

(1) The Secretary of the Interior (hereinafter in this subsection referred to as the "Secretary"), in cooperation with the Secretary of State, shall act on behalf of, and represent, the United States in all regards as required by the Convention on Nature Protection and Wildlife Preservation in the Western Hemisphere (56 Stat. 1354, T.S. 982, hereinafter in this subsection referred to as the "Western Convention"). In the discharge of these responsibilities, the Secretary and the Secretary of State shall consult with the Secretary of Agriculture, the Secretary of Commerce, and the heads of other agencies with respect to matters relating to or affecting their areas of responsibility.

(2) The Secretary and the Secretary of State shall, in cooperation with the contracting parties to the Western Convention and to the extent feasible and appropriate, with the participation of State agencies, take such steps as are necessary to implement the Western Convention. Such steps shall include, but not be limited to

(A) cooperation with contracting parties and international organizations

239

for the purpose of developing personnel resources and programs that will facilitate implementation of the Western Convention;

(B) identification of those species of birds that migrate between the United States and other contracting parties, and the habitats upon which those species depend, and the implementation of cooperative measures to ensure that such species will not become endangered or threatened; and

(C) identification of measures that are necessary and appropriate to implement those provisions of the Western Convention which address the protection of wild plants.

(3) No later than September 30, 1985, the Secretary and the Secretary of State shall submit a report to Congress describing those steps taken in accordance with the requirements of this subsection and identifying the principal remaining actions yet necessary for comprehensive and effective implementation of the Western Convention.

(4) The provisions of this subsection shall not be construed as affecting the authority, jurisdiction, or responsibility of the several States to manage, control, or regulate resident fish or wildlife under State law or regulations.

PROHIBITED ACTS
SEC. 9.

(a) GENERAL.

(1) Except as provided in sections 6(g)(2) and 10 of this Act, with respect to any endangered species of fish or wildlife listed pursuant to section 4 of this Act it is unlawful for any person subject to the jurisdiction of the United States to-

(A) import any such species into, or export any such species from the United States;

(B) take any such species within the United States or the territorial sea of the United States;

(C) take any such species upon the high seas;

(D) possess sell, deliver, carry, transport, or ship, by any means whatsoever, any such species taken in violation of subparagraphs (B) and (C);

(E) deliver, receive, carry, transport, or ship in interstate or foreign commerce, by any means whatsoever and in the course of a commercial activity, any such species;

(F) sell or offer for sale in interstate or foreign commerce any such species; or

(G) violate any regulation pertaining to such species or to any threatened species of fish or wildlife listed pursuant to section 4 of this Act and promulgated by the Secretary pursuant to authority provided by this Act. (2) Except as provided in sections 6(g)(2) and 10 of this Act, with respect to any endangered species of plants listed pursuant to section 4 of this Act, it is unlawful for any person subject to the jurisdiction of the United States to-

(A) import any such species into, or export any such species from, the United States;

(B) remove and reduce to possession any such species from areas under Federal jurisdiction; maliciously damage or destroy any such species on any such area; or remove, cut, dig up, or damage or destroy any such species on any other area in knowing violation of any law or regulation of any state or in the course of any violation of a state criminal trespass law;

(C) deliver, receive, carry, transport, or ship in interstate or foreign commerce, by any means whatsoever and in the course of a commercial activity, any such species;

(D) sell or offer for sale in interstate or foreign commerce any such species; or

(E) violate any regulation pertaining to such species or to any threatened species of plants listed pursuant to section 4 of this Act and promulgated by the Secretary pursuant to authority provided by this Act.

(b)(1) SPECIES HELD IN CAPTIVITY OR CONTROLLED ENVIRONMENT. The provisions of subsections (a)(l)(A) and (a)(l)(G) of this section shall not apply to any fish or wildlife which was held in captivity or in a controlled environment on (A) December 28. 1973, or

(B) the date of the publication in the Federal Register of a final regulation adding such fish or wildlife species to any list published pursuant to subsection (c) of section 4 of this Act: Provided, That such holding and any subsequent holding or use of the fish or wildlife was not in the course of a commercial activity. With respect to any act prohibited by subsections (a)(1)(A) and (a)(1)(G) of this section which occurs after a period of 180 days from

(i) December 28, 1973, or

(ii) the date of publication in the Federal Register of a final regulation adding such fish or wildlife species to any list published pursuant to subsection (c) of section 4 of this Act, there shall be a rebuttable presumption that the fish or wildlife involved in such act is not entitled to the exemption contained in this subsection.

(2)(A) The provisions of subsections (a)(I) shall not apply to-

(i) any raptor legally held in captivity or in a controlled environment on the effective date of the Endangered Species Act Amendments of 1978; or

(ii) any progeny of any raptor described in clause (i); until such time as any such raptor or progeny is intentionally returned to a wild state.

(B) Any person holding any raptor or progeny described in subparagraph (A) must be able to demonstrate that the raptor or progeny does, in fact, qualify under the provisions of this paragraph, and shall maintain and submit to the Secretary, on request, such inventories documentation, and records as the Secretary may by regulation require as being reasonably appropriate to carry out the purposes of this paragraph. Such requirements shall not unnecessarily duplicate the requirements of other rules and regulations promulgated by the Secretary.

(c) VIOLATION OF CONVENTION

(I) It is unlawful for any person subject to the jurisdiction of the United States to engage in any trade in any specimens contrary to the provisions of the Convention, or to possess any specimens traded contrary to the provisions of the Convention, including the definitions of terms in article I thereof

(2) Any importation into the United States of fish or wildlife shall, if-

(A) such fish or wildlife is not an endangered species listed pursuant to section 4 of this Act but is listed in Appendix II of the Convention:

(B) the taking and exportation of such fish or wildlife is not contrary to the provisions of the Convention and all other applicable requirements of the Convention have been satisfied;

(C) the applicable requirements of subsections (d), (e), and (f) of this section have been satisfied; and

(D) such importation is not made in the course of a commercial activity; be presumed to be an importation not in violation of any provision of this Act or any regulation issued pursuant to this Act.

(d) IMPORTS AND EXPORTS.-

(I) IN GENERAL.-It is unlawful for any person, without first having obtained permission from the Secretary, to engage in business-

(A) as an importer or exporter of fish or wildlife (other than shellfish and fishery products which

(i) are not listed pursuant to section 4 of this Act as endangered species

or threatened species, and

(ii) are imported for purposes of human or animal consumption or taken in waters under the jurisdiction of the United States or on the high seas for recreational purposes) or plants; or

(B) as an importer or exporter of any amount of raw or worked African elephant ivory.

(2) REQUIREMENTS.-Any person required to obtain permission under paragraph (I) of this subsection shall-

(A) keep such records as will fully and correctly disclose each importation or exportation of fish, wildlife, plants, or African elephant ivory made by him and the subsequent disposition made by him with respect to such fish, wildlife, plants, or ivory;

(B) at all reasonable times upon notice by a duly authorized representative of the Secretary, afford such representative access to his place of business, an opportunity to ex- amine his inventory of imported fish, wildlife, plants, or African elephant ivory and

the records required to be kept under subparagraph (A) of this paragraph, and to copy such records; and

(C) file such reports as the Secretary may require.

(3) REGULATIONS.-The Secretary shall prescribe such regulations as are necessary and appropriate to carry out the purposes of this subsection.

(4) RESTRICTION ON CONSIDERATION OF VALUE OR AMOUNT OF AFRICAN ELEPHANT IVORY IMPORTED OR EXPORTED.-In granting permission under this subsection for importation or exportation of African elephant ivory, the Secretary shall not vary the requirements for obtaining such permission on the basis of the value or amount of ivory imported or exported under such permission.

(e) REPORTS -It is unlawful for any person importing or exporting fish or wildlife (other than shellfish and fishery products) which

(I) are not listed pursuant to section 4 of this Act as endangered or threatened species, and

(2) are imported for purposes of human or animal consumption or taken in waters under the jurisdiction of the United States or on the high seas for recreational purposes) or plants to fail to file any declaration or report as the Secretary deems necessary to facilitate enforcement of this Act or to meet the obligations of the Convention.

(f) DESIGNATION OF PORTS-

(I) It is unlawful for any person subject to the jurisdiction of the United

States to import into or export from the United States any fish or wildlife (other than shellfish and fishery products which

(A) are not listed pursuant to section 4 of this Act as endangered species or threatened species, and

(B) are imported for purposes of human or animal consumption or taken in waters under the jurisdiction of the United States or on the high seas for recreational purposes) or plants, except at a port or pons designated by the Secretary of the Interior For the purposes of facilitating enforcement of this Act and reducing the costs thereof, the Secretary of the Interior, with approval of the Secretary of the Treasury and after notice and opportunity for public hearing, may, by regulation, designate ports and change such designations. The Secretary of the Interior, under such terms and conditions as he may prescribe, may permit the importation or exportation at nondesignated ports in the interest of the health or safety of the fish or wildlife or plants, or for other reasons if. in his discretion, he deems it appropriate and consistent with the purpose of this subsection.

(2) Any port designated by the Secretary of the Interior under the authority of section 4(d) of the Act of December 5, 1969 [16 U.S.C. 666cc 4(d)], shall, if such designation is in effect on the day before the date of the enactment of this Act, be deemed to be a port designated by the Secretary under paragraph (1) of this subsection until such time as the Secretary otherwise provides.

(g) Violations -It is Unlawful for any person subject to the jurisdiction of the United States to attempt to commit, solicit another to commit, or cause to be committed, any offense defined in this section.

EXCEPTIONS
SEC. I0.

(a) PERMITS-

(I) The Secretary may permit, under such terms and conditions as he shall prescribe-

(A) any act otherwise prohibited by section 9 for scientific purposes or to enhance the propagation or survival of the affected species, including, but not limited to, acts necessary for the establishment and maintenance of experimental populations pursuant subsection (j); or

(B) any taking otherwise prohibited by section 9(a)(I)(B) if such taking is incidental to, and not the purpose of, the carrying out of an otherwise lawful activity.

(2)(A) No permit may be issued by the Secretary authorizing any taking referred to in paragraph (1)(B) unless the applicant therefor submits to the Secretary a conservation plan that specifies-

(i) the impact which will likely result from such taking;

(ii) what steps the applicant will take to minimize and mitigate such impacts, and the funding that will be available to implement such steps;

(iii) what alternative actions to such taking the applicant considered and the reasons why such alternatives are not being utilized; and

(iv) such other measures that the Secretary may require as being necessary or appropriate for purposes of the plan.

(B) If the Secretary finds, after opportunity for public comment, with respect to a permit application and the related conservation plan that-

(i) the taking will be incidental;

(ii) the applicant will, to the maximum extent practicable, minimize and mitigate the impacts of such taking;

(iii) the applicant will ensure that adequate funding for the plan will be provided.

(iv) the taking will not appreciably reduce the likelihood of the survival and recovery of the species in the wild; and

(v) the measures. if any, required under subparagraph (A)(iv) will be met; and he has received such other assurances as he may require that the plan will be implemented, the Secretary shall issue the permit. The permit shall contain such terms and conditions as the Secretary deems necessary or appropriate to carry out the purposes of this paragraph, including. but not limited to, such reporting requirements as the Secretary deems necessary for determining whether such terms and conditions are being complied with.

(C) The Secretary shall revoke a permit issued under this paragraph if he finds that the permittee is not complying with the terms and conditions of the permit.

(b) HARDSHIP EXEMPTIONS.

(1) If any person enters into a contract with respect to a species of fish or wildlife or plant before the date of the publication in the Federal Register of notice of consideration of that species as an endangered species and the subsequent listing of that species as an endangered species pursuant to section 4 of this Act will cause undue hardship to such person under the contract, the Secretary. in order to minimize such hardship, may exempt such person from the application of section 9(a) of this Act to the extent the Secretary deems appropriate if such person

applies to him for such exemption and includes with such application such information as the Secretary may require to prove such hardship; except that (A) no such exemption shall be for a duration of more than one year from the date of publication in the Federal Register of notice of consideration of the species concerned, or shall apply to a quantity of fish or wildlife or plants in excess of that specified by the Secretary; (B) the one-year period for those species of fish or wildlife listed by the Secretary as endangered prior to the effective date of this Act shall expire in accordance with the terms of section 3 of the Act of December 5, 1969 (83 Stat. 275); and (C) no such exemption may be granted for the importation or exportation of a specimen listed in Appendix I of the Convention which is to be used in a commercial activity.

(2) As used in this subsection, the term "undue economic hardship" shall include, but not be limited to:

(A) substantial economic loss resulting from inability caused by this Act to perform contracts with respect to species of fish and wildlife entered into prior to the date of publication in the Federal Register of a notice of consideration of such species as an endangered species;

(B) substantial economic loss to persons who, for the year prior to the notice of consideration of such species as an endangered species, derived a substantial portion of their income from the lawful taking of any listed species, which taking would be made unlawful under this Act; or

(C) curtailment of subsistence taking made unlawful under this Act by persons

(i) not reasonably able to secure other sources of subsistence; and

(ii) dependent to a substantial extent upon hunting and fishing for subsistence; and

(iii) who must engage in such curtailed taking for subsistence purposes.

(3) The Secretary may make further requirements for a showing of undue economic hardship as he deems fit. Exceptions granted under this section may be limited by the Secretary in his discretion as to time, area, or other factor of applicability.

(c) NOTICE AND REVIEW.-The Secretary shall publish notice in the Federal Register of each application for an exemption or permit which is made under this section. Each notice shall invite the submission from interested parties, within thirty days after the date of the notice, of written data, views, or arguments with respect to the application; except that such thirty-day period may be waived by the Secretary in an emergency situation where the health or life of an endangered animal is threatened and no reasonable alternative is available to the applicant, but notice of any such waiver shall be published by the Secretary in the Federal Register within ten days following the issuance of the exemption or permit. Information received by the Secretary as part of any application shall be available to the public as a matter of public record at every stage of the proceeding.

247

(d) PERMIT AND EXEMPTION POLICY.-The Secretary may grant exceptions under subsections (a)(I)(A) and (b) of this section only if he finds and publishes his finding in the Federal Register that

(I) such exceptions were applied for in good faith,

(2) if granted and exercised will not operate to the disadvantage of such endangered species, and

(3) will be consistent with the purposes and policy set forth in section 2 of this Act.

(e) ALASKA NATIVES-

(I) Except as provided in paragraph (4) of this subsection the provisions of this Act shall not apply with respect to the taking of any endangered species or threatened species, or the importation of any such species taken pursuant to this section, by-

(A) any Indian, Aleut, or Eskimo who is an Alaskan Native who resides in Alaska; or

(B) any non-native permanent resident of an Alaskan native village; if such taking is primarily for subsistence purposes. Non-edible byproducts of species taken pursuant to this section may be sold in interstate commerce when made into authentic native articles of handicrafts and clothing; except that the provisions of this subsection shall not apply to any non-native resident of an Alaskan native village found by the Secretary to be not primarily dependent upon the taking of fish and wildlife for consumption or for the creation and sale of authentic native articles of handicrafts and clothing.

(2) Any taking under this subsection may not be accomplished in a wasteful manner.

(3) As used in this subsection-

(i) The term "subsistence" includes selling any edible portion of fish or wildlife in native villages and towns in Alaska for native consumption within native villages or towns; and

(ii) The term "authentic native articles of handicrafts and clothing" means items composed wholly or in some significant respect to natural materials, and which are produced, decorated or fashioned in the exercise of traditional native handicrafts without the use of pantographs, multiple carvers, or other mass copying devices. Traditional native handicrafts include, but are not limited to, weaving, carving, stitching, sewing, lacing, beading, drawing, and painting.

(4) Notwithstanding the provisions of paragraph (I) of this subsection, whenever the Secretary determines that any species of fish or wildlife which is subject to taking under the provisions of this subsection is an endangered species or threatened species, and that such taking materially and negatively affects the threatened or endangered species, he may prescribe regulations upon the taking of such species by any such Indian, Aleut, Eskimo, or non-native Alaskan resident of an Alaskan native village. Such regulations may be established with reference to species, geographical description of the area included, the season for taking, or any other factors related to the reason for establishing such regulations and consistent with the policy of this Act. Such regulations shall be prescribed after a notice and hearings in the affected judicial districts of Alaska and as otherwise required by section 103 of the Marine Mammal Protection Act of 1972, and shall be removed as soon as the Secretary determines that the need for their impositions has disappeared.

(f)(I) As used in this subsection-

(A) The term "Pre-Act endangered species part" means-

(i) any sperm whale oil, including derivatives thereof, which was lawfully held within the United States on December 28, 1973, in the course of a commercial activity; or

(ii) any finished scrimshaw product, if such product or the raw material for such product was lawfully held within the United States on December 28, 1973, in the course of a commercial activity.

(B) The term "scrimshaw product" means any art form which involves the substantial etching or engraving of designs upon, or the substantial carving of figures, patterns, or designs from, any bone or tooth of any marine mammal of the order Cetacea. For purposes of this subsection, polishing or the adding of minor superficial markings does not constitute substantial etching, engraving, or carving.

(2) The Secretary, pursuant to the provisions of this subsection, may exempt, if such exemption is not in violation of the Convention, any pre-Act endangered species part from one or more of the following prohibitions:

(A) The prohibition on exportation from the United States set forth in section 9(a)(I)(A) of this Act.

(B) Any prohibition set forth in section 9(a)(I) (E) or (F) of this Act.
(3) Any person seeking an exemption described in paragraph (2) of this subsection shall make application therefor to the Secretary in such form and manner as he shall prescribe, but no such application may be considered by the Secretary unless the application-

(A) is received by the Secretary before the close of the one year period beginning on the date on which regulations promulgated by the Secretary to carry out this subsection first take effect;

249

(3) contains a complete and detailed inventory of all pre-Act endangered species parts for which the applicant seeks exemption;

(C) is accompanied by such documentation as the Secretary may require to prove that any endangered species part or product claimed by the applicant to be a pre-Act endangered species part is in fact such a part; and

(D) contains such other information as the Secretary deems necessary and appropriate to carry out the purposes of this subsection.

(4) If the Secretary approves any application for exemption made under this subsection, he shall issue to the applicant a certificate of exemption which shall specify-

(A) any prohibition in section 9(a) of this Act which is exempted;

(B) the pre-Act endangered species parts to which the exemption applies;

(C) the period of time during which the exemption is in effect, but no exemption made under this subsection shall have force and effect after the close of the three-year period beginning on the date of issuance of the certificate unless such exemption is renewed under paragraph (8); and

(D) any term or condition prescribed pursuant to paragraph (5)(A) or (B), or both, which the Secretary deems necessary or appropriate.

(5) The Secretary shall prescribe such regulations as he deems necessary and appropriate to carry out the purposes of this subsection. Such regulations may set forth-

(A) terms and conditions which may be imposed on applicants for exemptions under this subsection (including, but not limited to, requirements that applicants register inventories, keep complete sales records, permit duly authorized agents of the Secretary to inspect such inventories and records, and periodically file appropriate reports with the Secretary); and

(B) terms and conditions which may be imposed on any subsequent purchaser of any pre-Act endangered species pan covered by an exemption granted under this subsection; to insure that any such part so exempted is adequately accounted for and not disposed of contrary to the provisions of this Act. No regulation prescribed by the Secretary to carry out the purposes of this subsection shall be subject to section 4(f)(2)(A)(i) of this Act.

(6)(A) Any contract for the sale of pre-Act endangered species parts which is entered into by the Administrator of General Services prior to the effective date of this subsection and pursuant to the notice published in the Federal Register on January 9, 1973, shall not be rendered invalid by virtue of the fact that fulfillment of such contract may be prohibited under section 9(a)(1)(F).

(B) In the event that this paragraph is held invalid, the validity of the remainder of the Act, including the remainder of this subsection. shall not be affected.

(7) Nothing in this subsection shall be construed to-

(A) exonerate any person from any act committed in violation of paragraphs (1)(A), (1)(E), or (1)(F) of section 9(a) prior to the date of enactment of this subsection; or

(B) immunize any person from prosecution for any such act. (8)(A)(i) Any valid certificate of exemption which was renewed after October 13, 1982, and was in effect on March 31, 1988, shall be deemed to be renewed for a 6-month period beginning on the date of enactment of the Endangered Species Act Amendments of 1988. Any person holding such a certificate may apply to the Secretary for one additional renewal of such certificate for a period not to exceed 5 years beginning on the date of such enactment.

(B) If the Secretary approves any application for renewal of an exemption under this paragraph, he shall issue to the applicant a certificate of renewal of such exemption which shall provide that all terms, conditions, prohibitions, and other regulations made applicable by the previous certificate shall remain in effect during the period of the renewal.

(C) No exemption or renewal of such exemption made under this subsection shall have force and effect after the expiration date of the certificate of renewal of such exemption issued under this paragraph.

(D) No person may, after January 31, 1984, sell or offer for sale in interstate or foreign commerce, any pre-Act finished scrimshaw product unless such person holds a valid certificate of exemption issued by the Secretary under this subsection, and unless such product or the raw material for such product was held by such person on October 13, 1982.

(g) In connection with any action alleging a violation of section 9, any person claiming the benefit of any exemption or permit under this Act shall have the burden of proving that the exemption or permit is applicable, has been granted and was valid and in force at the time of the alleged violation.

(h) CERTAIN ANTIQUE ARTICLES.-

(1) Sections 4(d), 9(a), and 9(c) do not apply to any article which-

(A) is not less than 100 years of age;

(B) is composed in whole or in part of any endangered species or threatened species listed under section 4.

(C) has not been repaired or modified with any Dart of any such species on or after the date of the enactment of this Act and (D) is entered at a port designated under paragraph (3).

(2) Any person who wishes to import an article under the exception provided by this subsection shall submit to the customs officer concerned at the time of entry of the article such documentation as the Secretary of the Treasury, after consultation with the Secretary of the Interior, shall by regulation require as being necessary to establish that the article meets the requirements set forth in paragraph (1) (A), (B), and (C).

(3) The Secretary of the Treasury, after consultation with the Secretary of the Interior, shall designate one port within each customs region at which articles described in paragraph

(1) (A), (B), and (C) must be entered into the customs territory of the United States.

(4) Any person who imported, after December 27, 1973, and on or before the date of the enactment of the Endangered Species Act Amendments of 1978, any article described in paragraph (1) which-

(A) was not repaired or modified after the date of importation with any part of any endangered species or threatened species listed under section 4;

(B) was forfeited to the United States before such date of the enactment, or is subject to forfeiture to the United States on such date of enactment. pursuant to the assessment of a civil penalty under section 11; and

(C) is in the custody of the United States on such date of enactment;

may, before the dose of the one-year period beginning on such date of enactment make application to the Secretary for return of the article. Application shall be made in such form and manner~and contain such documentation, as the Secretary prescribes. If on the basis of any such application which is timely filed, the Secretary is satisfied that the requirements of this paragraph are met with respect to the article concerned, the Secretary shall return the article to the applicant and the importation of such article shall, on and after the date of return, be deemed to be a lawful importation under this Act.

(i) NONCOMMERCIAL TRANSSHIPMENTS.-Any importation into the United States of fish or wildlife shall, if-

(1) such fish or wildlife was lawfully taken and exported from the country of origin and country of reexport, if any;

(2) such fish or wildlife is in transit or transshipment through any place subject to the jurisdiction of the United States en route to a country where such fish or wildlife may be lawfully imported and received;

(3) the exporter or owner of such fish or wildlife gave explicit instructions not to ship such fish or wildlife through any place subject to the jurisdiction of the United States, or did all that could have reasonably been done to prevent transshipment, and the circumstances leading to the transshipment were beyond the exporter's or owner's control;

(4) the applicable requirements of the Convention have been satisfied; and

(5) such importation is not made in the course of a commercial activity, be an importation not in violation of any provision of this Act or any regulation issued pursuant to this Act while such fish or wildlife remains in the control of the United States Customs Service.

(j) EXPERIMENTAL POPULATIONS.

(1) For purposes of this subsection, the term "experimental population" means any population (including any offspring arising solely therefrom) authorized by the Secretary for release under paragraph (2), but only when, and at such times as, the population is wholly separate geographically from nonexperimental populations of the same species.

(2)(A) The Secretary may authorize the release (and the related transportation) of any population (including eggs, propagules, or individuals) of an endangered species or a threatened species outside the current range of such species if the Secretary determines that such release will further the conservation of such species.

(B) Before authorizing the release of any population under subparagraph (A), the Secretary shall by regulation identify the population and determine, on the basis of the best available information, whether or not such population is essential to the continued existence of an endangered species or a threatened species.

(C) For the purposes of this Act, each member of an experimental population shall be treated as a threatened species; except that-

(i) solely for purposes of section 7 (other than subsection (a)(1) thereof), an experimental population determined under subparagraph (B) to be not essential to the continued existence of a species shall be treated, except when it occurs in an area within the National Wildlife Refuge System or the National Park System, as a species proposed to be listed under section 4; and

253

(ii) critical habitat shall not be designated under this Act for any experimental population determined under subparagraph (B) to be not essential to the continued existence of a species.

(3) The Secretary, with respect to populations of endangered species or threatened species that the Secretary authorized, before the date of the enactment of this subsection, for release in geographical areas separate from the other populations of such species, shall determine by regulation which of such populations are an experimental population for the purposes of this subsection and whether or not each is essential to the continued existence of an endangered species or a threatened species.

PENALTIES AND ENFORCEMENT
SEC. 11.
(a) CIVIL PENALTIES.-
(1) Any person who knowingly violates, and any person engaged in business as an importer or exporter of fish, wildlife, or plants who violates, any provision of this Act, or any provision of any permit or certificate issued hereunder, or of any regulation issued in order to implement subsection (a)(1)(A), (B), (C), (D), (E), or (F), (a)(2)(A)7 (B), (C), or (D) (c), (d) (other than regulation relating to recordkeeping or filing of reports), (f), or (g) of section 9 of this Act, may be assessed a civil penalty by the Secretary of not more than $25,000 for each violation. Any person who knowingly violates, and any person engaged in business as an importer or exporter of fish, wildlife, or plants who violates, any provision of any other regulation issued under this Act may be assessed a civil penalty by the Secretary of not more than $12,000 for each such violation. Any person who otherwise violates any provision of this Act, or any regulation, permit, or certificate issued hereunder, may be assessed a civil penalty by the Secretary of not more than $500 for each such violation. No penalty may be assessed under this subsection unless such person is given notice and opportunity for a hearing with respect to such violation. Each violation shall be a separate offense. Any such civil penalty may be remitted or mitigated by the Secretary. Upon any failure to pay a penalty assessed under this subsection, the Secretary may

request the Attorney General to institute a civil action in a district court of the United States for any district in which such person is found, resides, or transacts business to collect the penalty and such court shall have jurisdiction to hear and decide any such action. The court shall hear such action on the record made before the Secretary and shall sustain his action if it is supported by substantial evidence on the record considered as a whole.

(2) Hearings held during proceedings for the assessment of civil penalties by paragraph (I) of this subsection shall be conducted in accordance with section 554 of title 5, United States Code. The Secretary may issue subpoenas for the attendance and testimony of witnesses and the production of relevant papers, books. and documents. and administer oaths. Witnesses summoned shall be paid the same fees and mileage that are paid to witnesses in the courts of the United States. In case of contumacy or refusal to obey a subpoena served upon any person pursuant to this paragraph, the district court of the United States for any district in which such person is found or resides or transacts business, upon application by the United States and after notice to such person. shall have jurisdiction to issue an order requiring such person to appear and give testimony before the Secretary or to appear and produce documents before the Secretary, or both, and any failure to obey such order of the court may be punished by such court as a contempt thereof.

(3) Notwithstanding any other provision of this Act, no civil penalty shall be imposed if it can be shown by a preponderance of the evidence that the defendant committed an act based on a good faith belief that he was acting to protect himself or herself, a member of his or her family, or any other individual from bodily harm. from any endangered or threatened species.

(b) CRIMINAL VIOLATIONS.-

(I) Any person who knowingly violates any provision of this Act, of any permit or certificate issued hereunder, or of any regulation issued in order to implement subsection (a)(l)(A), (B), (C), (D), (E), or (F); (a)(2)(A), (B), (C), or (D), (c). (d) (other than a regulation relating to recordkeeping, or filing of reports), (f), or (g) of section 9 of this Act shall, upon conviction, be fined not more than $50,000 or imprisoned for not more than one year, or both. Any person who knowingly violates any provision of any other regulation issued under this Act shall, upon conviction, be fined not more than $25,000 or imprisoned for not more than six months, or both.

(2) The head of any Federal agency which has issued a lease, license, permit, or other agreement authorizing a person to import or export fish, wildlife, or plants, or to operate a quarantine station for imported wildlife, or authorizing the use of Federal lands, including grazing of domestic livestock to any person who is convicted of a criminal violation of this Act or any regulation, permit, or certificate issued hereunder may immediately modify, suspend, or revoke each lease, license, permit, or other agreement. The Secretary shall also suspend for a period of up to one year, or cancel, any Federal hunting or fishing permits or stamps issued to any person who is convicted of a criminal violation of any provision of this Act or any regulation, permit, or certificate issued hereunder. The United States shall not be liable for the payments of any compensation. reimbursement, or damages in connection with the modification, suspension, or revocation of any leases, licenses permits stamps, or other agreements pursuant to this section.

(3) Notwithstanding any other provision of this Act, it shall be a defense to prosecution under this subsection if the defendant committed the offense based on a good faith belief that he was acting to protect himself or herself, a member of his or her family, or any other individual, from bodily harm from any endangered or threatened species.

(c) DISTRICT COURT JURISDICTION.-The several district courts of the United States; including the courts enumerated in section 460 of title 28, United States Code, shall have jurisdiction over any actions arising under this Act. For the purpose of this Act, American Samoa shall be included within the judicial district of the District Court of the United States for the District of Hawaii.

(d) REWARDS AND CERTAIN INCIDENTAL EXPENSES.-The Secretary or the Secretary of the Treasury shall pay, from sums received as penalties, fines, or forfeitures of properly for any violation of this chapter or any regulation issued hereunder

(1) a reward to any person who furnishes information which leads to an arrest, a criminal conviction, civil penalty assessment, or forfeiture of property for any violation of this chapter or any regulation issued hereunder, and

(2) the reasonable and necessary costs incurred by any person in providing temporary care for any fish, wildlife, or plant pending the disposition of any civil or criminal proceeding alleging a violation of this chapter with respect to that fish, wildlife, or plant. The amount of the reward, if any, is to be designated by the Secretary or the Secretary of the

Treasury, as appropriate. Any officer or employee of the United States or any State or local government who furnishes information or renders service in the performance of his official duties is ineligible for payment under this subsection. Whenever the balance of sums received under this section and section 6(d) of the Act of November 16, 1981 (16 U.S.C. 3375(d)) as penalties or fines, or from forfeitures of property, exceed $500,000, the Secretary of the Treasury shall deposit an amount equal to such excess balance in the cooperative endangered species conservation fund established under section 6(i) of this Act.

(e) ENFORCEMENT.

(1) The provisions of this Act and any regulations or permits issued pursuant thereto shall be enforced by the Secretary. the Secretary of the Treasury, or the Secretary of the Department in which the Coast Guard is operating, or all such Secretaries. Each such Secretary may utilize by agreement, with or without reimbursement, the personnel, services, and facilities of any other Federal agency or any State agency for purposes of enforcing this Act.

(2) The judges of the district courts of the United States and the United States magistrates may within their respective jurisdictions, upon proper oath or affirmation showing probable cause, issue such warrants or other process as may be required for enforcement of this Act and any regulation issued thereunder.

(3) Any person authorized by the Secretary, the Secretary of the Treasury, or the Secretary of the Department in which the Coast Guard is operating, to enforce this Act may detain for inspection and inspect any package, crate, or other container, including its contents, and all accompanying documents, upon importation or exportation. Such persons may make arrests without a warrant for any violation of this Act if he has reasonable grounds to believe that the person to be arrested is committing the violation in his presence or view and may execute and serve any arrest warrant, search warrant, or other warrant or civil or criminal process issued by any officer or court of competent jurisdiction for enforcement of this Act. Such person so authorized may search and seize, with or without a warrant, as authorized by law. Any fish, wildlife, property, or item so seized shall be held by any person authorized by the Secretary, the Secretary of the Treasury, or the Secretary of the Department in which the Coast Guard is operating pending disposition of civil or criminal proceedings, or the institution of an action in rem for forfeiture of such fish, wildlife, property, or item pursuant to para-

graph (4) of the subsection; except that the Secretary may, in lieu of holding such fish, wildlife, property, or item, permit the owner or consignee to post a bond or other surety satisfactory to the Secretary, but upon forfeiture of any such property to the United States, or the abandonment or waiver of any claim to any such property, it shall be disposed of (other than by sale to the general public) by the Secretary in such a manner, consistent with the purposes of this Act, as the Secretary shall by regulation prescribe.

257

(4)(A) All fish or wildlife or plants taken, possessed sold purchased offered for sale or purchase, transported, delivered, received, carried, shipped, exported, or imported contrary to the provisions of this Act, any regulation made pursuant thereto, or any permit or certificate issued hereunder shall be subject to forfeiture to the United States.

(B) All guns, traps, nets, and other equipment, vessels, vehicles, aircraft, and other means of transportation used to aid the taking, possessing, selling, purchasing, offering for sale or purchase, transporting, delivering, receiving, carrying, shipping, exporting, or importing of any fish or wildlife or plants in violation of this Act, any regulation made pursuant thereto, or any permit or certificate issued thereunder shall be subject to forfeiture to the United States upon conviction of a criminal violation pursuant to section I l(b)(l) of this Act.

(5) All provisions of law relating to the seizure, forfeiture, and condemnation of a vessel for violation of the customs laws, the disposition of such vessel or the proceeds from the sale thereof, and the remission or mitigation of such forfeiture, shall apply to the seizures and forfeitures incurred, or alleged to have been incurred, under the provisions of this Act, insofar as such provisions of law are applicable and not inconsistent with the provisions of this Act; except that all powers, rights, and duties conferred or imposed by the customs laws upon any officer or employee of the Treasury Department shall, for the purposes of this Act, be exercised or performed by the Secretary or by such persons as he may designate.

(6) The Attorney General of the United States may seek to enjoin any person who is alleged to be in violation of any provision of this Act or regulation issued under authority thereof.

(f) REGULATIONS.-The Secretary, the Secretary of the Treasury, and the Secretary of the Department in which the Coast Guard is operating, are authorized to promulgate such regulations as may be appropriate to enforce this Act, and charge reasonable fees for expenses to the

Government connected with permits or certificates authorized by this Act including processing applications and reasonable inspections, and with the transfer, board handling, or storage of fish or wildlife or plants and evidentiary items seized and forfeited under this Act. All such fees collected pursuant to this subsection shall be deposited in the Treasury to the credit of the appropriation which is current and chargeable for the cost of furnishing the services. Appropriated funds may be expended pending reimbursement from parties in interest.

(g) CITIZEN SUITS.-

(1) Except as provided in paragraph (2) of this subsection any person may commence a civil suit on his own behalf-

(A) to enjoin any person, including the United States and any other governmental instrumentality or agency (to the extent permitted by the eleventh amendment to the Constitution), who is alleged to be in violation of any provision of this Act or regulation issued under the authority thereof; or

(B) to compel the Secretary to apply, pursuant to section 6(g)(2)(B)(ii) of this Act, the prohibitions set forth in or authorized pursuant to section 4(d) or section 9(a)(1)(B) of this Act with respect to the taking of any resident endangered species or threatened species within any State; or

(C) against the Secretary where there is alleged a failure of the Secretary to perform any act or duty under section 4 which is not discretionary with the Secretary.

The district courts shall have jurisdiction, without regard to the amount in controversy or the citizenship of the parties, to enforce any such provision or regulation or to order the Secretary to perform such act or duty, as the case may be. In any civil suit commenced under subparagraph (B) the district court shall compel the Secretary to apply the prohibition sought if the court finds that the allegation that an emergency exists is supported by substantial evidence.

(2)(A) No action may be commenced under subparagraph (1)(A) of this section-

(i) prior to sixty days after written notice of the violation has been given to the Secretary, and to any alleged violator of any such provision or regulation;

(ii) if the Secretary has commenced action to impose a penalty pursuant to subsection (a) of this section; or

(iii) if the United States has commenced and is diligently prosecuting a criminal action in a court of the United States or a State to redress a violation of any such provision or regulation.

(B) No action may be commenced under subparagraph (I)(B) of this section-

(i) prior to sixty days after written notice has been given to the Secretary setting forth the reasons why an emergency is thought to exist with respect to an endangered species or a threatened species in the State concerned; or

(ii) if the Secretary has commenced and is diligently prosecuting action under section 6(g)(2)(B)(ii) of this Act to determine whether any such emergency exists.

(C) No action may be commenced under subparagraph (I)(C) of this section prior to sixty days after written notice has been given to the Secretary; except that such action may be brought immediately after such notification in the case of an action under this section respecting an emergency posing a significant risk to the well-being of any species of fish or wildlife or plants.

(3)(A) Any suit under this subsection may be brought in the judicial district in which the violation occurs.

(B) In any such suit under this subsection in which the United States is not a party, the Attorney General, at the request of the Secretary, may intervene on behalf of the United States as a manner of right.

(4) The court, in issuing any final order in any suit brought pursuant to paragraph (I) of this subsection, may award costs of litigation (including reasonable attorney and expert witness fees) to any party, whenever the court determines such award is appropriate.

(5) The injunctive relief provided by this subsection shall not restrict any right which any person (or class of persons) may have under any statute or common law to seek enforcement of any standard or limitation or to seek any other relief (including relief against the Secretary or a State agency).

(h) COORDINATION WITH OTHER LAWS.-The Secretary of Agriculture and the Secretary shall provide for appropriate coordination of the administration of this Act with the administration of the animal quarantine laws (21 U.S.C. 101-105, 111-135b, and 612-614) and section 306 of the Tariff Act of 1930 (19 U.S.C. 1306). Nothing in this Act or any amendment made by this Act shall be construed as superseding or limiting in any manner the functions of the Secretary of Agriculture under any other law relating to prohibited or restricted importations or possession of animals and other articles and no proceeding or determination under this Act shall preclude any proceeding or be considered determinative of any issue of fact or law in any proceeding under any Act administered by the Secretary of Agriculture. Nothing in this Act shall be construed as superseding or limiting in any manner the functions and responsibilities of the Secretary of the Treasury under the Tariff Act of 1930, including, without limitation, section 527 of that Act (19 U.S.C. 1527), relating to the importation of wildlife taken, killed, possessed, or exported to the United States in violation of the laws or regulations of a foreign country.

ENDANGERED PLANTS
SEC. 12. The Secretary of the Smithsonian Institution, in conjunction with other affected agencies, is authorized and directed to review (1) species of plants which are now or may become endangered, or threatened and (2) methods of adequately conserving such species, and to report to Congress, within one year after the date of the enactment of this Act, the results of such review including recommendations for new legislation or the amendment of existing legislation.

CONFORMING AMENDMENTS
SEC. 13.
(a) Subsection 4(c) of the Act of October 15, 1966 (80 Stat. 928, 16 U.S.C. 668dd(c)), is further amended by revising the second sentence thereof to read as follows: "With the exception of endangered species and threatened species listed by the Secretary pursuant to section 4 of the Endangered Species Act of 1973 in States wherein a cooperative agreement does not exist pursuant to section 6(c) of that Act, nothing in this Act shall be construed to authorize the Secretary to control or regulate hunting or fishing of resident fish and wildlife on lands not within the system."
(b) Subsection 10(a) of the Migratory Bird Conservation Act (45 Stat. 1224, 16 U.S.C. 715i(a)) and subsection 401(a) of the Act of June 15, 1935 (49 Stat. 383, 16 U.S.C. 715s(a)) are each amended by striking out "threatened with extinction," and inserting in lieu thereof the following: "listed pursuant to section 4 of the Endangered Species Act of 1973 as endangered species or threatened species."
(c) Section 7(a)(1) of the Land and Water Conservation Fund Act of 1965 (16 U.S.C. 4601-9(a)(1)) is amended by striking out:

"THREATENED SPECIES.-For any national area which may be authorized for the preservation of species of fish or wildlife that are threatened with extinction." and inserting in lieu thereof the following: "ENDANGERED SPECIES AND THREATENED SPECIES -For lands, waters, or interests therein, the acquisition of which is authorized under section 5(a) of the Endangered Species Act of 1973, needed for the purpose of conserving endangered or threatened species of fish or wildlife or plants."

(d) The first sentence of section 2 of the Act of September 28, 1962, as amended (76 Stat. 653, 16 U.S.C. 460k-1), is amended to read as follows:

"The Secretary is authorized to acquire areas of land, or interests therein, which are suitable for-

"(1) incidental fish and wildlife-oriented recreational development;

"(2) the protection of natural resources;

"(3) the conservation of endangered species or threatened species listed by the Secretary pursuant to section 4 of the Endangered Species Act of 1973; or

"(4) carrying out two or more of the purposes set forth in paragraphs (1) through (3) of this section, and are adjacent to, or within, the said conservation areas, except that the acquisition of any land or interest therein pursuant to this section shall be accomplished only with such funds as may be appropriated therefor by the Congress or donated for such purposes, but such property shall not be acquired with funds obtained from the sale of Federal migratory bird hunting stamps."

(e) The Marine Mammal Protection Act of 1972 (16 U.S.C. 13611407) is amended-

(1) by striking out "Endangered Species Conservation Act of 1969" in section 3(1)(B) thereof and inserting in lieu thereof the following: Endangered Species Act of 1973";

(2) by striking out "pursuant to the Endangered Species Conservation Act of 1969" in section 101(a)(3)(B) thereof and inserting in lieu thereof the following: "or threatened species pursuant to the Endangered Species Act of 1973";

(3) by striking out "endangered under the Endangered Species Conservation Act of 1969" in section 102(b)(3) thereof and inserting in lieu thereof the following: "an endangered species or threatened species pursuant to the Endangered Species Act of 1973"; and

(4) by striking out "of the interior and revisions of the Endangered

Species List, authorized by the Endangered Species Conservation Act of 1969," in section 202(a)(6) thereof and inserting in lieu thereof the following: "such revisions of the endangered species list and threatened species list published pursuant to section 4(c)(1) of the Endangered Species Act of 1973". (f) Section 2(1) of the Federal Environmental Pesticide Control Act of 1972 (Public Law 92-516) is amended by striking out the words "by the Secretary of the Interior under Public Law 91 - 135" and inserting in lieu thereof the words "or threatened by the Secretary pursuant to the Endangered Species Act of 1973."

REPEALER
SEC. 14.
The Endangered Species Conservation Act of 1969 (sections 1 through 3 of the Act of October 15, 1966, and sections 1 through 6 of the Act of December 5, 1969; 16 U.S.C. 668aa-668cc-6), is repealed.

AUTHORIZATION OF APPROPRIATIONS
SEC. 15.
(a) IN GENERAL -Except as provided in subsections (b), (c), and (d), there are authorized to be appropriated(1 not to exceed $35,000,000 for fiscal year 1988, $36,500,000 for fiscal year 1989, $38,000,000 for fiscal year 1990. $39.500.000 for fiscal year 1991, and $41,500,000 for fiscal year 1992 to enable the Department of the Interior to carry out such functions and responsibilities as it may have been given under this Act:
(2) not to exceed $5,750,000 for fiscal year 1988, $6,250,000 for each of fiscal years 1989 and 1990, and $6.750.000 for each of fiscal years 1991 and 1992 to enable the Department of Commerce to carry out such functions and responsibilities as it may have been given under this Act; and
(3) not to exceed $2,200,000 for fiscal year 1988, $2,400,000 for each of fiscal years 1989 and 1990, and $2,600,000 for each of fiscal years 1991 and 1992, to enable the Department of Agriculture to carry out its functions and responsibilities with respect to the enforcement of this Act and the Convention which pertain to the importation or exportation of plants.
(b) EXEMPTIONS FROM ACT.-There are authorized to be appropriated to the Secretary to assist him and the Endangered Species Committee in carrying out their functions under section 7 (e), (g) and

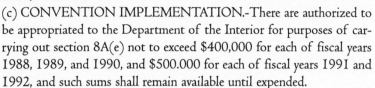

(h) not to exceed $600,000 for each for fiscal years 1988, 1989, 1990, 1991, and 1992.

(c) CONVENTION IMPLEMENTATION.-There are authorized to be appropriated to the Department of the Interior for purposes of carrying out section 8A(e) not to exceed $400,000 for each of fiscal years 1988, 1989, and 1990, and $500.000 for each of fiscal years 1991 and 1992, and such sums shall remain available until expended.

263

EFFECTIVE DATE
SEC. 16.
This Act shall take effect on the date of its enactment.

MARINE MAMMAL PROTECTION ACT OF 1972
SEC. 17.
Except as otherwise provided in this Act, no provision of this Act shall take precedence over any more restrictive conflicting provision of the Marine Mammal Protection Act of 1972.

ANNUAL COST ANALYSIS BY THE FISH AND WILDLIFE SERVICE
SEC. 18.
On or before January 15, 1990, and each January 15 thereafter, the Secretary of the Interior, acting through the Fish and Wildlife Service, shall submit to the Congress an annual report covering the preceding fiscal year which shall contain

(1) an accounting on a species by species basis of all reasonably identifiable Federal expenditures made primarily for the preservation of endangered or threatened species pursuant to this Act; and

(2) an accounting on a species by species basis for all reasonably identifiable expenditures made primarily for the conservation of endangered or threatened species pursuant to this Act by states receiving grants under section 6.

ENDANGERED SPECIES LIST—MAMMALS

(alphabetical by common name)
Published in the Federal Register—current through April 1995.

Common Name: Bat, gray
Scientific Name: Myotis grisescens
Historic Range: Central and southeastern U.S.A.
Status: E
When Listed: 13
Vertebrate Pop: Entire
Critical Habitat: NA
Special Rule: NA

Common Name: Bat, Hawaiian hoary
Scientific Name: Lasiurus cinereus semotus
Historic Range: U.S.A. (HI)
Status: E
When Listed: 2
Vertebrate Pop: Entire
Critical Habitat: NA
Special Rule: NA

Common Name: Bat, lesser (=Sanborn's) long-nosed
Scientific Name: Leptonycteris curasoae (=sanborni) yerbabuenae
Historic Range: U.S.A. (AZ, NM), Mexico, Central America
Status: E
When Listed: 336
Vertebrate Pop: Entire
Critical Habitat: NA
Special Rule: NA

Common Name: Bat, little Mariana fruit
Scientific Name: Pteropus tokudae
Historic Range: Western Pacific Ocean—U.S.A. (Guam)
Status: E
When Listed: 156
Vertebrate Pop: Entire
Critical Habitat: NA
Special Rule: NA

Common Name: Bat, Mariana fruit
Scientific Name: Pteropus mariannus mariannus
Historic Range: Western Pacific Ocean—U.S.A. (Guam, Rota, Tinian, Saipan, Agiguan)
Status: E
When Listed: 156
Vertebrate Pop: Guam
Critical Habitat: NA
Special Rule: NA

Common Name: Bat, Mexican long-nosed
Scientific Name: Leptonycteris nivalis
Historic Range: U.S.A. (NM, TX), Mexico, Central America
Status: E
When Listed: 336
Vertebrate Pop: Entire
Critical Habitat: NA
Special Rule: NA

Common Name: Bat, Ozark big-eared
Scientific Name: Plecotus townsendii ingens
Historic Range: U.S.A. (MO, OK, AR)
Status: E
When Listed: 85
Vertebrate Pop: Entire
Critical Habitat: NA
Special Rule: NA

Common Name: Bat, Virginia big-eared
Scientific Name: Plecotus townsendii virginianus
Historic Range: U.S.A. (KY, NC, WV, VA)
Status: E
When Listed: 85
Vertebrate Pop: Entire
Critical Habitat: 17.95(a)
Special Rule: NA

Common Name: Bear, Louisiana black
Scientific Name: Ursus americanus luteolus
Historic Range: U.S.A. (LA, MS, TX)
Status: T
When Listed: 456
Vertebrate Pop: Entire
Critical Habitat: NA
Special Rule: 17.40(i)

Common Name: Caribou, woodland
Scientific Name: Rangifer tarandus caribou
Historic Range: U.S.A. (AK, ID, ME, MI, MN, MT, NH, VT, WA, WI), Canada
Status: E
When Listed: 128E, 136E, 143
Vertebrate Pop: U.S.A. (ID, WA), Canada (that part of S.E. British Columbia bounded by the U.S.-Can. border, Columbia R., Kootenay R., Kootenay L., and Kootenai R.)
Critical Habitat: NA
Special Rule: NA

Common Name: Deer, Columbian white-tailed
Scientific Name: Odocoileus virginianus leucurus
Historic Range: U.S.A. (WA, OR)
Status: E
When Listed: 1
Vertebrate Pop: Entire
Critical Habitat: NA
Special Rule: NA

Common Name: Deer, key
Scientific Name: Odocoileus virginianus clavium
Historic Range: U.S.A. (FL)
Status: E
When Listed: I
Vertebrate Pop: Entire
Critical Habitat: NA
Special Rule: NA

Common Name: Dugong
Scientific Name: Dugong dugon
Historic Range: East Africa to southern Japan, including U.S.A. (Trust Territories)
Status: E
When Listed: 4
Vertebrate Pop: Entire, except U.S.A
Critical Habitat: NA
Special Rule: NA

Common Name: Ferret, black-footed
Scientific Name: Mustela nigripes
Historic Range: Western U.S.A., western Canada
Status: E
When Listed: I, 3, 433
Vertebrate Pop: Entire, except where listed as an experimental population below
Critical Habitat: NA
Special Rule: NA

Common Name: Ferret, black-footed
Scientific Name: Mustela nigripes
Historic Range: Western U.S.A., western Canada
Status: XN
When Listed: 433, 545, 546
Vertebrate Pop: U.S.A. (specific portions of MT, SD, and WY, see 17.84(g))
Critical Habitat: NA
Special Rule: 17.84(g)

Common Name: Fox, northern swift
Scientific Name: Vulpes velox hebes
Historic Range: U.S.A. (northern plains), Canada
Status: E
When Listed: 3
Vertebrate Pop: Canada
Critical Habitat: NA
Special Rule: NA

Common Name: Fox, San Joaquin kit
Scientific Name: Vulpes macrotis mutica
Historic Range: U.S.A. (CA)
Status: E
When Listed: I
Vertebrate Pop: Entire
Critical Habitat: NA
Special Rule: NA

Common Name: Jaguar
Scientific Name: Panthera onca
Historic Range: U.S.A. (AZ, NM, TX), Central and South America
Status: E
When Listed: 5
Vertebrate Pop: Mexico southward
Critical Habitat: NA
Special Rule: NA

267

Common Name: Jaguarundi
Scientific Name: Felis yagouaroundi cacomitli
Historic Range: U.S.A. (TX), Mexico
Status: E
When Listed: 15
Vertebrate Pop: Entire
Critical Habitat: NA
Special Rule: NA

Common Name: Jaguarundi
Scientific Name: Felis yagouaroundi tolteca
Historic Range: U.S.A. (AZ), Mexico
Status: E
When Listed: 15
Vertebrate Pop: Entire
Critical Habitat: NA
Special Rule: NA

Common Name: Kangaroo rat, Fresno
Scientific Name: Dipodomys nitratoides exilis
Historic Range: U.S.A. (CA)
Status: E
When Listed: 170
Vertebrate Pop: Entire
Critical Habitat: 17.95(a)
Special Rule: NA

Common Name: Kangaroo rat, giant
Scientific Name: Dipodomys ingens
Historic Range: U.S.A. (CA)
Status: E
When Listed: 251
Vertebrate Pop: Entire
Critical Habitat: NA
Special Rule: NA

Common Name: Kangaroo rat, Morro Bay
Scientific Name: Dipodomys heermanni morroensis
Historic Range: U.S.A. (CA)
Status: E
When Listed: 2
Vertebrate Pop: Entire
Critical Habitat: 17.95(a)
Special Rule: NA

Common Name: Kangaroo rat, Stephens'
Scientific Name: Dipodomys stephensi (incl. D. cascus)
Historic Range: U.S.A. (CA)
Status: E
When Listed: 338
Vertebrate Pop: Entire
Critical Habitat: NA
Special Rule: NA

Common Name: Kangaroo rat, Tipton
Scientific Name: Dipodomys nitratoides nitratoides
Historic Range: U.S.A. (CA)
Status: E
When Listed: 312
Vertebrate Pop: Entire
Critical Habitat: NA
Special Rule: NA

Common Name: Manatee, West Indian (=Florida)
Scientific Name: Trichechus manatus
Historic Range: U.S.A. (southeastern), Caribbean Sea, South America
Status: E
When Listed: I, 3
Vertebrate Pop: Entire
Critical Habitat: 17.95(a)
Special Rule: 17.108(a)

Common Name: Margay
Scientific Name: Felis wiedii
Historic Range: U.S.A. (TX), Central and South America
Status: E
When Listed: 5
Vertebrate Pop: Mexico southward
Critical Habitat: NA
Special Rule: NA

Common Name: Mountain beaver, Point Arena
Scientific Name: Aplodontia rufa nigra
Historic Range: U.S.A. (CA)
Status: E
When Listed: 454
Vertebrate Pop: Entire
Critical Habitat: NA
Special Rule: NA

Common Name: Mouse, Alabama beach
Scientific Name: Peromyscus polionotus ammobates
Historic Range: U.S.A. (AL)
Status: E
When Listed: 183
Vertebrate Pop: Entire
Critical Habitat: 17.95(a)
Special Rule: NA

Common Name: Mouse, Anastasia Island beach
Scientific Name: Peromyscus polionotus phasma
Historic Range: U.S.A. (FL)
Status: E
When Listed: 349
Vertebrate Pop: Entire
Critical Habitat: NA
Special Rule: NA

269

Common Name: Mouse, Choctawahatchee beach
Scientific Name: Peromyscus polionotus allophrys
Historic Range: U.S.A. (FL)
Status: E
When Listed: 183
Vertebrate Pop: Entire
Critical Habitat: 17.95(a)
Special Rule: NA

Common Name: Mouse, Key Largo cotton
Scientific Name: Peromyscus gossypinus allapaticola
Historic Range: U.S.A. (FL)
Status: E
When Listed: 131E, 160
Vertebrate Pop: Entire
Critical Habitat: NA
Special Rule: NA

Common Name: Mouse, Pacific pocket
Scientific Name: Perognathus longimembris pacificus
Historic Range: U.S.A. (CA)
Status: E
When Listed: 526E,554
Vertebrate Pop: Entire
Critical Habitat: NA
Special Rule: NA

Common Name: Mouse, Perdido Key beach
Scientific Name: Peromyscus polionotus trissyllepsis
Historic Range: U.S.A. (AL, FL)
Status: E
When Listed: 183
Vertebrate Pop: Entire
Critical Habitat: 17.95(a)
Special Rule: NA

Common Name: Mouse, salt marsh harvest
Scientific Name: Reithrodontomys raviventris
Historic Range: U.S.A. (CA)
Status: E
When Listed: 2
Vertebrate Pop: Entire
Critical Habitat: NA
Special Rule: NA

Common Name: Mouse, southeastern beach
Scientific Name: Peromyscus polionotus niveiventris
Historic Range: U.S.A. (FL)
Status: T
When Listed: 349
Vertebrate Pop: Entire
Critical Habitat: NA
Special Rule: NA

Common Name: Ocelot
Scientific Name: Felis pardalis
Historic Range: U.S.A. (AZ, TX) to Central and South America
Status: E
When Listed: 5, 119
Vertebrate Pop: Entire
Critical Habitat: NA
Special Rule: NA

Common Name: Otter, southern sea
Scientific Name: Enhydra lutris nereis
Historic Range: West Coast, U.S.A. (CA, OR, WA) south to Mexico (Baja California)
Status: T
When Listed: 21, 284
Vertebrate Pop: Entire, except where listed below
Critical Habitat: NA
Special Rule: NA

Common Name: Otter, southern sea
Scientific Name: Enhydra lutris nereis
Historic Range: West Coast, U.S.A. (CA, OR, WA) south to Mexico (Baja California)
Status: See 17.84(d)
When Listed: 21, 284
Vertebrate Pop: All areas subject to U.S. jurisdiction south of Pt. Conception, CA
(34¡26.9' N. Lat.) [Note—status governed by Pub. L. 99-625, 100 Stat. 3500.]
Critical Habitat: NA
Special Rule: 17.84(d)

Common Name: Panther, Florida
Scientific Name: Felis concolor coryi
Historic Range: U.S.A. (LA and AR east to SC and FL)
Status: E
When Listed: 1
Vertebrate Pop: Entire
Critical Habitat: NA
Special Rule: NA

Common Name: Prairie dog, Utah
Scientific Name: Cynomys parvidens
Historic Range: U.S.A. (UT)
Status: T
When Listed: 6, 149
Vertebrate Pop: Entire
Critical Habitat: NA
Special Rule: 17.40(g)

Common Name: Pronghorn, Sonoran
Scientific Name: Antilocapra americana sonoriensis
Historic Range: U.S.A. (AZ), Mexico
Status: E
When Listed: 1, 3
Vertebrate Pop: Entire
Critical Habitat: NA
Special Rule: NA

Common Name: Rabbit, Lower Keys
Scientific Name: Sylvilagus palustris hefneri
Historic Range: U.S.A. (FL)
Status: E
When Listed: 390
Vertebrate Pop: Entire
Critical Habitat: NA
Special Rule: NA

Common Name: Rice rat (=silver rice rat)
Scientific Name: Oryzomys palustris natator (=O. argentatus)
Historic Range: U.S.A. (FL)
Status: E
When Listed: 421
Vertebrate Pop: Lower FL Keys (west of Seven Mile Bridge)
Critical Habitat: 17.95(a)
Special Rule: NA

Common Name: Sea-lion, Steller (=northern)
Scientific Name: Eumetopias jubatus
Historic Range: U.S.A. (AK, CA, OR, WA), Canada, Russia; North Pacific Ocean
Status: T
When Listed: 384E, 408
Vertebrate Pop: Entire
Critical Habitat: NA
Special Rule: 227.12

Common Name: Seal, guadalupe fur
Scientific Name: Arctocephalus townsendi
Historic Range: U.S.A. (Farallon Islands of CA) south to Mexico (Islas Revillagigedo)
Status: T
When Listed: 1, 2D, 212
Vertebrate Pop: Entire
Critical Habitat: NA
Special Rule: 227.11

Common Name: Seal, Hawaiian monk
Scientific Name: Monachus schauinslandi
Historic Range: U.S.A. (HI)
Status: E
When Listed: 18
Vertebrate Pop: Entire
Critical Habitat: 226.11
Special Rule: NA

Common Name: Shrew, Dismal Swamp southeastern
Scientific Name: Sorex longirostris fisheri
Historic Range: U.S.A. (VA, NC)
Status: T
When Listed: 246
Vertebrate Pop: Entire
Critical Habitat: NA
Special Rule: NA

Common Name: Squirrel, Carolina northern flying
Scientific Name: Glaucomys sabrinus coloratus
Historic Range: U.S.A. (NC, TN)
Status: E
When Listed: 189
Vertebrate Pop: Entire
Critical Habitat: NA
Special Rule: NA

Common Name: Squirrel, Delmarva Peninsula fox
Scientific Name: Sciurus niger cinereus
Historic Range: U.S.A. (Delmarva Peninsula to southeastern PA)
Status: E
When Listed: 1, 161, 168
Vertebrate Pop: Entire, except Sussex Co., DE
Critical Habitat: NA
Special Rule: NA

Common Name: Squirrel, Delmarva Peninsula fox
Scientific Name: Sciurus niger cinereus
Historic Range: U.S.A. (Delmarva Peninsula to southeastern PA)
Status: XN
When Listed: 161
Vertebrate Pop: U.S.A. (DE—Sussex Co.)
Critical Habitat: NA
Special Rule: 17.84(a)

Common Name: Squirrel, Mount Graham red
Scientific Name: Tamiasciurus hudsonicus grahamensis
Historic Range: U.S.A. (AZ)
Status: E
When Listed: 268
Vertebrate Pop: Entire
Critical Habitat: 17.95(a)
Special Rule: NA

Common Name: Squirrel, Virginia northern flying
Scientific Name: Glaucomys sabrinus fuscus
Historic Range: U.S.A. (VA, WV)
Status: E
When Listed: 189
Vertebrate Pop: Entire
Critical Habitat: NA
Special Rule: NA

Common Name: Vole, Amargosa
Scientific Name: Microtus californicus scirpensis
Historic Range: U.S.A. (CA)
Status: E
When Listed: 166
Vertebrate Pop: Entire
Critical Habitat: 17.95(a)
Special Rule: NA

Common Name: Vole, Florida salt marsh
Scientific Name: Microtus pennsylvanicus dukecampbelli
Historic Range: U.S.A. (FL)
Status: E
When Listed: 415
Vertebrate Pop: Entire
Critical Habitat: NA
Special Rule: NA

Common Name: Vole, Hualapai Mexican
Scientific Name: Microtus mexicanus hualpaiensis
Historic Range: U.S.A. (AZ)
Status: E
When Listed: 292
Vertebrate Pop: Entire
Critical Habitat: NA
Special Rule: NA

Common Name: Wolf, red
Scientific Name: Canis rufus
Historic Range: U.S.A. (SE U.S.A., west to central TX)
Status: E
When Listed: 1, 248, 449
Vertebrate Pop: Entire, except where listed as experimental populations below
Critical Habitat: NA
Special Rule: NA

Common Name: Wolf, red
Scientific Name: Canis rufus
Historic Range: U.S.A. (SE U.S.A., west to central TX)
Status: XN
When Listed: 248, 449
Vertebrate Pop: U.S.A. (portions of NC and TN—see 17.84(c)(9))
Critical Habitat: NA
Special Rule: 17.84(c)

Common Name: Woodrat, Key Largo
Scientific Name: Neotoma floridana smalli
Historic Range: U.S.A. (FL)
Status: E
When Listed: 131E, 160
Vertebrate Pop: Entire
Critical Habitat: NA
Special Rule: NA

ENDANGERED SPECIES LIST—BIRDS

(alphabetical by common name)
Published in the Federal Register—current through April 1995.

Common Name: `Akepa, Hawaii (honeycreeper)
Scientific Name: Loxops coccineus coccineus
Historic Range: U.S.A. (HI)
Status: E
When Listed: 2
Vertebrate Pop: Entire
Critical Habitat: NA
Special Rule: NA

Common Name: `Akepa, Maui (honeycreeper)
Scientific Name: Loxops coccineus ochraceus
Historic Range: U.S.A. (HI)
Status: E
When Listed: 2
Vertebrate Pop: Entire
Critical Habitat: NA
Special Rule: NA

Common Name: `Akialoa, Kauai (honeycreeper)
Scientific Name: Hemignathus procerus
Historic Range: U.S.A. (HI)
Status: E
When Listed: 1
Vertebrate Pop: Entire
Critical Habitat: NA
Special Rule: NA

Common Name: `Akiapola`au (honeycreeper)
Scientific Name: Hemignathus munroi (=wilsoni)
Historic Range: U.S.A. (HI)
Status: E
When Listed: 1
Vertebrate Pop: Entire
Critical Habitat: NA
Special Rule: NA

Common Name: Albatross, short-tailed
Scientific Name: Diomedea albatrus
Historic Range: North Pacific Ocean—Japan, Russia, U.S.A. (AK, CA, HI, OR, WA)
Status: E
When Listed: 3
Vertebrate Pop: Entire, except U.S.A
Critical Habitat: NA
Special Rule: NA

Common Name: Blackbird, yellow-shouldered
Scientific Name: Agelaius xanthomus
Historic Range: U.S.A. (PR)
Status: E
When Listed: 17
Vertebrate Pop: Entire
Critical Habitat: 17.95(b)
Special Rule: NA

Common Name: Bobwhite, masked (quail)
Scientific Name: Colinus virginianus ridgwayi
Historic Range: U.S.A. (AZ), Mexico (Sonora)
Status: E
When Listed: 1, 3
Vertebrate Pop: Entire
Critical Habitat: NA
Special Rule: NA

Common Name: Broadbill, Guam
Scientific Name: Myiagra freycineti
Historic Range: Western Pacific Ocean—U.S.A. (Guam)
Status: E
When Listed: 156
Vertebrate Pop: Entire
Critical Habitat: NA
Special Rule: NA

Common Name: Caracara, Audubon's crested
Scientific Name: Polyborus plancus audubonii
Historic Range: U.S.A. (AZ, FL, LA, NM, TX) south to Panama; Cuba
Status: T
When Listed: 280
Vertebrate Pop: U.S.A. (FL)
Critical Habitat: NA
Special Rule: NA

Common Name: Condor, California
Scientific Name: Gymnogyps californianus
Historic Range: U.S.A. (CA, OR), Mexico (Baja California)
Status: E
When Listed: 1
Vertebrate Pop: U.S.A. only
Critical Habitat: 17.95(b)
Special Rule: NA

Common Name: Coot, Hawaiian (=`alae-ke`oke`o)
Scientific Name: Fulica americana alai
Historic Range: U.S.A. (HI)
Status: E
When Listed: 2
Vertebrate Pop: Entire
Critical Habitat: NA
Special Rule: NA

Common Name: Crane, Mississippi sandhill
Scientific Name: Grus canadensis pulla
Historic Range: U.S.A. (MS)
Status: E
When Listed: 6
Vertebrate Pop: Entire
Critical Habitat: I7.95(b)
Special Rule: NA

Common Name: Crane, whooping
Scientific Name: Grus americana
Historic Range: Canada, U.S.A. (Rocky Mountains east to Carolinas), Mexico
Status: E
When Listed: I, 3, 487
Vertebrate Pop: Entire, except where listed as an experimental population
Critical Habitat: I7.95(b)
Special Rule: NA

Common Name: Crane, whooping
Scientific Name: Grus americana
Historic Range: Canada, U.S.A. (Rocky Mountains east to Carolinas), Mexico
Status: XN
When Listed: 487
Vertebrate Pop: U.S.A. (FL)
Critical Habitat: NA
Special Rule: I7.84.(h)

Common Name: Creeper, Hawaii
Scientific Name: Oreomystis (=Loxops) mana
Historic Range: U.S.A. (HI)
Status: E
When Listed: I0
Vertebrate Pop: Entire
Critical Habitat: NA
Special Rule: NA

Common Name: Creeper, Molokai (=kakawahie)
Scientific Name: Paroreomyza (=Oreomystis, =Loxops) flammea
Historic Range: U.S.A. (HI)
Status: E
When Listed: 2
Vertebrate Pop: Entire
Critical Habitat: NA
Special Rule: NA

Common Name: Creeper, Oahu (=alauwahio)
Scientific Name: Paroreomyza (=Oreomystis, =Loxops) maculata
Historic Range: U.S.A. (HI)
Status: E
When Listed: 2
Vertebrate Pop: Entire
Critical Habitat: NA
Special Rule: NA

Common Name: Crow, Hawaiian (=`alala)
Scientific Name: Corvus hawaiiensis (=tropicus)
Historic Range: U.S.A. (HI)
Status: E
When Listed: 1
Vertebrate Pop: Entire
Critical Habitat: NA
Special Rule: NA

Common Name: Crow, Mariana
Scientific Name: Corvus kubaryi
Historic Range: Western Pacific Ocean—U.S.A. (Guam, Rota)
Status: E
When Listed: 156
Vertebrate Pop: Entire
Critical Habitat: NA
Special Rule: NA

Common Name: Crow, white-necked
Scientific Name: Corvus leucognaphalus
Historic Range: U.S.A. (PR), Dominican Republic, Haiti
Status: E
When Listed: 419
Vertebrate Pop: Entire
Critical Habitat: NA
Special Rule: NA

Common Name: Duck, Hawaiian (=koloa)
Scientific Name: Anas wyvilliana
Historic Range: U.S.A. (HI)
Status: E
When Listed: 1
Vertebrate Pop: Entire
Critical Habitat: NA
Special Rule: NA

Common Name: Duck, Laysan
Scientific Name: Anas laysanensis
Historic Range: U.S.A. (HI)
Status: E
When Listed: 1
Vertebrate Pop: Entire
Critical Habitat: NA
Special Rule: NA

Common Name: Eider, spectacled
Scientific Name: Somateria (=Arctonetta,=Lampronetta) fischeri
Historic Range: U.S.A. (AK), Russia
Status: T
When Listed: 503
Vertebrate Pop: Entire
Critical Habitat: NA
Special Rule: NA

Common Name: Falcon, northern aplomado
Scientific Name: Falco femoralis septentrionalis
Historic Range: U.S.A. (AZ, NM, TX), Mexico, Guatemala
Status: E
When Listed: 216
Vertebrate Pop: Entire
Critical Habitat: NA
Special Rule: NA

Common Name: Finch, Laysan (honeycreeper)
Scientific Name: Telespyza (=Psittirostra) cantans
Historic Range: U.S.A. (HI)
Status: E
When Listed: 1
Vertebrate Pop: Entire
Critical Habitat: NA
Special Rule: NA

Common Name: Finch, Nihoa (honeycreeper)
Scientific Name: Telespyza (=Psittirostra) ultima
Historic Range: U.S.A. (HI)
Status: E
When Listed: 1
Vertebrate Pop: Entire
Critical Habitat: NA
Special Rule: NA

Common Name: Gnatcatcher, coastal California
Scientific Name: Polioptila californica californica
Historic Range: U.S.A. (CA), Mexico
Status: T
When Listed: 496
Vertebrate Pop: Entire
Critical Habitat: NA
Special Rule: NA

Common Name: Goose, Aleutian Canada
Scientific Name: Branta canadensis leucopareia
Historic Range: U.S.A. (AK, CA, OR, WA), Japan
Status: T
When Listed: 1, 3, 410
Vertebrate Pop: Entire
Critical Habitat: NA
Special Rule: NA

Common Name: Goose, Hawaiian (=nene)
Scientific Name: Nesochen (=Branta) sandvicensis
Historic Range: U.S.A. (HI)
Status: E
When Listed: 1
Vertebrate Pop: Entire
Critical Habitat: NA
Special Rule: NA

Common Name: Hawk, Hawaiian (=io)
Scientific Name: Buteo solitarius
Historic Range: U.S.A. (HI)
Status: E
When Listed: 1
Vertebrate Pop: Entire
Critical Habitat: NA
Special Rule: NA

Common Name: Hawk, Puerto Rican broad-winged
Scientific Name: Buteo platypterus brunnescens
Historic Range: U.S.A. (PR)
Status: E
When Listed: 550
Vertebrate Pop: Entire
Critical Habitat: NA
Special Rule: NA

Common Name: Hawk, Puerto Rican sharp-shinned
Scientific Name: Acipiter striatus venator
Historic Range: U.S.A. (PR)
Status: E
When Listed: 550
Vertebrate Pop: Entire
Critical Habitat: NA
Special Rule: NA

Common Name: Honeycreeper, crested (=`akohekohe)
Scientific Name: Palmeria dolei
Historic Range: U.S.A. (HI)
Status: E
When Listed: 1
Vertebrate Pop: Entire
Critical Habitat: NA
Special Rule: NA

Common Name: Jay, Florida scrub
Scientific Name: Aphelocoma coerulescens coerulescens
Historic Range: U.S.A. (FL)
Status: T
When Listed: 267
Vertebrate Pop: Entire
Critical Habitat: NA
Special Rule: NA

Common Name: Kingfisher, Guam Micronesia
Scientific Name: Halcyon cinnamomina cinnamomina
Historic Range: West Pacific Ocean—U.S.A. (Guam)
Status: E
When Listed: 156
Vertebrate Pop: Entire
Critical Habitat: NA
Special Rule: NA

Common Name: Kite, Everglade snail
Scientific Name: Rostrhamus sociabilis plumbeus
Historic Range: U.S.A. (FL), Cuba
Status: E
When Listed: I
Vertebrate Pop: U.S.A. (FL)
Critical Habitat: 17.95(b)
Special Rule: NA

Common Name: Mallard, Mariana
Scientific Name: Anas oustaleti
Historic Range: West Pacific Ocean—U.S.A. (Guam, Mariana Islands)
Status: E
When Listed: 23
Vertebrate Pop: Entire
Critical Habitat: NA
Special Rule: NA

Common Name: Megapode, Micronesian (=La Perouse's)
Scientific Name: Megapodius laperouse
Historic Range: West Pacific Ocean—U.S.A. (Palau Island, Mariana Islands)
Status: E
When Listed: 3
Vertebrate Pop: Entire
Critical Habitat: NA
Special Rule: NA

Common Name: Millerbird, Nihoa (old world warbler)
Scientific Name: Acrocephalus familiaris kingi
Historic Range: U.S.A. (HI)
Status: E
When Listed: I
Vertebrate Pop: Entire
Critical Habitat: NA
Special Rule: NA

Common Name: Monarch, Tinian (old world flycatcher)
Scientific Name: Monarcha takatsukasae
Historic Range: West Pacific Ocean—U.S.A. (Mariana Islands)
Status: T
When Listed: 3, 261
Vertebrate Pop: Entire
Critical Habitat: NA
Special Rule: NA

Common Name: Moorhen (=gallinule), Hawaiian common
Scientific Name: Gallinula chloropus sandvicensis
Historic Range: U.S.A. (HI)
Status: E
When Listed: I
Vertebrate Pop: Entire
Critical Habitat: NA
Special Rule: NA

Common Name: Moorhen (=gallinule), Mariana common
Scientific Name: Gallinula chloropus guami
Historic Range: West Pacific Ocean—U.S.A. (Guam, Tinian, Saipan, Pagan)
Status: E
When Listed: 156
Vertebrate Pop: Entire
Critical Habitat: NA
Special Rule: NA

Common Name: Murrelet, marbled
Scientific Name: Brachyramphus marmoratus marmoratus
Historic Range: U.S.A. (AK, CA, OR, WA), Canada (B.C.)
Status: T
When Listed: 479
Vertebrate Pop: U.S.A. (CA, OR, WA)
Critical Habitat: NA
Special Rule: NA

Common Name: Nightjar, Puerto Rican (=whip-poor-will)
Scientific Name: Caprimulgus noctitherus
Historic Range: U.S.A. (PR)
Status: E
When Listed: 6
Vertebrate Pop: Entire
Critical Habitat: NA
Special Rule: NA

Common Name: Nukupu`u (honeycreeper)
Scientific Name: Hemignathus lucidus
Historic Range: U.S.A. (HI)
Status: E
When Listed: 1, 2
Vertebrate Pop: Entire
Critical Habitat: NA
Special Rule: NA

Common Name: `O`o, Kauai (=`o`o `a`a) (honeyeater)
Scientific Name: Moho braccatus
Historic Range: U.S.A. (HI)
Status: E
When Listed: 1
Vertebrate Pop: Entire
Critical Habitat: NA
Special Rule: NA

Common Name: `O`u (honeycreeper)
Scientific Name: Psittirostra psittacea
Historic Range: U.S.A. (HI)
Status: E
When Listed: 1
Vertebrate Pop: Entire
Critical Habitat: NA
Special Rule: NA

Common Name: Owl, Mexican spotted
Scientific Name: Strix occidentalis lucida
Historic Range: U.S.A. (AZ, CO, NM, TX, UT), Mexico
Status: T
When Listed: 494
Vertebrate Pop: Entire
Critical Habitat: NA
Special Rule: NA

Common Name: Owl, northern spotted
Scientific Name: Strix occidentalis caurina
Historic Range: U.S.A. (CA, OR, WA), Canada (B.C.)
Status: T
When Listed: 393
Vertebrate Pop: Entire
Critical Habitat: 17.95(b)
Special Rule: NA

Common Name: Palila (honeycreeper)
Scientific Name: Loxioides (=Psittirostra) bailleui
Historic Range: U.S.A. (HI)
Status: E
When Listed: 1
Vertebrate 'Pop: Entire
Critical Habitat: 17.95(b)
Special Rule: NA

Common Name: Parrot, Puerto Rican
Scientific Name: Amazona vittata
Historic Range: U.S.A. (PR)
Status: E
When Listed: 1
Vertebrate Pop: Entire
Critical Habitat: NA
Special Rule: NA

Common Name: Parrot, thick-billed
Scientific Name: Rhynchopsitta pachyrhyncha
Historic Range: Mexico, U.S.A. (AZ, NM)
Status: E
When Listed: 3
Vertebrate Pop: Mexico
Critical Habitat: NA
Special Rule: NA

Common Name: Parrotbill, Maui (honeycreeper)
Scientific Name: Pseudonestor xanthophrys
Historic Range: U.S.A. (HI)
Status: E
When Listed: 1
Vertebrate Pop: Entire
Critical Habitat: NA
Special Rule: NA

Common Name: Pelican, brown
Scientific Name: Pelecanus occidentalis
Historic Range: U.S.A (Carolinas to TX, CA, OR, WA), West Indies, coastal Central and South America
Status: E
When Listed: 2, 3, 171
Vertebrate Pop: Entire, except U.S. Atlantic coast, FL, AL
Critical Habitat: NA
Special Rule: NA

Common Name: Petrel, Hawaiian dark-rumped
Scientific Name: Pterodroma phaeopygia sandwichensis
Historic Range: U.S.A. (HI)
Status: E
When Listed: 1
Vertebrate Pop: Entire
Critical Habitat: NA
Special Rule: NA

Common Name: Pigeon, Puerto Rican plain
Scientific Name: Columba inornata wetmorei
Historic Range: U.S.A. (PR)
Status: E
When Listed: 2
Vertebrate Pop: Entire
Critical Habitat: NA
Special Rule: NA

Common Name: Plover, piping
Scientific Name: Charadrius melodus
Historic Range: U.S.A. (Great Lakes, northern Great Plains, Atlantic and Gulf coasts, PR, VI), Canada, Mexico, Bahamas, West Indies
Status: E
When Listed: 211
Vertebrate Pop: Great Lakes watershed in States of IL, IN, MI, MN, NY, OH, PA, and WI and Canada (Ont.)
Critical Habitat: NA
Special Rule: NA

Common Name: Plover, piping
Scientific Name: Charadrius melodus
Historic Range: U.S.A. (Great Lakes, northern Great Plains, Atlantic and Gulf coasts, PR, VI), Canada, Mexico, Bahamas, West Indies
Status: T
When Listed: 211
Vertebrate Pop: Entire, except those areas where listed as endangered above
Critical Habitat: NA
Special Rule: NA

Common Name: Plover, western snowy
Scientific Name: Charadrius alexandrinus nivosus
Historic Range: U.S.A. (AZ, CA, CO, KS, NM, NV, OK, OR, TX, UT, WA), Mexico
Status: T
When Listed: 493
Vertebrate Pop: U.S.A. (CA, OR, WA), Mexico (Within 50 miles of Pacific coast)
Critical Habitat: NA
Special Rule: NA

Common Name: Po`ouli (honeycreeper)
Scientific Name: Melamprosops phaeosoma
Historic Range: U.S.A. (HI)
Status: E
When Listed: 10
Vertebrate Pop: Entire
Critical Habitat: NA
Special Rule: NA

Common Name: Prairie-chicken, Attwater's greater
Scientific Name: Tympanuchus cupido attwateri
Historic Range: U.S.A. (TX)
Status: E
When Listed: 1
Vertebrate Pop: Entire
Critical Habitat: NA
Special Rule: NA

Common Name: Rail, California clapper
Scientific Name: Rallus longirostris obsoletus
Historic Range: U.S.A. (CA)
Status: E
When Listed: 2
Vertebrate Pop: Entire
Critical Habitat: NA
Special Rule: NA

Common Name: Rail, Guam
Scientific Name: Rallus owstoni
Historic Range: Western Pacific Ocean—U.S.A. (Guam)
Status: E
When Listed: 146E, 156
Vertebrate Pop: Entire, except Rota
Critical Habitat: NA
Special Rule: NA

Common Name: Rail, Guam
Scientific Name: Rallus owstoni
Historic Range: Western Pacific Ocean—U.S.A. (Guam)
Status: XN
When Listed: 371
Vertebrate Pop: Rota
Critical Habitat: NA

Special Rule: 17.84(f)
Common Name: Rail, light-footed clapper
Scientific Name: Rallus longirostris levipes
Historic Range: U.S.A. (CA), Mexico (Baja California)
Status: E
When Listed: 2
Vertebrate Pop: U.S.A. only
Critical Habitat: NA
Special Rule: NA

Common Name: Rail, Yuma clapper
Scientific Name: Rallus longirostris yumanensis
Historic Range: Mexico, U.S.A. (AZ, CA)
Status: E
When Listed: 1
Vertebrate Pop: U.S.A. only
Critical Habitat: NA
Special Rule: NA

Common Name: Shearwater, Newell's Townsend's (formerly Manx) (=`a`o)
Scientific Name: Puffinus auricularis (=puffinus) newelli
Historic Range: U.S.A. (HI)
Status: T
When Listed: 10
Vertebrate Pop: Entire
Critical Habitat: NA
Special Rule: NA

Common Name: Shrike, San Clemente loggerhead
Scientific Name: Lanius ludovicianus mearnsi
Historic Range: U.S.A. (CA)
Status: E
When Listed: 26
Vertebrate Pop: Entire
Critical Habitat: NA
Special Rule: NA

Common Name: Sparrow, Cape Sable seaside
Scientific Name: Ammodramus (=Ammospiza) maritimus mirabilis
Historic Range: U.S.A. (FL)
Status: E
When Listed: 1
Vertebrate Pop: Entire
Critical Habitat: 17.95(b)
Special Rule: NA

Common Name: Sparrow, Florida grasshopper
Scientific Name: Ammodramus savannarum floridanus
Historic Range: U.S.A. (FL)
Status: E
When Listed: 239
Vertebrate Pop: Entire
Critical Habitat: NA

Special Rule: NA
Common Name: Sparrow, San Clemente sage
Scientific Name: Amphispiza belli clementeae
Historic Range: U.S.A. (CA)
Status: T
When Listed: 26
Vertebrate Pop: Entire
Critical Habitat: NA
Special Rule: NA

Common Name: Stilt, Hawaiian (=ae`o)
Scientific Name: Himantopus mexicanus (=himantopus) knudseni
Historic Range: U.S.A. (HI)
Status: E
When Listed: 2
Vertebrate Pop: Entire
Critical Habitat: NA
Special Rule: NA

Common Name: Stork, wood
Scientific Name: Mycteria americana
Historic Range: U.S.A., (CA, AZ, TX, to Carolinas), Mexico, C. and S. America
Status: E
When Listed: 142
Vertebrate Pop: U.S.A. (AL, FL, GA, NC, SC)
Critical Habitat: NA
Special Rule: NA

Common Name: Swiftlet, Mariana gray (=vanikoro)
Scientific Name: Aerodramus (=Collocalia) vanikorensis bartschi
Historic Range: Western Pacific Ocean—U.S.A. (Guam, Rota, Tinian, Saipan, Agiguan)
Status: E
When Listed: 156
Vertebrate Pop: Entire
Critical Habitat: NA
Special Rule: NA

Common Name: Tern, California least
Scientific Name: Sterna antillarum (=albifrons) browni
Historic Range: Mexico, U.S.A. (CA)
Status: E
When Listed: 2, 3
Vertebrate Pop: Entire
Critical Habitat: NA
Special Rule: NA

Common Name: Tern, least
Scientific Name: Sterna antillarum
Historic Range: U.S.A. (Atlantic and Gulf coasts, Miss. R. Basin, CA), Greater and
Lesser Antilles, Bahamas, Mexico; winters Central America, northern South America
Status: E
When Listed: 182
Vertebrate Pop: U.S.A. (AR, CO, IA, IL, IN, KS, KY, LA—Miss. R. and tribs. N of
Baton Rouge, MS—Miss. R., MO, MT, ND, NE, NM, OK, SD, TN, TX—except
within 50 miles of coast)
Critical Habitat: NA
Special Rule: NA

Common Name: Thrush, large Kauai
Scientific Name: Myadestes (=Phaeornis) myadestinus
Historic Range: U.S.A. (HI)
Status: E
When Listed: 2
Vertebrate Pop: Entire
Critical Habitat: NA
Special Rule: NA

Common Name: Thrush, Molokai (=oloma`o)
Scientific Name: Myadestes (=Phaeornis) lanaiensis (=obscurus) rutha
Historic Range: U.S.A. (HI)
Status: E
When Listed: 2
Vertebrate Pop: Entire
Critical Habitat: NA
Special Rule: NA

Common Name: Thrush, small Kauai (=puaiohi)
Scientific Name: Myadestes (=Phaeornis) palmeri
Historic Range: U.S.A. (HI)
Status: E
When Listed: 1
Vertebrate Pop: Entire
Critical Habitat: NA
Special Rule: NA

Common Name: Towhee, Inyo California (=brown)
Scientific Name: Pipilo crissalis (=fuscus) eremophilus
Historic Range: U.S.A. (CA)
Status: T
When Listed: 282
Vertebrate Pop: Entire
Critical Habitat: 17.95(b)
Special Rule: NA

Common Name: Vireo, black-capped
Scientific Name: Vireo atricapillus
Historic Range: U.S.A. (KS, LA, NE, OK, TX), Mexico.
Status: E
When Listed: 294
Vertebrate Pop: Entire
Critical Habitat: NA
Special Rule: NA

Common Name: Vireo, least Bell's
Scientific Name: Vireo bellii pusillus
Historic Range: U.S.A. (CA), Mexico
Status: E
When Listed: 228
Vertebrate Pop: Entire
Critical Habitat: 17.95(b)
Special Rule: NA

Common Name: Warbler (wood), Bachman's
Scientific Name: Vermivora bachmanii
Historic Range: U.S.A. (Southeastern), Cuba
Status: E
When Listed: 1, 3
Vertebrate Pop: Entire
Critical Habitat: NA
Special Rule: NA

Common Name: Warbler (wood), golden-cheeked
Scientific Name: Dendroica chrysoparia
Historic Range: U.S.A. (TX), Mexico, Guatemala, Honduras, Nicaragua, Belize
Status: E
When Listed: 387E, 411
Vertebrate Pop: Entire
Critical Habitat: NA
Special Rule: NA

Common Name: Warbler (wood), Kirtland's
Scientific Name: Dendroica kirtlandii
Historic Range: U.S.A. (principally MI), Canada, West Indies—Bahama Islands
Status: E
When Listed: 1, 3
Vertebrate Pop: Entire
Critical Habitat: NA
Special Rule: NA

Common Name: Warbler (Old World), nightingale reed
Scientific Name: Acrocephalus luscinia
Historic Range: West Pacific Ocean—U.S.A. (Guam, Alamagan, Saipan)
Status: E
When Listed: 3, 4
Vertebrate Pop: U.S.A. (Mariana Islands)
Critical Habitat: NA
Special Rule: NA

Common Name: White-eye, bridled
Scientific Name: Zosterops conspicillatus conspicillatus
Historic Range: Western Pacific Ocean—U.S.A. (Guam)
Status: E
When Listed: 156
Vertebrate Pop: Entire
Critical Habitat: NA
Special Rule: NA

Common Name: Woodpecker, ivory-billed
Scientific Name: Campephilus principalis
Historic Range: U.S.A. (southcentral and southeastern), Cuba
Status: E
When Listed: 1, 3
Vertebrate Pop: Entire
Critical Habitat: NA
Special Rule: NA

Common Name: Woodpecker, red-cockaded
Scientific Name: Picoides (=Dendrocopos) borealis
Historic Range: U.S.A. (southcentral and southeastern)
Status: E
When Listed: 2
Vertebrate Pop: Entire
Critical Habitat: NA
Special Rule: NA

ENDANGERED SPECIES LIST—FISH

(alphabetical by common name)
Published in the Federal Register—current through April 1995.

Common Name: Catfish, Yaqui
Scientific Name: Ictalurus pricei
Historic Range: U.S.A. (AZ), Mexico
Status: T
When Listed: 157
Vertebrate Pop: Entire
Critical Habitat: 17.95(e)
Special Rule: 17.44(g)

Common Name: Cavefish, Alabama
Scientific Name: Speoplatyrhinus poulsoni
Historic Range: U.S.A. (AL)
Status: E
When Listed: 28, 328
Vertebrate Pop: Entire
Critical Habitat: 17.95(e)
Special Rule: NA

290

Common Name: Cavefish, Ozark
Scientific Name: Amblyopsis rosae
Historic Range: U.S.A. (AR, MO, OK)
Status: T
When Listed: 164
Vertebrate Pop: Entire
Critical Habitat: NA
Special Rule: NA

Common Name: Chub, bonytail
Scientific Name: Gila elegans
Historic Range: U.S.A. (AZ, CA, CO, NV, UT, WY)
Status: E
When Listed: 92
Vertebrate Pop: Entire
Critical Habitat: 17.95(e)
Special Rule: NA

Common Name: Chub, Borax Lake
Scientific Name: Gila boraxobius
Historic Range: U.S.A. (OR)
Status: E
When Listed: 94E, 124
Vertebrate Pop: Entire
Critical Habitat: 17.95(e)
Special Rule: NA

Common Name: Chub, Chihuahua
Scientific Name: Gila nigrescens
Historic Range: U.S.A. (NM), Mexico (Chihuahua)
Status: T
When Listed: 132
Vertebrate Pop: Entire
Critical Habitat: NA
Special Rule: 17.44(g)

Common Name: Chub, humpback
Scientific Name: Gila cypha
Historic Range: U.S.A. (AZ, CO, UT, WY)
Status: E
When Listed: 1
Vertebrate Pop: Entire
Critical Habitat: 17.95(e)
Special Rule: NA

Common Name: Chub, Hutton tui
Scientific Name: Gila bicolor ssp.
Historic Range: U.S.A. (OR)
Status: T
When Listed: 174
Vertebrate Pop: Entire
Critical Habitat: NA
Special Rule: 17.44(j)

Common Name: Chub, Mohave tui
Scientific Name: Gila bicolor mohavensis
Historic Range: U.S.A. (CA)
Status: E
When Listed: 2
Vertebrate Pop: Entire
Critical Habitat: NA
Special Rule: NA

Common Name: Chub, Oregon
Scientific Name: Oregonichthys (=Hybopsis) crameri
Historic Range: U.S.A. (OR)
Status: E
When Listed: 520
Vertebrate Pop: Entire
Critical Habitat: NA
Special Rule: NA

Common Name: Chub, Owens tui
Scientific Name: Gila bicolor snyderi
Historic Range: U.S.A. (CA)
Status: E
When Listed: 195
Vertebrate Pop: Entire
Critical Habitat: 17.95(e)
Special Rule: NA

Common Name: Chub, Pahranagat roundtail (=bonytail)
Scientific Name: Gila robusta jordani
Historic Range: U.S.A. (NV)
Status: E
When Listed: 2
Vertebrate Pop: Entire
Critical Habitat: NA
Special Rule: NA

Common Name: Chub, slender
Scientific Name: Erimystax (=Hybopsis) cahni
Historic Range: U.S.A. (TN, VA)
Status: T
When Listed: 28
Vertebrate Pop: Entire
Critical Habitat: 17.95(e)
Special Rule: 17.44(c)

Common Name: Chub, Sonora
Scientific Name: Gila ditaenia
Historic Range: U.S.A., (AZ), Mexico
Status: T
When Listed: 227
Vertebrate Pop: Entire
Critical Habitat: 17.95(e)
Special Rule: 17.44(o)

Common Name: Chub, spotfin (=turquoise shiner)
Scientific Name: Cyprinella (=Hybopsis) monacha
Historic Range: U.S.A. (AL, GA, NC, TN, VA)
Status: T
When Listed: 28
Vertebrate Pop: Entire
Critical Habitat: 17.95(e)
Special Rule: 17.44(c)

Common Name: Chub, Virgin River
Scientific Name: Gila robusta seminuda
Historic Range: U.S.A. (AZ, NV, UT)
Status: E
When Listed: 361
Vertebrate Pop: Entire
Critical Habitat: NA
Special Rule: NA

Common Name: Chub, Yaqui
Scientific Name: Gila purpurea
Historic Range: U.S.A. (AZ), Mexico
Status: E
When Listed: 157
Vertebrate Pop: Entire
Critical Habitat: 17.95(e)
Special Rule: NA

Common Name: Cui-ui
Scientific Name: Chasmistes cujus
Historic Range: U.S.A. (NV)
Status: E
When Listed: 1
Vertebrate Pop: Entire
Critical Habitat: NA
Special Rule: NA

Common Name: Dace, Ash Meadows speckled
Scientific Name: Rhinichthys osculus nevadensis
Historic Range: U.S.A. (NV)
Status: E
When Listed: 117E, 127E, 130
Vertebrate Pop: Entire
Critical Habitat: 17.95(e)
Special Rule: NA

Common Name: Dace, blackside
Scientific Name: Phoxinus cumberlandensis
Historic Range: U.S.A. (KY, TN)
Status: T
When Listed: 273
Vertebrate Pop: Entire
Critical Habitat: NA
Special Rule: NA

Common Name: Dace, Clover Valley speckled
Scientific Name: Rhinichthys osculus oligoporus
Historic Range: U.S.A. (NV)
Status: E
When Listed: 370
Vertebrate Pop: Entire
Critical Habitat: NA
Special Rule: NA

Common Name: Dace, desert
Scientific Name: Eremichthys acros
Historic Range: U.S.A. (NV)
Status: T
When Listed: 1, 2D, 210
Vertebrate Pop: Entire
Critical Habitat: 17.95(e)
Special Rule: 17.44(m)

Common Name: Dace, Foskett speckled
Scientific Name: Rhinichthys osculus ssp.
Historic Range: U.S.A. (OR)
Status: T
When Listed: 174
Vertebrate Pop: Entire
Critical Habitat: NA
Special Rule: 17.44(j)

Common Name: Dace, Independence Valley speckled
Scientific Name: Rhinichthys osculus lethoporus
Historic Range: U.S.A. (NV)
Status: E
When Listed: 370, 372
Vertebrate Pop: Entire
Critical Habitat: NA
Special Rule: NA

Common Name: Dace, Kendall Warm Springs
Scientific Name: Rhinichthys osculus thermalis
Historic Range: U.S.A. (WY)
Status: E
When Listed: 2
Vertebrate Pop: Entire
Critical Habitat: NA
Special Rule: NA

Common Name: Dace, Moapa
Scientific Name: Moapa coriacea
Historic Range: U.S.A. (NV)
Status: E
When Listed: 1
Vertebrate Pop: Entire
Critical Habitat: NA
Special Rule: NA

Common Name: Darter, amber
Scientific Name: Percina antesella
Historic Range: U.S.A. (AL, GA, TN)
Status: E
When Listed: 196
Vertebrate Pop: Entire
Critical Habitat: 17.95(e)
Special Rule: NA

Common Name: Darter, bayou
Scientific Name: Etheostoma rubrum
Historic Range: U.S.A. (MS)
Status: T
When Listed: 10
Vertebrate Pop: Entire
Critical Habitat: NA
Special Rule: 17.44(b)

Common Name: Darter, bluemask (=jewel)
Scientific Name: Etheostoma (Doration) sp.
Historic Range: U.S.A. (TN)
Status: E
When Listed: 525
Vertebrate Pop: Entire
Critical Habitat: NA
Special Rule: NA

Common Name: Darter, boulder (=Elk River)
Scientific Name: Etheostoma wapiti
Historic Range: U.S.A. (AL, TN)
Status: E
When Listed: 322
Vertebrate Pop: Entire
Critical Habitat: NA
Special Rule: NA

Common Name: Darter, Cherokee
Scientific Name: Etheostoma (Ulocentra) sp.
Historic Range: U.S.A. (GA)
Status: T
When Listed: 569
Vertebrate Pop: Entire
Critical Habitat: NA
Special Rule: NA

Common Name: Darter, duskytail
Scientific Name: Etheostoma (Catonotus) sp.
Historic Range: U.S.A. (TN, VA)
Status: E
When Listed: 502
Vertebrate Pop: Entire
Critical Habitat: NA
Special Rule: NA

Common Name: Darter, Etowah
Scientific Name: Etheostoma etowahae
Historic Range: U.S.A. (GA)
Status: E
When Listed: 569
Vertebrate Pop: Entire
Critical Habitat: NA
Special Rule: NA

Common Name: Darter, fountain
Scientific Name: Etheostoma fonticola
Historic Range: U.S.A. (TX)
Status: E
When Listed: 2
Vertebrate Pop: Entire
Critical Habitat: 17.95(e)
Special Rule: NA

Common Name: Darter, goldline
Scientific Name: Percina aurolineata
Historic Range: U.S.A. (AL, GA, TN)
Status: T
When Listed: 462
Vertebrate Pop: Entire
Critical Habitat: NA
Special Rule: NA

Common Name: Darter, leopard
Scientific Name: Percina pantherina
Historic Range: U.S.A. (AR, OK)
Status: T
When Listed: 31
Vertebrate Pop: Entire
Critical Habitat: 17.95(e)
Special Rule: 17.44(d)

Common Name: Darter, Maryland
Scientific Name: Etheostoma sellare
Historic Range: U.S.A. (MD)
Status: E
When Listed: 1
Vertebrate Pop: Entire
Critical Habitat: 17.95(e)
Special Rule: NA

Common Name: Darter, Niangua
Scientific Name: Etheostoma nianguae
Historic Range: U.S.A. (MO)
Status: T
When Listed: 185
Vertebrate Pop: Entire
Critical Habitat: 17.95(e)
Special Rule: 17.44(k)

Common Name: Darter, Okaloosa
Scientific Name: Etheostoma okaloosae
Historic Range: U.S.A. (FL)
Status: E
When Listed: 6
Vertebrate Pop: Entire
Critical Habitat: NA
Special Rule: NA

Common Name: Darter, relict
Scientific Name: Etheostoma (Catonotus) chienense
Historic Range: U.S.A. (KY)
Status: E
When Listed: 525
Vertebrate Pop: Entire
Critical Habitat: NA
Special Rule: NA

Common Name: Darter, slackwater
Scientific Name: Etheostoma boschungi
Historic Range: U.S.A. (AL, TN)
Status: T
When Listed: 28
Vertebrate Pop: Entire
Critical Habitat: 17.95(e)
Special Rule: 17.44(c)

Common Name: Darter, snail
Scientific Name: Percina tanasi
Historic Range: U.S.A. (AL, GA, TN)
Status: T
When Listed: 12, 150
Vertebrate Pop: Entire
Critical Habitat: NA
Special Rule: NA

Common Name: Darter, watercress
Scientific Name: Etheostoma nuchale
Historic Range: U.S.A. (AL)
Status: E
When Listed: 2
Vertebrate Pop: Entire
Critical Habitat: NA
Special Rule: NA

Common Name: Gambusia, Big Bend
Scientific Name: Gambusia gaigei
Historic Range: U.S.A. (TX)
Status: E
When Listed: 1
Vertebrate Pop: Entire
Critical Habitat: NA
Special Rule: NA

Common Name: Gambusia, Clear Creek
Scientific Name: Gambusia heterochir
Historic Range: U.S.A. (TX)
Status: E
When Listed: 1
Vertebrate Pop: Entire
Critical Habitat: NA
Special Rule: NA

Common Name: Gambusia, Pecos
Scientific Name: Gambusia nobilis
Historic Range: U.S.A. (NM, TX)
Status: E
When Listed: 2
Vertebrate Pop: Entire
Critical Habitat: NA
Special Rule: NA

Common Name: Gambusia, San Marcos
Scientific Name: Gambusia georgei
Historic Range: U.S.A. (TX)
Status: E
When Listed: 98
Vertebrate Pop: Entire
Critical Habitat: 17.95(e)
Special Rule: NA

Common Name: Goby, tidewater
Scientific Name: Eucyclogobius newberryi
Historic Range: U.S.A. (CA)
Status: E
When Listed: 527
Vertebrate Pop: Entire
Critical Habitat: NA
Special Rule: NA

Common Name: Logperch, Conasauga
Scientific Name: Percina jenkinsi
Historic Range: U.S.A. (GA, TN)
Status: E
When Listed: 196
Vertebrate Pop: Entire
Critical Habitat: 17.95(e)
Special Rule: NA

Common Name: Logperch, Roanoke
Scientific Name: Percina rex
Historic Range: U.S.A. (VA)
Status: E
When Listed: 359
Vertebrate Pop: Entire
Critical Habitat: NA
Special Rule: NA

Common Name: Madtom, Neosho
Scientific Name: Noturus placidus
Historic Range: U.S.A. (KS, MO, OK)
Status: T
When Listed: 388
Vertebrate Pop: Entire
Critical Habitat: NA
Special Rule: NA

Common Name: Madtom, pygmy
Scientific Name: Noturus stanauli
Historic Range: U.S.A. (TN)
Status: E
When Listed: 502
Vertebrate Pop: Entire
Critical Habitat: NA
Special Rule: NA

Common Name: Madtom, Scioto
Scientific Name: Noturus trautmani
Historic Range: U.S.A. (OH)
Status: E
When Listed: 10
Vertebrate Pop: Entire
Critical Habitat: NA
Special Rule: NA

Common Name: Madtom, smoky
Scientific Name: Noturus baileyi
Historic Range: U.S.A. (TN)
Status: E
When Listed: 163
Vertebrate Pop: Entire
Critical Habitat: 17.95(e)
Special Rule: NA

Common Name: Madtom, yellowfin
Scientific Name: Noturus flavipinnis
Historic Range: U.S.A. (TN, VA)
Status: T
When Listed: 28, 317
Vertebrate Pop: Entire, except where listed as an experimental population below
Critical Habitat: 17.95(e)
Special Rule: 17.44(c)

Common Name: Madtom, yellowfin
Scientific Name: Noturus flavipinnis
Historic Range: U.S.A. (TN, VA)
Status: XN
When Listed: 317
Vertebrate Pop: N. Fork Holston R., VA, TN; S. Fork Holston R., upstream to Ft.
Patrick Henry Dam, TN; Holston R., downstream to John Sevier Detention Lake
Dam, TN; and all tributaries thereto
Critical Habitat: NA
Special Rule: 17.84(e)

Common Name: Minnow, loach
Scientific Name: Rhinichthys (=Tiaroga) cobitis
Historic Range: U.S.A. (AZ, NM), Mexico
Status: T
When Listed: 247
Vertebrate Pop: Entire
Critical Habitat: 17.95(e)
Special Rule: 17.44(q)

Common Name: Minnow, Rio Grande silvery
Scientific Name: Hybognathus amarus
Historic Range: U.S.A. (NM, TX), Mexico
Status: E
When Listed: 543
Vertebrate Pop: Cyprinidae
Critical Habitat: NA
Special Rule: NA

Common Name: Poolfish (=killifish), Pahrump
Scientific Name: Empetrichthys latos
Historic Range: U.S.A. (NV)
Status: E
When Listed: 1
Vertebrate Pop: Entire
Critical Habitat: NA
Special Rule: NA

Common Name: Pupfish, Ash Meadows Amargosa
Scientific Name: Cyprinodon nevadensis mionectes
Historic Range: U.S.A. (NV)
Status: E
When Listed: 117E, 127E, 130
Vertebrate Pop: Entire
Critical Habitat: 17.95(e)
Special Rule: NA

Common Name: Pupfish, Comanche Springs
Scientific Name: Cyprinodon elegans
Historic Range: U.S.A. (TX)
Status: E
When Listed: 1
Vertebrate Pop: Entire
Critical Habitat: NA
Special Rule: NA

Common Name: Pupfish, desert
Scientific Name: Cyprinodon macularius
Historic Range: U.S.A. (AZ, CA) Mexico
Status: E
When Listed: 222
Vertebrate Pop: Entire
Critical Habitat: 17.95(e)
Special Rule: NA

Common Name: Pupfish, Devils Hole
Scientific Name: Cyprinodon diabolis
Historic Range: U.S.A. (NV)
Status: E
When Listed: 1
Vertebrate Pop: Entire
Critical Habitat: NA
Special Rule: NA

Common Name: Pupfish, Leon Springs
Scientific Name: Cyprinodon bovinus
Historic Range: U.S.A. (TX)
Status: E
When Listed: 102
Vertebrate Pop: Entire
Critical Habitat: 17.95(e)
Special Rule: NA

Common Name: Pupfish, Owens
Scientific Name: Cyprinodon radiosus
Historic Range: U.S.A. (CA)
Status: E
When Listed: 1
Vertebrate Pop: Entire
Critical Habitat: NA
Special Rule: NA

Common Name: Pupfish, Warm Springs
Scientific Name: Cyprinodon nevadensis pectoralis
Historic Range: U.S.A. (NV)
Status: E
When Listed: 2
Vertebrate Pop: Entire
Critical Habitat: NA
Special Rule: NA

Common Name: Salmon, chinook
Scientific Name: Oncorhynchus tshawytscha
Historic Range: North Pacific Basin from U.S.A. (CA) to Japan
Status: E
When Listed: 383E, 407
Vertebrate Pop: Sacramento R. (U.S.A.—CA) winter run, wherever found
Critical Habitat: 226.21
Special Rule: NA

Common Name: Salmon, chinook
Scientific Name: Oncorhynchus tshawytscha
Historic Range: North Pacific Basin from U.S.A. (CA) to Japan
Status: T
When Listed: 516
Vertebrate Pop: Snake R. (U.S.A.—ID,OR,WA) mainstem and the following sub-basins—Tucannon R., Grande Ronde R., Imnaha R., and Salmon R.; spring/summer run, natural population(s), wherever found
Critical Habitat: NA
Special Rule: 227.21

Common Name: Salmon, chinook
Scientific Name: Oncorhynchus tshawytscha
Historic Range: North Pacific Basin from U.S.A. (CA) to Japan
Status: T
When Listed: 516
Vertebrate Pop: Snake R. (U.S.A.—ID, OR, WA) mainstem and the following sub-basins—Tucannon R., Grande Ronde R., Imnaha R., Salmon R, and Clearwater R.; fall run, natural populations(s), wherever found
Critical Habitat: NA
Special Rule: 227.21

Common Name: Salmon, sockeye (=red, =blueback)
Scientific Name: Oncorhynchus nerka
Historic Range: North Pacific Basin from U.S.A. (CA) to Russia
Status: E
When Listed: 455
Vertebrate Pop: U.S.A. (Snake River, ID stock wherever found.)
Critical Habitat: NA
Special Rule: NA

Common Name: Sculpin, pygmy
Scientific Name: Cottus pygmaeus
Historic Range: U.S.A. (AL)
Status: T
When Listed: 365
Vertebrate Pop: Entire
Critical Habitat: NA
Special Rule: 17.44(u)

Common Name: Shiner, beautiful
Scientific Name: Cyprinella (=Notropis) formosa
Historic Range: U.S.A. (AZ, NM), Mexico
Status: T
When Listed: 157
Vertebrate Pop: Entire
Critical Habitat: 17.95(e)
Special Rule: 17.44(g)

Common Name: Shiner, blue
Scientific Name: Cyprinella (=Notropis) caerulea
Historic Range: U.S.A. (AL, GA, TN)
Status: T
When Listed: 462
Vertebrate Pop: Entire
Critical Habitat: NA
Special Rule: NA

Common Name: Shiner, Cahaba
Scientific Name: Notropis cahabae
Historic Range: U.S.A. (AL)
Status: E
When Listed: 405
Vertebrate Pop: Entire
Critical Habitat: NA
Special Rule: NA

302

Common Name: Shiner, Cape Fear
Scientific Name: Notropis mekistocholas
Historic Range: U.S.A. (NC)
Status: E
When Listed: 290
Vertebrate Pop: Entire
Critical Habitat: 17.95(e)
Special Rule: NA

Common Name: Shiner, Palezone
Scientific Name: Notropis sp.
Historic Range: U.S.A. (AL, KY, TN)
Status: E
When Listed: 502
Vertebrate Pop: Entire
Critical Habitat: NA
Special Rule: NA

Common Name: Shiner, Pecos bluntnose
Scientific Name: Notropis simus pecosensis
Historic Range: U.S.A. (NM)
Status: T
When Listed: 258
Vertebrate Pop: Entire
Critical Habitat: 17.95(e)
Special Rule: 17.44(r)

Common Name: Silverside, Waccamaw
Scientific Name: Menidia extensa
Historic Range: U.S.A. (NC)
Status: T
When Listed: 265
Vertebrate Pop: Entire
Critical Habitat: 17.95(e)
Special Rule: 17.44(s)

Common Name: Smelt, delta
Scientific Name: Hypomesus transpacificus
Historic Range: U.S.A. (CA)
Status: T
When Listed: 492
Vertebrate Pop: Entire
Critical Habitat: NA
Special Rule: NA

Common Name: Spikedace
Scientific Name: Meda fulgida
Historic Range: U.S.A. (AZ, NM), Mexico
Status: T
When Listed: 236
Vertebrate Pop: Entire
Critical Habitat: 17.95(e)
Special Rule: 17.44(p)

Common Name: Spinedace, Big Spring
Scientific Name: Lepidomeda mollispinis pratensis
Historic Range: U.S.A. (NV)
Status: T
When Listed: 173
Vertebrate Pop: Entire
Critical Habitat: 17.95(e)
Special Rule: 17.44(i)

303

Common Name: Spinedace, Little Colorado
Scientific Name: Lepidomeda vittata
Historic Range: U.S.A. (AZ)
Status: T
When Listed: 287
Vertebrate Pop: Entire
Critical Habitat: 17.95(e)
Special Rule: 17.44(t)

Common Name: Spinedace, White River
Scientific Name: Lepidomeda albivallis
Historic Range: U.S.A. (NV)
Status: E
When Listed: 203
Vertebrate Pop: Entire
Critical Habitat: 17.95(e)
Special Rule: NA

Common Name: Springfish, Hiko White River
Scientific Name: Crenichthys baileyi grandis
Historic Range: U.S.A. (NV)
Status: E
When Listed: 206
Vertebrate Pop: Entire
Critical Habitat: 17.95(e)
Special Rule: NA

Common Name: Springfish, Railroad Valley
Scientific Name: Crenichthys nevadae
Historic Range: U.S.A. (NV)
Status: T
When Listed: 224
Vertebrate Pop: Entire
Critical Habitat: 17.95(e)
Special Rule: 17.44(n)

Common Name: Springfish, White River
Scientific Name: Crenichthys baileyi baileyi
Historic Range: U.S.A. (NV)
Status: E
When Listed: 206
Vertebrate Pop: Entire
Critical Habitat: 17.95(e)
Special Rule: NA

Common Name: Squawfish, Colorado
Scientific Name: Ptychocheilus lucius
Historic Range: U.S.A. (AZ, CA, CO, NM, NV, UT, WY), Mexico
Status: E
When Listed: I, 193
Vertebrate Pop: Entire, except Salt and Verde R. drainages, AZ
Critical Habitat: 17.95(e)
Special Rule: NA

Common Name: Squawfish, Colorado
Scientific Name: Ptychocheilus lucius
Historic Range: U.S.A. (AZ, CA, CO, NM, NV, UT, WY), Mexico
Status: XN
When Listed: 193
Vertebrate Pop: Salt and Verde R. drainages, AZ
Critical Habitat: NA
Special Rule: 17.84(b)

Common Name: Stickleback, unarmored threespine
Scientific Name: Gasterosteus aculeatus williamsoni
Historic Range: U.S.A. (CA)
Status: E
When Listed: 2
Vertebrate Pop: Entire
Critical Habitat: NA
Special Rule: NA

Common Name: Sturgeon, Gulf
Scientific Name: Acipenser oxyrhynchus desotoi
Historic Range: U.S.A. (AL, FL, GA, LA, MS)
Status: T
When Listed: 444
Vertebrate Pop: Entire
Critical Habitat: NA
Special Rule: 17.44(v)

Common Name: Sturgeon, pallid
Scientific Name: Scaphirhynchus albus
Historic Range: U.S.A. (AR, IA, IL, KS, KY, LA, MO, MS, MT, ND, NE, SD, TN)
Status: E
When Listed: 399
Vertebrate Pop: Entire
Critical Habitat: NA
Special Rule: NA

Common Name: Sturgeon, shortnose
Scientific Name: Acipenser brevirostrum
Historic Range: U.S.A. and Canada (Atlantic Coast)
Status: E
When Listed: I
Vertebrate Pop: Entire
Critical Habitat: NA
Special Rule: NA

Common Name: Sturgeon, white (Kootenai River pop.)
Scientific Name: Acipenser transmontanus
Historic Range: U.S.A. (ID, MT), Canada (B.C.)
Status: E
When Listed: 549
Vertebrate Pop: Entire
Critical Habitat: NA
Special Rule: NA

305

Common Name: Sucker, June
Scientific Name: Chasmistes liorus
Historic Range: U.S.A. (UT)
Status: E
When Listed: 223
Vertebrate Pop: Entire
Critical Habitat: 17.95(e)
Special Rule: NA

Common Name: Sucker, Lost River
Scientific Name: Deltistes luxatus
Historic Range: U.S.A. (CA, OR)
Status: E
When Listed: 313
Vertebrate Pop: Entire
Critical Habitat: NA
Special Rule: NA

Common Name: Sucker, Modoc
Scientific Name: Catostomus microps
Historic Range: U.S.A. (CA)
Status: E
When Listed: 184
Vertebrate Pop: Entire
Critical Habitat: 17.95(e)
Special Rule: NA

Common Name: Sucker, razorback
Scientific Name: Xyrauchen texanus
Historic Range: U.S.A. (AZ, CA, CO, NM, NV, UT, WY), Mexico
Status: E
When Listed: 447
Vertebrate Pop: Entire
Critical Habitat: 17.95(e)
Special Rule: NA

Common Name: Sucker, shortnose
Scientific Name: Chasmistes brevirostris
Historic Range: U.S.A. (CA, OR)
Status: E
When Listed: 313
Vertebrate Pop: Entire
Critical Habitat: NA
Special Rule: NA

Common Name: Sucker, Warner
Scientific Name: Catostomus warnerensis
Historic Range: U.S.A. (OR)
Status: T
When Listed: 205
Vertebrate Pop: Entire
Critical Habitat: 17.95(e)
Special Rule: 17.44(I)

Common Name: Topminnow, Gila (incl. Yaqui)
Scientific Name: Poeciliopsis occidentalis
Historic Range: U.S.A. (AZ, NM), Mexico
Status: E
When Listed: I
Vertebrate Pop: U.S.A. only
Critical Habitat: NA
Special Rule: NA

Common Name: Trout, Apache (=Arizona)
Scientific Name: Oncorhynchus (=Salmo) apache
Historic Range: U.S.A. (AZ)
Status: T
When Listed: I, 8
Vertebrate Pop: Entire
Critical Habitat: NA
Special Rule: 17.44(a)

Common Name: Trout, Gila
Scientific Name: Oncorhynchus (=Salmo) gilae
Historic Range: U.S.A. (AZ, NM)
Status: E
When Listed: I
Vertebrate Pop: Entire
Critical Habitat: NA
Special Rule: NA

Common Name: Trout, greenback cutthroat
Scientific Name: Oncorhynchus (=Salmo) clarki stomias
Historic Range: U.S.A. (CO)
Status: T
When Listed: I, 38
Vertebrate Pop: Entire
Critical Habitat: NA
Special Rule: 17.44(f)

Common Name: Trout, Lahontan cutthroat
Scientific Name: Oncorhynchus (=Salmo) clarki henshawi
Historic Range: U.S.A. (CA, NV, OR, UT)
Status: T
When Listed: 2, 8
Vertebrate Pop: Entire
Critical Habitat: NA
Special Rule: 17.44(a)

Common Name: Trout, Little Kern golden
Scientific Name: Oncorhynchus (=Salmo) aguabonita whitei
Historic Range: U.S.A. (CA)
Status: T
When Listed: 37
Vertebrate Pop: Entire
Critical Habitat: 17.95(e)
Special Rule: 17.44(e)

Common Name: Trout, Paiute cutthroat
Scientific Name: Oncorhynchus (=Salmo) clarki seleniris
Historic Range: U.S.A. (CA)
Status: T
When Listed: 1, 8
Vertebrate Pop: Entire
Critical Habitat: NA
Special Rule: 17.44(a)

Common Name: Woundfin
Scientific Name: Plagopterus argentissimus
Historic Range: U.S.A. (AZ, NV, UT)
Status: E
When Listed: 2, 193
Vertebrate Pop: Entire, except Gila R. drainage, AZ, NM
Critical Habitat: NA
Special Rule: NA

Common Name: Woundfin
Scientific Name: Plagopterus argentissimus
Historic Range: U.S.A. (TN, VA)
Status: XN
When Listed: 193
Vertebrate Pop: Gila R. drainage, AZ, NM
Critical Habitat: NA
Special Rule: 17.84(b)

ENDANGERED SPECIES LIST—REPTILES

(alphabetical by common name)
Published in the Federal Register—current through April 1995.

Common Name: Alligator, American
Scientific Name: Alligator mississippiensis
Historic Range: Southeastern U.S.A.
Status: T(S/A)
When Listed: 1, 11, 20, 47, 51, 60, 113, 134, 186, 269
Vertebrate Pop: Entire
Critical Habitat: NA
Special Rule: 17.42(a)

Common Name: Anole, Culebra Island giant
Scientific Name: Anolis roosevelti
Historic Range: U.S.A. (PR—Culebra Island)
Status: E
When Listed: 25
Vertebrate Pop: Entire
Critical Habitat: 17.95(c)
Special Rule: NA

Common Name: Boa, Mona
Scientific Name: Epicrates monensis monensis
Historic Range: U.S.A. (PR)
Status: T
When Listed: 33
Vertebrate Pop: Entire
Critical Habitat: 17.95(c)
Special Rule: NA

Common Name: Boa, Puerto Rican
Scientific Name: Epicrates inornatus
Historic Range: U.S.A. (PR)
Status: E
When Listed: 2
Vertebrate Pop: Entire
Critical Habitat: NA
Special Rule: NA

Common Name: Crocodile, American
Scientific Name: Crocodylus acutus
Historic Range: U.S.A. (FL), Mexico, Caribbean, Central and South America
Status: E
When Listed: 10, 87
Vertebrate Pop: Entire
Critical Habitat: 17.95(c)
Special Rule: NA

Common Name: Crocodile, saltwater (=estuarine)
Scientific Name: Crocodylus porosus
Historic Range: Southeast Asia, Australia, Papua New Guinea, Pacific Islands, U.S.A. (Palau)
Status: E
When Listed: 87
Vertebrate Pop: Entire, except Papua New Guinea
Critical Habitat: NA
Special Rule: NA

Common Name: Gecko, Monito
Scientific Name: Sphaerodactylus micropithecus
Historic Range: U.S.A. (PR)
Status: E
When Listed: 125
Vertebrate Pop: Entire
Critical Habitat: 17.95(c)
Special Rule: NA

Common Name: Iguana, Mona ground
Scientific Name: Cyclura stejnegeri
Historic Range: U.S.A. (PR—Mona Island)
Status: T
When Listed: 33
Vertebrate Pop: Entire
Critical Habitat: 17.95(c)
Special Rule: NA

Common Name: Lizard, blunt-nosed leopard
Scientific Name: Gambelia (=Crotaphytus) silus
Historic Range: U.S.A. (CA)
Status: E
When Listed: 1
Vertebrate Pop: Entire
Critical Habitat: NA
Special Rule: NA

Common Name: Lizard, Coachella Valley fringe-toed
Scientific Name: Uma inornata
Historic Range: U.S.A. (CA)
Status: T
When Listed: 105
Vertebrate Pop: Entire
Critical Habitat: 17.95(c)
Special Rule: NA

Common Name: Lizard, Island night
Scientific Name: Xantusia (=Klauberina) riversiana
Historic Range: U.S.A. (CA)
Status: T
When Listed: 26
Vertebrate Pop: Entire
Critical Habitat: NA
Special Rule: NA

Common Name: Lizard, St. Croix ground
Scientific Name: Ameiva polops
Historic Range: U.S.A. (VI)
Status: E
When Listed: 24
Vertebrate Pop: Entire
Critical Habitat: 17.95(c)
Special Rule: NA

Common Name: Rattlesnake, New Mexican ridge-nosed
Scientific Name: Crotalus willardi obscurus
Historic Range: U.S.A. (NM), Mexico
Status: T
When Listed: 43
Vertebrate Pop: Entire
Critical Habitat: 17.95(c)
Special Rule: NA

Common Name: Skink, bluetail (=blue-tailed) mole
Scientific Name: Eumeces egregius lividus
Historic Range: U.S.A. (FL)
Status: T
When Listed: 299
Vertebrate Pop: Entire
Critical Habitat: NA

310 Special Rule: 17.42(d)

Common Name: Skink, sand
Scientific Name: Neoseps reynoldsi
Historic Range: U.S.A. (FL)
Status: T
When Listed: 299
Vertebrate Pop: Entire
Critical Habitat: NA
Special Rule: 17.42(d)

Common Name: Snake, Atlantic salt marsh
Scientific Name: Nerodia clarkii (=fasciata) taeniata
Historic Range: U.S.A. (FL)
Status: T
When Listed: 30
Vertebrate Pop: Entire
Critical Habitat: NA
Special Rule: NA

Common Name: Snake, Concho water
Scientific Name: Nerodia paucimaculata (=harteri p.)
Historic Range: U.S.A. (TX)
Status: T
When Listed: 241
Vertebrate Pop: Entire
Critical Habitat: 17.95(c)
Special Rule: NA

Common Name: Snake, eastern indigo
Scientific Name: Drymarchon corais couperi
Historic Range: U.S.A. (AL, FL, GA, MS, SC)
Status: T
When Listed: 32
Vertebrate Pop: Sntire
Critical Habitat: NA
Special Rule: NA

Common Name: Snake, giant garter
Scientific Name: Thamnophis gigas
Historic Range: U.S.A. (CA)
Status: T
When Listed: 522
Vertebrate Pop: Entire
Critical Habitat: NA
Special Rule: NA

Common Name: Snake, San Francisco garter
Scientific Name: Thamnophis sirtalis tetrataenia
Historic Range: U.S.A. (CA)
Status: E
When Listed: I
Vertebrate Pop: Entire
Critical Habitat: NA
Special Rule: NA

311

Common Name: Tortoise, desert
Scientific Name: Gopherus (=Xerobates, =Scaptochelys) agassizii
Historic Range: U.S.A. (AZ, CA, NV, UT), Mexico
Status: T
When Listed: I03, 357E, 378
Vertebrate Pop: Entire, except AZ south and east of Colorado R., and Mexico
Critical Habitat: I7.95(c)
Special Rule: NA

Common Name: Tortoise, desert
Scientific Name: Gopherus (=Xerobates, =Scaptochelys) agassizii
Historic Range: U.S.A. (AZ, CA, NV, UT), Mexico
Status: T(S/A)
When Listed: 357E, 378
Vertebrate Pop: AZ south and east of Colorado R., and Mexico, when found outside
of Mexico or said range in AZ
Critical Habitat: NA
Special Rule: I7.42(e)

Common Name: Tortoise, gopher
Scientific Name: Gopherus polyphemus
Historic Range: U.S.A. (AL, FL, GA, LA, MS, SC)
Status: T
When Listed: 28I
Vertebrate Pop: Wherever found west of Mobile and Tombigbee Rivers in AL, MS,
and LA
Critical Habitat: NA
Special Rule: NA

Common Name: Turtle, Alabama redbelly (=red-bellied)
Scientific Name: Pseudemys alabamensis
Historic Range: U.S.A. (AL)
Status: E
When Listed: 278
Vertebrate Pop: Entire
Critical Habitat: NA
Special Rule: NA

Common Name: Turtle, flattened musk
Scientific Name: Sternotherus depressus
Historic Range: U.S.A. (AL)
Status: T
When Listed: 272
Vertebrate Pop: Black Warrior R. system upstream from Bankhead Dam
Critical Habitat: NA
Special Rule: NA

Common Name: Turtle, Plymouth redbelly (=red-bellied)
Scientific Name: Pseudemys (=Chrysemys) rubriventris bangsi
Historic Range: U.S.A. (MA)
Status: E
When Listed: 90
Vertebrate Pop: Entire
Critical Habitat: 17.95(c)
Special Rule: NA

312

Common Name: Turtle, ringed map (=sawback)
Scientific Name: Graptemys oculifera
Historic Range: U.S.A. (LA, MS)
Status: T
When Listed: 250
Vertebrate Pop: Entire
Critical Habitat: NA
Special Rule: NA

Common Name: Turtle, yellow-blotched map (=sawback)
Scientific Name: Graptemys flavimaculata
Historic Range: U.S.A. (MS)
Status: T
When Listed: 416
Vertebrate Pop: Entire
Critical Habitat: NA
Special Rule: NA

ENDANGERED SPECIES LIST—AMPHIBIANS

(alphabetical by common name)
Published in the Federal Register—current through Jan 1995.

Common Name: Coqui, golden
Scientific Name: Eleutherodactylus jasperi
Historic Range: U.S.A. (PR)
Status: T
When Listed: 29
Vertebrate Pop: Entire
Critical Habitat: 17.95(d)
Special Rule: NA

Common Name: Salamander, Cheat Mountain
Scientific Name: Plethodon nettingi
Historic Range: U.S.A. (WV)
Status: T
When Listed: 358
Vertebrate Pop: Entire
Critical Habitat: NA
Special Rule: NA

Common Name: Salamander, desert slender
Scientific Name: Batrachoseps aridus
Historic Range: U.S.A. (CA)
Status: E
When Listed: 6
Vertebrate Pop: Entire
Critical Habitat: NA
Special Rule: NA

Common Name: Salamander, Red Hills
Scientific Name: Phaeognathus hubrichti
Historic Range: U.S.A. (AL)
Status: T
When Listed: 19
Vertebrate Pop: Entire
Critical Habitat: NA
Special Rule: NA

Common Name: Salamander, San Marcos
Scientific Name: Eurycea nana
Historic Range: U.S.A. (TX)
Status: T
When Listed: 98
Vertebrate Pop: Entire
Critical Habitat: 17.95(d)
Special Rule: 17.43(a)

Common Name: Salamander, Santa Cruz long-toed
Scientific Name: Ambystoma macrodactylum croceum
Historic Range: U.S.A. (CA)
Status: E
When Listed: 1
Vertebrate Pop: Entire
Critical Habitat: NA
Special Rule: NA

Common Name: Salamander, Shenandoah
Scientific Name: Plethodon shenandoah
Historic Range: U.S.A. (VA)
Status: E
When Listed: 358
Vertebrate Pop: Entire
Critical Habitat: NA
Special Rule: NA

Common Name: Salamander, Texas blind
Scientific Name: Typhlomolge rathbuni
Historic Range: U.S.A. (TX)
Status: E
When Listed: 1
Vertebrate Pop: Entire
Critical Habitat: NA
Special Rule: NA

Common Name: Toad, Arroyo southwestern
Scientific Name: Bufo microscaphus californicus
Historic Range: U.S.A. (CA), Mexico.
Status: E
When Listed: 568
Vertebrate Pop: Entire
Critical Habitat: NA
Special Rule: NA

314

Common Name: Toad, Houston
Scientific Name: Bufo houstonensis
Historic Range: U.S.A. (TX)
Status: E
When Listed: 2
Vertebrate Pop: Entire
Critical Habitat: 17.95(d)
Special Rule: NA

Common Name: Toad, Puerto Rican crested
Scientific Name: Peltophryne lemur
Historic Range: U.S.A. (PR), British Virgin Islands
Status: T
When Listed: 283
Vertebrate Pop: Entire
Critical Habitat: NA
Special Rule: NA

Common Name: Toad, Wyoming
Scientific Name: Bufo hemiophrys baxteri
Historic Range: U.S.A. (WY)
Status: E
When Listed: 138
Vertebrate Pop: Entire
Critical Habitat: NA
Special Rule: NA

ENDANGERED SPECIES LIST—INVERTEBRATE ANIMALS

(U.S. Listed Invertebrate Animal Species Index By Lead Region and Status as of November 30, 1995)

LEAD REGION—STATUS—COMMON NAME (SCIENTIFIC NAME)
U.S. Listed Clams
4 — E — Acornshell, southern (Epioblasma othcaloogensis)
4 — E — Clubshell, black (=Curtus' mussel) (Pleurohema curtum)
4 — E — Clubshell, ovate (Pleurobema perovatum)
4 — E — Clubshell, southern (Pleurobema decisum)
5 — E — Clubshell (Pleurobema clava)
4 — E — Combshell, southern (=penitent mussel) (Epioblasma penita)
4 — E — Combshell, upland (Epioblasma metastnata)
4 — E — Elktoe, Appalachian (Alasmidonta raveneliana)
4 — E — Fanshell (Cyprogenia stegaria)

4 — T — Fatmucket, Arkansas (Lampsilis powelli)
4 — E — Heelsplitter, Carolina (Lasmigona decorata)
4 — T — Heelsplitter, inflated (Potamilus inSlatus)
4 — E — Kidneyshell, triangular (Ptychobranchus greeni)
4 — -E — Lampmussel, Alabama (Lampsilis virescens)
4 — T — Moccasinshell, Alabama (Medionidus acuh'ssimus)
4 — E — Moccasinshell, Coosa (Medionidus parvulus)
4 — T — Mucket, orange-nacre (Lampsilis perovalis)
5 — E — Mussel, dwarf wedge (Alasmidonta heterodon)
4 — E — Mussel, ring pink (=golf stick pearly) (Obovaria retusa)
3 — E — Mussel, winged mapleleaf (Quadrula fragosa)
4 — T — Pearlshell, Louisiana (Margaritifera hembeli)
4 — E — Pearlymussel, Appalachian monkeyface (Quadrula sparsa)
4 — E — Pearlymussel, birdwing (Conradilla caelata)
4 — E — Pearlymussel, cracking (Hemistena lata)
4 — E — Pearlymussel, Cumberland bean (Villosa trabalis)
4 — E — Pearlymussel, Cumberland monkeyface (Quadrula intermedia)
3 — E — Pearlymussel, Curtis' (Epioblasma (=Dysnomia) florentina curtisi)
4 — E — Pearlymussel, dromedary (Dromus dromas)
4 — E — Pearlymussel, green-blossom (Epioblasma torulosa gubernaculum)
3 — E — Pearlymussel, Higgins' eye (Lampsilis higginsi)
4 — E — Pearlymussel, little-wing (Pegias fabula)
4 — E — Pearlymussel, orange-foot pimple back (Plethobasus cooperianus)
4 — E — Pearlymussel, pale lilliput (Toxolasma cylindrellus)
4 — E — Pearlymussel, pink mucket (Lampsilis abrupta)
4 — E — Pearlymussel, purple cat's paw (Epioblasma obliquata obliquata)
4 — E — Pearlymussel, tubercled-blossom (Epioblasma torulosa torulosa)
4 — E — Pearlymussel, turgid-blossom (Epioblasma turgidula)
3 — E — Pearlymussel, white cat's paw (Epioblasma obliquata perobliqua (=sulcata delicata))
4 — E — Pearlymussel, white wartyback (Plethobasus cicatricosus)
4 — E — Pearlymussel, yellow-blossom (Epioblasma florentina florentina)
4 — E — Pigtoe, Cumberland (=Cumberland pigtoe mussel) (Pleurobema gibberum)
4 — E — Pigtoe, dark (Pleurobema furvum)
4 — E — Pigtoe, fine-rayed (Fusconaia cuneolus)
4 — E — Pigtoe, flat (=Marshall's mussel) (Pleurobema marshalli)
4 — E — Pigtoe, heavy (=Judge Tait's mussel) (Pleurobema taitianum)
4 — E — Pigtoe, rough (Pleurobema plenum)
4 — E — Pigtoe, shiny (Fusconaia cor (=edgariann
4 — E — Pigtoe, southern (Pleurobema georgianum)
4 — E — Pocketbook, fat (Potamilus (=Proptera) capax)
4 — T — Pocketbook, fine-lined (Lampsilis altilis)
4 — E — Pocketbook, speckled (Lampsilis streckeri)
5 — E — Riffleshell, northern (Epioblasmu Ivrulosa rangiunu)
4 — E — Riffleshell, tan (Epioblasma walkeri)
2 — E — Rock-pocketbook, Ouachita (=Wheeler's pearly mussel) (Arkansia wheeleri)
5 — E — Spinymussel, James River (=Virginia) (Pleurobema collina)
4 — E — Spinymussel, Tar River (Ellipho steinstansana)
4 — E — Stirrupshell (Quadrula stapes)
U.S. Listed Snails

315

6 — E — Ambersnail, Kanab (Oxyloma haydeni kanabensis)
I — E — Limpet, Banbury Springs (Lanx sp.)
4 — E — Marstonia (snail), royalobese) (Pyrgulopsis (=Marstonia) ogmoraphe)
4 — E — Riversnail, Anthony's (Athearnia anthonyi)
4 — T — Shagreen, Magazine Mountain (Mesodon magazinensis)
I — T — Snail, Bliss Rapids (Taylorconcha serpenticola)
5 — T — Snail, Chittenango ovate amber (Succinea chittenangoensis)
5 — T — Snail, flat-spired three-toothed (Triodopsis platysayoides)
3 — E — Snail, Iowa Pleistocene (Discus macclintocki)
I — E — Snail, Morro shoulderband (=banded dune) (Helminthoglypta walkeriana)
4 — T — Snail, noonday (Azlesodon clarki nantahala)
4 — T — Snail, painted snake coiled forest (Anguispira picta)
I — E — Snail, Snake River physa (Physa natricina)
4 — T — Snail, Stock Island tree (Orthalicus reses (not incl. nesodryas))
4 — E — Snail, tulotoma (-Alabama live-bearing) (Tulotoma magnifica)
I — E — Snail, Utah valvata (Valvata utahensis)
5 — E — Snail, Virginia fringed mountain (Polygyriscus virginianus)
I — E — Snails, Oahu tree (Achatinella spp.)
2 — E — Springsnail, Alamosa (Tryonia alamosae)
I — E — Springsnail, Bruneau Hot (Pyrgulopsis bruneauensis)
I — E — Springsnail, Idaho (Fontelicella idahoensis)
2 — E — Springsnail, Socorro (Pyrgulopsis neomexicana)

U.S. Listed Insects

5 — E — Beetle, American burying (=giant carrion) (Nicrophorus americanus)
2 — E — Beetle, Coffin Cave mold (Batrisodes texanus)
I — T — Beetle, delta green ground (Elaphrus viridis)
3 — E — Beetle, Hungerford's crawling water (Brychius hungerfordi)
2 — E — Beetle, Kretschmarr Cave mold (Texamaurops reddelli)
5 — T — Beetle, northeastern beach tiger (Cicindela dorsalis dorsalis)
S — T — Beetle, Puritan tiger (Cicindela puritana)
2 — E — Beetle, Tooth Cave ground (Rhadine persephone)
I — T — Beetle, valley elderberry longhorn (Desmocerus californicus dimorphus)
I — T — Butterfly, bay checkerspot (Euphydryas editha bayensis)
I — E — Butterfly, El Segundo blue (Euphilotes battoides allyni)
5 — E — Butterfly, Karner blue (Lycaeides melissa samuelis)
I — E — Butterfly, Lange's metalmark (Apodemia mormo langei)
I — E — Butterfly, lotis blue (Lycaeides argyrognomon lotis)
I — E — Butterfly, mission blue (Icaricia icarioides missionensis)
3 — E — Butterfly, Mitchell's satyr (Neonympha mitchellii mitchellii)
I — E — Butterfly, Myrtle's silverspot (Speyeria zerene myrtleae)
I — T — Butterfly, Oregon silverspot (Speyeria zerene hippolyta)
I — E — Butterfly, Palos Verdes blue (Glaucopsyche lygdamus palosverdesensis)
I — E — Butterfly, Saint Francis' satyr (Neonympha mitchellii francisci)
I — E — Butterfly, San Bruno elfin (Callophrys mossii bayensis)
4 — E — Butterfly, Schauzs swallowtail (Heraclides (=Papilio) aristodemus ponceanus)
I — E — Butterfly, Smith's blue (Euphilotes enoptes smithi)
6 — E — Butterfly, Uncompahgre fritillary (Boloria acrocnema)
3 — E — Dragonfly, Hine's emerald (Somatochlora hineana)
I — E — Fly, Delhi Sands flower loving (Rhaphiomidas terminatus abdominalis)

I — T — Moth, Kern primrose sphinx (Euproserpinus euterpe)
I — T — Naucorid, Ash Meadows (Ambrysus amargosus)
6 — T — Skipper, Pawnee montane (Hesperia leonardus (=pawnee) montana)

U.S. Listed Arachnids
2 — E — Harvestman, Bee Creek Cave (Texella reddelli)
2 — E — Harvestman, Bone Cave (Texella reyesi)
2 — E — Pseudoscorpion, Tooth Cave (Microcreagris texana)
4 — E — Spider, spruce-fir moss (Microhexura montivaga)
2 — E — Spider, Tooth Cave (Leptoneta myopica)

U.S. Listed Crustaceans
5 — E — Amphipod, Hay's Spring (Stygobromus hayi)
4 — E — Crayfish, cave [no common name] (Cambarus aculabrum)
4 — E — Crayfish, cave [no common name] (Cambarus zophonastes)
4 — E — Crayfish, Nashville (Orconectes shoupi)
I — E — Crayfish, Shasta (=placid) (Pacifastacus fortis)
I — E — Fairy shrimp, Conservancy (Branchinecta conservatio)
I — E — Fairy shrimp, longhorn (Branchinecta longiantenna)
I — E — Fairy shrimp, riverside (Streptocephalus woottoni)
I — T — Fairy shrimp, vernal pool (Branchinecta lynchi)
5 — E — Isopod, Lee County cave (Lirceus usdagalun)
5 — T — Isopod, Madison Cave (Antrolana lira)
2 — E — Isopod, Socorro (Thermosphaeroma (=Exosphaeroma) thermophilus)
4 — E — Shrimp, Alabama cave (Palaemonias alabamae)
I — E — Shrimp, California freshwater (Syncaris pacifica)
4 — E — Shrimp, Kentucky cave (Palaemonias ganteri)
4 — T — Shrimp, Squirrel Chimney Cave (=Florida cave) (Palaemonetes cummingi)
I — E — Tadpole shrimp, vernal pool (Lepidurus packardi)

ENDANGERED SPECIES LIST—NON-FLOWERING PLANTS
(U.S. Listed Non-Flowering Plant Species Index By Lead Region and Status as of November 30, 1995)

LEAD REGION—-STATUS—-COMMON NAME (SCIENTIFIC NAME)
U.S. Listed Conifers & Cycads
I — E — Santa Cruz cypress (Cupressus abramsiana)
4 — E — Florida torreya (Torreya taxiffolia)

U.S. Listed Ferns & Allies
I — E — Pendant kihi fern (Adenophorus periens)
4 — E — Adiantum vivesii (Fern, no common name)
3 — T — American hart's-tongue fern (Asplenium scolopendrium var. americanum)
I — E — Asplenium fragile var. insulare (Fern, no common name)
I — E — Pauoa (Ctenitis squamigera)
4 — E — Elfin tree fern (Cyathea dryopteroides)
I — E — Asplenium-leaved diellia (Diellia erecta)
I — E — Diellia falcata (Fern, no common name)
I — E — Diellia pallida (Fern, no common name)
I — E — Diellia unisora (Fern, no common name)
I — E — Diplazium molokaiense (Fern, no common name)

317

4 — E — Elaphoglossum serpens (Fern, no common name)
I — E — Wawae'iole (Huperzia mannii)
I — E — Louisiana quillwort (Isoetes louisianensis)
4 — E — Black-spored quillwort (Isoetes melanospora)
4 — E — Mat-forming quillwort (Isoetes tegetiformans)
I — E — Wawae'iole (Lycopodium nutans)
I — E — 'Ihi'ihi (Marsilea villosa)

318

7 — -E — Aleutian shield-fern (=Aleutian holly-fern) (Polystichum aleuticum)
4 — E — Polystichum calderonense (Fern, no common name)
I — E — Pteris lidgatei (Fern, no common name)
4 — E — Tectaria estremerana (Fern, no common name)
4 — T — Alabama streak-sorus fern (Thelypteris pilosa var alabamensis)
4 — E — Thelypteris inabonensis (Fern, no common name)
4 — E — Thelypteris verecunda (Fern, no common name)
4 — E — Thelyypteris yaucoensis (Fern, no common name)

U.S. Listed Lichens
4 — E — Florida perforate cladonia (Cladonia perforata)
4 — E — Rock gnome lichen (Gymnoderma lineare)

ENDANGERED SPECIES LIST—FLOWERING PLANTS
(U.S. Listed Flowering Plant Species Index By Lead Region and Status, as of November 30, 1995)

LEAD REGION—-STATUS—-COMMON NAME (SCIENTIFIC NAME)
U.S. Listed Flowering Plants
2 — E — Large-fruited sand-verbena (Abronia macrocarpa)
I — E — Abutilon eremitopetalum (Plant, no common name)
I — E — Ko'oloa'ula (Abutilon menziesii)
I — E — Abutilon sandwicense (Plant, no common name)
I — E — Liliwai (Acaena exigua)
I — E — San Mateo thornmint (Acanthomintha obovata ssp. duttonii)
I — E — Round-leaved chaff-flower (Achyranthes splendens var. rotundata)
3 — T — Northern wild monkshood (Aconiturm noveboracense)
4 — T — Sensitive joint-vetch (Aeschynomene virginica)
5 — E — Sandplain gerardia (Agalinis acuta)
2 — E — Arizona agave (Agave arizonica)
I — E — Mahoe (Alectryon macrococcus)
I — E — Alsinidendron obovatum (Plant, no common name)
I — E — Alsinidendron trinerve (Plant, no common name)
4 — T — Seabeach amaranth (Amaranthus pumilus)
2 — E — South Texas ambrosia (Ambrosia cheiranthifolia)
4 — E — Crenulate lead-plant (Amorpha crenulata)
4 — T — Little amphianthus (Amphianthus pusillus)
I — E — Large-flowered fiddleneck (Amsinckia grandiflora)
2 — E — Kearney's blue-star (Amsonia kearneyana)
2 — E — Tobusch fishhook cactus (Ancistrocuctus tobuschii)
3 — T — Price's potato-bean (Apios priceana)
I — E — McDonald's rock-cress (Arabis mcdonaldiana)
4 — E — Rock cress (Arabis perstellata)
5 — E — Shale barren rock-cress (Arabis serotina)

6 — E — Dwarf bear-poppy (Arctomecon humilis)
I — E — Presidio (=Raven's) manzanita (Arctostaphylos hookeri var. ravendi)
I — T — Morro manzanita (Arctostaphylos morroensis)
4 — E — Cumberland sandwort (Arenaria cumberlandensis)
I — E — Marsh sandwort (Arenaria paludicola)
2 — E — Sacramento prickly-poppy (Argemone pleiacantha ssp. pinnatisecta)
I — E — Ka'u silversword (Argyroxiphiurm kauense)
I — E — 'Ahinahina (=Haleakala silversword) (Argyroxiphium sandwicense ssp. macrocephalum)
I — E — 'Ahinahina (=Mauna Kea silversword) (Argyroxiphium sandwicense ssp. sandwicense)
4 — E — Aristida chaseae (PIant, no common name)
4 — E — Pelos del diablo (Aristida portoricensis)
3 — T — Mead's miLkweed (Asclepias meadii)
6 — T — Welsh's milkweed (Asclepias welshii)
4 — E — Four-petal pawpaw (Asimina tetramera)
I — E — Cushenbury milk-vetch (Astragalus albens)
I — E — Applegate's milk-vetch (Astragalus applegatei)
4 — E — Pyne's (=Guthrie's) ground-plum (Astragalus bibullatus)
2 — E — Sentry milk-vetch (Astragalus cremnophylax var. cremnophylax)
2 — E — Mancos milk-vetch (Astragalus humillimus)
6 — T — Heliotrope milk-vetch (Astragalus montii)
6 — E — Osterhout milk-vetch (Astragalus osterhoutii)
I — T — Ash Meadows milk-vetch (Astragalus phoenix)
5 — E — Jesup's milk-vetch (Astragalus robbinsii var. jesupi)
2 — E — Star cactus (Astrophytum asterias)
4 — E — Auerodendron pauciflorum (Plant, no common name)
2 — E — Texas ayenia (Ayenia limitaris)
4 — E — Palo de Ramón (Banara vanderbiltii)
4 — E — Hairy rattleweed (Baptisia arachnifera)
I — E — Truckee barberry (Berberis sonnei)
5 — T — Virginia round-leaf birch (Betula uber)
I — E — Cuneate bidens (Bidens cuneata)
I — E — Ko'oko'olau (Bidens micrantha ssp. kalealaha)
I — E — Ko'oko'olau (Bidens wiebkei)
I — E — Sonoma sunshine (=Baker's stickyseed) (Blennosperma bakeri)
3 — T — Decurrent false aster (Boltonia decurrens)
4 — T — Florida bonamia (Bonamia grandiflora)
I — E — Bonamia menziesii (Plant, no common name)
I — E — 'Olulu (Brighamia insignis)
I — E — Pua'ala (Brighamia rockii)
4 — E — Vahl's boxwood (Buxus vahlii)
I — E — Uhiuhi (Caesalpinia kavaiense)
4 — E — Capá rosa (=péndula cimarrona) (Callicarpa ampla)
2 — E — Texas poppy-mallow (Callirhoe scabriuscula)
I — T — Tiburon mariposa lily (Calochorlus tiburonensis)
4 — E — Calyptranthes thomasiana (Plant, no common name)
4 — T — Palma de manaca or manac palm (Calyptronoma rivalis)
I — T — San Benito evening-primrose (Camissonia benitensis)
4 — E — Brooksville (=Robins') bellflower (Campanula robinsiae)
I — E — 'Awikiwiki (Canavalia molokaiensis)

4 — E — Small-anthered bittercress (Cardamine micranthera)
2 — T — Navajo sedge (Carex specuicola)
I — E — Tiburon paintbrush (Castilleja affinis ssp. neglecta)
I — E — San Clemente Island Indian paintbrush (Castilleja grisea)
I — E — California jewelflower (Caulanthus californicus)
I — E — Coyote ceanothus (=Coyote Valley California-lilac) (Ceanothus ferrisae)
I — T — Spring-loving centaury (Centurium namophilum)
I — E — 'Awiwi (Centaurium sebaeoides)
4 — E — Fragrant prickly-apple (Cereus eriophorus var. fragrans)
4 — E — Chamaecrista glandulosa var. mirabilis (=Cassia mirabilis) (Plant, no common name)
4 — E — Deltoid spurge (Chamaesyce deltoidea ssp. deltoidea)
I — E — 'Akoko (Chamaesyce deppeana (=Euphorbia d.))
4 — T — Garber's spurge (Chamaesyce garberi)
I — E — 'Ewa Plains 'akoko (Chamaesyce skottsbergii var. kalaeloana)
I — E — 'Akoko (Chamaesyce celastroides var. kaenana)
I — E — Chamaesyce halemanui (Plant, no common name)
I — E — 'Akoko (Chamaesyce kuwaleana)
4 — E — Pygmy fringe-tree (Chionanthus pygmaeus)
I — E — Howell's spineflower (Chorizanthe howellii)
I — E — Ben Lomond spineflower (Chorizanthe pungens var. hartwegiana)
I — T — Monterey spineflower (Chorizanthe pungens var. pungens)
I — E — Robust spineflower (includes Scotts Valley spineflower) (Chorizanthe robusta)
I — E — Sonoma spineflower (Chonzanthe valida)
4 — E — Florida golden aster (Chrysopsis floridana)
I — E — Fountam thistle (Cirsium fontinale var. fontinale)
I — E — Chorro Creek bog thistle (Cirsium fontinale obispoense)
3 — T — Pitcher's thistle (Cirsium pitcheri)
2 — T — Sacramento Mountains thistle (Cirsium vinaceum)
I — E — Presidio clarkia (Clarkia franciscana)
I — E — Pismo clarkia (Clarkia speciosa immaculata)
4 — E — Morefield's leather-flower (Clematis morefieldii)
4 — E — Alabama leather-flower (Clematis socialis)
I — E — 'Oha wai (Clermontia lindseyana)
I — E — 'Oha wai (Clermontia oblongifolia ssp. brevipes)
I — E — 'Oha wai (Clermontia oblongifolia ssp. mauiensis)
I — E — 'Oha wai (Clermontia peleana)
I — E — 'Oha wai (Clermontia pyrularia)
I — T — Pigeon wings (Clitoria fragrans)
I — E — Kauila (Colubrina oppositifolia)
I — E — Short-leaved rosemary (Conradina brevifolia)
4 — E — Etonia rosemary (Conradina etonia)
4 — E — Apalachicola rosemary (Conradina glabra)
4 — T — Cumberland rosemary (Conradina verticillata)
I — E — Salt marsh bird's-beak (Cordylanthus marismus ssp. maritismus)
I — E — Palmate-bracted bird's-beak (Cordylanthus palmatus)
I — E — Pennell's bird's-beak (Cordylanthus tenuis ssp. capillaris)
4 — E — Palo de nigua (=cap jug_erilla) (Cornutia obovata)
2 — T — Cochise pincushion cactus (Coryphantha (=Escobaria) robbinsorwm)
2 — E — Nellie cory cactus (Coryphantha (=Escobaria) minima)

2 — T — Bunched cory cactus (Coryphantha ramillosa)
2 — E — Pima pineapple cactus (Coryphantha scheeri var. robustispina)
2 — T — Lee pincushion cactus (Coryphantha sneedii var leei)
2 — E — Sneed pincushion cactus (Coryphantha sneedii var. sneedii)
4 — E — Cranichis ricartii (Plant, no common name)
4 — E — Higuero de Sierra (Crescenha portoricensis)
1 — E — Avon Park harebells (Crotalaria avonensis)
2 — E — Terlingua Creek cats-eye (Cryptantha crassipes)
4 — E — Okeechobee gourd (Cucurbita okeechobeensis ssp. okeechobeensis)
1 — E — Haha (Cyanea asarifolia)
1 — E — Haha (Cyanea copelandii ssp. copelandii)
1 — E — Haha (Cayanea grimesiana ssp. obatae)
1 — E — Haha (Cyanea hamatiflora ssp. carlsonii)
1 — E — Haha (Cyanea lobata)
1 — E — Cyanea macrostegia ssp. gibsonii (Plant, no common name)
1 — E — Haha (Cyanea mannii)
1 — E — Haha (Cyanea mceldowneyi)
1 — E — Haha (Cyanea pinnatifda)
1 — E — Haha (Cyvanea procera)
1 — E — Haha (Cyanea shipmannii)
1 — E — Haha (Cyanea stictophylla)
1 — E — Cyanea superba (Plant, no common name)
1 — E — Haha (Cyanea truncata)
1 — E — Cyanea undulata (Plant. no common name)
2 — T — Jones cycladenia (Cycladenia humilis var. jonesii)
1 — E — Ha'iwale (Cyrtandra crenata)
1 — E — Ha'iwale (Cyrtandra giffardii)
1 — T — Ha'iwale (Cyrtandra limahuliensis)
1 — E — Ha'iwale (Cvrtandra munroi)
1 — E — Ha'iwale (Cyrtandra polyantha)
1 — E — Ha'iwale (Cyrtandra hntinnabula)
3 — E — Leafy prairie-clover (Dalea (=Petalostemum) foliosa)
4 — E — Daphnopsis hellerana (Plant, no common name)
4 — E — Beautiful pawpaw (Deeringothamnus pulchellus)
4 — E — Rugel's pawpaw (Deeringothamnus rugelii)
1 — E — Delissea rhyndosperma (Plant, no common name)
1 — E — San Clemente Island larkspur (Delphinium variegatum ssp. kinkiense)
4 — E — Garrett's mint (Dicerandra christmanii)
4 — E — Longspurred mint (Dicerandra cornutissima)
4 — E — Scrub mint (Dicerandra frutescens)
4 — E — Lakela's mint (Dicerandra immaculata)
1 — E — Slender-horned spineflower (Dodecahema leptoceras)
1 — E — Na'ena'e (Dubautia herbstobatae)
1 — E — Dubautia latifolia (Plante no common name)
1 — E — Dubautia pauciflorula (Plant, no common name)
1 — E — Santa Clara Valley dudleya (Dudleya setchellii)
1 — E — Santa Barbara Island liveforever (Dudleya traskiae)
4 — E — Smooth coneflower (Echinacea laevigata)
4 — E — Tennessee purple coneflower (Echinacea tennesseensis)
2 — E — Nichol's Turk's head cactus (Echinocactus horizonthalonius var. nicholii
2 — T — Chisos Mountain hedgehog cactus (Echinocereus chisoensis var. chisoensis)

2 — E — Kuenzler hedgehog cactus (Echinocereus fendleri var. kuenzleri)

2 — E — Lloyd's hedgehog cactus (Echinocereus lloydii)

2 — E — Black lace cactus (Echinocereus reichenbachii (=melanocentrus) var. albertii)

2 — E — Arizona hedgehog cactus (Echinocereus triglochidiatus var. arizonicus)

2 — E — Davis' green pitaya (Echinocereus viridiflorus var. davisii)

2 — T — Lloyd's Mariposa cactus (Echinomastus (=Sclerocactus) mariposensis)

1 — T — Ash Meadows sunray (Enceliopsis nudicaulis var. corrugata)

1 — E — Kern mallow (Eremalche kernensis)

1 — E — Santa Ana River woolly-star (Eriastrum densifolium ssp. sanctorum)

1 — T — Hoover's woolly-star (Eriastrum hooveri)

6 — E — Maguire daisy (Erigeron maguirei var. maguirei)

1 — T — Parish's daisy (Erigeron parishii)

2 — T — Zuni (=rhizome) fleabane (Erigeron rhizomatus)

1 — E — Indian Knob mountain balm (Eriodictwon altissimum)

2 — T — Gypsum wild-buckwheat (Eriogonum gypsophilum)

4 — T — Scrub buckwheat (Eriogonum longifolium var. gnaphalifolium)

1 — E — Cushenbury buckwheat (Eriogonum ovalifolium var. vineum)

1 — E — Steamboat buckwheat (Eriogonum ovalifolium var. williamsiae)

6 — E — Clay-loving wild-buckwheat (Eriogonum pelinophilum)

1 — E — San Mateo woolly sunflower (Eriophyllum latilobum)

1 — E — San Diego button-celery (Eryngium aristulatum var. parishii)

1 — E — Loch Lomond coyote-thistle (Eryngium constancei)

4 — E — Snakeroot (Eryngium cuneifolium)

1 — E — Contra Costa wallflower (Ezysimum capitatum var. angustatum)

1 — E — Menzies' wallflower (Erysimum menziesii)

1 — E — Ben Lomond wallflower (Erysimum teretifolium)

3 — E — Minnesota trout lily (Erythronium propullans)

4 — E — Uvillo (Eugenia haematocarpa)

1 — E — Nioi (Eugenia koolauensis)

4 — E — Eugenia woodburyana (Plant, no common name)

4 — T — Telephus spurge (Euphorbia telephioides)

6 — T — Penland alpine fen mustard (Eutrema penlandii)

1 — E — Heau (Exocarpos luteolus)

1 — E — Mehamehame (Flueggea neowawraea)

2 — E — Johnston's frankenia (Frankenia johnstonii)

1 — E — Gahnia lanaiensis (Plant, no common name)

4 — E — Small's milkpea (Galactia smallii)

1 — E — Na'u or Hawaiian gardenia (Gardenia brighamii)

3 — T — Geocarpon minimum (Plant, no common name)

1 — E — Hawaiian red-flowered geranium (Geranium arboreum)

1 — E — Nohoanu (Geranium multiflorum)

1 — T — Gesneria pauciflora (Plant, no common name)

4 — E — Spreading avens (Geum radiatum)

1 — E — Monterey gilia (Gilia tenuiflora ssp. arenaria)

4 — E — Beautiful goetzea or matabuey (Goetzea elegans)

1 — E — Gouania hillebrandii (Plant, no common name)

1 — E — Gouania meyenii (Plant, no common name)

1 — E — Gouania vitifolia (Plant, no common name)

1 — T — Ash Meadows gumplant (Grindelia fraxino-pratensis)

1 — E — Haplostachys haplostachya (Plant, no common name)

4 — E — Harper's beauty (Harperocallis flava)
4 — T — Higo chumbo (Harrisia portoricensis)
2 — E — Todsen's pennyroyal (Hedeoma todsenii)
1 — E — 'Awiwi (Hedyotis cookiana)
1 — E — Kio' ele (Hedyotis coriacea)
1 — E — Hedyotis degeneri (Plant, no common name)
1 — E — Pilo (Hedyotis mannii)
1 — E — Hedyotis parvula (Plant, no common name)
4 — E — Roan Mountain bluet (Hedyotis purpurea var. montana)
1 — E — Na Pali beach hedyotis (Hedyotis st. johnii)
4 — E — Schweinitz's sunflower (Helianthus schweinitzii)
5 — T — Swamp pink (Helonias bullata)
1 — E — Marin dwarf-flax (Hesperolinon congestum)
1 — E — Hesperomannia arborescens (Plant, no common name)
1 — E — Hesperomannia arbuscula (Plant, no common name)
1 — E — Hesperomannia lydgatei (Plant, no common name)
4 — T — Dwarf-flowered heartleaf (Hexastylis naniflora)
1 — E — Kauai hau kuahiwi (Hibiscadelphus distans)
1 — E — Koki'o ke'oke'o (Hibiscus arnottianus ssp. immaculatus)
1 — E — Ma'o hau hele (Hibiscus brackenridgei)
1 — E — Clay's hibiscus (Hibiscus clayi)
2 — E — Slender rush-pea (Hoffmannseggia tenella)
6 — T — Water howellia (Howellia aquatilis)
4 — T — Mountain golden heather (Hudsonia montana)
3 — T — Lakeside daisy (Hymenoxys herhacea)
2 — E — Texas prairie dawn-flower (=Texas bitterweed) (Hymenoxys texana)
4 — E — Highlands scrub hypericum (Hypericum cumulicola)
4 — E — Cook's holly (Ilex cookii)
4 — E — Ilex sintenisii (Plant, no common name)
5 — E — Peter's Mountain mallow (Iliamna corei)
2 — E — Holy Ghost ipomopsis (Ipomopsis sancti-spiritus)
3 — T — Dwarf lake iris (Iris lacustris)
1 — E — Hilo ischaemum (Ischaemum byrone)
1 — E — Aupaka (Isodendrion hosakae)
1 — E — Wahine noho kula (Isodendrion pyrifolium)
3 — T — Small whorled pogonia (Isotria medeoloides)
1 — T — Ash Meadows ivesia (Ivesia kingii var. eremica)
4 — E — Beach jacquemontia (Jacquemontia reclinata)
1 — E — Cooley's water-willow (Justicia cooleyi)
1 — E — Cooke's koki'o (Kokia cookei)
1 — E — Koki'o (=hau-hele'ula or Hawaii tree cotton) (Kokia drynarioides)
1 — E — Kamakahala (Labordia lydgatei)
1 — E — Burke's goldfields (Lasthenia burkei)
1 — E — Beach layia (Layia carnosa)
1 — E — San Joaquin wooly-threads (Lembertia congdonii)
4 — E — Lepanthes eltoroensis (Plant, no common name)
6 — E — Barneby ridge-cress (=peppercress) (Lepidium barnebyanum)
4 — E — Leptocereus grantianus (Plant, no common name)
3 — T — Prairie bush-clover (Lespedeza leptostachya)
6 — T — Dudley Bluffs bladderpod (Lesquerella congesta)
3 — E — Missouri bladderpod (Lesquerella filiformis)

I — E — San Bernardino Mountains bladderpod (Lesquerella kingii ssp. bernardina)
4 — T — Lyrate bladderpod (Lesquerella lyrata)
2 — E — White bladderpod (Lesquerella pallida)
6 — E — Kodachrome bladderpod (Lesquerella tumulosa)
4 — T — Heller's blazingstar (Liatris helleri)
I — E — Scrub blazingstar (Liatris ohlingerae)
I — E — Western lily (Lilium occidental)
I — E — Butte County meadowfoam (Limnanthes floccosa ssp. californica)
I — E — Sebastopol meadowfoam (Limnanthes vinculans)
3 — E — Pondberry (Lindera melissifolia)
I — E — Nehe (Lipochaeta fauriei)
I — E — Nehe (Lipochaeta kamolensis)
I — E — Nehe (Lipochaeta lobata var. leptophylla)
I — E — Nehe (Lipochaeta micrantha)
I — E — Nehe (Lipochaeta tenuifolia)
I — E — Lipochaeta venosa (Plant, no common name)
I — E — Nehe (Lipochaeta waimeaensis)
I — E — Lobelia niihauensis (Plant, no common name)
I — E — Lobelia oahuensis (Plant, no common name)
I — E — Bradshaw's desert-parsley (=lomatium) (Lomatium bradshawii)
I — E — San Clemente Island broom (Lotus dendroideus ssp. traskiae)
4 — E — Scrub lupine (Lupinus aridorum)
I — E — Clover lupine (Lupinus tidestromii)
4 — E — Lyonia truncata var. proctorii (Plant, no common name)
4 — E — Rough-leaved loosestrife (Lysimachia asperulaefolia)
I — E — Lysimachia filifolia (Plant, no common name)
I — E — Lysimachia lydgatei (Plant, no common name)
4 — T — White birds-in-a-nest (Macbridea alba)
I — E — San Clemente Island bush-mallow (Malacothamnus clementinus)
2 — E — Walker's manioc (Manihot walkerae)
I — E — Mariscus fauriei (Plant, no common name)
I — E — Mariscus pennatiformis (Plant, no common name)
4 — T — Mohr's Barbara's buttons (Marshallia mohrii)
I — E — Alani (Melicope lydgatei)
I — E — Alani (Melicope mucronulata)
I — E — Alani (Melicope adscendens)
I — E — Alani (Melicope ballonii)
I — E — Alani (Melicope haupuensis)
I — E — Alani (Melicope knudsenii)
I — E — Alani (Melicope ovalis)
I — E — Alani (Melicope pallida)
I — E — Alani (Melicope quadangularis)
I — E — Alani (Melicope reflexa)
I — T — Ash Meadows blazing-star (Mentzelia leucophylla)
3 — E — Michigan monkey-flower (Mimulus glabratus var. michiganensis)
I — E — MacFarlane's four-o'clock (Mirabilis macfarlanei)
4 — E — Mitracarpus maxwelliae (Plant, no common name)
4 — E — Mitracarpus polycladus (Plant, no common name)
I — E — Munroidendron racemosum (Plant, no common name)
4 — E — Myrcia paganii (Plant, no common name)
I — E — Neraudia angulata (Plant, no common name)

I — E — Neraudia sericea (Plant, no common name)
I — E — Amargosa niterwort (Nitrophila mohavensis)
4 — E — Britton's beargrass (Nolina brittoniana)
I — E — 'Aiea (Nothocestrum breviflorum)
I — E — 'Aiea (Nothocestrum peltatum)
I — E — Kulu'i (Nototrichium humile)
I — E — Holei (Ochrosia kilaueaensis)
I — E — Eureka Valley evening-primrose (Oenothera avita ssp. eurekensis)
I — E — Antioch Dunes evening-primrose (Oenothera deltoides ssp. howellii)
I — E — Bakersfield cactus (Opunta treleasei)
I — E — California Orcutt grass (Orcuttia californica)
4 — E — Palo de rosa (Ottoschulzia rhodoxylon)
4 — E — Canby's dropwort (Oxypolis canbyi)
I — E — Cushenbury oxytheca (Oxytheca parishii var. goodmaniana)
3 — T — Fassett's locoweed (Oxytropis campestris var. chartacea)
I — E — Carter's panicgrass (Panicumfauriei var. carteri)
4 — T — Papery whitlow-wort (Paronychia chartacea)
5 — E — Furbish lousewort (Pedicularis furbishiae)
2 — T — Siler pincushion cactus (Pediocactus sileri)
2 — E — Peebles Navajo cactus (Pediocactus peeblesianus var. peeblesianus)
2 — E — Brady pincushion cactus (Pediocactus bradyi)
2 — E — Knowlton cactus (Pediocactus knowltonii)
6 — E — San Rafael cactus (Pediocactus despainii)
6 — E — Blowout penstemon (Penstemon haydenii)
6 — E — Penland beardtongue (Penstemon penlandii)
I — E — White-rayed pentachaeta (Pentachaeta bellidiflora)
4 — E — Wheeler's peperomia (Peperomia wheeleri)
I — T — Makou (Peucedanum sandwicense)
6 — E — Clay phacelia (Phacelia argillacea)
6 — E — North Park phacelia (Phacelia formosula)
2 — E — Texas trailing phlox (Phlox nivalis ssp. texensis)
I — E — Phyllostegia glabra var. lanaiensis (Plant, no common name)
I — E — Phyllostegia mannii (Plant, no common name)
I — E — Phyilostegia mollis (Plant, no common name)
I — E — Phyllostegia waimeae (Plant, no common name)
6 — T — Dudley Bluffs twinpod (Physaria obcordata)
4 — E — Key tree-cactus (Pilosocereus robinii (=Cereus r.))
4 — T — Godfrey's butterwort (Pinguicula ionantha)
4 — E — Ruth's golden aster (Pityopsis (=Heterotheca =Chrysopsis) ruthii)
I — E — Laukahi kuahiwi (Plantago hawaiensis)
I — E — Laukahi kuahiwi (Plantago princeps)
3 — T — Eastern prairie fringed orchid (Platanthera leucophaea) 2 — T — Western prairie fringed orchid (Platanthera praeclara) 4 — E — Chupacallos (=Chupagallo) (Pleodendron macranthum)
I — E — Mann's bluegrass (Poa mannii)
I — E — Hawaiian bluegrass (Poa sandvicensis)
I — E — Poa siphonoglossa (Plant, no common name)
I — E — San Diego mesa mint (Pogogyne abramsii)
I — E — Otay mesa mint (Pogogyne nudiuscula)
4 — E — Lewton's polygala (Polygala lewtonii)
4 — E — Tiny polygala (Polygala smallii)

4 — E — Wireweed (Polygonella basiramia)
4 — E — Sandlace (Polygonella myriophylla)
1 — E — Po'e (Portulaca sclerocarpa)
2 — E — Little Aguja pondweed (Potamogeton clystocarpus)
5 — E — Robbins' cinquefoil (Potentlla robbinsiana)
6 — T — Maguire primrose (Primula maguirei)
1 — E — Loulu (Pritchardia affinis)
1 — E — Loulu (Pritchardia munroi)
4 — E — Scrub plum (Prunus geniculata)
1 — E — Kaulu (Pteralyxia kauaiensis)
5 — E — Harperella (ptilimnium nodosum (—fluviatile))
2 — E — Arizona cliffrose (Purshia subintegra)
2 — T — Hinckley's oak (Quercus hinckleyi)
6 — E — Autumn buttercup (Ranunculus acriformis var. aeshvalis)
1 — E — Remya kauaiensis (Plant, no common name)
1 — E — Maui remya (Remvva mauiensis)
1 — E — Remya montgomeryi (Plant, no common name)
4 — E — Chapman rhododendron (Rhododendron chapmanii)
4 — E — Michaux's sumac (Rhus michauxii)
5 — T — Knieskern's beaked-rush (Rhynchospora knieskernii)
4 — T — Miccosukee gooseberry (Ribes echinellum)
1 — E — Rollandia crispa (Plant, no conunon name)
1 — E — Gambel's watercress (Rorippa gambellii)
4 — E — Bunched arrowhead (Sagittaria fasciculata)
4 — T — Kral's water-plantain (Sagittaria secundifolia)
1 — E — Sanicula mariversa (Plant, no common name)
1 — E — Lanai sandalwood or 'iliahi (santalum freycinehanum var. lanaiense)
4 — E — Green pitcher-plant (Sarracenia oreophila)
4 — E — Alabama canebrake pitcher-plant (Sarracenia rubra ssp. alabamensis)
4 — E — Mountain sweet pitcher-plant (Sarracenia rubra ssp. jonesii)
1 — E — Dwarf naupaka (Scaevola coriacea)
1 — E — Diamond Head schiedea (Schiedea adamantis)
1 — E — Ma'oli'oli (Schiedea apokremnos)
1 — E — Schiedea haleakalenisis (Plant, no common name)
1 — E — Schiedea kaalae (Plant, no common name)
1 — E — Schiedea lydgatei (Plant, no common name)
1 — E — Schiedea spergulina var. leiopoda (Plant, no common name)
1 — T — Schiedea spergulina var. spergulina (Plant, no common name)
6 — E — Shrubby reed-mustard (=toad-flax cress) (Schoenocrambe suffutescens)
6 — T — Clay reed-mustard (Schoenocrambe argillacea)
6 — E — Barneby reed-mustard (Schoenocrambe barnebyi)
4 — T — Schoepfia arenaria (Plant, no common name)
4 — E — American chaffseed (Schwalbea americana)
5 — E — Northeastern (=Barbed bristle) bulrush (Scirpus ancistrochaetus)
2 — T — Mesa Verde cactus (Sclerocactus mesae-verdae)
6 — T — Uinta Basin hookless cactus (Sclerocactus glaucus)
6 — E — Wright fishhook cactus (Sclerocactus wrightiae)
4 — T — Florida skullcap (Scutellaria floridana)
4 — E — Large-flowered skullcap (Scutellaria montana)
3 — T — Leedy's roseroot (Sedum integrifolium ssp. leedyi)
2 — T — San Francisco Peaks groundsel (Senecio franciscanus)

I — E — Hayun lagu (Guam), Tronkon guafi (Rota) (Serianthes nelsonii)
I — E — ʻOhai (Sesbania tomentosa)
I — T — Nelson's checker-mallow (Sidalcea nelsoniana)
I — E — Pedate checker-mallow (Sidalcea pedata)
I — E — Silene alexandri (Plant, no common name)
I — T — Silene hawaiiensis (Plant, no common name)
I — E — Silene lanceolata (Plant, no common name)
I — E — Silene perlmanii (Plant, no common name)
4 — E — Fringed campion (Silene polypetala)
4 — E — White irisette (Sisyrinchium dichotomum)
4 — E — Erubia (Solanum drymophilum)
I — E — Popolo ku mai (Solanum incompletum)
I — E — ʻAiakeakua, popolo (Solanum sandwicense)
4 — T — White-haired goldenrod (Solidago albopilosa)
3 — T — Houghton's goldenrod (Solidago houghtonii)
4 — E — Short's goldenrod (Solidago shortii)
4 — T — Blue Ridge goldenrod (Solidago spithamaea)
I — E — Spermolepis hawaiiensis (Plant, no common name)
4 — E — Gentian pinkroot (Spigelia gentianoides)
4 — T — Virginia spiraea (Spiraea virginiana)
6 — T — Ute ladies'-tresses (Spiranthes diluvialis)
2 — E — Navasota ladies'-tresses (Spiranthes parksii)
4 — T — Cóbana negra (Stahlia monosperma)
I — E — Stenogyne angustifolia (Plant, no common name)
I — E — Stenogyne bifida (Plant, no common name)
I — E — Stenogyne campanulata (Plant, no common name)
I — E — Stenogyne kanehoana (Plant, no common name)
I — E — Malheur wire-lettuce (Stephanomeria malheurensis)
I — E — Metcalf Canyon jewelflower (Streptanthus albidus ssp albidus)
I — E — Tiburon jewelflower (Streptanthus niger)
I — E — Palo de jazmin (Styrax portoricensis)
2 — E — Texas snowbells (Styrax texana)
I — E — California seablite (Suaeda californica)
I — E — Eureka Dune grass (Swallenia alexandrae)
I — E — Palo colorado (Ternstroemia luquillensis)
4 — E — Ternstroemia subsessilis (Plant, no common name)
I — E — Tetramolopium arenarium (Plant, no common name)
I — E — Pamakani (Tetramolopium capillare)
I — E — Tetramolopium filiforme (Plant, no common name)
I — E — Tetramolopium lepidotum ssp. lepidotum (Plant, no common name)
I — E — Tetramolopium remyi (Plant, no common name)
I — T — Tetramolopium rockii (Plant, no common name)
I — E — ʻOheʻohe (Tetraplasandra gymnocarpa)
4 — E — Cooley's meadowrue (Thalictrum cooleyi)
I — E — Slender-petaled mustard (Thelypodium stenopetalum)
2 — E — Ashy dogweed (Thymophylla tephroleuca)
6 — T — Last Chance townsendia (Townsendia aprica)
4 — E — Bariaco (=guayabacon) (Trichilia triacantha)
3 — E — Running buffalo clover (Trifolium stoloniferum)
4 — E — Persistent trillium (Trillium persistens)
4 — E — Relict trillium (Trillium reliquum)

327

I — E — Solano grass (Tuctoria mucronata)
I — E — Opuhe (Urera kaalae)
4 — E — Vernonia proctorii (Plant, no common name)
I — E — Hawaiian vetch (Vicia menziesii)
I — E — Vigna o-wahuensis (Plant, no common name)
I — E — Pamakani (Viola chamissoniana chamissoniana)
I — E — Viola helenae (Plant, no common name)
I — E — Viola lanaiensis (Plant, no common name)
4 — E — Wide-leaf warea (Warea amplexifolia)
4 — E — Carter's mustard (Warea carteri)
I — E — Dwarf iliau (Wilkesia hobdyi)
I — E — Xylosma crenatum (Plant, no common name)
4 — E — Tennessee yellow-eyed grass (Xyris tennesseensis)
I — E — A'e (Zanthoxylum hawaiiense)
4 — E — St. Thomas prickly-ash (Zanthoxylum thomasianum)
2 — E — Texas wild-rice (Zizania texana)
4 — E — Florida ziziphus (Ziziphus celata)

Dr. Donald Wolberg, is a paleontologist and the former secretary of the prestigious Paleontological Society, the oldest and largest paleontological organization in the world. He earned his Ph.D. in geology and vertebrate paleontology from the University of Minnesota in 1978. Dr. Wolberg has worked with fossils from Montana, North Dakota, South Dakota, Colorado, Minnesota, Alabama, Wisconsin, Illinois, New York, New Jersey, and New Mexico. He also participated in archeological digs in Greece and elsewhere. He has published more than 200 articles dealing with living animals, fossils, geology, mineralogy, anthropology, and archeology.

As paleontologist for the New Mexico Bureau of Mines and Mineral Resources in Socorro, New Mexico, from 1978 to 1993, Dr. Wolberg became fluent in the language of bureaucratic permits necessary for his paleontological explorations and excavations. He worked on a daily basis with Native American tribes, the BLM, the U.S. Forest Service, the Army Corps of Engineers, the Department of Defense, the Bureau of Reclamation, the National Park Service, and the New Mexico State Land Office. He also served on the New Mexico Coal Surface Mining Commission, and in other advisory roles to state government.

He served as a member of the Academy of Sciences Committee on Guidelines for Paleontological Collecting from 1985-1987 which made its own recommendations discussed in this book under "Pending Federal Legislation" in Chapter 3. He also has been consulted by the authors of two of the bills on fossils now before Congress. Dr. Wolberg is asked frequently to lecture or give advice on difficulties collectors have encountered with federal or state laws and is personally familiar with many of the cases discussed in this book. He testified as an expert on the condition of "Sue" in the infamous 1992 FBI seizure of a *Tyrannosaurus rex* from the Black Hills Geological Institute. He is also familiar with the international export and import of fossils, a subject of another book.

Dr. Wolberg is now best known as the creator of Dinofest™ an annual or bi-annual travelling natural history festival. The last Dinofest was hosted by Arizona State University of Tempe, Arizona, in April, 1996, and the next is scheduled for Philadelphia in 1998.

Patsy Reinard is a licensed attorney and has a private practice in the State of New Mexico. She and Wolberg have been married for eighteen years and have eight children. As legal counsel for ESTA (Earth Sciences Trade Association), a national trade association of commercial collectors,

Ms. Reinard has become familiar with some of the legal problems facing collectors today, including the potential for criminal prosecution. As a former ACLU attorney, she is familiar with the constitutional pitfalls of vagueness and overbreadth in drafting legislation.

The authors can honestly say that they have personally experienced, or know the people who experienced, many of the cases discussed in this book. They form a unique husband-wife team, with the skills and experience that make this book a knowledgeable commentary on the law rather than a mere technical recitation. It is a valuable resource, not only to collectors, but to those who write and administer the laws as well.